Hiroshima Revisited

The evidence that napalm and mustard gas helped fake the atomic bombings

by Michael Palmer, MD

with a Foreword by Franklin Stahl

©Michael Palmer, MD (2020)

ISBN: 978-0-9937882-2-2

This work is licensed under the Creative Commons Attribution-NonCommercial-ShareAlike 4.0 International License (CC BY-NC-SA 4.0). This means that you are free to share, adapt, and reuse the content, but only for non-commercial purposes. In any such case, you must give appropriate credit to this source, provide a link to the license, and indicate if changes were made. For commercial adaptations, including translations to other languages, please contact the author.

Exempt from these requirements is the use of small portions of this work which amounts to fair use. Also exempt are images and quotes in this work which were taken from various other works as indicated. The author considers the use of these materials in this book to be permissible under fair use rules.

For further details, visit:

https://creativecommons.org/licenses/by-nc-sa/4.0/.

This is version 1.12 (March 11, 2025). To check for updated versions of this document, visit its homepage:

https://mpalmer.heresy.is/webnotes/HR/

A German translation of this text is available at the same URL.

If you make use of significant portions of the content, or comment on it in a substantial manner, be it critically or favorably, I would be grateful for a notification by email to

mpalmer@heresy.is

Email is my preferred method of contact—I am not active on social media.

Cover design by Jana Rade (impactstudiosonline.com).

*To the witnesses and the scientists who preserved the truth
even if they could not tell it*

Contents

List of Figures	xi
List of Tables	xv
Foreword	xvii
Preface	xix
Acknowledgments	xxi

1 Why doubt the nuclear bombings of Hiroshima and Nagasaki? ... 1
  1.1 An expert witness on the signs of destruction in Hiroshima ... 3
  1.2 The missing uranium ... 6
  1.3 Eyewitness accounts of the attack ... 8
  1.4 What really happened on that day? ... 10
  1.5 The evidence in the case ... 16
  1.6 A brief guide to the remaining chapters of this book ... 21

2 A primer on ionizing radiation and radioactivity ... 23
  2.1 Atoms and subatomic particles ... 23
  2.2 Chemical bonds and molecules ... 25
  2.3 Radioactivity ... 26
  2.4 Interaction of ionizing radiation with matter ... 30
  2.5 Nuclear fission ... 34
  2.6 Ionizing radiation unrelated to radioactivity or nuclear fission ... 38
  2.7 Attenuation of ionizing radiation by matter ... 39
  2.8 Measurement of ionizing radiation ... 43
  2.9 Radiation dose ... 46
  2.10 Forms of radiation released by fission bombs ... 48
  2.11 Biological radiation effects ... 50

3 The nuclear fallout at Hiroshima and Nagasaki — 55
- 3.1 Uranium isotopes in soil samples — 56
- 3.2 Cesium and uranium in samples collected shortly after the bombing — 60
- 3.3 Cesium and plutonium in soil samples from the Hiroshima fallout area — 61
- 3.4 Variability of isotope ratios in the Hiroshima fallout — 64
- 3.5 Cesium and plutonium in sediments from the Nishiyama reservoir near Nagasaki — 66
- 3.6 Enrichment of uranium to bomb grade: was it feasible in 1945? — 68
- 3.7 Did the first atomic test explosion really use a plutonium bomb? — 71
- 3.8 Conclusion — 75

4 Early measurements of residual radioactivity — 77
- 4.1 Timeline and findings of early field measurements — 78
- 4.2 Shimizu's sulfur activation measurements — 81
- 4.3 Conclusion — 83

5 γ-Ray dosimetry by thermoluminescence — 85
- 5.1 Calibration of thermoluminescence measurements — 86
- 5.2 Signal shape and stability — 88
- 5.3 Sample inactivation by heat from the bomb and the fire — 90
- 5.4 Appraisal of reported luminescence data — 94
- 5.5 Conclusion — 96

6 The evidence of neutron radiation — 99
- 6.1 Neutron dose estimates in the T65D and DS86 dosimetry schemes — 99
- 6.2 Measurements of isotopes induced by low-energy neutrons — 107
- 6.3 Sulfur activation measurements — 109
- 6.4 Comparative cobalt and europium activation studies — 118
- 6.5 New and improved measurements: everything finally falls into place — 122
- 6.6 The generational model of fakery — 126
- 6.7 Conclusion — 127

7	**Sulfur mustard and napalm**	**129**
	7.1 Physicochemical properties	130
	7.2 Mode of action and toxicokinetics	131
	7.3 Clinical and pathological manifestations	135
	7.4 Napalm	145
8	**Statistical observations on acute 'radiation' sickness in Hiroshima and Nagasaki**	**147**
	8.1 Physical assumptions	148
	8.2 Manifestations of acute radiation sickness	149
	8.3 Acute radiation doses in Hiroshima and Nagasaki	152
	8.4 Observed distance distribution of ARS in Hiroshima	154
	8.5 Observed distance distribution of ARS in Nagasaki	159
	8.6 ARS symptoms in people shielded by concrete buildings	159
	8.7 ARS in people who were outside Hiroshima at the time of the bombing	161
	8.8 Late-onset ARS	163
	8.9 ARS symptoms and official radiation dose estimates	165
	8.10 Diarrhea as an early symptom of ARS	166
	8.11 The curse of the pharaohs	168
9	**Skin burns in survivors**	**171**
	9.1 Classification of skin burns	172
	9.2 Statistical observations on burns in Hiroshima and Nagasaki	174
	9.3 Fast and slow burns	179
	9.4 Evidence of napalm burns	181
	9.5 Chemical burns by mustard gas	185
	9.6 Appendix: experimental flash burns to the skin	186
10	**Early clinical and pathological findings in the bombing victims**	**189**
	10.1 Clinical picture in early fatalities	190
	10.2 Acute retinal burns: the dog that didn't bark	202
	10.3 Other acute eye lesions	211
	10.4 Lungs	213
	10.5 Neck organs	215
	10.6 Gastrointestinal tract	216

10.7 Other organs 218

11 The radiation dose estimates used in studies on survivors 219
11.1 The Atomic Bomb Casualty Commission (ABCC) . . 220
11.2 Establishment of individual dose estimates 221
11.3 Correlation of radiation dose estimates with ARS symptoms 223
11.4 Dose estimates and somatic chromosome aberrations 225
11.5 The DS86 dosimetry scheme 232
11.6 Conclusion 235

12 Disease in long-term survivors 237
12.1 Malformations and malignant disease in prenatally exposed survivors 238
12.2 Cancer and leukemia 248
12.3 Long-term disease other than cancer 262
12.4 Conclusion 266

13 How was it done? 267
13.1 The make-believe nuclear detonation 268
13.2 The conventional attack and its concealment 278
13.3 Japanese collusion 283
13.4 Censorship and propaganda 292
13.5 Special effects 296
13.6 Additional evidence against the nuclear detonation 298

14 Why was it done? 305
14.1 The object was not to obtain Japan's surrender . . . 305
14.2 The purpose of the fake bombings was not to intimidate Stalin 309
14.3 The faked nuclear bombings as terror acts 312
14.4 Two competing views on modern history 315

Afterword 319

References 323

List of Figures

1.1	Portrait of Alexander P. de Seversky	5
1.2	Plaster board contaminated with black rain streaks .	7
2.1	Bohr model of atomic structure	24
2.2	Time course of activity for three hypothetical nuclides with different half-lives	28
2.3	Neutron capture cross sections of ^{59}Co and ^{235}U . . .	33
2.4	Fission products of ^{239}Pu and ^{235}U	35
2.5	Nuclear stability as a function of proton and neutron numbers	36
2.6	Radiosensitivity and differentiation of cells in tissues	52
3.1	Area affected by black rain near Hiroshima	57
3.2	α-Ray spectra of uranium extracted from soil samples	58
3.3	γ-Ray spectrum of one of the samples collected on August 9th 1945 by Yoshio Nishina	61
3.4	Cesium and plutonium activities in soil samples from Hiroshima	63
3.5	Variability of isotope ratios in studies on fallout from Hiroshima	65
3.6	Radioactive fallout in sediments from Nishiyama reservoir near Nagasaki	67
4.1	Estimates and measurements of induced radioactivity in Hiroshima	81
5.1	Thermoluminescence curves of brick or tile samples	88
5.2	Depth profile of thermoluminescence intensity in a laboratory-irradiated brick, and roof tile from Nagasaki with surface damaged by heat	89
5.3	Three of many burnt-out buildings	92

List of Figures

5.4	Sample thermoluminescence, calibration factors, and γ-dosages as functions of distance from the hypocenters in Hiroshima and Nagasaki	95
6.1	Neutron fluence observed in a 'typical bomb test' . .	101
6.2	Neutron source spectrum of the Hiroshima bomb . .	103
6.3	Neutron relaxation lengths in the T65D and the DS02 models	106
6.4	Ratio of measured to calculated neutron activation as a function of distance from the epicenter	109
6.5	Measurements and calculations of ^{32}P formation through capture of fast neutrons at Hiroshima	114
6.6	Estimation of fast neutron relaxation length λ from measurements of ^{32}P induced in sulfur samples in Hiroshima	117
6.7	Estimating the date of neutron activation by comparing calculated fluences for various isotopes	120
6.8	Measurements of fast neutron fluence at Hiroshima by ^{63}Ni induced in metallic copper samples	125
7.1	Structures of sulfur mustard and of lewisite	130
7.2	Cross-linking of guanine bases in DNA by sulfur mustard	132
7.3	Metabolism of sulfur mustard	136
7.4	Ocular symptoms of mustard gas exposure	139
7.5	Skin lesions in mustard gas victims	141
7.6	Clothes or hair do not protect from mustard gas . .	143
8.1	Estimated radiation doses at Hiroshima and Nagasaki	153
8.2	Location of survivors of the Hiroshima bombing by shielding and distance from the hypocenter	155
8.3	Symptoms of ARS in 525 persons who were outside Hiroshima during the bombing	162
8.4	Time of onset of purpura and oropharyngeal lesions in Hiroshima bombing victims, and blood cell counts in accidentally irradiated patients	164
8.5	Numbers of survivors grouped by dose values, and incidence of ARS symptoms among those assigned an estimated dose of 6 Gy	166

List of Figures

8.6	Time of onset of diarrhea and vomiting in Hiroshima bombing victims	168
9.1	Radiant heat and incidence of burns as functions of distance from the hypocenters at Hiroshima and Nagasaki	175
9.2	Burns of the skin limited to areas that had been covered with clothing	176
9.3	Skin lesions in Hiroshima bombing victims ascribed to 'flash burn'	178
9.4	Two cases of 'nuclear flash burn' from Nagasaki	180
9.5	Victims of the napalm attack at Trang Bang, South Vietnam, on June 8th 1972	182
9.6	Splash burn to the face and neck caused by napalm and gasoline	183
10.1	Patient with capillary leak syndrome	196
10.2	Effects of pupil diameter and of object distance on retinal images	204
10.3	Nuclear flash burns of the retina in a human and in a rabbit	205
10.4	Thermal energy density and diameter of retinal images of the Hiroshima and Nagasaki nuclear bombs	206
10.5	Denuded corneal epithelium	212
10.6	Lung emphysema (excessive inflation) and atelectasis (excessive deflation) in an early fatality from Hiroshima	214
10.7	Focal necrosis, inflammation, and hemorrhage in the lungs of bombing victims	215
11.1	Mortality due to experimental irradiation in mice and rhesus monkeys, and incidence of ARS symptoms vs. estimated radiation doses in A-bomb survivors	224
11.2	Induction of chromosome aberrations by DNA damage	226
11.3	Chromosome aberrations in peripheral blood lymphocytes observed in A-bomb survivors	229
11.4	Leukemia rates in Hiroshima and Nagasaki vs. radiation dose estimates	233
11.5	Chromosome aberrations in bombing survivors vs. T65D and DS86 dose estimates	234

12.1 Time correlation of mouse and human embryonic development, and time-dependent effect of prenatal irradiation on brain growth in rats	239
12.2 Embryotoxic effects of X-rays and of alkylating agents	241
12.3 Mental retardation in children exposed in utero at Hiroshima and Nagasaki	242
12.4 Microcephaly and mental retardation in children who were exposed *in utero*: time of exposure vs. distance from hypocenter	245
12.5 Cancer and leukemia risk vs. radiation dose estimates and clinical symptoms	249
12.6 Cancer risk of Hiroshima bombing survivors compared to control groups from outside the city	252
12.7 Cancer risk in subjects directly exposed to the Hiroshima bombing and in early entrants to the city . .	257
12.8 Distribution of cancer risk about the hypocenter in Hiroshima	260
13.1 Photograph of downtown Hiroshima, taken by Alexander P. de Seversky during his visit in early September 1945	288
13.2 Wind speed of the pressure wave of a 'nominal' atomic bomb	299
13.3 Shadows on the Bantai bridge: observation vs. prediction	300
13.4 Purported effects of the Hiroshima bomb on tombstones in the city	301
13.5 The "Trinity" bomb test	303

List of Tables

2.1	Relative biological effectiveness (RBE) of different types of ionizing radiation	48
4.1	Early measurements of environmental radioactivity in Hiroshima	79
5.1	Thermoluminescence measurements on tiles and bricks in Hiroshima and Nagasaki	87
6.1	Neutron radiation in Hiroshima: relaxation lengths determined from studies preceding the DS02 report	107
6.2	The Kyoto sulfur activation measurements	112
6.3	Neutron fluence estimates obtained from a roof tile sample in Hiroshima	119
6.4	Nuclear data and measurements used to calculate the timing of neutron activation	121
6.5	Comparison of three neutron activation studies using multiple isotopes	123
8.1	Prevalence of acute radiation sickness in Hiroshima patients 20 days after the bombing	157
8.2	Attenuation of γ-rays and fast neutrons by different materials	160
12.1	Association of death due to cancer or leukemia with burns	250
12.2	Incidence of leukemia in early entrants to Hiroshima	256
12.3	Cataract incidence in Hiroshima survivors by distance from the hypocenter	265

Foreword

In this well researched and eminently readable book, Palmer has corralled the available evidence that the war-ending bombs dropped on Hiroshima and Nagasaki in August 1945 were not atom bombs.

What? What's that you say?

Your family and friends, like mine, may find this notion incredible. If they do, ask them to read the book; it's free online (see URL on the imprint page). I predict that most of those who take your suggestion will agree that the conventional Manhattan Project history may well be a contender for the *Greatest Hoax of all Time*. During the reading, readers both old enough to have experienced and young enough to remember those times may experience some *Ah ha!* moments. Palmer kicks off his study by analyzing physical data that reveal the hoax. In this, he makes good use of the recent book by Akio Nakatani: *Death Object: Exploding the Nuclear Weapons Hoax* [1], which draws upon reports by those who have examined the scene and assert that the destruction of those two cities was, by all appearances, the result of fire-bombing, like that which had already destroyed most of Japan's major cities.

Palmer reviews and expands on this convincing physical evidence, and then complements it by analyzing the effects of the bomb on people. He concludes that the reported 'radiation effects' expected from an atom bomb are, instead, effects of sulfur mustard gas and napalm. It is not surprising that government documents regarding medical effects among victims and survivors remain classified for reasons of 'national security'. Several chapters provide primers on elementary aspects of nuclear physics and human physiology that will be appreciated by those who aim for a critical understanding of Palmer's thesis.

Thanks to this book, I can now understand a pair of perplexing conversations I had in the 1960s. The first, which took place in the new Institute for Molecular Biology at the University of Oregon, was with its founding director who told me that one of his activities in the Manhattan project was to collect soil samples from the site of the

Trinity test a few hours after the explosion. An interesting story, but how come he was alive to tell it? Wasn't the site lethally radioactive from a ground level explosion of a plutonium bomb?

The other puzzling conversation occurred during a flight to the west coast. A noted geneticist was angry with a world-famous chemist who, he claimed, grossly exaggerated the genetic damage from the Hiroshima atrocity. Why would the chemist, whom I knew and trusted, do such a thing? Palmer's book provided the *Ah ha!* moments for both these puzzles.

The young director was not killed by intensely radioactive soil at the site simply because the test bomb had not been an atom bomb. The chemist, relying on physicists' estimates of the bomb's radiation intensity, used experimentally derived relations between radiation dose and mutation rates to predict the genetic damage to Hiroshima survivors and their offspring. The geneticist, on the other hand, had made direct observations on children born to survivors and not found the level of damage that the chemist had estimated—in fact, such studies have found only slight and non-significant increases of genetic disease in the offspring of survivors.

Some readers will acknowledge that Palmer has made a strong scientific case for the fakery but will resist it without answers to "How was it done?" and "Why?". In the final two chapters, the author takes on those questions with arguments that are, by necessity, speculative. Please don't cheat by reading these chapters first. Their conclusions are likely to appear reasonable only after you have acknowledged the possibility of the book's primary conclusion, that We the People have been taken in by this enormous hoax.

Franklin Stahl

Preface

> We ought in fairness to fight our case with no help beyond the bare facts: nothing, therefore, should matter except the proof of those facts.
>
> Aristotle, Rhetoric

If you are even considering to read this book, you are most likely already aware that mainstream history is not always truthful. Therefore, we can skip that part and jump right in. This book explores the scientific evidence pertaining to the 'atomic' bombings of Hiroshima and Nagasaki. My inquiry into this subject began one morning when, on the web, I stumbled upon someone's assertion that the nuclear bombings had been a hoax; I don't recall now who had said it or where. However, I remember that, when trying to learn more, I found Swedish engineer and entrepreneur Anders Björkman. On his website, Anders argues that atomic bombs won't work in principle. Having trained as an MD only, I will abstain from judging the merit of this far-reaching claim. Nevertheless, Anders also shares some intriguing personal experiences with direct bearing on the story of the Japanese 'atomic' bombings and on the early stages of nuclear arms development. It thus was Anders' work which first convinced me that at least the story of the Hiroshima and Nagasaki bombings must be false.

Of course, if one believes that, then the question arises: what is the matter with all the science which surrounds these two events? What about the fallout, the cancer, the radiation sickness? There cannot be two truths: either Anders is crazy and the science is right, or Anders is right and the science is crazy.

The book before you argues that indeed the science is *kaput*, and that this has been so since the very beginning of the 'atomic age'. It considers both the physical and the medical evidence, supplemented where necessary with eyewitness testimony, to unequivocally reject the story of the atomic bombings of both cities. In its place, the book develops a scenario of conventional killing and destruction with poison gas, napalm, and high explosives. In detail, this interpretation may be incomplete or mistaken, but overall it fits the available evidence far better than the atomic tall tale. The final chapter examines the motives behind the staged bombing; while the result is less solidly grounded than the analysis of the scientific evidence, I felt that this question should not be left out.

This treatise attempts to get at the truth, but cannot lay claim to the whole truth; too much evidence remains hidden from view, even 75 years after the events. While it contains no deliberate falsehoods, it most likely will contain some errors. If you find one, be it in substance or in detail, I will be grateful to you for pointing it out, so that the book can be improved.

Acknowledgments

I owe a debt of gratitude to a number of people who read earlier versions of the manuscript and offered suggestions, useful criticism, and encouragement. Franklin Stahl not only contributed the foreword and suggested the title for the book, but he also repeatedly went through the whole manuscript, raising important questions and pointing out errors of fact and of judgment. Hans Vogel gave freely of his time to share insights into the political and historical context; he alerted me to several important references which found their way into the concluding chapters of the book. He also made valuable suggestions concerning some of the technical and scientific aspects, as did Jurek Bem. Two physicists who prefer to remain anonymous helped with proofreading some of the physical chapters. A colleague from Japan, Teruichi Harada, helped with procuring several Japanese references and translating them into English; he also made multiple corrections to this text. Another colleague, who is a native speaker of Russian, helped with translations from that language. Jana Rade created a cover graphic that captures vividly the atrocious events this investigation has brought to light.

Among the members of my own family, the manuscript found a decidedly mixed reception—I appreciate both their encouragement and their rejection, because they showed me early on what kind of echo to expect when trying to tell this 'far-out' story.

1 Why doubt the nuclear bombings of Hiroshima and Nagasaki?

> It's got nothing to do with atoms.
>
> Werner Heisenberg [2]

The detonation of the nuclear bomb above Hiroshima marks the beginning of the 'atomic age.' Isn't this an incontrovertible historic fact? Most people probably would say so. Yet, there were those who refused to believe it, at least in the beginning; and among them were leading nuclear physicists, including Werner Heisenberg [2, p. 116]. In time, however, they and the world at large were persuaded that the story was true. Why doubt it?

The story of the atomic bomb is certainly replete with astonishing achievements. The principle of nuclear fission was discovered only in 1938. At that time, no methods existed for isolating the fissile isotope ^{235}U,[1] which is only a minor constituent of natural uranium, but which must be almost pure for building a bomb. Even if highly enriched ^{235}U had immediately been available, one would think that first investigating its properties and behavior, then applying this new knowledge to the design of a novel bomb, and finally testing that bomb, should have taken considerable time. Indeed, some fairly preliminary experiments were going on as late as 1944. Morton Camac, a physicist who had just joined the 'Manhattan Project' fresh out of college, recounts:[2]

> *I participated in an experiment in which Uranium 235 placed in a plastic bag was dropped down the middle of a sphere with hydro-*

---

[1] The concept of isotopes and the notation used to describe them are explained in Section 2.1.

[2] The cited document [3] was obtained from a website that supports the official narrative, but I have been unable to connect it with any other of Camac's writings. Nevertheless, I tentatively judge it authentic, since it does tie in with his CV, and it is written in the jaunty yet precise style that is characteristic of reminiscing scientists. It contains some other statements that might surprise you—well worth a read.

carbons. The purpose was to determine the critical setup using only the neutrons from the reaction and not from the radioactive atoms. ... The amount of Uranium was increased with each dropping. In the final dropping the neutron growth rate was so fast that the plastic melted ... We were lucky that we were not killed.

This simple procedure of trial and error differs a little from the mental picture I had formed, which featured genius theoreticians with furrowed brows, deducing the exact critical mass and the time course of the detonation from first principles alone; equipped with only chalk and blackboard, and with the largest coffeemaker the world had ever seen. Yet, only one year after this venturesome experiment, American ingenuity emerged triumphant: the first ever uranium bomb, though never once tested before,[3] went off without a hitch to obliterate Hiroshima. Does this really sound true to life, or rather like something out of Hollywood? Should we censure Heisenberg for spontaneously calling it a bluff?

Of course, this question cannot be settled by insinuations, but only by the evidence; and that is what I will attempt in this book. Before going any further, however, I should point out that the book before you is not the first one to argue that the 'nuclear bomb' in Hiroshima was a fraud. A recent work entitled *Death Object: Exploding the Nuclear Weapons Hoax* [1] makes the same case, yet goes beyond it to reject the existence of nuclear weapons altogether. Its author, Akio Nakatani (apparently a pen name), claims to be an expert in applied mathematics, and furthermore to have carried out his own computer simulations of the Hiroshima and Nagasaki bomb designs, which show that these bombs could not have worked. He does, however, not describe these calculations in detail:

Though I could nuke the entire orthodoxy with the scientific result ... unfortunately due to archaic USA national security laws ... I cannot present that openly, [therefore] I am doing the next best thing, which is to compile ... the voluminous circumstantial evidence.

Nakatani generalizes his findings to conclude that nuclear bombs are impossible in principle. He indeed presents ample evidence to

---

[3] The 'Trinity' test explosion in New Mexico is said to have been a plutonium bomb resembling that used at Nagasaki.

demonstrate that the systematic fakery goes well beyond Hiroshima and Nagasaki, and I highly recommend his book. However, I will here take a somewhat different approach: instead of addressing the subject of atomic weapons in its entirety, which I am not competent to do,[4] I will focus on the scientific and medical evidence pertaining to Hiroshima and Nagasaki, which I will examine at greater depth. The findings will neither supersede nor merely duplicate Nakatani's work, but rather they will complement it.

Apart from some general works, several of which I hesitate to call 'nonfiction', the sources for this book are mostly scientific books and peer-reviewed articles, all of which are publicly available and have been carefully referenced. In this chapter, I will present some selected pieces of evidence; each of the topics thus introduced, and others, will be treated at greater length in later chapters.

1.1 An expert witness on the signs of destruction in Hiroshima

Alexander P. de Seversky (Figure 1.1) was a Russian-American pilot and also an eminent aeronautical engineer. After the end of World War II, he was sent on an official mission to report on the results of the Allied bombing campaigns in Germany and Japan. On this tour, he also visited Hiroshima and Nagasaki. He describes his impressions from this visit in his work *Air power: key to survival* [5]. The following is quoted from the ninth chapter of his book:

> I WAS *keyed up for my first view of an atom-bombed city, prepared for the radically new sights suggested by the exciting descriptions I had read and heard. But to my utter astonishment, Hiroshima from the air looked exactly like all the other burned-out cities I had observed!*
>
> *Within an area defined by black, undestroyed houses there was the familiar pink carpet, about two miles in diameter. What is more, precisely as in Yokohama, Osaka, or Kobe, it was dotted with buildings still standing erect, with charred trees, poles, and other*

---

[4]I would note, however, that regardless of the viability of the Hiroshima and Nagasaki bomb designs, I consider nuclear detonations to be possible in principle, and also to have actually occurred during later bomb tests. Whether the designs, explosive yields, and suitability as weapons of such test devices are realistically described in the literature [4] is a separate question which this book will not attempt to answer.

> objects.[5] *All but one of the steel and concrete bridges were intact. A cluster of modern concrete buildings in the downtown section stood upright and seemingly undamaged. ...*
>
> *I had heard about buildings instantly consumed by unprecedented heat. Yet here were buildings structurally intact, with outside and stone facings in place. What is more, I found them topped by undamaged flag poles, lightning rods, painted railings, air-raid sirens, and other fragile objects. Clearly they had weathered the blast and somehow escaped the infernal heat, as well as the alleged super-hurricane thousand-mile-an-hour wind.*
>
> *For two days I examined Hiroshima. I drove to T Bridge, which had been the aiming point for the atomic bomb. In its environs I looked for the bald spot where everything presumably had been vaporized or boiled to dust in the twinkling of an eye. It wasn't there or anywhere else in the city. I searched for other traces of phenomena that could reasonably be tagged "unusual." I couldn't find them.*

In his subsequent chapter, entitled *Atomic hysteria and common sense*, de Seversky writes about the reactions to his report from Hiroshima in the United States:

> THE STORY *sketched in the preceding chapter obviously was different from the one then being told virtually in unison by press, radio, and scientists. Against the prevailing hyperbole it must have sounded more incredible than I suspected. But it was the only story I could conscientiously tell when I was questioned by newspapermen in Tokyo and back home in America.*
>
> *I did not "underrate" the atom bomb or dispute its future potential. Certainly I did not dismiss lightly the infernal horror visited on Hiroshima and Nagasaki. As an engineer, I limited myself to an analysis of the demolition accomplished by particular bombs exploded in a particular way. These one-man observations I em-*

---

[5] Elsewhere, de Seversky invokes 'rusted metal' to account for the commonly observed 'pink carpet'. However, most buildings in Hiroshima, and in many other bombed cities, were of wooden construction and most likely contained only small amounts of iron that could have been oxidized and dispersed in the fire. It seems more likely that the fires caused the oxidation of inorganic iron already contained in the ground; the same effect causes gray bricks to turn red when fired. An alternate explanation which points specifically to napalm is considered in the footnote on page 145.

Figure 1.1: Alexander P. de Seversky at his desk. A photograph that shows him with Harry Truman is in the background, and a copy of his book cited here [5] is in the foreground. The Wikipedia page on de Seversky lists several of his books, but this one is conspicuous by its absence.

> bodied in a formal report to the Secretary of War, who released it to the public. In addition I wrote several articles on the subject.
>
> Whereupon all hell broke loose over my sinful head. My findings were pounced upon by all sorts of people in angry fury, on the air, in the press, at public forums; scientists who hadn't been within five thousand miles of the atomized cities solemnly issued condemnations of my heretical views. Almost for the first time in my career I found myself in the position of a "conservative" under fire from "extremists."

As is clear from de Seversky's protestations, he did not question the reality of the atomic bombs. His only 'sin' was to faithfully report the lack of evidence of their distinct and apocalyptic effects; the bombed cities of Hiroshima and Nagasaki had impressed him in much the same way as the many cities destroyed by conventional air bombing which he had visited before.

We will return to the question of what visible traces a nuclear blast should or should not have left behind in Chapter 13; here, we will simply note that the visible signs of Hiroshima's destruction were compatible with a conventional bombing raid. Let us now sample some proper, quantifiable physical evidence.

1.2 The missing uranium

The Hiroshima bomb ('Little Boy') purportedly contained some 64 kg of total uranium, within which the fissile ^{235}U isotope was enriched to 80%; this corresponds to approximately 50 kg of ^{235}U. Furthermore, of those 50 kg, less than 1 kg is said to actually have fissioned. Where did the other 49 kg go?[6]

Several scientific studies have looked for this uranium, but all have come up short. One such study was carried out by Shizuma et al. [6]. The authors obtained samples from an interior plaster board of a house whose roof had been blown off in the attack, and which had been soiled by the notorious 'black rain' that came down a short while after the bombing. The plaster board in question is shown in Figure 1.2.

The traces left by the black rain were analyzed for uranium using mass spectrometry, which separates chemical elements and their isotopes according to atomic weight. Because uranium has significant abundance in nature,[7] the question arises how much, if any, of the uranium detected in the samples might be due to natural background, and how much is derived from the bomb. Since natural uranium contains > 99% ^{238}U, while bomb uranium should be 80% ^{235}U, this question can readily be answered: the higher the isotope ratio $^{235}U/^{238}U$ in the sample, the greater the fraction of bomb uranium.

What is the answer?

In most of the samples studied, the isotope ratio deviated only very slightly from the natural one, indicating negligible amounts of bomb-derived uranium. The highest ratio was observed with a sample taken from the upper edge of the plaster board, which unlike the face of the board had not been wiped down by the house's residents. The ratio observed in this sample—0.88%, vs. 0.72% in natural uranium—indicates

---

[6] One can find somewhat different numbers for the exact amount of uranium contained in the bomb and its degree of isotopic enrichment, but none seem to have been endorsed by any relevant government or international agency.

[7] Since the natural abundance of ^{235}U in uranium ore is only about 0.72%—with most of the rest being ^{238}U—preparing that amount is no mean feat in itself. In Section 3.6, I will argue that the technology most likely did not exist at the time; however, for now this question will be set aside.

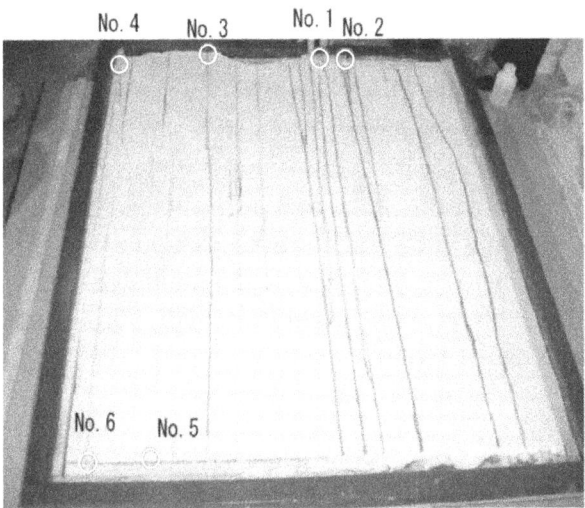

Figure 1.2: Plaster board contaminated with black rain streaks (photograph taken from [6]). Circles indicate locations that were sampled. Sample 3—the sample that yielded the highest amounts of the telltale isotopes (see text)—is located not on the face of the board but rather on its upper edge.

that, of the total uranium in the sample, *just 0.2% would be derived from the bomb*.

This value surely is surprisingly low; so low, in fact, that one might wonder if these samples contained any bomb-derived uranium at all. Could it be that those black stripes were not what they were believed to be—that they had no relation to the black rain at all? Two arguments can be raised against this. Firstly, mass spectrometry is highly accurate—a deviation in the uranium isotope ratio as high as observed would not arise through a statistical fluke.

Secondly, in addition to ^{235}U, the authors also found small amounts of radioactive cesium (^{137}Cs) in those same samples. This isotope is one of the main products of nuclear fission. Its radioactive half-life is much shorter than those of ^{235}U and ^{238}U—only 30 years. This is far too short for it to occur in nature; therefore, ^{137}Cs is a telltale sign of artificial, man-made nuclear fission.

Should neither of the above arguments satisfy you, be advised that the number reported by Shizuma et al. [6]—bomb-derived uranium amounting to just 0.2% of the natural background—is the *highest* figure reported in any of the studies on Hiroshima fallout that I could find.

Thus, if we reject this number as invalid for being too low, we must reject all those other studies also, and we are left without any evidence at all of ^{235}U in the fallout.

We can conclude that both ^{235}U and ^{137}Cs fell upon Hiroshima on August 6, 1945. The very low abundance of ^{235}U in the fallout, however, fits very poorly with the story of the purported nuclear blast, and indeed this notion will be laid to rest altogether by a more in-depth analysis of published scientific data in Chapter 3. For now, let us turn to some witness testimony about the event itself. Surely, those dramatic accounts of a singularly violent explosion will tell the story, and obviate the need to puzzle over dirt on plaster boards?

1.3 Eyewitness accounts of the attack

Eye witnesses of the bomb are unanimous that the atomic bomb produced an intense, blinding flash, quickly followed by an enormous bang. Or are they? Consider this quote from John Hersey's famous book, *Hiroshima* [7]:

> *Then a tremendous flash of light cut across the sky. Mr. Tanimoto has a distinct recollection that it traveled from east to west, from the city towards the hills. It seemed a sheet of sun. ... He felt a sudden pressure, and then splinters and pieces of board and fragments of tile fell on him. He heard no roar. (Almost no one in Hiroshima recalls hearing any noise of the bomb. But a fisherman ... saw the flash and heard a tremendous explosion; he was nearly twenty miles from Hiroshima.)*

Whether nuclear or not, it is astonishing that an explosion should be audible from twenty miles away, but inaudible from almost directly underneath it. Could it be that all those close to the detonation simply had their ears shattered before they even could perceive the sound? Apparently not—Ishikawa et al. [8, p. 126] state that only 1% of all hospitalized patients in Hiroshima had ruptured eardrums (but 8% of those in Nagasaki; both values are within the range observed in conventional bombings [9]).

Another interesting source is Keller [10], an American physician who was working in Japan during the fall of 1945. He writes:

> *The information presented in this report was obtained from studies on 21 patients who were admitted to the Osaka University Hospi-*

tal in late August and early September 1945 suffering from an alarming malady designated atomic bomb disease by the Japanese. I observed, examined and followed approximately half of the patients, while information on the remaining patients was taken from the hospital records.

Only 5 patients recalled experiencing a definite concussion wave at the time of the atomic bomb explosion. One of the 5 who was in a wooden building about 50 meters from the center of the explosion was thrown 12 feet by the blast as the building collapsed. The 2 victims who were outdoors had contrasting experience in that 1 was knocked unconscious while the other 1 felt no blast.

Three patients recall hearing a noise "like the sound of an explosion." One described a noise that sounded "like a falling bomb," and 2 said the noise they heard at the time of the atomic bomb explosion was a sound "like rain." Two stated that they heard no definite sound of an explosion, while the remaining 13 were uncertain.

Nine patients were conscious of a "flash of light" when the bomb exploded. One of the 9 described the light as being green. Three of the remaining 12 patients experienced no sensation of light, while the other 9 case records do not specify one way or the other.

There is no need to belabor the stark contrasts in this testimony, but I do want to draw your attention to the first of Keller's patients—the one who was just 50 meters from the hypocenter, shielded from radiation by nothing more than a wooden house. If there had indeed been a proper nuclear detonation, he should have been killed immediately, or at least very rapidly, by the blast, the heat, and the radiation; but here he is, some four weeks later: hospitalized and 'alarmingly' ill, but alive enough to tell the tale.[8]

The remainder of Keller's article consists of clinical and laboratory findings on what he interprets as radiation sickness. When examined in detail, such observations also fail to support crucial aspects of the official story, as will be shown in Chapter 8. For now, we note that the available witness testimony on the blast and the flash expected of a proper nuclear detonation is inconsistent.

---

[8]While one might dismiss a single such case report as spurious, Chapter 8 will show that there are more.

One aspect that we have not yet considered is the 'mushroom cloud' that rose above Hiroshima during and after the attack. The first thing to note is that such clouds—referred to as *flammagenitus* or *pyrocumulus* clouds—are not limited to nuclear detonations, but are also seen above wildfires or burning cities. In fact, even the New York Times, in a piece entitled *The Hiroshima Mushroom Cloud That Wasn't* [11], has claimed that the mushroom cloud above Hiroshima was caused by the burning of the city rather than the nuclear detonation. However, eyewitnesses report that a large, mushroom-like cloud formed very early on in the attack, before large-scale fires had broken out in the city. Various ingredients likely to have been used in the creation of this cloud will be discussed in Section 13.1.4.

1.4 What really happened on that day?

If we maintain that no actual nuclear blast occurred at Hiroshima, we must provide an alternate explanation for the destruction, the radioactive fallout (small as it may be), and also for the medical findings in numerous victims that broadly resemble those of exposure to intense irradiation. These questions are also discussed by Nakatani [1], who proposes that the city was destroyed by a conventional bombing raid.

1.4.1 Phony nuclear detonations. Nakatani discusses a non-nuclear pyrotechnical scenario for the 'flash', which, even though not perceived by all witnesses, does seem to figure more commonly in victim testimony than the 'bang'. He suggests that photoflash bombs were used—perhaps of the AN-M46 type. Indeed, quite a few witnesses liken the impression to that of a photographer's flash, such as for example Toyofumi Ogura [12, p. 15]:

> *I saw, or rather felt, an enormous bluish white flash of light, as when a photographer lights a dish of magnesium.*

Spectacular though it was, the light emitted by this flash must have been considerably less intense than that of a real nuclear detonation, as we will see in Section 10.2.

The 'bang' was probably not created by a single detonation but by several separate large bombs burst in the air. This is discussed in some more detail in Section 13.1.2.

1.4.2 Destruction of the cities with incendiary bombs. Most buildings in Japanese cities were constructed from wood. Consequently, in their conventional bombing raids, the Americans relied mostly on incendiaries, which according to the U.S. Strategic bombing survey [13] included both 'oil-gel' (napalm) and thermite-magnesium bombs. As we shall see later, only the use of napalm is supported by strong evidence. Even though scattered, some witness reports of incendiary bombs falling on Hiroshima and Nagasaki can be found; but as will be discussed in Section 13.2, most bombs were likely detonated already in the air, and only a small number reached the ground.

1.4.3 Dispersal of reactor waste to create some fallout. Finally, Nakatani posits that some radioactivity—probably reactor waste—was dispersed using conventional explosives, relating that such a device—known as a 'dirty bomb'—had previously been tested in New Mexico. Chapter 3 will show that scattered reactor waste fits the published scientific findings on 'Little Boy's' radioactive fallout much better than does the official story of a nuclear detonation.

1.4.4 Use of mustard gas to fake 'radiation sickness'. Keller [10] reports that many Hiroshima victims suffered from bone marrow suppression and other symptoms that are commonly observed in patients exposed to strong irradiation, be it by accident or for treatment; and these statements are confirmed by many other medical case studies and surveys. The very low amount of dispersed radioactive material apparent from studies such as Shizuma et al. [6] cannot account for these observations.

Nakatani recognizes this incongruity and proposes that clinical reports of radiation sickness are mostly fabricated, although he suggests that a dirty bomb might have produced some real cases. I concur in principle that much of the science that surrounds this event is fraudulent, and I will discuss some specific examples in later chapters. However, the medical reports are too numerous and come from too many independent sources to be so nonchalantly dismissed, and in fact they can be readily explained by the use of poison gas. Eyewitness testimony from Hiroshima is replete with references to poisonous gas and its deleterious effects. Among 105 witnesses who experienced the Hiroshima bombing as school age children, and whose memories were collected and published by the Japanese teacher Arata Osada [14], 13 explicitly mention poisonous gas or fumes.[9] One of them, Hisato Itoh, died shortly after writing his account, which contains this statement:

Both my mother and I had been through a great deal of strain during this time ... and then we also started to feel listless and began to lose our hair because we had breathed the gases when the atom bomb fell.

The possible use of poison gas was brought up early on by Dr. Masao Tsuzuki, the leading Japanese member on the U.S.-Japanese 'Joint Commission' of medical scientists convened to investigate the aftermath of the bombing. The historian Sey Nishimura [15] quotes from a 1945 article by Tsuzuki:

Immediately after the explosion of the atomic bomb, some gas permeated, which appeared like white smoke with stimulating odor. Many reported that when inhaled, it caused acute sore throat or suffocating pain.

According to Nishimura, Tsuzuki's position concerning the gas attracted the attention of the U.S. military censors, who, for violation of their rule that "news must be factual, devoid of conjecture," struck out the following passage from his manuscript:

Considering from various points, generation of something like poisonous gas accompanying the explosion operation is conceivable, and it is not hard to conjecture that there were perhaps war victims who died of these poisons. At present we have no clue whether it was devised on purpose so as to radiate something like poisonous gas. If I have a chance, I'd like to put a question to America on this matter.

Again according to Nishimura, Tsuzuki nevertheless reaffirmed his position in another report six years later:

Everyone experienced inhalation of a certain indescribable malodorous gas. This may be considered city stench, which was induced by fierce wind from the explosion; a part of it might have originated from electrolytes generated by application of radioactivity to air. What this so-called "gas" is, is not clear. But it is not unthinkable that it could be invasive to the human body.

---

[9] Several more of these are quoted in Section 13.4.2.

Tsuzuki's conjecture on the radiogenic origin of the gas is sound in principle: ionizing radiation traveling through air can indeed produce pungent, aggressive gases such as ozone and oxides of nitrogen. However, assuming that no nuclear detonation actually happened, we can rule out this possibility, which means that any poisonous gas present must have been dropped in finished form during the air raid. It is interesting to note that the first independent journalist to report from Hiroshima, the Australian Wilfred Burchett [16],[10] also brings up poison gas:

My nose detected a peculiar odour unlike anything I have ever smelled before. It is something like sulphur, but not quite. I could smell it when I passed a fire that was still smouldering, or at a spot where they were still recovering bodies from the wreckage. But I could also smell it where everything was still deserted.

The gas plagued the people even four weeks after the event:

And so the people of Hiroshima today are walking through the forlorn desolation of their once proud city with gauze masks over their mouths and noses.

The Japanese interviewed by Burchett conflated it with radioactivity:

They believe it [the smell] is given off by the poisonous gas still issuing from the earth soaked with radioactivity released by the split uranium atom.

Their conjecture on the origin of the gas must be false, for there is no plausible mechanism by which radiation or fallout from a nuclear bomb could produce this sort of lingering fumes.[11] However, this should not mislead us into discounting their perceptions altogether; surely no one toiling in hot summer weather will wear a face mask without reason. What kind of gas would fit this entire scenario?

The most likely candidate is sulfur mustard, which had been used as a chemical weapon in World War I, and which was so used again more recently by Iraq in its war against Iran. Sulfur mustard mimics both the acute and the chronic effects of radiation on the human

---

[10]This report first appeared under the byline 'Peter Burchett' in the *Daily Express* on September fifth, 1945.

[11]As stated above, some ozone and nitrogen oxides might well be produced in a nuclear blast, but they would be short-lived.

body. In particular, like radiation, mustard gas damages the bone marrow, the hair follicles, and other rapidly proliferating tissues; and this commonality was already well understood at the time [17].[12]

An oily fluid, sulfur mustard can evaporate slowly over time; its smell resembles that of 'garlic, addled eggs, or oil-roasted vegetables' [19] and is also sometimes described as sulfuric. It can persist in the environment for considerable periods of time [20], which would explain that Burchett still noted its stench and its effects when he visited Hiroshima in early September.

1.4.5 Preparedness of the U.S. military for the use of mustard gas. The U.S. had stockpiled sulfur mustard in World War II and had even conducted experiments on some of their own soldiers.[13]

In 1943, numerous U.S. servicemen and civilians had been killed by the poison in the Italian port city of Bari after a German air attack struck an American military transport ship which had carried a large consignment of aerial bombs filled with mustard gas.[14] This disaster would have been fresh on the minds of the military brass when plans for the fake nuclear bombings were first sketched out.[15]

While the effects of mustard gas resemble those of radiation in several ways, there nonetheless are differences between the two. A nuclear detonation will produce radiation predominantly in the form of γ-rays and of neutrons, both of which are highly penetrating and thus have marked effects on rapidly proliferating tissues deep inside the body; they will destroy the bone marrow at dosages well below those that will severely harm the skin, the lungs, and even the intestines,

---

[12]Substances with such properties are sometimes referred to as *radiomimetic* [18]; and the cytotoxic effects of both radiation and radiomimetic chemicals are exploited in the treatment of cancers and leukemias.

[13]According to the book *Veterans at Risk: The Health Effects of Mustard Gas and Lewisite* [21], this program involved more than 60,000 military personnel; in a later survey of these subjects, only 12 out of 257 respondents reported no adverse health effects.

[14]Alexander, the medical officer who oversaw the treatment of the mustard victims at Bari, writes that 83 servicemen died of the poison in hospitals [22], but also indicates that the overall death toll was likely higher (e.g., he states that all those aboard the ship that had carried the sulfur mustard were killed). The civilian death toll was likely much higher [23, 24].

[15]Interestingly, according to Brodie [25], research on reactor development, military use of fission products, and mustard gas toxicity were all concentrated at the University of Chicago in the early 1940s. In some of these studies, the effects of mustard gas and of nuclear fission products on lung tissue were compared side-by-side in animal experiments [26].

although these are second in susceptibility only to the bone marrow. Mustard gas, in contrast, must be taken up through the skin or the mucous membranes of the lungs or intestines, and in the process it will produce marked and early symptoms of damage to these organs. You may have read accounts like the following, again taken from John Hersey [7]:

> *The eyebrows of some were burned off and skin hung from their faces and hands. ... He reached down and took a woman by the hands, but her skin slipped off in huge, glove-like pieces.*

While standard lore explains such lesions as thermal 'flash burns' caused by the light radiating from the bomb, they really do not fit that description. Instead, they are strikingly similar to those described by the military physician Alexander [22] in the mustard gas victims at Bari:

> *In many cases large areas of the superficial layers of the epidermis were separated from their deeper layers and torn loose ... The pathologists repeatedly noted that these layers of the skin were dislodged upon handling of the body ... As the superficial skin layers were stripped loose they often took their surface hair with them.*

Similar descriptions were given by other physicians [27, 28]. The characteristic skin lesions are but one sign that distinguishes mustard gas poisoning from true radiation sickness; there are others, which may be less graphic yet are no less specific and decisive. As we will see later, clinical and pathological reports from Hiroshima contain a wealth of evidence that clearly points to sulfur mustard or a closely similar poisonous gas, rather than radiation, as the cause of 'radiation sickness' among the victims in Hiroshima.

Alexander further notes:

> *Thermal burns were readily distinguished from the chemical burns. There were a small number of cases that sustained minor thermal burns in addition to their mustard injuries.*

Thermal burns must have occurred in those victims in Hiroshima and Nagasaki whose wooden houses had been set afire and collapsed around them. In addition, however, it is likely that many of the burns were inflicted by napalm or a similar incendiary; this will be discussed in more detail in Chapter 9.

In summary, therefore, the thesis of this book as to what happened in Hiroshima and Nagasaki is similar to that of Nakatani [1], but augmented with sulfur mustard, which was used to mimic in the victims the symptoms of exposure to strong radiation.

1.5 The evidence in the case

While the physical and medical evidence will be more fully presented in later chapters, it is useful to consider beforehand how different kinds of findings relate to the overall case.

1.5.1 Evidence that directly disproves the nuclear detonation. Some findings prove that physical and medical effects expected of the purported nuclear detonation did not in fact occur. Among the examples introduced above, we can cite the absence of characteristic signs of destruction in the city (Section 1.1), the lack of ^{235}U in the fallout (Section 1.2), and the survival of people who were practically right at the hypocenter, protected from the blast and the radiation by nothing more than a Japanese style wooden house (Section 1.3).

Another important finding in this category is the absence of retinal lesions in survivors who reported having looked directly at the flash. As we will see in Section 10.2, there are both case reports and experimental studies to show that these survivors should all have had their retinas severely burned and scarred, had they indeed looked at a real nuclear detonation.

1.5.2 Evidence that cannot be accounted for by the atomic bomb. The official story of Hiroshima states that the city was destroyed by a single atomic bomb and nothing else. Thus, any kind of destruction or trauma that is *not* explained by this single bomb also contradicts the official story, even though it does not disprove the detonation of an atomic bomb outright.

A crucial finding in this category is the occurrence of 'radiation sickness' among those who were not close to the alleged bomb detonation. All orthodox sources on the effects of the Hiroshima bomb—see for example Okajima et al. [29] and Cullings et al. [30]—agree that levels of radiation sufficient to induce acute radiation sickness occurred only during the detonation itself, and within at most 2,000 m of the hypocenter;[16] in contrast, the residual radioactivity due to fallout and neutron capture remained below this threshold both at the hypocenter and in the Koi area of the city, which is some 2 km from the hypocenter yet received the highest levels of fallout. Nevertheless, numerous cases of 'radiation sickness' have been reported in people who were more than 2,000 m away from the 'blast' or even outside the city altogether. The victims within this group often fell sick after participating in rescue and recovery efforts in the inner city shortly after the bombing. Two such cases, both with deadly outcome, are described in an early report by the International Red Cross [32]. Larger statistics that amply support this contention can be found in reports by Oughterson et al. [33] and Sutou [34].

1.5.3 Evidence of the use of mustard gas. This category is a special case of the previous one, but it is important enough to be highlighted separately. In addition to the skin forming blisters and being torn loose (Section 1.4), there is abundant evidence of immediate, acute affliction of the airways and the intestines, which in the course of acute radiation sickness should be affected only at a later stage or not at all. The involvement of these organs is clear both from clinical descriptions and from autopsies of bombing victims.

Importantly, mustard gas also mimics the typical manifestations of radiation sickness such as bone marrow suppression and epilation, and it can persist in the environment for weeks or even months [17, 35]. Thus, mustard gas accounts for 'radiation sickness' not only in those who were in the city at the time of the bombing, but also in those who entered it in the aftermath. Moreover, it can account for some atypical symptoms which do not fit the textbook pattern of true radiation sickness; it explains the entire picture and succeeds where nuclear radiation falls short.

1.5.4 Experimental evidence of the nuclear detonation. The case *for* the nuclear bomb is, of course, supported by an endless stream of government-sponsored scientific studies. For example, there are dozens of reports on the formation of ^{60}Co and other radioactive isotopes near the hypocenter, which is ascribed to the capture of neutrons emitted

---

[16]The minimum dose to induce acute radiation sickness is approximately 1 Sv, and characteristic symptoms require at least 2 Sv [31]. Lower doses might cause long-term effects such as increased incidence of leukemia and cancer, but this does not matter in the current context.

by the nuclear detonation. Similarly, thermoluminescence in samples of ceramic materials is adduced as proof of the γ-irradiation released by the detonation.

Taken at face value, such experimental studies indeed prove that a large amount of both γ-rays and neutrons was released at Hiroshima, which clearly supports the story of the nuclear detonation and flatly contradicts the negative evidence discussed above. We are thus forced to choose sides. On what basis can we make this choice?

If we assume that no blast occurred, then we must conclude that the evidence of neutron and γ-radiation is fabricated. This is not technically difficult; in fact, the studies in question commonly employ control and calibration samples that were produced by exposing inactive precursor materials to defined doses of laboratory-generated neutron and γ-radiation. The only difficulty is a *moral* one—we must accuse either the scientists themselves or a third party, such as a government or its secret service, of substituting artificial samples for the real ones. In this context, it is worth noting that none of the studies I have seen documents the chain of custody of its samples; it is not clear who had access to the samples at which times.

If, on the other hand, we assume that a nuclear blast *did* occur, and furthermore that *only* this blast occurred, then we have to conclude that some people inexplicably survived deadly doses of radiation, whereas others succumbed to acute radiation sickness without significant exposure. A third miracle is needed to explain that all people who looked at the flash of the detonation escaped with their retinas unhurt.[17]

Between moral embarrassment and scientific impossibility, the only sound choice is the former. We all expect the fortitude to make such choices correctly in the members of a jury; here, we should expect the same of ourselves.

1.5.5 Missing evidence. Evidence that has been lost or was not collected in the first place cannot, of course, directly support either side of an argument. It will matter only on a meta-plane, and only to those who would entertain the possibility of its deliberate suppression; readers familiar with the controversies surrounding the Kennedy murders or the twin tower collapses will likely recognize the theme. While in my

---

[17]There are reports of transient loss of vision, which are entirely consistent with the known effect of mustard gas on the cornea of the eye. In contrast, retinal damage should have been irreversible.

own view the missing evidence rounds out the case, it is not a logically essential element.

Some choice examples of disappearing evidence are provided by the physicist John A. Auxier [36]. While he remarks that "it is difficult to realize the passion that prevailed after the war for secrecy about all information concerning nuclear bombs," he nevertheless accepts at face value the official story that had to be nurtured by such secrecy, and he dedicated a large part of his own career to the arduous work of filling the gaps in the accepted picture of the radiation doses released and received at Hiroshima and Nagasaki.

Considering the great novelty of the atomic bombs, the U.S. military would certainly have been highly interested in measuring exactly the force of their detonations. To this end, the planes dropping these bombs were accompanied by others that dropped instruments for recording the shock waves of the explosions. Since the strength of the shock wave decreases with distance, it was important to know precisely the distance between the bombs and these instruments. However, according to Auxier, this information is missing from the official records:

> *If there are need, interest, and credentials, information about bombing missions in World War II can be obtained in great detail from Air Force records. For a given mission, the aircraft identification numbers, names of crew members, types of bombs, bombing altitude, winds aloft, approach direction, and indicated and true airspeed can be found. There are, however, at least two exceptions to this ... The records for the two most important bombing missions in history are incomplete and inaccurate to a degree beyond comprehension.*

In addition to the strength of the explosion, the intensity of the radiation produced should also have been of great interest. It is therefore peculiar that radiation measurements in Hiroshima by American teams began only in October, at a time when most of the radioactivity left behind by the bomb would already have vanished. However, several Japanese teams had on their own initiative performed measurements shortly after the bombings. Among them was a group from Kyoto University that included the physicist Sakae Shimizu, who carried out some very early measurements pertaining to the dose of very high energy neutrons [37]. How did the Americans treat this valuable evidence? Says Auxier:

> *Unfortunately, soon after the war ended and while Dr. Shimizu's studies were still underway, the U.S. occupation force confiscated the cyclotron and all apparatus and records that laymen would consider to be related to atomic bomb research. Included in the latter were the radium source [required for calibrating instruments for measuring radiation] and all the notebooks of data. Through the handwritten receipt that had been given Dr. Shimizu, the confiscating officer was identified some 12 years later, and, by the cooperation by the Army records staff, he was located in civilian life. However, soon after receiving the materials from Dr. Shimizu, the officer was ordered back to the United States with little time for an orderly changeover. He turned everything over to a lieutenant colonel or major whose name he could not recall. Further research through Army records has failed to identify this man or to locate any trace of the notebooks or radium source.*

Surely an astonishing imbroglio of mishaps and incompetence. It should be added that the Kyoto cyclotron was not merely 'confiscated' but physically destroyed, as was every single cyclotron in the country [38, 39]. This draconian measure of course severely crippled the Japanese scientists' ability to carry out any sort of in-depth study on the physical effects of the atomic bombs.[18] At the same time, their investigations into the medical effects were hamstrung by the confiscation of all tissue and organ samples that had been collected from bombing victims by Japanese pathologists [41]. These materials were returned to Japan only several decades later; and while in American custody, they made only a single appearance, limited and belated, in the scientific literature [42].

The examples in this section may suffice to outline a map on which to place the various kinds of evidence in the case. In the subsequent chapters, we will explore this evidence at greater depth.

---

[18] According to the Japanese nuclear physicist Nishina [39], the American Secretary of War Patterson blamed the destruction of the cyclotrons on the 'mistake' of a nameless Pentagon underling. In his book *Now it can be told* [40], Manhattan Project chief Leslie Groves outs himself as that underling, but he finds a way to pass the buck to other nameless underlings in turn. Apparently, nobody was held responsible.

1.6 A brief guide to the remaining chapters of this book

Most chapters in this book focus on various aspects of the relevant physical and medical evidence. These chapters are necessarily quite technical in nature. Some background that may help readers to better understand the physical arguments is given in Chapter 2. The most important physical findings are presented in Chapter 3; this evidence alone suffices to reject the story of the nuclear detonations. The remaining physical chapters mostly deal with data which are offered as proof of the nuclear detonation, and which seem to be largely fabricated.

As to the medical evidence, Chapter 7 provides background on mustard gas and napalm, the two key weapons used in the bombings. The evidence presented in Chapters 8 and 9 is sufficient to prove the case for mustard gas and napalm and against nuclear detonations. I believe that they can be understood without much medical background, while Chapters 12 and particularly 10 are more demanding in this regard. Chapter 11 combines physical and medical aspects; its most significant contribution is to illuminate the scientific malfeasance that is used to maintain the deception.

The book concludes with two chapters on the methods and the motives, respectively, of the staged bombings. The arguments presented there are of a more general, less scientific nature than those in the preceding parts. The case presented in the final chapter, in particular, is based largely on inference and plausibility; readers who disagree with its conclusions are asked to judge its merit separately from that of the other, more evidence-based chapters.

2 A primer on ionizing radiation and radioactivity

This chapter is intended solely to explain some fundamental scientific concepts that will be used in later chapters; it does not go into any specifics on the atomic bombs purportedly dropped on Japan. Readers with the required scientific background may safely skip it.

2.1 Atoms and subatomic particles

Radioactivity involves the building blocks of individual atoms, so this is where we will start our guided tour. Each atom has a nucleus, which contains one or more protons and zero or more neutrons, and it also has a shell, which contains electrons (Figure 2.1). The number of protons in the nucleus determines which chemical element the atom belongs to. The atoms of a given chemical element may, however, differ by the number of neutrons; atoms of the same element that also share the same number of neutrons belong to the same *isotope*. For example, hydrogen has three isotopes, each of which has one proton. Protium, the most abundant hydrogen isotope, has no neutrons; deuterium and tritium have one and two neutrons, respectively. Nuclei that share the same number of protons and neutrons are also said to belong to the same *nuclide*.[1] This term is synonymous with 'isotope' but typically used when the focus is on the properties of atomic nuclei, rather than on specific chemical elements; for example, Figure 2.1 illustrates three different nuclides.

A common shorthand notation for the composition of a nuclide uses the symbol of the chemical element, for example H for hydrogen, prefixed with a subscript that indicates the number of protons and a superscript for the number of *nucleons*, by which we mean both protons and neutrons. For example, the isotopes of Hydrogen are ^1_1H,

---

[1] This definition of 'nuclide' ignores some finer distinctions that have to do with different energetic states of atomic nuclei. There will be several more instances of simplified treatment in this chapter, which is intended for quick orientation but not as a definitive reference.

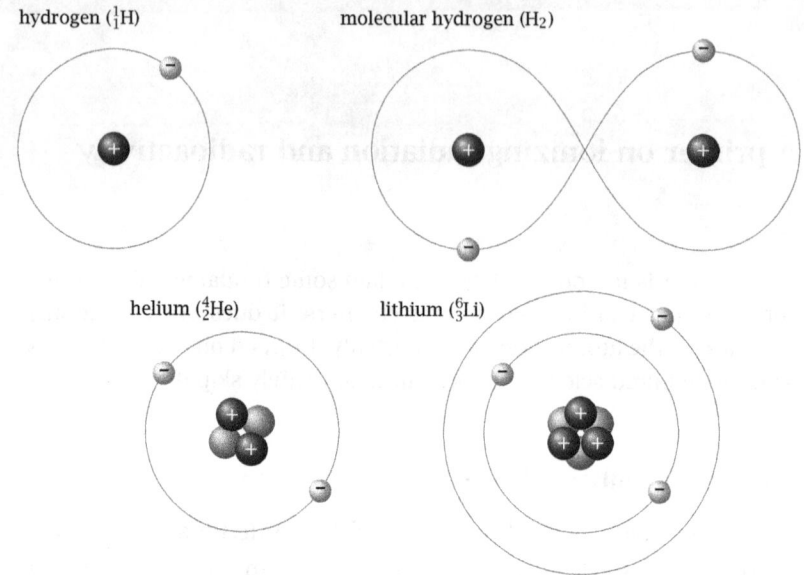

Figure 2.1: Bohr model of atomic structure. The atom consists of protons (+), neutrons (unlabeled), and electrons (-). Protons and neutrons are located in the nucleus; they have similar mass, but only the protons carry a positive charge. Prefixed subscripts indicate the number of protons, and superscripts the sum of protons and neutrons (i.e., nucleons). Electrons are negatively charged and are found in the shell. They prefer to form pairs, either within single atoms (e.g. helium, He) or within molecules composed of two or more atoms (e.g. H_2). See text for further details.

^2_1H, and ^3_1H, while the two major isotopes of uranium are $^{238}_{92}U$ and $^{235}_{92}U$. Since the number of protons is also implicit in the element, the corresponding prefix is often omitted, as in ^{235}U instead of $^{235}_{92}U$ or ^3H instead of ^3_1H.

Protons and neutrons are similar in mass but differ in electric (coulombic) charge. Neutrons are uncharged, whereas each proton carries a single positive charge. The magnitude of this charge equals that of the electron; however, the latter's charge is negative. In the common case that the number of protons in the nucleus equals that of the electrons in the shell, the atom has no net charge. On the other hand, if the atom is short of electrons or has surplus ones, it will have a positive or negative net charge. Atoms (and also molecules) that are in a charged state are called *ions*.

2.2 Chemical bonds and molecules

In everyday chemistry—including biochemistry, that is, the kind of chemical reactions that occur in the human body and other living organisms—only the electron shells of the atoms take an active part; the nuclei are merely passengers. There is a number of rules that govern the behavior of the electrons, and therefore the chemical reactivity of each element. One of these rules states that electrons prefer to form pairs. If all electrons of an atom can form pairs within that atom's shell, then the element in question typically has low reactivity. An example is helium (shown in Figure 2.1), which occurs in nature as a one-atomic gas. On the other hand, hydrogen and lithium have unpaired electrons in their shells, and they are therefore more reactive. Two hydrogen atoms can mutually satisfy their preference for electron pairing by sharing their electrons within in a joint, dumbbell-shaped orbit (the chemical term is *orbital*). The shared electron pair constitutes a chemical bond between the two hydrogen atoms, which thus have become a single hydrogen molecule (H_2). Lithium can react analogously with other atoms, although two lithium atoms will not form a stable molecule.

The atoms of some elements have more than one unpaired electron in their shells; for example, oxygen has two, and nitrogen has three. With nitrogen, all of these can be paired in a diatomic nitrogen molecule (N_2). To indicate that this molecule contains three shared electron pairs or bonds, N_2 may be written as $N \equiv N$, while H_2 with its single bond is written as $H-H$.

In contrast to nitrogen, molecular oxygen (O_2) does not manage to properly pair all electrons; its electronic structure may be written as $^\bullet O - O^\bullet$ to indicate that one stable electron pair is formed, while the other two electrons, represented by the dots, remain 'lonely.' This difference in internal electron pairing explains the very different reactivities of oxygen and nitrogen, for example *vis-a-vis* hydrogen: while N_2 can be coaxed into reacting with hydrogen only at very high pressure and temperature,[2] oxygen requires only a spark to explosively react with hydrogen. The product of this reaction ($2 H_2 + O_2 \longrightarrow 2 H_2O$) is of course water; its bond structure may be written as $H-O-H$, which

---

[2]The reaction of molecular nitrogen and hydrogen at high pressure and temperature—namely, $N_2 + 3 H_2 \longrightarrow 2 NH_3$, with NH_3 representing ammonia—is the Haber-Bosch process. It is industrially important for the production of nitrogen-based fertilizers and explosives.

means that in this molecule all the electron pairing needs of oxygen are satisfied. Water is therefore a fairly stable molecule. Oxygen also reacts with carbon (C) to form a stable product, carbon dioxide (CO_2, or O=C=O), again with the release of energy; and similarly with many other elements. The wide scope of oxygen's reactivity is reflected in the familiar observations of combustion and corrosion.

The association between unpaired electrons and chemical reactivity is not limited to the oxygen molecule. Below, we will see that ionizing radiation can break up electron pairs within initially stable atoms and molecules, which thereby become reactive. Before considering the biological significance of this effect, we will first consider the physical basis of radiation and radioactivity.

2.3 Radioactivity

While chemical reactivity is determined by the electron shell, radioactivity is a property of the atomic nucleus alone. Most of the atomic nuclei that occur in nature are stable, but some are not; these will at some point in time decay. The stability of a nucleus depends on the ratio of neutrons to protons which it contains, as well as on its overall size, that is, its overall count of protons plus neutrons.

We have already encountered the three isotopes of hydrogen (see Section 2.1). Protium and deuterium are stable, whereas tritium is not, because it has too many neutrons. It therefore decays through the emission of an electron (e^-):

$$^{3}_{1}H \longrightarrow \, ^{3}_{2}He + e^- \qquad (2.1)$$

The emission of the negatively charged electron is balanced by changing one neutron to a proton, which creates a positive charge. The neutron excess is thereby remedied; the resulting nucleus, which now belongs to a different element (Helium, He), is therefore stable.[3]

The electron produced by the decay is catapulted out of the nucleus with considerable energy, which it will dissipate by colliding with atoms and molecules in its path. The energy transferred in these

---

[3] The reaction also releases an antineutrino (written as $\overline{\nu_e}$), a subatomic particle with no charge and very small mass. It will carry off a substantial share of the energy released in the decay, but it is otherwise inconsequential in the context of biological radiation effects.

collisions causes additional electrons to be ejected from those atoms and molecules, which will thereby turn into ions. The formation of ions along the path of the emitted particle can be readily detected; hence, this phenomenon is known as *ionizing radiation*, and nuclides that produce it are called *radioactive*.

2.3.1 Radioactive half-life and activity. The exact time at which an individual nucleus will decay is unpredictable, but the probability that it will decay within a certain time period can be determined, and this is a fixed and characteristic property of the isotope in question. Processes that follow this pattern—decay or conversion of a species at a rate that is directly proportional to its own abundance—can be described by an exponential function:

$$N_t = N_0 \, e^{-t/\tau} \qquad (2.2)$$

In this equation, N_0 is the number of atoms at time zero ($t = 0$), and N_t is the number remaining after some time interval t. The *lifetime* τ is the time required to reduce a given number of atoms (N_0) of the nuclide in question to the residue N_0/e. Alternatively, we can use the nuclide's *radioactive half-life* ($t_{1/2}$), which is the time required to reduce N_0 by half.[4] In the case of tritium, the half-life is 12.3 years.

Equation 2.2 states that the residual number N_t of a nuclide is an exponential function of time. The first derivative of N_t is the *activity* (A_t) of the nuclide:

$$A_t = \frac{dN}{dt} = -\frac{N_0}{\tau} e^{-t/\tau} \qquad (2.3)$$

The activity is measured in units of seconds^{-1}, which in this context[5] is referred to as *Becquerel* (Bq):

$$1\,\text{Bq} = 1\,\text{sec}^{-1}$$

The derived unit milli-Becquerel (mBq) denotes one thousandth of a Becquerel.

---

[4] There is a simple relationship between both time parameters: $t_{1/2} = \ln 2 \, \tau \approx 0.693\, \tau$. Furthermore, the inverse of τ is defined as the rate constant, k. Thus, we can write $N_t = N_0 \, e^{-kt}$.

[5] In the context of wave frequencies, the same basic unit (second^{-1}) is named Hertz (Hz).

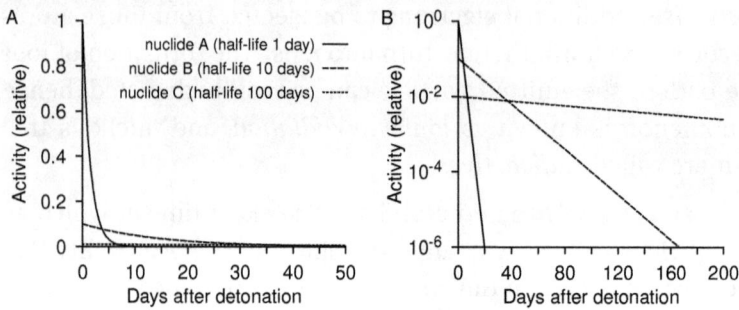

Figure 2.2: Time course of activity for three hypothetical nuclides with different half-lives. At time zero, the amounts of nuclides A-C are identical, but the activity is highest for nuclide A, which has the shortest half-life. After three weeks, however, A is practically gone, and after 200 days only nuclide C is still present at appreciable levels. Panels A and B depict the same hypothetical decays, but the semilogarithmic plot format in B better displays activities of very different magnitude.

The relationship stated in Equation 2.3 is illustrated in Figure 2.2 for three hypothetical nuclides, which at $t = 0$ are present at the same amounts (N_0). Because the lifetime occurs in the denominator of the pre-exponential term, the nuclide with the lowest lifetime—or the shortest half-life; in our example, one day—shows the highest activity per quantity of nuclide, or *specific activity*. However, after 20 days—that is, after 20 successive half-lives—its activity has dropped to about one millionth of the initial value. On the other hand, the nuclide with the longest half-life (100 days) is still present at appreciable levels even after 200 days.

The half-lives of nuclides occurring in nature or being formed in artificial nuclear reactions vary to a much greater extent than those in our example—namely, from fractions of a second to billions of years. Accordingly, they have vastly different specific activities. Some of the nuclides that are formed by nuclear fission have very short half-lives, and thus cause a 'flash in the pan' with very high activity for a very short time, sometimes lasting no longer than the blast itself. Others can be detected for many years afterwards, but because of their relatively low specific activity don't contribute significantly to the acute radiation dosage.

2.3.2 Types of radioactive decay.
The form of decay observed with tritium—conversion of a neutron to a proton, with the ejection of

an electron from the nucleus—is very common, and it is particularly important with the fission products of uranium and plutonium (see later). It is referred to as β-decay, and more specifically as β⁻-decay, since the ejected electron is negatively charged.

Some nuclides that undergo β-decay may concomitantly also emit a neutron. While this is comparatively rare, it does occur among the fragment nuclei that result from nuclear fission, and these *delayed* neutrons form part of the neutron radiation released by nuclear bombs.

In many cases, a nucleus undergoing β-decay does not get rid of all available energy in the process. In these cases, the remainder is emitted, usually a short time later, as a γ-particle, which is a *photon*—a particle of the same nature as light, but with much higher energy (and correspondingly shorter wavelength). γ-Particles, or γ-rays, can also be produced by nuclei that need to offload surplus energy originating from other processes, including α-decay, nuclear fission, or the non-elastic collision with neutrons (see below).

While the nuclei of tritium and of most nuclear fission products contain excess neutrons and thus undergo β⁻-decay, the opposite case also occurs. Unstable isotopes that have too few neutrons may achieve stability by 'reverse' β-decay, or *electron capture*. Here, the nucleus picks up an electron from the atomic shell, and one of the protons is thereby converted to a neutron. The nucleus may again release excess energy through γ-radiation. An example is the iodine isotope ^{125}I, which decays to an isotope of tellurium (Te):[6]

$$^{125}_{53}\text{I} + e^- \longrightarrow {}^{125}_{52}\text{Te} \qquad (2.4)$$

In α-decay, the emitted particle is much larger and heavier than in β-decay—it contains 2 protons and 2 neutrons, and therefore is identical with the nucleus of the stable helium isotope ^{4}He. α-Decay is particularly important with very heavy elements[7] such as radium,

---

[6]The γ-radiation emitted by ^{125}I is very convenient to work with. It is soft enough to be easily shielded with a thin layer of lead, yet hard enough not to be trapped inside inhomogeneous samples, and the half-life of the isotope (59 days) offers a good trade-off between sensitivity and sample stability. Moreover, it is easy to couple ^{125}I to protein or drug molecules of interest. It is therefore widely used as a tracer in biochemical experiments.

[7]The word 'heavy' in this context refers to the mass of individual nuclei rather than the density of the element as a solid material. However, both are correlated—elements with heavy nuclei also have high densities.

thorium, uranium, and the artificially produced elements that exceed the atomic number—that is, the proton count—of uranium. These 'transuranes' include in particular plutonium, which is produced in nuclear reactors from the uranium isotope ^{238}U through neutron capture and two subsequent β-decays (see below). α-Decay may also be accompanied by the release of γ-radiation.

2.3.3 Decay chains. The products of radioactive decay may themselves be unstable and decay in their turn, and successive decays may form a chain that continues for multiple generations. An important natural decay chain begins with $^{238}_{92}$U and ends with lead ($^{206}_{82}$Pb), which is stable. The total number of nucleons declines by 32, which corresponds to 8 α-particles overall. 8 α-Decays would reduce the number of protons by 16, but the actual difference is only 10, which means that 6 neutrons must be converted to protons through β-decay. Accordingly, the total number of α- and β-decays is 14.

The half-life of ^{238}U, at 4.47 billion years, is much longer than those of all intermediate species. This has the interesting consequence that the *activities*, that is, the number of decays per unit of time, of all chain members in a natural, undisturbed uranium ore sample will be virtually equal. To see why, assume that you start with a sample of pure ^{238}U. As the uranium undergoes α-decay with very low, virtually constant activity, its daughter nuclide (^{234}Th, an isotope of thorium) will accumulate. ^{234}Th has a half-life of only 24 days and will therefore decay rapidly; it can accumulate only until the rate of its own decay—its activity—reaches the rate of its formation, which is of course identical with the activity of ^{238}U. The same principle applies to all subsequent decay intermediates, including the uranium isotope ^{234}U, which is formed two β-decays downstream of ^{234}Th. Therefore, in natural uranium, the activities of ^{238}U and ^{234}U should be equal, even though ^{234}U is much less abundant. We will make use of this relationship when considering studies on the fallout of the Hiroshima bombing (see Section 3.1).

2.4 Interaction of ionizing radiation with matter

As briefly stated above, all types of particles released by radioactive decay will cause ionization: as they collide with atoms and molecules along their path, they will transfer some of their initially ample energy to the electrons of those targets, and the electrons will thereby be ejected from their atomic shells, turning the atoms and molecules into ions. Since these ions are readily observed in *ionization chambers* (see below), all of these disparate particles came to be known as 'ionizing radiation'. However, they cause other effects beyond ionization, and some of these affect living organisms.

2.4.1 Radical formation. Ejection of electrons can happen not only with individual atoms but also with molecules, which may thereby be broken up. A straightforward example is the cleavage of water molecules, which may be written as

$$H-O-H \longrightarrow H^+ + e^- + {}^\bullet O-H \qquad (2.5)$$

What happened here? One electron (e^-) that was part of an O–H bond has been ejected. The hydrogen atom has been ionized (H^+), and the second bond electron is retained by the residue of the molecule ($^\bullet O-H$, or $^\bullet OH$), whose dot represents this now unpaired electron. An atom or molecule with an unpaired electron is referred to as a *radical*.

Due to their unpaired electrons, radicals tend to be highly reactive, and none is more so than the hydroxyl radical ($^\bullet OH$). Since water is abundant in living organisms, $^\bullet OH$ is the predominant product of irradiation and the most important mediator of its deleterious effects (see later).[8]

2.4.2 Interactions of γ-rays with matter. For the most part, γ-rays cause ionization and radical formation as described above. Most commonly, the interaction with electrons in target atoms will take the form of *Compton scattering*—the γ-photon collides with an atom or molecule and ejects one of its electrons. In the process, it also transfers some of its kinetic energy to the electron, which causes the γ-photon itself to change direction. This can repeat a number of times until the energy of the γ-photon is depleted.

Since γ-rays dissipate their energy through successive collisions with electrons, it follows that sufficiently thick layers of matter, which contain a large enough number of electrons, can act as a shield against γ-radiation. Since atoms contain equal numbers of electrons and protons,

---

[8] The oxygen molecule ($^\bullet O-O^\bullet$) is a radical, too, and it can react like one. For example, if you have ever patched a bicycle tire, you have observed radical polymerization induced by molecular oxygen, which causes the rapid hardening of the glue.

heavy elements make particularly good shields; lead is very commonly used for this purpose.[9]

2.4.3 Interaction of α- and β-particles with matter. Due to their slower speed and their electric charge, α- and β-particles interact with electrons more effectively than do γ-rays. Thus, after entering a target, both particle types produce many secondary ions in rapid succession, at a high local density, and in so doing quickly exhaust their energy. They therefore do not penetrate matter very deeply (see Section 2.7.1).

2.4.4 Neutron interactions with matter. Unlike the other particles considered here, neutrons don't interact with electrons directly, but only with atomic nuclei. The collision of a neutron with a nucleus may have three different outcomes:

1. the neutron may bounce off, such that the overall amount of kinetic energy is preserved, but some part of it is transferred to the nucleus. This is known as *elastic neutron scattering*.
2. it may be 'swallowed up' by the nucleus. This is known as *neutron capture*;
3. it may be captured briefly but immediately ejected again. This is referred to as *non-elastic neutron scattering*.

In both elastic and non-elastic scattering, the neutrons will not only lose part of their energy but also change direction.

When neutrons of sufficient energy are scattered elastically by hydrogen nuclei, the latter will be yanked loose from the molecules that they are part of and sent flying; these so-called 'recoil protons' then cause the actual ionization and radical formation. This effect mediates most of the biological effects of neutron radiation and also is important for its detection.

Virtually any nuclide can capture a neutron, but the probability varies both with the composition of the target nucleus and the kinetic energy of the neutron. With most nuclides, neutrons of very low energy are captured the most readily. These are called *thermal neutrons*, since their kinetic energy is in equilibrium with that of the surrounding atoms,

---

[9]Another interesting effect that occurs with γ-photons of sufficiently high energy is that of *pair production*—the γ-photon is converted to an electron-positron pair (e^- + e^+). The positron will swiftly bump into another electron, which will cause annihilation of both particles and give rise to two γ-photons. Thus, for practical purposes, pair-production can be considered a transitory stage in the dissipation of γ-ray energy.

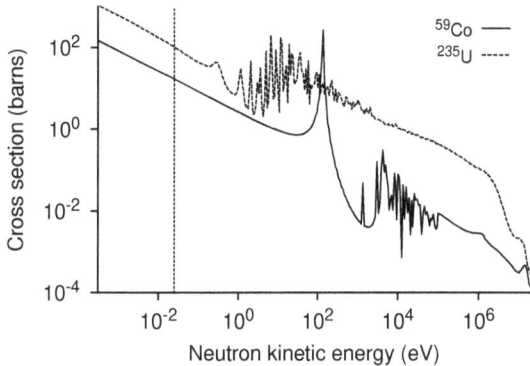

Figure 2.3: Neutron capture cross sections of ^{59}Co and ^{235}U, as a function of neutron kinetic energy. The cross section has the dimension of an area but really measures the probability of capture. The vertical dotted line indicates the typical energy of a thermal neutron (0.025 eV). Data taken from [43].

whose kinetic energy reflects the temperature of the system. Figure 2.3 illustrates how the probability of capture varies with the energy of the neutron on the loose with two different nuclides, cobalt-59 and uranium-235. These two neutron capture reactions can be written as follows:

$$^{59}_{27}\text{Co} + \text{n} \longrightarrow {}^{60}_{27}\text{Co} \tag{2.6}$$

$$^{235}_{92}\text{U} + \text{n} \longrightarrow {}^{236}_{92}\text{U} \tag{2.7}$$

The products of neutron capture are often unstable, and this is the case with both of the above examples. ^{60}Co undergoes radioactive β- and γ-decay with a half-life of 5.27 years. The γ-particles emitted by ^{60}Co are quite high in energy; they can be used e.g. for the irradiation treatment of cancer or for sterilizing medical equipment. With ^{236}U, most nuclei immediately undergo fission (see below); however, a minor fraction of nuclei don't fission but instead 'simmer down' and undergo radioactive decay with a rather long half-life (23.4 million years).

In both the capture and the non-elastic scattering of neutrons, the atomic nuclei are transiently promoted to more energy-rich states; they release this surplus energy in the form of γ-radiation. These secondary γ-rays contribute to the biological effects of neutron radiation.

2.5 Nuclear fission

As an alternative to α- or β-decay, some unstable nuclides may undergo nuclear fission. In this process, the nucleus breaks up into two large fragments of somewhat variable size and composition, plus two or three individual neutrons. Most of the nuclear energy released by the fission is converted to kinetic energy, causing the two fission fragments and the neutrons to dash off like scalded cats; some more energy is released in the form of γ-radiation.

Some nuclides may fission spontaneously, while others fission only upon neutron capture. Among the latter, some are fissioned only by neutrons of high energy, whereas others are readily fissioned by any neutrons at all, regardless of their kinetic energy. This leads to the following distinction:

1. a *fissionable* nuclide releases neutrons which are too low in energy to fission other nuclei of the same nuclide.
2. a *fissile* nuclide releases neutrons which *can* fission other nuclei of the same nuclide; thus, with these nuclides, fission can potentially occur as a chain reaction.

Among the isotopes of uranium, ^{238}U is fissionable, whereas ^{235}U is fissile. ^{235}U is indeed the *only* fissile nuclide with useful natural abundance. However, additional ones can be produced artificially from certain precursor nuclides; these are called *fertile*. The most important fertile nuclides are ^{238}U and ^{232}Th, which upon neutron capture undergo two sequential β-decays to turn into the fissile nuclides ^{239}Pu and ^{233}U, respectively.[10] In so-called 'breeder' reactors, fissile and fertile nuclides are mixed on purpose, and a fraction of the neutrons produced by the ongoing chain reaction is diverted to 'breed' more fissile nuclides for use as reactor fuel or bomb material.

While ^{232}Th is more abundant than ^{238}U, there are some technical obstacles to the use of its fissile derivative ^{233}U as bomb material. This leaves ^{235}U and ^{239}Pu as candidates for such use; the Hiroshima bomb ('Little Boy') is said to have contained ^{235}U, whereas the Nagasaki bomb ('Fat Man') purportedly contained ^{239}Pu.

---

[10] You may notice that ^{238}U is both fertile and fissionable. The outcome of a capture event depends on the energy of the captured neutron; fast neutrons tend to induce fission, while slow ones will initiate conversion to ^{239}Pu.

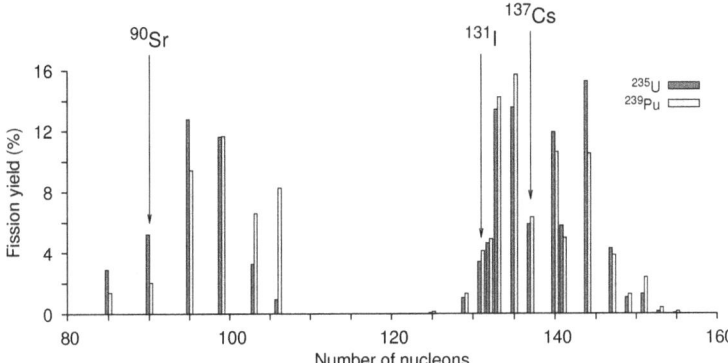

Figure 2.4: Products of ^{239}Pu and ^{235}U when undergoing fission induced by fast neutrons. Nuclides with the same numbers of nucleons were lumped together in this graph, but the three highlighted nuclides all have unique nucleon numbers. ^{90}Sr chemically resembles calcium and accumulates in bone, whereas ^{131}I accumulates in the thyroid gland. ^{137}Cs resembles potassium and may accumulate diffusely in tissues. In addition, it is also commonly used as an environmental marker of nuclear fallout. Data from [44].

2.5.1 Products of nuclear fission. Each fissile nuclide gives rise to a *distribution* of fission products rather than two distinct species. The shape of the distribution varies somewhat between nuclides and also with the energy of the neutrons that bring about the fission; in particular, it differs between nuclear reactors and bombs, which use low and high energy neutrons, respectively. Figure 2.4 shows the distributions produced by ^{235}U and ^{239}Pu when fissioned with fast neutrons, that is, under conditions similar to those that would prevail in a fission bomb. The fission products fall into two clusters centered near 140 and 95 nucleons, respectively. The two nuclides produce a similar amount of ^{137}Cs, which was already introduced in Chapter 1 as a marker of fallout in environmental samples. In both cases, ^{137}Cs is produced in approximately 6% of all fission events; thus, from the abundance of ^{137}Cs in the fallout, it is possible to estimate the total amount of bomb fuel that must have fissioned.

^{131}I (iodine) and ^{90}Sr (strontium) are fission products that may accumulate in specific organs and potentially cause disease. ^{90}Sr chemically resembles calcium and accumulates in bone mineral; its proximity to the bone marrow may contribute to the causation of leukemia. Its half-

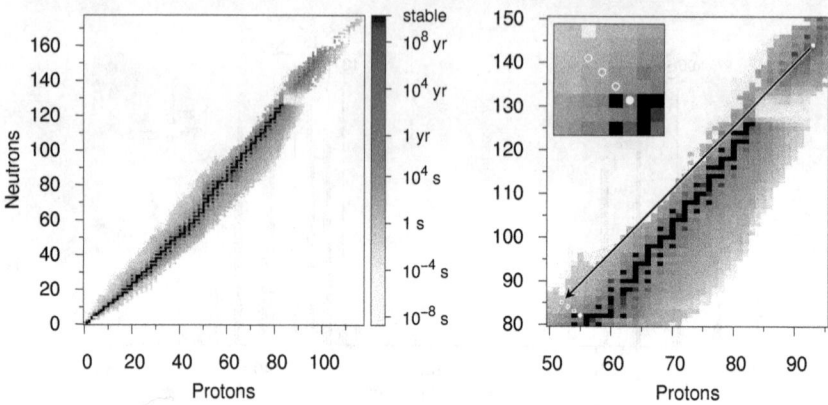

Figure 2.5: Nuclear stability as a function of proton and neutron numbers. Left: For almost all proton numbers (or elements) up to 82, there is at least one neutron number that will result in a stable nucleus (black). Radioactive isotopes with long half-lives (darker shades) are typically found close to this region of stability, which is curved slightly upwards. Right: a ^{235}U nucleus may produce, as one of its fission products, a nuclide with 52 protons and 85 neutrons (^{137}Te; arrow). Within minutes of its formation, this highly unstable species will undergo three successive β-decays to become ^{137}Cs (filled circle; see inset). While still radioactive, ^{137}Cs is long-lived enough to remain detectable in the fallout for many decades. Figure adapted from [46].

life is 28.8 years, which means that it remains detectable in the bone for significant lengths of time. In contrast, the half-life of ^{131}I is only about a week. This is nevertheless long enough for it to be dispersed with the fallout and to accumulate in thyroid gland tissue. Release and dispersal of ^{131}I in the Chernobyl disaster caused numerous cases of thyroid cancers in the adjacent areas of Ukraine and Belarus [45].

Another point to note is that fission products such as the three discussed above will typically not be formed directly. Instead, the immediate fission products tend to be very short-lived and decay into longer-lived ones through one or more β-decays; this is illustrated in Figure 2.5. The γ-rays emitted as part of these secondary decays contribute significantly to the immediate radiation of the bomb. Some of these decay events will also release neutrons; while such 'slow neutrons' make only a minor contribution to the bomb radiation, they are crucial for controlling chain reactions inside nuclear reactors.

2.5.2 Fission bombs.
The detonation of a fission bomb occurs through a chain reaction, which starts when the first ^{235}U or ^{239}Pu atom captures a neutron—supplied by a small neutron source built into the bomb—and undergoes fission. As stated above, this produces two fragment nuclei and 2 or 3 neutrons. Each of the neutrons can potentially be captured by another fissile nucleus and cause it to fission in turn. The likelihood of such secondary fission events depends on the number of fissile nuclei within reach of each liberated neutron. Once this likelihood becomes so high that, on average, each fissioning nucleus will give rise to more than one fission event in the next generation, the chain reaction will be rapidly amplified and cause the detonation. To make this happen, we need to pack enough fissile nuclei next to each other—the amount needed will vary with the identity and the purity of the fissile isotope in question and is referred to as its *critical mass*.

From the foregoing, we can understand in outline what the consequences of a nuclear detonation will be. The copious kinetic energy of the fission products and neutrons is converted to heat. The heat produces a flash of light, and it also drives expansion of the surrounding air, which gives rise to a pressure shock wave. Much of the γ-rays and some of the neutrons will escape from the detonating bomb core and cause an intense pulse of ionizing radiation. In contrast, the β-particles released by short-lived fission intermediates have only short free path lengths and remain confined within the core. In summary, the immediate long-range effects of a detonating fission bomb comprise intense radiant heat, a shock wave, and ionizing γ- and neutron radiation.

2.5.3 Fission yield.
We had noticed in Section 1.2 that with the alleged uranium bomb detonated above Hiroshima only about 1 kg ^{235}U of 50 kg had undergone fission, whereas the remainder is said to have been scattered about. Why did this happen?

The chain reaction will only be sustained as long as the critical mass stays together. As soon as the chain reaction begins, it will release heat, which will tend to blow the critical mass apart. A key problem in the construction of fission bombs is to keep the critical mass together long enough for the chain reaction to reach enough of the fissile material. The fraction of the fissile material actually fissioned before the critical mass breaks up is referred to as the *fission yield*.

2.6 Ionizing radiation unrelated to radioactivity or nuclear fission

The particles released by radioactive decay are ionizing primarily due to their high energies; the source of that energy—in this case, the atomic nuclei undergoing decay—is not important. Other, artificial means for endowing particles with similarly high energies exist, and the energy-rich particles thus generated will be every bit as ionizing as those arising from radioactivity.

There is no need for a comprehensive survey of such techniques for our purposes, but some examples are relevant and useful. The process always begins by accelerating a charged particle in a vacuum using high voltage. The easiest such process involves the acceleration of electrons, which then strike a metal target. Within that target, they will collide with other electrons, to which they will transfer some of their energy. The transferred energy is then released in the form of X-rays, which are electromagnetic radiation of high energy. The particle energy of this radiation depends on the strength of the electric field used for electron acceleration, and it can match or even exceed that of γ-rays. Such high-energy X-rays can be used interchangeably with γ-rays in technical or medical applications. Similarly, the accelerated electrons themselves can be used to mimic β-radiation.

The artificial generation of neutrons in the laboratory can be accomplished by stripping some atomic nucleus of electrons and then using an electric field to accelerate it and slam it into another nucleus. Most commonly, this is done with two isotopes of hydrogen (deuterium and tritium); the collision of the two nuclei will produce helium and a free neutron. In the early days, including those following the alleged atomic bombings, the production of neutrons in quantity required cyclotrons, but in the meantime smaller, simpler devices have been invented. Such artificial neutron sources can be used to mimic, and thus to study, the effects of neutron radiation from atomic bombs.

The process of charged particle acceleration by an electric field also makes plain the meaning of the physical unit electron volt (eV)—it is equivalent to the energy which an electron, or another particle with a single charge, will acquire while traveling through a vacuum from one electrode to another when a potential of 1 V exists between the two. The energies of particles released by radioactive decay are typically stated in kilo-eV (keV) and mega-eV (MeV; one million eV). For example, the decay of ^{60}Co produces β-radiation with 317 keV as well as γ-radiation with 1.17 MeV and 1.33 MeV. We can mimic those β-particles by sending electrons down a field with 317 kV, and the γ-radiation by accelerating electrons using 1.17 or 1.33 MV and then converting them to X-rays by slamming them into a metal target.[11]

2.7 Attenuation of ionizing radiation by matter

When a particle of ionizing radiation impinges on some target matter, it will begin to ionize the atoms and molecules within; and since each ionization event requires some energy, the ionizing particle itself will eventually run out of energy and come to rest or vanish. To what depth the particle can penetrate before this occurs obviously depends on its initial energy; in addition, however, it also depends on its nature, which determines at what range it can interact with individual electrons or nuclei in the target matter.

2.7.1 Distinctions between particle types. The interaction with the longest range is the Coulomb force; accordingly, α- and β-particles, which are electrically charged, interact the most readily and produce the greatest number of ions along a certain path length. This also means that they shed their energy very quickly and thus penetrate the target matter only to a very shallow depth. Among the two, the α-particles are heavier and slower; they thus spend more time in the vicinity of a given single electron and stand a greater chance of exerting enough pull to pry it loose from its host atom. Therefore, α-particles exhibit the highest density of ionization, which implies the shallowest depth of penetration; in fact, they cannot even penetrate intact human skin deep enough to reach its basal layer of vital, regenerating cells. Isotopes that emit α-radiation thus can harm humans only when ingested or inhaled.

The lighter β-particles move faster and do not ionize quite as many atoms or molecules along a given stretch of path within the target, which results in somewhat deeper penetration. Even they, however, will penetrate human skin to a depth of only a few millimeters; thus, while β-emitting radionuclides may burn the skin from without, they may cause damage to interior organs only after they have been taken up.

---

[11] Note that in this case some, but not all the X-ray photons will receive the full amount of energy. A better way to mimic energetically homogeneous γ-rays is through synchrotron radiation.

This is illustrated by the aforementioned fission products ^{131}I and ^{90}Sr, which will cause disease only after accumulation in the thyroid gland or bone matrix, respectively.[12]

In contrast to α- and β-particles, γ-photons have no charge, and they thus will interact with electrons only when they hit them straight on. Thus, on average, a γ-photon will travel a much longer distance between two consecutive ionization events; it will shed its energy more slowly and penetrate the target to a much greater depth, or even traverse it. The depth of penetration will be inversely proportional to the number of electrons per volume segment of target matter; thus, matter that consists of comparably light atoms, for example water or soft tissues, will be penetrated most readily, whereas matter that contains heavier atoms such steel or bone mineral stop γ-rays more readily.[13]

Neutrons are uncharged as well; unlike γ-rays, they interact primarily with the nuclei of the target matter, and moreover they lose energy more readily by colliding with lighter nuclei than with heavier ones. Like γ-rays, however, they can penetrate the walls of buildings and human tissues to considerable depths. Both neutrons and γ-rays thus contribute to the total radiation dose due to a nuclear detonation.

2.7.2 Linear energy transfer. We just saw that ionizing particles differ in their depth of penetration into a target, and we explained this in terms of faster or slower depletion of a particle's energy. This can be expressed quantitatively as the amount of energy transferred from the impinging particle to the matter in the target as it traverses a certain specified distance. This quantity, the particle's *linear energy transfer*, correlates inversely to its depth of penetration.

2.7.3 Quantitative treatment of attenuation. Let us first consider a parallel beam of radiation that strikes a block of matter, whose surface is perpendicular to the beam. As a first approximation, we can consider the block of matter as composed of many stacked layers of uniform thickness, and then postulate that each layer attenuates the impinging

---

[12]It is, however, possible to achieve deeper electron penetration by accelerating them to very high energies. Such artificial high-energy electron radiation is used in the radiation therapy of cancer.

[13]Remember that γ-rays are of the same nature as X-rays. Bones show up white on an X-ray film because the heavier elements (calcium and phosphorus) in bone mineral stop the X-rays. In contrast, the X-rays traverse the surrounding soft tissues and blacken the film.

radiation by a constant fraction or percentage. This results in an exponential relationship: just as we can determine a lifetime for the effect of time on radiation intensity, we can determine a *relaxation length* for the shielding effect of matter:

$$R_d = R_0 \, e^{-d/\lambda} \tag{2.8}$$

In this equation, R_0 is the unattenuated radiation intensity at the surface, d is a certain depth of penetration, R_d is the radiation intensity observed at that depth, and the relaxation length λ is the layer thickness of the given material that will reduce R by a factor of $1/e$. In analogy to the half-life that describes the effect of time, we can also define a *half-thickness* that will reduce radiation intensity by a factor of $1/2$. Furthermore, one may find values tabulated for layer thicknesses that attenuate radiation by 90%; this latter value will be approximately 3 times the half-thickness.[14]

From the preceding sections, it will be clear that the actual values of relaxation lengths and half-thicknesses will vary greatly both with the type of radiation and the shielding material. The principle applies not only to solids or liquids, but also to gases, including the atmosphere; the difference is simply that the shielding half-widths or relaxation lengths in the atmosphere will be far larger than for example in water, soil, or concrete. While the exponential approximation thus is quite versatile in practice, there are some effects that limit its accuracy:

- Particle energies are usually inhomogeneous, and particles with higher energies will penetrate more deeply.[15]
- Even if all particles strike the surface of the block of matter in question from the same direction, they may be scattered rather than fully stopped; they will thus change both their energy and their direction.
- Some primary particles, when stopped, will produce secondary radiation: stopped β-particles or fast electrons will produce X-rays, and stopped neutrons will produce γ-rays. These secondary rays

---

[14] Consider that $0.5^3 = 0.125$, or 12.5%; therefore, three stacked layers of half-thickness will attenuate the radiation by $100\% - 12.5\% = 87.5\%$.

[15] This has been exploited for the 'hardening' of X-rays: passing the beam generated by an X-ray tube through some metal filters first will preferentially attenuate the low-energy part of the spectrum; this reduces radiation doses to the skin, which would otherwise disproportionately absorb and be damaged by this 'soft' fraction.

will typically be more penetrating than the primary particles that produced them.

These effects need to be taken into account in order to accurately determine the dosages received for example by persons located inside a house during a nuclear detonation, as discussed by Auxier [36]. Nevertheless, the exponential approximation is useful at least for orientation.

2.7.4 Concomitant attenuation and radial divergence. Equation 2.8 describes the attenuation of a parallel beam of radiation. However, in the detonation of a bomb, the radiation propagates in all directions, diverging radially from the center. Let us assume a nuclear bomb goes off in outer space, where there is no matter that could attenuate its radiation. Then, due to the radial divergence, the radiation intensity R_d will still decrease with increasing distance d:

$$R_d = \frac{1}{d^2} R_0 \tag{2.9}$$

If we assume that d is given in meters, then R_0 is the radiation intensity at a distance of 1 m from the center of the detonation, since here $1/d^2 = 1$. This assumption treats the exploding bomb as a point source, which is of course not realistic; however, in practice we are only interested in the radiation intensity at much larger distances from the bomb, where the point source assumption is good enough.

When a bomb goes off in the atmosphere, both attenuation and divergence must be considered. We can account for their combined effects with the following formula:

$$R_d = \frac{1}{d^2} R_0 \, e^{-d/\lambda} \tag{2.10}$$

R_0 has the same meaning as in the preceding formula. Equation 2.10 applies to both neutron and γ-radiation released by a bomb, but of course each kind of radiation has its own characteristic λ value. Furthermore, the equation can be used to estimate both the number of ionizing particles per unit area, referred to as the *fluence* of the radiation, and the *dose* received by some body of matter struck by these particles (see Section 2.9). We can rearrange Equation 2.10 as follows:

$$R_d \, d^2 = R_0 \, e^{-d/\lambda} \tag{2.11}$$

The product $R_d\, d^2$ is a simple exponential function of d, which in a semilogarithmic plot will yield a straight line. From the slope of this line, we can obtain λ. This approach will be used in Section 6.1.1.

2.8 Measurement of ionizing radiation

In order to detect and quantify ionizing radiation, we must observe some of its interactions with matter; and to do so sensitively, we must find ways to amplify the initial signal generated in this interaction. Several different physical principles are exploited for these measurements.

2.8.1 Ionization. This effect is observed in an *ionization chamber*, an enclosure that is filled with some noble gas and also hosts two electrodes, between which a high voltage is applied. When an ionizing particle traverses this chamber, it will collide with gas atoms and knock electrons out of their shells. In the strong electric field, the ions and the electrons will become separated and be attracted toward the two opposite electrodes, where they will cause an electric signal. The magnitude of this signal will be proportional to the number of ions that were generated; and this number will vary depending on the type and energy of the ionizing particle as outlined above.

In what form exactly the signal is received depends on the experimental setup. If the voltage between the electrodes is applied only initially but not renewed, then each detected burst of ions and electrons will decrease that initial voltage. This means that the measurement will be cumulative—we will know how many ions were generated, but not by how many ionizing particles. If the voltage is kept constant, then the signal is the current required to restore the voltage to its preset level after each ionization event; and since this restoration will occur quickly, it will be possible to count the number of ionizing particles over a certain time interval.

Even though it may be counterintuitive, the signal can be amplified by reducing the gas pressure inside the chamber. A low pressure will reduce the number of collisions between the ionizing particle and the gas atoms, and therefore the number of ions and electrons released; however, while traveling toward their respective target electrodes, these secondary ions will gather more speed before colliding with other gas atoms, and due to this greater speed they will be able to ionize those gas atoms in turn. The overall result will be a cascading proliferation of charged particles and therefore amplification of the electrical signal. There are two ways to exploit this mode of amplification:

- The amplification may be limited in extent, such that the final signal is still constrained by the number of ions and electrons generated directly by the ionizing particle. Then, the signal will retain information about the nature and energy of the ionizing particle.
- The amplification may be saturating—each event is amplified to the same, maximal extent, regardless of the strength of the original ionization. This will maximize sensitivity, but on the other hand the ability to discriminate between different particle types is lost. This latter principle is applied in the widely used Geiger counters.

Both modes of detection have their uses. Generally speaking, counting devices optimized for sensitivity tend to be simpler and are more suitable for field use. Instruments that can discriminate different particle types are more complex and mostly used in the lab. The key advantage is that particle energies can be used to discriminate and identify different radionuclides in complex mixtures such as soil, which may contain both natural background and nuclear fallout; Figure 3.3 shows an example.

2.8.2 Scintillation. Like ionization, this physical effect begins with a collision of an ionizing particle with an electron of some other atom or molecule. However, in scintillation, the electron is not knocked free but only transiently promoted to a higher state of energy within its host particle. When it falls back to its initial level, the surplus energy which it received in the collision is released as light (a single photon). The light can be focused onto a photomultiplier and quantified; the intensity of the flash of light will be proportional to the number of scintillating atoms or molecules and thus to the energy of the ionizing particle. γ-Rays induce intense scintillation in materials such as crystalline sodium iodide, and this is exploited for their detection.

2.8.3 Thermoluminescence. Some materials, in particular ceramics, may show a peculiar response to ionizing radiation: the dislocated electrons may migrate through the material for some distance and become trapped in a *metastable state*, that is, a state that is high in energy, yet unlike most other high-energy states does not spontaneously fall back to a lower energy level. It can, however, be induced to give back its energy in the form of light by heating the material. This heat-induced light signal is called *thermoluminescence*.[16]

The metastable state can persist for potentially very long periods of time, which means that it gives the material a 'memory' for the ionizing radiation it was exposed to in the past. Ceramic material is fairly dense and thus will not be significantly penetrated by α- or β-radiation. Neutrons and γ-rays may penetrate it, but of these only γ-rays interact with electrons effectively; thus, in practice, all the observed thermoluminescence activity can be attributed to γ-rays.

An interesting application of thermoluminescence concerns the dating of ceramics recovered in archaeological excavations [47]. Firing a new piece of pottery will purge the clay of any previously accumulated luminescence energy and thus 'reset the clock', and its repeated heating on a fire while in use will do the same. Once it becomes emplaced underground, however, its pent-up thermoluminescence will increase at a steady rate due to the decay of natural radioactive isotopes such as ^{40}K within the material itself and in the soil around it. When the piece is heated again after its recovery, the amount of light released will be proportional to the number of γ-particles that struck it, and therefore to the time elapsed, since it became buried.

When applied to tiles and bricks of recent manufacture, the luminescence induced by natural radiation should of course only amount to negligible background, and in a sample from Hiroshima or Nagasaki, the lion's share of the signal should come from the intense flash of γ-rays that it was exposed to when the bomb went off. We will consider experimental studies of this kind in Chapter 5.

2.8.4 Mass spectrometry. This method does not measure radiation as such, but it can nevertheless be used to determine the presence and abundance of radionuclides in a sample. As the name suggests, mass spectrometry simply distinguishes atoms—or, in other applications, molecules—according to their mass; it can therefore be used with both stable and unstable nuclides. The method requires that all atoms be

---

[16]For a simple analogy, consider a pinball machine. The plunger is the ionizing particle, and the ball is the electron. When you pull and release the plunger, the ball receives energy and starts rolling. Most of the time, the ball will roll on all the way to the exit; but every so often, it may get stuck at some obstacle along the course instead. To get it rolling again, you have to supply some activation energy by punching the table. In thermoluminescence, the heat provides the punch that frees the electrons trapped in metastable states.

converted into single ions, then accelerated in an electric field, and finally captured in a detector. The crucial step for identification is the acceleration: it must overcome inertia, which is proportional to mass; therefore, between two atoms of equal charge but different mass, the lighter one will reach the detector before the heavier one.[17]

Mass spectrometry is very powerful and versatile; nevertheless, it has not fully replaced radiation counting. To understand the respective advantage of either method, consider that radioactive isotopes decay on vastly different time scales (Section 2.3.1). Among the fission products of ^{235}U, a short-lived nuclide is ^{131}I, which has a half-life of 8 days, whereas a long-lived one is ^{129}I, which has a half-life of 16 million years. (Both are isotopes of iodine.)

Assume we have a sample that contains 1 ppm (one millionth) of ^{131}I, while the remainder is ^{129}I. Mass spectrometry will simply count the atoms as they are at any given moment, and will give us the true abundance right away—but the very small fraction of ^{131}I in our sample might get lost in the noise. On the other hand, if we use radiation counting, the far shorter half-life of ^{131}I means that many more of its atoms will decay during the time interval of the measurement—indeed, even at these odds, its signal will be about 700 times higher than that of ^{129}I; and with a small sample, we might entirely miss the ^{129}I. This effect is no mere curiosity; for example, in order to measure uranium isotopes in soil samples, radiation counting would be preferred with the relatively short-lived ^{234}U, whereas mass spectrometry would be more suitable for the longer lived isotopes ^{235}U or ^{238}U.

2.9 Radiation dose

We have seen that ionizing particles can interact in various ways with matter. While these distinctions are often important, it is also useful to have a global measure of the overall dose of radiation received by a target, and in particular by living organisms. Since each of the interactions between radiation and matter involves some transfer of energy, we can use the sum of all the energy transferred to measure the total dose. The unit of measure is the Gray, or Gy for short; 1 Gy is defined as $1 J/1 kg$.

---

[17]This is the principle of separation in *time of flight* (TOF) mode, which is the easiest to understand; however, mass spectrometry has other modes of operation as well.

To understand how much, or rather how little, energy 1 Gy actually amounts to, consider this: 1 J is approximately equal to 0.25 cal, and thus will heat one gram of water by 0.25°C. Accordingly, a kilogram of water that receives a radiation dosage of 1 Gy will thereby be heated by approximately 0.00025°C. With γ-radiation, the lethal dose in humans is on the order of 8 Gy; therefore, a lethal dosage of γ-radiation will heat up the body by an entirely imperceptible 0.002°C. Thus, the total energy associated with a lethal radiation dose is minuscule; it is the very high energy associated with each of the individual ionizing particles that makes them so fearfully effective.

2.9.1 Dose and Kerma. We just saw that the dose is defined in terms of energy transferred from ionizing particles to a unit of target mass. In this context, one can make a subtle distinction: the energy thus transferred may remain in that target mass unit, or it may escape it in the form of secondary radiation (see Section 2.7.3). The escaping fraction of the energy is included in the *kerma*, which is an acronym for 'kinetic energy released per unit mass', but it is excluded from the dose.

How important is this distinction with human bodies? We have relatively large bodies; therefore, much of the energy that will escape one kg-sized portion of our body will end up in the next, and vice versa. Therefore, fruit flies and silkworms probably have more reason to worry about the difference than we do; for the purpose of this book, we can treat the two as approximately equivalent.

2.9.2 Biological effectiveness of different particle types. Qualitatively, all types of radiation induce the same kinds of genetic damage in cells (see below); however, if we use identical doses of each as measured in Gy, then the extent of the damage will vary considerably. To account for this, biological weighting factors have been distilled empirically for each type of radiation from experimental observations (Table 2.1). These weighting factors go by various names; we will here adopt *relative biological effectiveness* (RBE). In order to estimate the biological effect of a given physical dose of radiation, one multiplies the physical dose in Gy with the appropriate RBE:

$$\text{biological dose (Sv)} = \text{RBE} \times \text{physical dose (Gy)} \qquad (2.12)$$

Table 2.1: Relative biological effectiveness (RBE) of different types of ionizing radiation

Radiation type	RBE
α-particles	20
β-particles	1
photons (γ-rays and X-rays)	1
neutrons	5

Since the RBE factors are dimensionless, the unit of the biological dose—the *Sievert*, or Sv for short—is also equal to $1\,\text{J}/1\,\text{kg}$, as is the Gray. Which unit to use depends on the context. It probably goes without saying that the numbers listed in Table 2.1 are approximations. With neutrons, there is considerable debate about the most appropriate value. In Figure 8.1, we will use the dose-adjusted RBE described by Sasaki et al. [48], but the neutron RBE value listed here, 5, is a reasonable approximation in the relatively high dose range that matters most in this book.

2.10 Forms of radiation released by fission bombs

While fission bombs may of course be detonated anywhere, we will confine the discussion to air bursts at considerable altitude, as allegedly occurred in Hiroshima and Nagasaki.

2.10.1 Immediate radiation: γ-rays and neutrons.
While inside the bomb itself there is a veritable stew of particles (see Section 2.5), the β-particles and the fission fragments have low ranges within the bomb and even within air, and they will not contribute to radiation on the ground. In contrast, both γ-rays and neutrons can escape the bomb and strike the ground; it is these two particles that account for the intense yet short-lived burst of immediate radiation from the bomb. Exactly what share of the neutrons will escape the bomb and contribute to radiation on the ground remains uncertain and contentious. For several decades after the event, it was proclaimed that at Hiroshima the biological dose due to neutrons had roughly been on par with that due to γ-irradiation, but later on the neutron dose was revised downward to an almost negligible quantity [49]. This strange story will be examined in Section 11.5.

2.10.2 Nuclear fallout. With fission bombs of the size said to have been used in Japan, the fireball of the detonation is expected to reach a maximum diameter of approximately 200 m. Since both bombs were set off at an altitude of at least 500 m, the fireball did not touch the ground.[18] Most of the radioactive witches' brew therefore would not have come down in the targeted cities themselves, but instead have been carried upward in and away by the thermal updraft that was caused by the heat released by the bomb itself. However, some radioactivity *did* reach the ground as local fallout, carried at least in part by the black rain already mentioned in Section 1.2.

2.10.3 Induced radioactivity. Some of the neutrons released by the detonation will strike the ground and, often after first losing most of their energy through a series of collisions, they will be captured by some nuclides on the ground. In many cases, the new nuclides formed by the capture will be radioactive; and since they will tend to have a neutron surplus, they will undergo β^--decay, which is often accompanied by significant γ-radiation. Interest in this *induced radiation* is twofold:

- at least for a short time after the detonation, some very short-lived nuclides may contribute to the radiation dosage received by people on the ground;
- since radionuclides will be induced in proportion to the intensity of the neutron radiation from the blast, the abundance of the longer-lived isotopes can be used to estimate the neutron dosages that would have been received during the blast.

As noted in Section 2.4.4, the efficiency of neutron capture varies both with neutron energy and with the precursor nuclide in question; some precursors capture only high-energy neutrons, others only or preferentially low-energy neutrons. Comparing within a single sample the abundance of nuclides induced by neutrons of low and high energy, respectively, can give an indication of the neutron energy spectrum of the detonation. Studies which applied this approach to tile or rock samples from Hiroshima have yielded conflicting results (see Section 6.4.2).

---

[18] In contrast, the 'Trinity' test explosion in New Mexico is said to have been detonated at low altitude and to have caused intense radioactivity on the ground (see Section 13.6.4).

2.11 Biological radiation effects

2.11.1 DNA damage and repair. We have already seen that ionizing radiation converts molecules to radicals (Section 2.4.1). An abundant and particularly reactive radical species is •OH, which is formed from water. While •OH reacts with virtually anything in the cell, including protein molecules and cell membranes, its most significant target is DNA. This is not due to any particular chemical reactivity of DNA, but solely to its special biological function. Other molecules, when damaged, can always be replaced, but DNA cannot—it is passed on from one generation of each cell and each organism to the next, and thus it must be safeguarded from any damage, since even a small chemical change to a stretch of DNA (a gene) can cause a heritable *mutation* with potentially grave consequences.

Living organisms have been exposed to natural radiation throughout evolution, and accordingly they have developed a fairly elaborate machinery for coping with DNA damage by radiation. This machinery continually scans the DNA for damage. If it is found, the response to it depends on the extent of the damage. If it is deemed limited, then the cell will attempt to repair it. In many cases, this repair will be completely successful and restore the native, intact state of the DNA; the chances for this are good if one of the two DNA strands has remained unaltered and can therefore serve as a template in the repair of the other. On the other hand, if *both* strands of a DNA molecule are severed, the cell may still succeed in repairing the break and restoring an intact DNA molecule, but the all-important nucleotide sequence may have been altered on both strands. Once this happens, the lesion will have become permanent—a mutation has occurred that will now be passed on to all daughter cells.

An •OH radical can readily break a single DNA strand, and if the local concentration of such radicals is high enough, then two breaks may occur simultaneously on opposite strands, producing the double strand break situation described above. This is the reason why α-particles, which deposit all their energy along a very short distance and therefore produce a high local •OH concentration, have a very high relative biological effectiveness. Thus, overall, •OH radicals are a chief mediator or DNA damage caused by ionizing radiation.[19]

2.11.2 Apoptosis. While DNA repair may seem like an 'obvious' coping strategy, a more surprising one is *apoptosis*, or programmed cell death. Each cell in the human body that contains DNA[20] will commit *harakiri* when the load of DNA damage, and therefore the chance of harmfully mutated progeny, becomes too great. A key effect observed in apoptotic cells is the destruction of the cell nucleus, which contains the DNA; this can be observed by conventional light microscopy, but also at the molecular level as DNA fragmentation.

Intriguingly, cells in different tissues differ significantly with respect to the level of DNA damage beyond which they will abandon repair and initiate apoptosis instead. This tissue-dependent threshold largely accounts for the observed order of organ damage by high doses of radiation. Among major organ systems, the bone marrow is affected first, and with it the regeneration of all types of blood cells; mucous membranes in the intestine are the second most susceptible. And again, since this response to DNA damage is built into the various tissues themselves, it is understandable that DNA-damaging agents other than radiation (such as sulfur mustard, of course) will produce a similar pattern of organ damage.

2.11.3 Cell proliferation rate and radiosensitivity. Differences in radiosensitivity exist not only between tissues but also within them. In a tissue that actively regenerates, the cells form a continuum of subpopulations, which ranges from rapidly dividing, undifferentiated cells to those that no longer divide but are fully differentiated (Figure 2.6). The most rapidly dividing cells are also the most sensitive to radiation; the differentiated cells, which have acquired all tissue-specific traits they need to function as that tissue's 'worker bees', have low sensitivity to radiation.

---

[19]There is, however, some argument concerning the requirement of only one or more than one •OH radical for the induction of a double strand break, as well as the contribution of direct interactions between ionizing particles and DNA molecules. Divergent findings seem to be influenced by the degree of chromatin condensation and the abundance of radical scavengers [50, 51].

[20]Red blood cells and blood platelets don't contain DNA, and thus are exempt. The precursor cells of both, however, which reside in the bone marrow, do contain DNA and accordingly are subject to apoptosis.

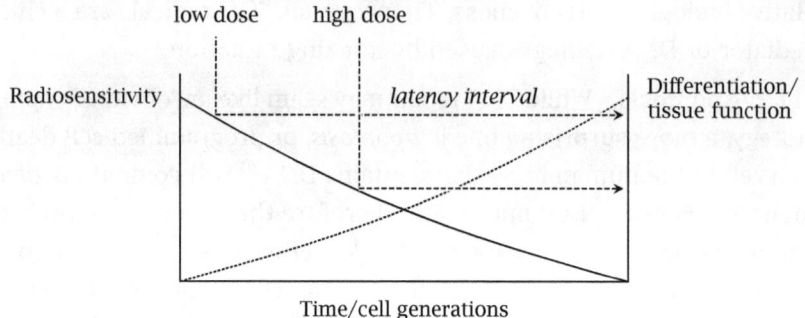

Figure 2.6: Radiosensitivity and differentiation of cells in tissues. Within most tissues, there exists a continuum of cells at different stages of differentiation. The least differentiated, most actively regenerating cells are also the most susceptible to radiation. At higher radiation doses, more highly differentiated cells will be depleted also, which will shorten the latency interval after which the lack of fully differentiated, functional cells becomes clinically manifest.

If the tissue is exposed to a relatively low radiation dose, then only the most sensitive, least differentiated cells may be killed off. The partially differentiated cells will go on maturing and sustain the tissue function a while; this corresponds to the clinical observation of a *latency period*, during which an irradiated patient may appear to be stable or improving. A higher dose will harm some partially differentiated cells also, and therefore shorten this clinical latency period. Moreover, it will more likely kill off every last one of the undifferentiated cells, the *stem cells*, from which all differentiated ones originate, and thereby cause irreversible, lethal damage to the tissue. These observations are directly relevant to acute radiation sickness.

2.11.4 Deterministic and stochastic radiation effects. While each individual event of DNA damage due to ionizing radiation is fundamentally stochastic, some of the overall biological effects are subject to the law of large numbers even in individuals, and they therefore manifest themselves in a predictable, deterministic manner. Any DNA lesion will promote apoptosis regardless of its exact location on the genome. All that is required to pull the trigger is that the number of DNA lesions exceed a certain cell type-specific threshold; and the number of lesions follows the radiation dose in a predictable manner. Furthermore, since apoptosis is the underlying mechanism of acute radiation sickness and of embryonic death or malformations, these, too are governed by deterministic dose-response relationships; both will become manifest in most individuals at doses above 2 Gy (see Sections 8.2 and 12.1). Also in this deterministic category is radiation-induced cataract (see Section 12.3.2).

In contrast, radiation-induced DNA damage has to affect very specific genes in specific ways in order to transform a normal cell to a cancerous or leukemic cell. Only a very small fraction of all damage events will have such specific effects; and therefore, cancer and leukemia are fairly rare even among those exposed to high doses of radiation. Furthermore, most cancers are initiated by cells that have undergone not one but several mutations before becoming manifestly malignant. Irradiation may have contributed some of these mutations, but additional ones were needed to express the malignant phenotype; therefore, cancers and leukemias become manifest with a delay of several years or even decades after the event, during which the cells in question will accumulate additional mutations.[21]

While cancer and leukemia are stochastic events in individuals regardless of the radiation dose, they should of course have their own law of large numbers in populations. However, the exact dose-response relationship between radiation exposure and cancer remains debated to this day, and not many studies can claim to have surveyed appropriately large populations (see Section 12.1.5).

2.11.5 Similarity of DNA damage induced by radiation and by sulfur mustard. We had noted above that DNA double strand breaks are the key mechanism by which ionizing radiation causes mutations and cell death. In this context, we should note that, although the underlying chemistry is different and no •OH radicals are involved, sulfur mustard can also produce DNA double strand breaks [52]. This observation can explain the striking similarities of its biological effects to those of radiation. The reaction of sulfur mustard with DNA and with other molecules in the human body will be considered in more detail in Chapter 7.

---

[21] The number of required mutations is lower in some forms of leukemia than in solid cancers, and therefore leukemias tend to occur sooner; this was also observed in Hiroshima and Nagasaki.

3 The nuclear fallout at Hiroshima and Nagasaki

> ... from January 1946 it would take one and one-half years to prove [plutonium extraction] ... three years to get plutonium in volume ...
>
> Arthur Compton, May 31st 1945 [53]

The radioactive fallout of the Hiroshima bombing, while weak, can be unequivocally detected. Its isotopic composition, however, indicates that it was not caused by the detonation of a ^{235}U bomb, but instead by the dispersal of reactor waste.

At Nagasaki, a high activity of plutonium is found in the sediments of a reservoir near the city. However, a stratigraphic study of these sediments shows that the plutonium entered the reservoir some time after the bombing; this agrees with the assessment by 'Manhattan Project' scientists, initially classified, that purification of plutonium had not yet been achieved in 1945. Moreover, the ratio of ^{239}Pu to ^{137}Cs contained in the sediment does not correspond to the purported fission yield of the Nagasaki bomb.

Collectively, the findings presented in this chapter suffice to conclusively reject the official story of the atomic bombings.

It is commonly believed that, while the atomic bombs in Japan exploded with unprecedented force, they were dwarfed by the much more powerful ones that were developed and tested in subsequent decades. According to Carter [54], the nuclear bomb tests during the 1950s, 60s, and 70s totaled 905 in number and 344 megatons in yield. Collectively, these tests produced a large amount of radioactive fallout, much of which was dispersed all over the Northern hemisphere, and which can be ubiquitously detected with modern, sensitive instruments.

If we want to determine how much fallout remains at Hiroshima and Nagasaki from the original bombs, we must distinguish it from the ubiquitous global fallout. There are two ways of doing so. Firstly, we can look for samples that were secured, or at least protected, early on, before they could become contaminated with the global fallout. Secondly, we can exploit the distinct nature of the purported Hiroshima bomb, which used highly enriched ^{235}U as its fuel, while the Nagasaki bomb, as well as the great majority of all later bomb tests used plutonium (^{239}Pu) instead.[1]

The fission products which form from ^{235}U and ^{239}Pu are quite similar; in particular, the widely used fallout tracer ^{137}Cs is found with both. However, unfissioned ^{235}U itself, when exceeding the natural isotope ratio relative to ^{238}U, would be a specific tracer for the Hiroshima bomb. The study by Shizuma et al. [6] cited earlier applied both of these principles: it quantified both ^{235}U and ^{238}U in samples touched only by local but not by global fallout. This circumstance earned it preferred treatment.

3.1 Uranium isotopes in soil samples

Apart from ^{235}U and ^{238}U, several other uranium isotopes exist that have low abundance, yet can be of value in understanding what did or did not happen at Hiroshima. Sakaguchi et al. [56] examined the abundance of ^{236}U, which forms from ^{235}U by neutron capture without fission. A complicating factor, however, is that ^{236}U also arises through radioactive decay of ^{240}Pu, the second most abundant plutonium isotope. Since ^{236}U decays very slowly and therefore has low specific activity, the method used in this study was mass spectrometry.

Starting from conventional estimates of bomb size, degree of ^{235}U enrichment, and fission yield, the authors estimate that 69 g ^{236}U should have been generated in the detonation, and they set out to look for it in the area affected by the black rain (see Figure 3.1).[2] At this point, you might not be surprised to learn that they do not find it; or more accurately, they do find some ^{236}U, but after comparison with plutonium levels and with samples from a control area in Japan taken

---

[1] Enriched uranium is said to have been used in some later tests, for example in the first Chinese atom bomb test in 1964, as well as in some American tests [4]. Non-enriched uranium can be used as a component of hydrogen bombs and has been detected in fallout shortly after such bombs were tested [55], but this will not cause upward deviations of the ^{235}U/^{238}U isotope ratio.

[2] Note that this quantity of ^{236}U is almost a thousand time less than that of unfissioned ^{235}U that should have been dispersed alongside the ^{236}U, and accordingly also been detected in this study. It is therefore noteworthy that the authors don't comment on the presence or absence of ^{235}U in their samples in any way.

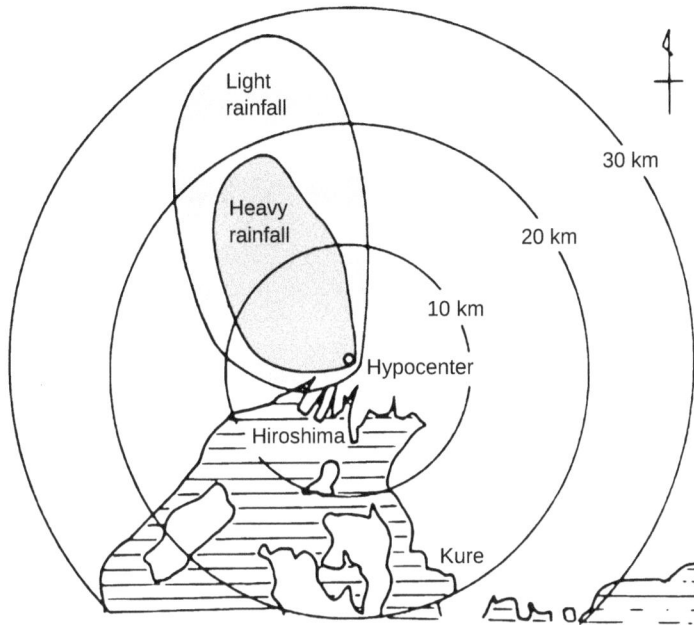

Figure 3.1: Area affected by black rain in and near Hiroshima. The areas of heavy and light black rainfall extend in NWN direction from the hypocenter. Concentric rings indicate distances of 10, 20, and 30 km from the hypocenter. Map adapted from [57]. The studies cited in this chapter mostly used soil samples from within the heavy black rain area.

to be unaffected by 'Little Boy', they conclude that all of it must be attributed to the global fallout. To explain the lack of a discernible local contribution, they assume that the black rain transported only a very small fraction of the radioactive matter generated in the blast.[3]

The major component of natural uranium, ^{238}U, undergoes α-decay, which is followed rapidly by two successive β-decays; this yields ^{234}U. The half-life of ^{238}U is very long (4.47 billion years), whereas that of ^{234}U is comparatively short (246,000 years). At steady state, ^{234}U will decay exactly as fast as it is formed through decay of ^{238}U (see Section 2.3.3). Therefore, if we stick a sample of natural uranium into a radiation counter, we should measure equal activities for these two isotopes. The relation should be different, however, with enriched uranium, as was supposedly used in the Hiroshima bomb. Because ^{234}U is close to ^{235}U

---

[3]The authors also found total fallout in the control area to be about twice *higher* than in Hiroshima. Readers with common sense surely will understand that this tells the story and skip the rest of this chapter; readers without it must persevere.

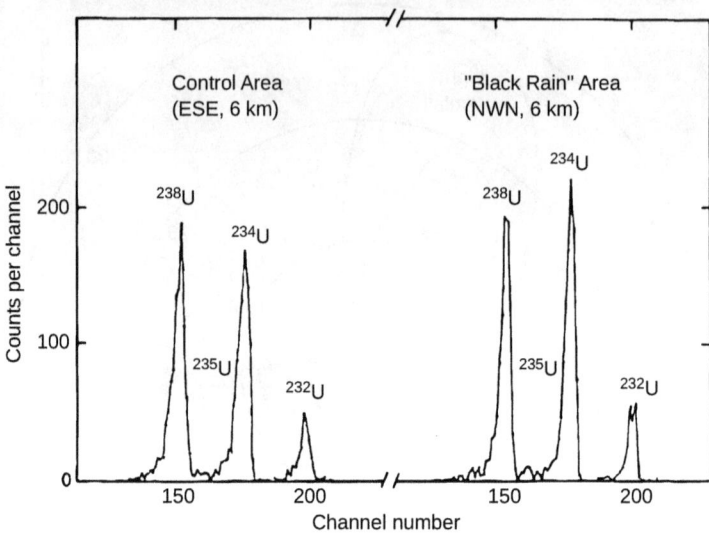

Figure 3.2: α-Ray spectra of uranium extracted from soil samples using 0.1 N nitric acid (taken from Takada et al. [57]). The α-particles emitted by the various uranium isotopes are distinguished by their characteristic energies, which correspond to 'channels' along the x-axis; the abundance of each isotope is represented by the area under its peak (rather than the peak height). See text for details.

in atomic weight, both isotopes should have been enriched together relative to ^{238}U. Assuming that in the Hiroshima bomb ^{234}U, like ^{235}U, was enriched by a factor of about 100 over its natural abundance, whereas ^{238}U was reduced by a factor of 5, the activity (but not the abundance) of ^{234}U in the bomb material should exceed that of ^{238}U by some 500 times. Therefore, the ^{234}U/^{238}U activity ratio should be a very sensitive probe for the detection of residual bomb uranium.

A very careful study that employed this probe was carried out by Takada et al. [57]. The samples consisted again of soil from the black rain area. What makes this study particularly interesting is the attempt to chemically separate bomb-derived uranium from that which constitutes the natural background. The bomb fallout should only adhere to the surface of the soil mineral particles, whereas the natural uranium should mostly reside within them. Thus, to extract the fallout, the soil samples were gently leached with dilute acid, which should strip only a shallow, superficial layer from the particles; the background was then recovered by dissolving the residue with concentrated acid.

In the fraction recovered with dilute acid, ^{234}U activity indeed exceeded that of ^{238}U—but only by a factor of approximately 1.15; compare this to the factor of about 500 expected for pure, highly enriched bomb uranium. This slight excess was observed only with samples from the black rain area, but not with those from a control area outside it.[4] The activity of ^{235}U, which in pure bomb-uranium should exceed that of ^{238}U some 25 times, remained very low in all samples (see Figure 3.2).

As with the study by Shizuma et al. [6] cited before (Section 1.2), we have evidence of a small yet distinct deviation from the natural uranium isotope distribution; and the magnitude is similar between the two studies. There are two explanations in principle—namely, either that a minuscule amount of highly enriched bomb uranium was diluted to near nothingness by natural background, or that the degree of ^{235}U enrichment in the dispersed artificial material was much lower than announced. Takada's failure to detect a higher degree of enrichment even when taking steps to concentrate the bomb uranium clearly militates in favor of the second alternative.

Considering this evidence, as well as the state of technology which then prevailed (see Section 3.6 below), I feel certain that no highly enriched ^{235}U was released at Hiroshima. However, here is how to prove me wrong: obtain a sample of pristine glacier ice, and analyze it for ^{235}U and ^{238}U. This has been done for both cesium and plutonium on a sample from Ellesmere Island in the Canadian arctic, and it is claimed that the imprint of the Nagasaki bomb is detectable in the layer of ice that was deposited in the year 1945 [58]. Such a sample should be largely free from terrestrial background, and using the exquisite sensitivity of modern mass spectrometry, the isotopic signature of 'Little Boy' should be unmistakable.[5]

---

[4] As discussed by Takada et al. [57], determination of the true ratio is complicated by the slight variation of the two isotopes' abundance in different types of soil, which is caused by a slight difference in solubility. However, in the current context, this minor variation is inconsequential.

[5] Some small amount of dust will be present, and natural uranium contained in it might reduce the isotope ratio to below 80%; but it should be clearly higher than in soil.

3.2 Cesium and uranium in samples collected shortly after the bombing

Since global fallout is rich in plutonium and in radioactive fission products such as ^{137}Cs, soil samples that were protected from it should have great value for examining the fallout from the Hiroshima event alone. Two studies on soil, rock, and roof tile samples that were preserved in 1945 in Hiroshima itself, and which were retrieved from storage several decades later, exhibited distinct yet very low ^{137}Cs activity [59, 60]. The latter study actually reexamined a series of samples which were reportedly collected by famed nuclear physicist Yoshio Nishina on his visit to Hiroshima only three days after the bombing. Among these samples, the spread in activity is very large. The two samples that had been collected the closest to the hypocenter gave no detectable ^{137}Cs activity. A single sample—obtained from the Koi area, which is located approximately 2 km from the hypocenter and is considered the zone most affected by fallout within the city limits—gave a value of 10.6 mBq/g; all other samples contained less than 1 mBq/g.

Figure 3.3 shows the γ-ray spectrum of one of the samples; the ^{137}Cs peak is indicated. Since the measurement was reported in 1996, approximately two thirds of the ^{137}Cs had decayed since the bombing. Most other peaks in the spectrum, particularly ^{40}K, are caused by natural background radioactivity. Concerning this background, Shizuma et al. [60] note:

> *In 1950, soil samples were repacked in air-tight glass vials. ... In the present measurement, soil samples were repacked in plastic containers ... to eliminate the ^{40}K gamma-ray background from the vial itself.*

Let that sink in for a moment—the radioactivity of fallout from 'Little Boy', collected in the city three days after the bombing, is obscured by that of the glass vials used to preserve it.

Nishina's samples have also been analyzed for uranium isotopes [61]. In this study, the isotope ratio ^{234}U/^{238}U was somewhat variable but always close to 1, whereas the abundance of ^{235}U was consistent with natural background. Therefore, these soil samples, which are untainted by global fallout and very likely were not exposed to rain other than the

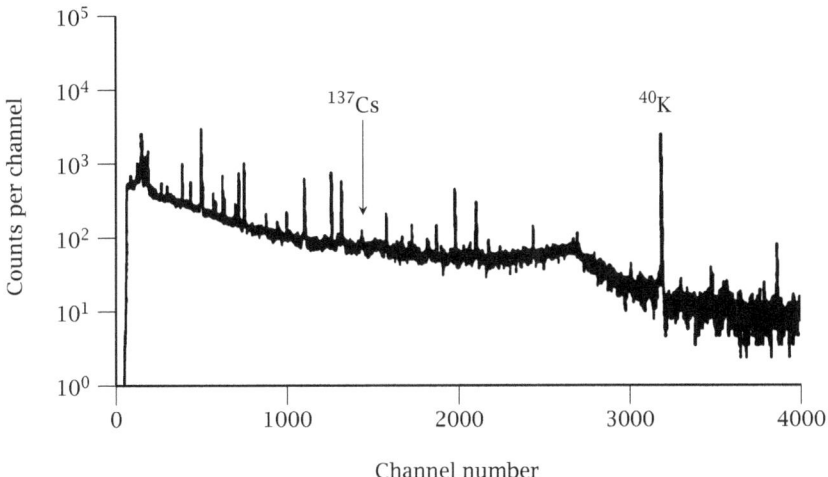

Figure 3.3: γ-Ray spectrum measured by Shizuma et al. [60] on one of the samples collected on August 9th 1945 by Yoshio Nishina. The ^{137}Cs peak is due to fallout, whereas the ^{40}K peak is part of the natural background.

black rain which transported the fallout,[6] fit into the general pattern of detectable but very low levels of ^{137}Cs, and negligible or absent bomb-derived ^{235}U.

3.3 Cesium and plutonium in soil samples from the Hiroshima fallout area

Yamamoto et al. [63] collected samples from soil underneath houses that had been erected throughout the black rain area after the Hiroshima bombing, but before 1950, and thus before most of the global fallout struck. All samples contained some ^{137}Cs. The levels scattered by almost two orders of magnitude; however, even the highest values, which were observed in samples from two houses built as early as 1946, remained well below those which are caused in unprotected soil near Hiroshima by the subsequent global fallout. Thus, even in the black rain area, the ^{137}Cs fallout from the Hiroshima bombing was small.

To explain the variability of their observed ^{137}Cs levels, the authors quite plausibly invoke the excavation that may have occurred in prepa-

---

[6]The physician Michihiko Hachiya notes in his diary that all days from the 6th to the 9th of August were clear and sunny [62]. It seems possible, however, that some of the sites sampled on the 9th by Nishina were drenched with water before that date by firefighters.

ration for construction in some of the buildings; however, they also state that

> *according to carpenters we interviewed, most of the wooden houses built around this time were built without causing major disturbance of the surface soil,*

which suggests that the fallout was indeed quite inhomogeneously distributed within what is considered the fallout area.

We will revisit the question how the fallout may have come to be distributed so unevenly in Section 13.1.5. Here, we only need to note the following crucial point: whether or not the soil was disturbed before construction, it should have been protected from any fallout once the houses had been completed. It is therefore remarkable that, in all of Yamamoto's presumably protected sub-floor samples, *plutonium is also found.*

Since the Hiroshima bomb is supposed to have consisted of enriched uranium, but not plutonium, its fallout should have contained at most minuscule amounts of plutonium.[7] The observed activity of plutonium (^{239}Pu + ^{240}Pu) activity was indeed only about 4% of that of ^{137}Cs (see Figure 3.4B). However, after accounting for the much longer half-lives of both plutonium isotopes, its molar amount—that is, the total number of its atoms—exceeds that of ^{137}Cs about 20-25 times on average.

A further consideration is the time of measurement. Plutonium has not decayed significantly since the bombing, but ^{137}Cs decays much faster and would have been reduced to about one fifth of the original amount between the event and the publication of Yamamoto's study; therefore, the ratio of abundance ($^{Pu}/_{Cs}$) at the time of the bombing would have been close to 4.

The authors, starting from the pious assumption that the official story of the bomb is true, stipulate that essentially no plutonium should have been present in pristine samples, and they ascribe that

---

[7] A small amount of plutonium would form during the detonation through neutron capture by ^{238}U. From the neutron cross sections for capture and fission of ^{235}U and ^{238}U, the presumed abundances of ^{235}U and ^{238}U in the bomb, and the fixed abundance of ^{137}Cs among the total fission products, it can be estimated that the amount of plutonium should have been some 15 times lower than observed. Moreover, virtually all of this plutonium should be ^{239}Pu. The fraction of ^{240}Pu, which in the small number of samples thus examined by Yamamoto et al. [63] ranged from 0.13 to 0.19 of the total, is typical of reactor fuel that has already burned up to a considerable degree; however, this much ^{240}Pu would not arise in the detonation of a ^{235}U bomb.

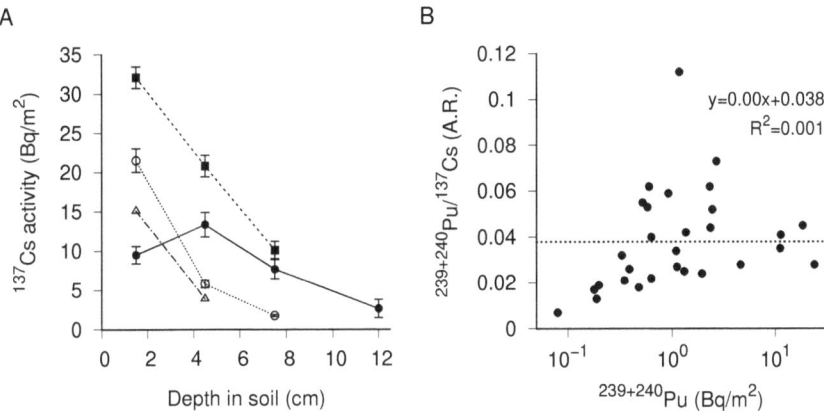

Figure 3.4: Cesium and plutonium activities in soil samples from Hiroshima. A: Activity vs. depth profiles of ^{137}Cs in soil samples retrieved from underneath buildings constructed in the Hiroshima black rain area in 1945-1949. All four individual samples shown by Sakaguchi et al. [64] are replotted here. B: Activity ratio (A.R., $^{Pu}/_{Cs}$) in similar samples, grouped by Pu activity. This graph contains all data points from Table 1 in Yamamoto et al. [63]. The equation and R^2 apply to the regression line.

which they find to contamination by the global fallout. Since this completely voids the very premise of their study—namely, that their samples should be free of such pollution—one would expect some effort on their part to explain this unexpected outcome. However, no such explanation is forthcoming. More importantly, the authors do not *test* their assumption that such contamination was possible, which they could have easily done by obtaining soil samples from underneath houses built in the same area *before* August 1945. If the original premise of the study held, such samples should have been protected from any fallout; on the other hand, according to the authors' revised hypothesis, fallout radioactivity should be present in all of these samples as well.

The only carrier I can think of that might transport some global fallout from soil outside a house to underneath it would be percolating rainwater. Note, however, that according to a preliminary report by the same authors [64] most of the radioactivity was found in a very shallow layer at the very top within the soil (Figure 3.4A). It is difficult to see how percolating water from outside the house would have produced such a distribution. Moreover, plutonium and cesium are not equally mobile within the soil; the aforementioned study by Sakaguchi et al. [56] shows that plutonium is carried downward faster than is cesium, and thus is more mobile. Hence, if indeed global fallout had been carried by percolating rainwater from soil outside to that underneath the house, the Pu/Cs ratio in the latter place should have been considerably increased. In this case, those among Yamamoto's samples which contain the highest plutonium activity, that is, presumably the highest contamination, should also have the highest ratio of plutonium to cesium activity. However, if we plot the ratio of plutonium activity to cesium activity against plutonium activity, then no such trend is apparent, but the scatter is very large (Figure 3.4B). Thus, percolating rainwater can be dismissed as a mechanism for the presumed contamination.

There is, of course, another explanation for the plutonium in samples that should not have been touched by global fallout—namely, that they *were indeed* not touched by it, and the plutonium was really contained in the fallout of the Hiroshima bombing. This hypothesis has the dual advantage of simplicity and physical plausibility; its only difficulty is that it runs counter to the official narrative.

3.4 Variability of isotope ratios in the Hiroshima fallout

Figure 3.4B showed that the ratio of ^{137}Cs to plutonium (^{239}Pu + ^{240}Pu) in the fallout of the Hiroshima bombing is subject to large variation. A very considerable variation is also reported by Shizuma et al. [6] in the ratio between ^{137}Cs and bomb-derived ^{235}U among the black rain samples taken from a single piece of plasterboard (see Figure 1.2). This isotope ratio should be proportional to the bomb's fission yield, which the authors peg at 1.2%; and according to their own calculations, the observed values of this ratio span a range of 0.62 to 8.1 times that yield. Similarly, the soil samples studied by Takada et al. [57], which were discussed in Section 3.1, show no clear correlation between the degree of ^{234}U enrichment to ^{137}Cs levels (Figure 3.5A).

In order to explain the marked variability in their observed isotope ratios, Shizuma et al. suggest that cesium and uranium were separated while being suspended in the air through "condensation," but they do not provide any details on this proposed mechanism. They also do not discuss the possibility that heterogeneous isotope abundance ratios would result from the detonation directly and persist until after the expansion stage.

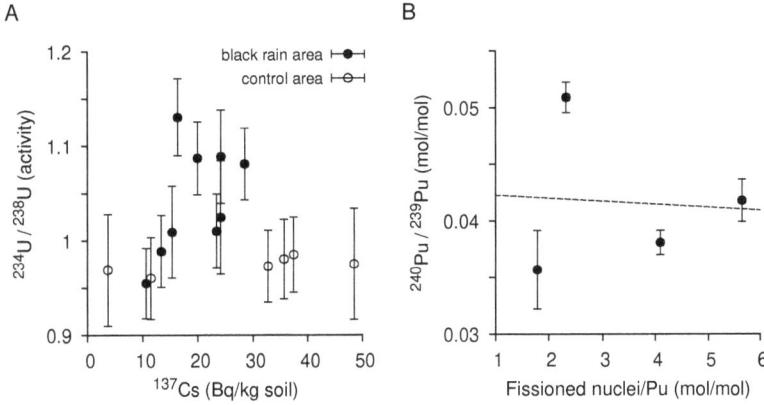

Figure 3.5: Variability of isotope ratios in studies on fallout from Hiroshima. A: Activity ratio of ^{234}U to ^{238}U vs. ^{137}Cs activity in fallout samples from within and outside the black rain area in Hiroshima. Replotted from Figure 5 in [57]. B: Molar ratio of ^{240}Pu to ^{239}Pu vs. molar ratio of fissioned nuclei to total plutonium [63]. Molar ratios are estimated from the activity ratios reported in the reference. The trend line is fitted without using errors; it would descend more steeply if errors were used.

In this context, it is noteworthy that the samples studied by Yamamoto et al. [63] show a substantial variation in the ratio of ^{240}Pu to ^{239}Pu (Figure 3.5B). If we suspend disbelief for a moment and assume that both plutonium isotopes indeed originated from a nuclear detonation, their variable ratio could not possibly be due to differential condensation during transport, since any such effect would have to be based on different chemical properties of the elements in question; thus, we could not expect it to separate different isotopes of the same element (and Shizuma et al. do not suggest that it does). We would therefore have to ascribe the observed variability of the ^{240}Pu/^{239}Pu ratio to inhomogeneity of the detonation itself.

We had seen earlier that ^{239}Pu arises from ^{238}U through the capture of a single neutron, whereas the formation of ^{240}Pu involves the successive capture of two neutrons, which must derive from separate fission events. We should therefore expect the proportion of ^{240}Pu to show a positive correlation with the ratio of fission events to total plutonium, but this is not observed (Figure 3.5B). Thus, the hypothetical condensation mechanism proposed by Shizuma et al. would have to account for the loss of a correlation not only between ^{235}U and ^{137}Cs, but also between ^{240}Pu and ^{137}Cs (which represents the number of fissioned nuclei).

How plausible is this hypothetical separation mechanism anyway? I have not seen this question addressed in the scientific literature; therefore, I will give my own reasoning. I assume that immediately after a nuclear detonation each of the resulting nuclides will be present in multiple states of ionization. It is the net charge of each ion which should dominate its interactions with other particles, rather than the chemical reactivity in the neutral state of the chemical element to which the ion belongs. This applies in particular to its association with water molecules, which will begin once the temperature has dropped sufficiently.

As soon as some of the ions have managed to attract and retain a hydration shell, the resulting aerosol particles will scavenge additional ions in their path, and they will ultimately coalesce into larger droplets. Both of these processes will tend to mix different nuclides, not to separate them. Overall, differential condensation seems ill-suited to explain the very pronounced variations in isotope ratios between the individual large black rain droplets whose residues were studied by Shizuma et al. [6].

3.5 Cesium and plutonium in sediments from the Nishiyama reservoir near Nagasaki

Since the Nagasaki bomb ('Fat Man') used ^{239}Pu, as did most nuclear bombs tested in the subsequent decades, isotopic signatures are less suitable for distinguishing local from global fallout in this case. However, there is one circumstance that makes up for it: at Nagasaki, the heaviest fallout reportedly occurred in and around the Nishiyama reservoir, a small body of water located some 3 km from the hypocenter. The timeline of fallout deposition was examined by Saito-Kokubu et al. [65], who analyzed the sediments at the bottom of this reservoir. The lowermost peaks of plutonium and cesium were found at a depth of 435-440 cm (Figure 3.6A); these must represent the earliest fallout.

The entire sediment core contains only a single layer of macroscopic charcoal particles, which the authors quite plausibly ascribe to the deposition of soot from the burning city. Intriguingly, however, this layer is found at approximately 450 cm. Since the study was published 63 years after the bombings, sedimentation had occurred with an av-

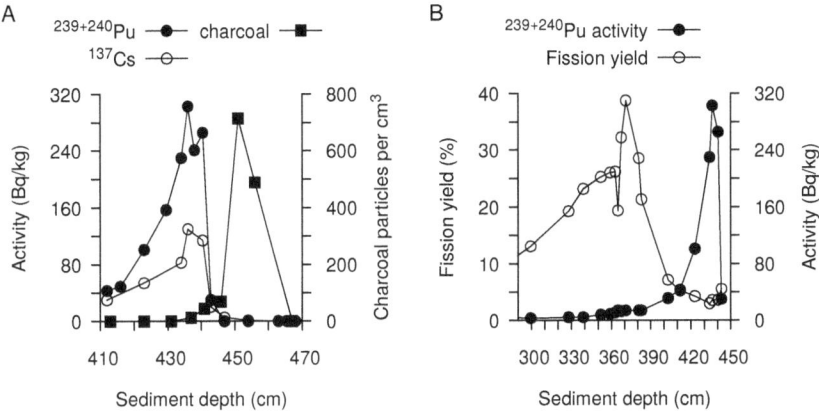

Figure 3.6: Radioactive fallout in sediments from Nishiyama reservoir near Nagasaki. A: Plutonium and cesium activities and charcoal particles vs. sediment depth. B: Plutonium and estimated fission yield vs. sediment depth. Data from Table 1 and Figure 2 in Saito-Kokubu et al. [65]. See text for details.

erage rate of close to 7 cm per year; assuming this rate to have been fairly uniform, a separation by 10-15 cm corresponds to a time interval of approximately two years.

The authors of the study acknowledge that the peaks are separated, but nevertheless ascribe the radioactivity to the Nagasaki bomb fallout. They do, however, not provide an explanation for the mechanism of separation beyond stating that it requires 'further study'. Considering the (macroscopic) size of the charcoal particles, we can assume that they are immobile within the sediment; thus, any separation would have to come about through upward migration of the radioactive isotopes. Such a migration, however, is very unlikely to have happened, for the following reasons:

1. It lacks a driving force. On dry land, isotopes may slowly be transported downward through the soil by percolating water; however, considering that the reservoir is already water-filled, there will be no upward movement of more water into it from the ground underneath.

2. The plutonium and cesium peaks are close to the charcoal layer, but they have practically no overlap with it. If the radioactivity had slowly leached out of the charcoal layer, then the radioactive peaks should be broader and exhibit more overlap with the charcoal layer.

3. The findings reported by Sakaguchi et al. [56] show that plutonium is carried by percolating water more rapidly than is cesium; therefore, in the reservoir, the plutonium peak should have moved upward further than the cesium peak. However, the peaks of the two isotopes coincide.

Another incongruity emerges if we examine the ratio of plutonium to cesium in the sediments. Using the half-lives of the three isotopes (^{239}Pu, ^{240}Pu, and ^{137}Cs), the age of a given layer of sediment, which can be estimated by interpolation from its depth, and the yield of ^{137}Cs per fission event (approximately 6%), we can calculate the fission yield of the bombs whose fallout is contained in that layer. In Figure 3.6B, this calculated fission yield is plotted vs. sediment depth, along with the plutonium content. We see a low plateau of plutonium activity between 360 and 390 cm; in this region, which most likely contains the fallout from nuclear bomb tests conducted after the war, we see fission yields in the range of 20-40%. As we go deeper and reach the large peak of the supposed Nagasaki bomb, however, the fission yield drops to 5% and below.

According to standard lore [4], the Nagasaki bomb ('Fat Man') contained 6.2 kg of plutonium, of which 1 kg is said to have fissioned; this amounts to a fission yield of 16%. Thus, the fission yield of at most 5%, which is evident from the isotope ratio observed in the sediment layers said to contain the 'Fat Man's' fallout, disagrees with the official narrative.[8]

As before, there is a politically incorrect but physically straightforward explanation for the observed discrepancies: charcoal and radioactivity are found in distinct layers of the sediment because they entered the reservoir at different times. The radioactivity was therefore not delivered by the 'Fat Man'; this also accounts for the discordant isotope ratio, which is at odds with the bomb's purported fission yield.

3.6 Enrichment of uranium to bomb grade: was it feasible in 1945?

We have seen above that no highly enriched ^{235}U can be demonstrated in the local fallout at Hiroshima, even though the bomb is said to

---

[8]The estimated fission yield is not materially affected by the presumed delayed dispersal of the plutonium; dating the lowermost stratum of sediment that contains plutonium and ^{137}Cs to 1945 will not reconcile the measured values to the official story.

have contained some 50 kg of it. We might therefore wonder if the technology for producing bomb-grade uranium even existed in 1945.

3.6.1 The state of the art according to Leslie Groves. The overall leader of the 'Manhattan Project', General Leslie Groves, asserts that everything came together in the nick of time, with both plutonium and bomb-grade uranium becoming available in quantity just days before they were needed. There is, however, good reason to doubt his story.

The enrichment of ^{235}U was carried out at Oak Ridge, Tennessee. According to Groves, three different plants were constructed for this purpose, each of which implemented a different physical principle of isotope separation. The first type was based on electromagnetic particle acceleration, the second on gaseous diffusion, and the final one on liquid thermal diffusion. In each case, construction was begun before the technical details of the process in question had been fully worked out. For example, with respect to the electromagnetic plant, Groves explains [40, p. 95 f]:

> *We then had to design, build and operate an extremely large plant with equipment of incredible complexity, without the benefit of any pilot plant or intermediate development: to save time we had early abandoned any idea of a pilot plant for this process. Always we were driven by the need to make haste. Consequently, research, development, construction and operation all had to be started and carried on simultaneously and without appreciable prior knowledge.*

Anyone with some experience in real-world research and development will understand that the chance of success of such a venture will be infinitesimally small. Groves, of course, claims that this plant was highly successful, as were both of the others.[9] To determine if this claim is credible, let's put ourselves in Groves' shoes and consider the following question: if our first isotope enrichment process is successful, will we scale it up, or will we gamble on a second process that has not yet been proven? If our first *two* processes work, will we scale up the more efficient one, or will we take our chances on a third?

---

[9]With none of the plants, however, does Groves give any numbers as to the degree of enrichment achieved, or the amounts of enriched materials obtained. Instead, he regales the reader with endless details on dollars spent, miles of pipes installed, watts of power consumed etc.

Groves chose to gamble on a new process at both times, which of course suggests that neither of the first two processes worked as intended. Furthermore, he reports that the third plant was shuttered shortly after the war, indicating that it, too, was a failure.

3.6.2 The state of the art according to Klaus Fuchs. In his book *Historical Dictionary of Atomic Espionage* [66], Glenmore Trenear-Harvey quotes from a conversation between the physicist Klaus Fuchs, a member of the Manhattan project and also a Soviet spy, with his spy handler Harry Gold from February 5th, 1944:

> *The work involves mainly separating the isotopes ... should the diffusion method prove successful, it will be used as a preliminary step in the separation, with the final work being done by the electronic method. They hope to have the electronic method ready early in 1945 and the diffusion method in July 1945, but K [Fuchs] says that the latter estimate is optimistic.*

Again according to Trenaer-Harvey, Fuchs met with another spy handler, Stepan Apresyan, in June 1944 and reported that

> *the ISLANDERS [British] and the TOWNSMEN [Americans] have finally fallen out as a result of the delay in research work on diffusion.*

Fuchs continued working for the Soviets throughout the war and afterwards, but he never could give them a description of a viable enrichment process. This is apparent from the technical development pursued during the late 1940s and early 1950s by the Soviets themselves. The German physicist Max Steenbeck, who played a leading role in this effort, gives a first-hand account of it in his autobiography [67]. Before the experimental work began, the Soviets conducted broad consultations to identify the most promising physical principles of separation, and indeed there were some false starts before the successful development of the gas centrifuge. Thus, even though the Soviets had supposedly come into possession of America's most prized atomic secrets, clearly those secret files did not tell them how to enrich ^{235}U.

Steenbeck, who had himself been kidnapped by the Soviets as a civilian in Berlin, recruited several German and Austrian scientists and technicians from Soviet POW camps; two of them, Zippe and Scheffel, stayed and worked with him throughout his whole time in the Soviet

Union. When finally all three men were allowed to return to Germany in the mid-1950s, Steenbeck joined his family at Jena in East Germany, whereas Zippe and Scheffel settled in the West. They were snapped up by Degussa, a metallurgical company with interests in nuclear fuel, for which they implemented the gas centrifugation technique on an industrial scale. Evidently, there was at the time no better or equally good process in place at this leading Western company. Centrifugation quickly superseded all other techniques for industrial ^{235}U enrichment and remains the standard method today. Overall, this bit of history strongly suggests that the technology for enriching uranium to bomb grade, in quantity, did not exist in 1945.[10]

3.7 Did the first atomic test explosion really use a plutonium bomb?

According to the official narrative, the "Trinity" test carried out on July 16, 1945 at Alamogordo (see Section 13.6.4) employed a plutonium bomb of the same type as the "Fat Man" bomb used on Nagasaki [40, p. 288]. However, this story is contradicted by some contemporaneous documents.

3.7.1 Arthur Compton in 1945: plutonium bomb several years away.
The 'Interim Committee' was a panel of leading scientists and politicians that was convened in 1945 to deliberate and advise on the future military and civilian use of atomic energy. Its affiliated scientific panel comprised leading physicists Robert Oppenheimer, Enrico Fermi, Arthur Compton, and Ernest Lawrence; all were present at the meeting in Washington, DC on May 31st, 1945. The following quote is taken from the protocol of this meeting [53]:

> *Dr. A. H. Compton explained the various stages of development. The first stage involved the separation of uranium 235. The*

---

[10] It is claimed that the 'Health Physics Research Reactor' (HPRR), which was used in 1961-62 during 'Operation Bren' to mimic the spectra of γ-rays and neutrons produced by the Hiroshima bomb (see Section 6.1.3), contained ^{235}U enriched to 93% [36]. This device was of course constructed *after* gas centrifugation technology had become available.

Considering that the critical mass of a sphere of enriched ^{235}U is on the order of 50 kg, we also have to wonder what sort of device exactly it was that Camac and his colleagues had been testing in 1944 (see page 1). Even assuming, counterfactually, that highly enriched ^{235}U was indeed available at the time, such an amount of the precious material would hardly have been expended on preliminary experiments of the kind described by Camac.

second stage involved the use of 'breeder' piles to produce enriched materials from which plutonium or new types of uranium could be obtained. The first stage was being used to produce material for the present bomb while the second stage would produce atomic bombs with a tremendous increase in explosive power over those now in production. Production of enriched materials was now on the order of pounds or hundreds of pounds and it was contemplated that the scale of operations could be expanded sufficiently to produce many tons. While bombs produced from the products of the second stage had not yet been proven in actual operation, such bombs were considered scientific certainty. It was estimated that from January 1946 it would take one and one-half years to prove this second stage in view of certain technical and metallurgical difficulties, that it would take three years to get plutonium in volume, and that it would take perhaps six years for any competitor to catch up with us.

Apparently, the somewhat bland wording of this excerpt caused the bureaucrats who declassified this originally 'top secret' file to miss its true import; however, the meaning is unmistakable.

Compton's first stage involves the isotopic enrichment of uranium. This comprises the production of both highly and weakly enriched ^{235}U. The highly enriched uranium is for building bombs of the Hiroshima type; remarkably, the protocol claims that such bombs are "now in production."

The second stage discussed by Compton concerns the production of plutonium. In this stage, he includes the generation of ^{239}Pu within weakly enriched uranium by letting the latter go critical inside an atomic reactor ('breeder pile'), as well as the subsequent purification of plutonium from the resulting complex mixture of uranium, ^{239}Pu and ^{240}Pu, and fission products.[11]

After these preliminaries, Compton discusses the prospects for the plutonium bomb. He states that the reactor-generated nuclide mixture

---

[11]Compton's term "enriched materials" refers not to a finished product but to this complex nuclide mixture. Compton also mentions that 'breeder piles' could, instead of ^{239}Pu, produce 'new types of uranium'. This refers to the conversion of ^{232}Th by neutron capture to ^{233}U, which like ^{235}U and ^{239}Pu is fissile and might in principle serve as bomb fuel. Elsewhere in the protocol, it is made clear that this reactor type has not yet reached the stage of technical realization.

is currently available on a scale of up to "pounds or hundreds of pounds."[12] However, this mixture will contain ^{239}Pu only in proportion to the amount of ^{235}U which was initially included in the pristine reactor fuel. In all likelihood, the ratio of ^{239}Pu formed to ^{235}U supplied was less than 1. Therefore, even 'hundreds of pounds' of the 'enriched material' would amount to several pounds of purified ^{239}Pu at best.

Compton further states that, counting from the beginning of 1946, it will take an estimated 1.5 years to "prove this second stage in view of certain technical and metallurgical difficulties." Since the first part of the second stage, namely, the production of 'enriched material', is already working, these difficulties must concern the purification of plutonium from it. Finally, he states that it will take yet more time to obtain plutonium 'in volume', which likely means in sufficient quantities for bomb manufacture. Even if we optimistically assume that 'proving the second stage' will already provide enough plutonium for a small number of bombs, Compton's words still imply that, counting from the time of the meeting, two more years must pass before the first plutonium bomb can be assembled. Thus, the inference is unavoidable that a plutonium bomb could not possibly have been ready a mere six weeks later for the fabled test at Alamogordo, or for the bombing of Nagasaki three weeks after that—or even for the 'Able' and 'Baker' alleged nuclear bomb tests at the Bikini Atoll in 1946.

Considering the report's surprising claim that ^{235}U bombs are already in production as of May 1945, we may wonder why so much emphasis is placed on the plutonium bomb. The explanation may be in the expected explosive yields of various bomb types, which Oppenheimer states at this meeting as up to 20 kt for the ^{235}U bomb, but up to 100 kt for the ^{239}Pu bomb—and even 100,000 kt for the 'third stage', by which is meant the hydrogen bomb.

Overall, this remarkable protocol collides with two important aspects of mainstream atomic bomb lore—namely, that 'Little Boy' was the only ^{235}U bomb available at the time, and that two ^{239}Pu bombs would have been ready for use at Alamogordo and at Nagasaki. Should we take seriously its claim that ^{235}U bombs "are now in production"?

---

[12] Between these two strangely divergent estimates, the lower one seems far more likely, since Enrico Fermi states at the same meeting that "approximately twenty pounds of the enriched material would be needed to carry on research in current engineering problems," which of course means that he does not currently have this amount.

The small amount available of 'enriched materials' indicates that even reactor-grade uranium was still in short supply; that much more highly enriched ^{235}U was available in the large quantities required for atomic bomb production is surely fiction.

We can assume that Leslie Groves and all of the scientists in attendance were aware of the true state of affairs. It thus seems that the fictional tale of uranium bombs already being in production was told at this meeting to keep some of the attending politicians and military officers in the dark. As among those present are listed Secretary of War Henry L. Stimson, James F. Byrnes, soon to be appointed as Secretary of State, and U.S. Army Chief of Staff George C. Marshall. However, even those participants who may have been deceived with respect to the uranium bombs must have understood soon after that the stories about the plutonium bombs having been detonated at Alamogordo and Nagasaki could not possibly be true. The protocol thus illuminates the striking extent of duplicity and deception engaged in alike by scientists, politicians, and military officers.[13]

3.7.2 Robert Wilson's last minute experiments on uranium fission.
The physicist Robert Wilson oversaw the experimental research division at Los Alamos. In a paper which was published 1947 in *Physical Review*, he describes a very ingenious experiment to observe the lag time between the capture of a neutron by a ^{235}U nucleus and the fission of that nucleus [69].

The manuscript of Wilson's published report had originally been confidential, but it was declassified in 1956. While the two texts are largely congruent, the following intriguing statement is found only in the declassified manuscript [70]:

The present experiment was done very hurriedly in the critical days before the first nuclear explosion was tried; the purpose was to be sure that no fissions were delayed as much as 10^{-8} sec, for such delays could have deleterious effects on the efficiency of the explosion.

---

[13] An electronic copy of the protocol of the Interim Committee meeting used to be hosted at the National Security Archive (NSA), but it has since been scrubbed from that website. The Wayback Machine archived a copy of the NSA's page in May 2022. Another electronic copy can be found through this book's reference list [53]. The excerpt used above is also quoted literally in the historic treatise by Alperovitz [68, p. 160], which will be used extensively in Chapter 14.

This sentence implies that even very shortly before the first atomic bomb test was carried out, a rather fundamental property of nuclear fission that might prevent the bomb from going off had not yet been established. It is of course hardly credible that the production of uranium bombs would have been begun, as the Interim Committee protocol asserts it had been, without this crucial experimental result in hand.

More pertinent in the current context, however, is the simple observation that Wilson's last minute studies concerned ^{235}U instead of ^{239}Pu. Apparently, he was under the impression that the imminent test explosion at Alamogordo would use a uranium rather than a plutonium bomb. While this agrees with Compton's statements before the Interim Committee, it is at odds with official atomic tradition. This conflict must have been the reason for scrubbing the quoted sentence from the manuscript before its publication in 1947.[14]

3.8 Conclusion

Studies from neither Hiroshima nor Nagasaki furnish any clear evidence of radioactive fallout commensurate with the purported nuclear detonations. Levels of plutonium and ^{137}Cs near Nagasaki are suitably high, but they do not agree with the bomb's stated fission yield. Moreover, they were apparently deposited approximately two years afterward, which corresponds well with Compton's estimated time of plutonium availability. The studies on the fallout of the Hiroshima bomb can be summed up as follows:

1. No evidence exists of highly enriched ^{235}U in the fallout. The measurements on soil samples indicate a very low degree of isotopic enrichment only, and those on black rain drops dried *in situ* suggest the same. A high degree of enrichment is only ever *stipulated*, and the calculations based on this premise result in vanishingly small absolute amounts of bomb uranium.

2. ^{137}Cs attributable to the Hiroshima bomb is readily detected. Its level remains well below the global fallout that arose from later bomb tests, but in most of the samples described in sufficient detail

---

[14]We will encounter Wilson again in the next chapter, laboring earnestly to estimate the amount of radiation that struck the two cities when the nuclear bombs went off, and commenting on the dearth of information available to him in this endeavor. From this, we can surmise that he was not in on the secret of the fraud.

it nevertheless exceeds the amount we should expect from ^{235}U measurements in conjunction with the key tenets of the official story of the bomb.

3. Samples protected from global fallout also contain plutonium, in amounts and isotopic compositions that are incompatible with its formation by a detonating ^{235}U bomb.

While none of these observations fit the 'Little Boy' narrative, all of them are consistent with the dispersal of reactor waste, for example by means of a 'dirty bomb'. We also note that measured isotope ratios are highly variable, suggesting the use of several different batches of radioactive waste, within which the weakly enriched ^{235}U had undergone fission to different degrees.

Overall, the findings and writings reviewed in this chapter consistently indicate that neither uranium nor plutonium were available in the required amounts and purities at the time of the alleged bombings, and that no atomic bombs were detonated. They also demonstrate inadequate, but determined efforts to forge the fallout of true nuclear detonations in both cities. With that in mind, let us now consider some of the physical studies adduced to prove that those nuclear bombings did indeed occur.

4 Early measurements of residual radioactivity

> General Farrell told us ... that our mission was to prove that there was no radioactivity from the bomb.
>
> Donald L. Collins [71]

This chapter examines reports on early field measurements in Hiroshima and Nagasaki by American and Japanese investigators. It concludes that the very limited evidence available does not substantiate the high initial levels of radioactivity on the ground that are implied by the conventional story of the nuclear bombings.

As explained in Section 2.10, most of the radiation produced by a nuclear bomb is released at the time of the detonation in the form of γ-rays and neutrons. Both can in principle be monitored in real time with suitable detectors [36], and the means were already available in 1945. The γ-radiation, in particular, should have been picked up by X-ray dosimeters, of which several types were already known in the 1940s [72], and at least the more modern hospitals in Hiroshima should have been equipped with them. I have not seen any reports of X-ray dosimeter readings that were taken during the bombing, but of course at that instant nobody had reason to suspect that an atomic bomb had been dropped. The upshot is that we have no record of an immediate, quantitative measurement of the radiation released during the blast.

In the absence of such direct measurements, one can try to reconstruct the radiation intensity during the detonation from indirect measurements of induced radioactivity (Section 2.10.3) and of thermoluminescence (Section 2.8.3). Here, we will consider measurements of radioactivity that occurred on-site in the days and weeks directly after the bombing. These measurements used Geiger counters or similar devices that could not identify radioactive isotopes, which also implies that they could not distinguish between the fission products carried by radioactive fallout and induced radioactivity. They are nevertheless of great value, since both fallout and induced radioactivity comprise mixtures of isotopes with very different half-lives. The very short-lived isotopes would produce high intensity beginning with the detonation but would drop to insignificant levels after time intervals ranging from hours to weeks; thereafter, the much slower decay of the longer-lived isotopes would sustain a residual activity somewhat above the natural background for several months to years (see Section 2.3.1). Thus, a high initial level of radioactivity which then rapidly drops by several orders of magnitude would be characteristic of a nuclear detonation. On the other hand, absence of the initial short phase of high activity would indicate that no such detonation had occurred.

4.1 Timeline and findings of early field measurements

Given the great potential value of early measurements, there is a striking shortage of actual data. The ^{235}U bomb supposedly dropped upon Hiroshima had never been tested before, and it has never been used again. Under these circumstances, one surely would expect that the Americans would have started their investigations at the earliest opportunity after the Japanese surrender; in fact, already *before* the surrender they might have advised the Japanese of the best ways to ascertain the nature and effect of the weapon. They might even have asked a neutral third party to assist the Japanese with the investigation, which would have been in the best interest of both sides. However, it seems the Japanese received no such assistance. Even more strikingly, after the capitulation it still took the Americans several weeks to send even some small advance parties of investigators; not before October did the Manhattan Engineers begin their own measurements (see Table 4.1).[1] Neither did they make up for lost time afterwards. The American physicist Robert Wilson, writing on the bomb radiation in 1951, began by summing up the state of this research [73]:[2]

---

[1]Among the team of Manhattan Engineers dispatched to Nagasaki was Donald L. Collins, whose rather interesting reminiscences [71] contain the quote preceding this chapter.

[2]Wilson's paper was published in 1956, but a footnote states that it was written in 1951 at the request of the Atomic Bomb Casualty Commission and declassified only in 1955. The paper repeatedly advises the reader that, due to the shortage of empirical data, the conclusions of this paper should be taken as educated guesses only. Wilson cites all of six references, which illustrates his limited access to information. I unsuccessfully tried to obtain one of these [74]—it remains in the poison cabinet to this day.

Table 4.1: Early measurements of environmental radioactivity in Hiroshima. Excerpted from Imanaka [75].

Team/University	Date	Location and findings
Osaka	August 11th	up to 5 times natural background several hundred meters from the hypocenter
Kyoto	August 11th	up to 10 times background several hundred meters from hypocenter
Kyoto	August 15th/16th	6 times natural background at Asahi bridge, otherwise weak activities
RIKEN	August 17th to October 20th	Imanaka [75] reports only relative readings; values in August and October are of similar magnitude
RIKEN	September	activity up to 6 times above background in fallout area
RIKEN	October 1-22	activity up to 9 times above background near hypocenter
RIKEN	January 1946	activity 6 times above background near hypocenter, 3 times background fallout area
Manhattan Engineers	October 1945	activity up to 15 times above background near hypocenter, up to 8 times in fallout area
Hiroshima	1948	activity up to 2.5 times background in fallout area

It is no simple problem to determine the X-ray and neutron dosages which were received at Hiroshima and Nagasaki. Much of the meager primary data that were written down has been dispersed or lost—that which existed but was not written down is mainly forgotten.

A timeline of early measurements, by both Japanese and American investigators, is given by Imanaka [75]. Table 4.1 provides a summary. While there is some variation in the results, all measurements agree that the level of activity is above the natural background but overall quite low, certainly nowhere near the levels required to induce acute radiation sickness (see Chapter 8). Among these results, the most important are those of August 11th, since they were obtained just five days after the bombing, and thus within a time period during which there should still have been substantial activity from short-lived isotopes.[3] This is illustrated in Figure 4.1A, which shows the hypothetical time course of induced radioactivity at the hypocenter, for the first three months after the bombing. The shape of this curve has been inferred from later experiments, in which soil samples from Hiroshima were irradiated with neutrons, and the activities of the major isotopes produced by neutron capture were measured.[4] The height of the curve was calibrated to a single reported measurement, which was taken 87 days after the bombing; according to Ishikawa et al. [8], and in keeping with the general trend evident from Table 4.1, this measured value amounted to ten times the natural background.

It is evident that the estimated activity changes very little after the 15th day. On the other hand, measurements within the first week should have shown a much higher activity. The question then is: did they? It seems that activity at the hypocenter was not measured within that time frame,[5] however, we can estimate it by comparing the two data series shown in Figure 4.1B. These data were collected at 5 days and 44 days, respectively, after the detonation. The measurement on day 5 is scaled in units of activity (Bq, or decays per second), while the measurement on day 44 is given in units of absorbed energy dose (µGy). They have been overlaid and scaled to show that they vary similarly with the distance from the hypocenter, as they should. We can use this similarity to estimate that the activity at the hypocenter on day 5 would have been approximately 4 Bq, which is some ten times above

---

[3]The only report I have found of an even earlier measurement is that by Toland [76], who states that Dr. Fumio Shigeto, then vice director of the Hiroshima Red Cross hospital, used an X-ray dosimeter to detect radiation at the hospital on the day after the bombing (August 7th) and found very little. Toland [76] and Liebow [77] also report that X-ray film stored in sealed packages within the same hospital was blackened after the bombing. This observation is often cited as evidence of ionizing radiation released in the blast, but while it may have prompted Dr. Shigeto's measurements, the negative outcome of the latter suggests that the films may have become blackened in some other manner, e.g. by exposure to heat when the hospital was burning. The physicist Robert Wilson considers this X-ray film evidence and concludes: "We must discard the film data because the analysis is much too complicated and difficult" [73].

[4]This graph was produced using the data in Table 9 in Okajima et al. [29], on which those authors also base their own 'official' estimate of induced radiation dosage. The single measured data point used to scale the curve is also given in that reference. A similar graph appears in Figure 5-2 of Ishikawa et al. [8].

[5]It is not clear who first determined the location of the hypocenter, or when; but in all likelihood it was not known or agreed upon at such a short time after the bombing.

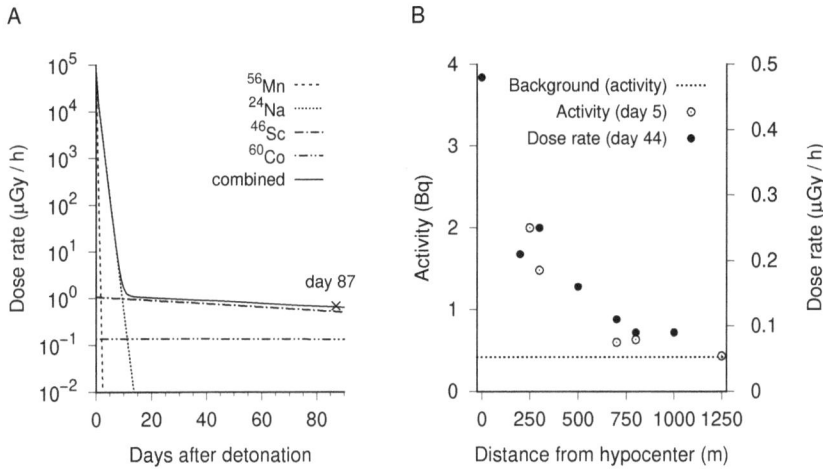

Figure 4.1: Estimates and measurements of induced radioactivity in Hiroshima. A: Induced radioactivity at the hypocenter as a function of time, extrapolated from a single measured data point (day 87) according to Okajima et al. [29]. The solid line is the sum of all individual isotope activities. See text for further explanation. B: Two data series shown by Takeshita [78]. The measurements after 5 days are given in Bq, whereas those on day 44 are given in µGy/h.

the natural background.[6] The single measured data point in panel A, at 87 days, was also about 10 times above the natural background [8]. Thus, while the neutron activation experiment shown in panel A indicates that between day 5 and day 87 the level of radioactivity should have decreased by a factor of 100, the observed factor is 1—that is, no decrease has occurred. Even though both of these factors are approximations, they cannot be reconciled; one must be false.

4.2 Shimizu's sulfur activation measurements

Against the various accounts of weak observed activity throughout the early period, one report stands out—that by Sakae Shimizu [37], one of the researchers from Kyoto University who undertook several expeditions to Hiroshima in August and September (see Table 4.1). The key pieces of his evidence are a magnetic piece of iron, a horse

---

[6]This plot combines panels A and B from Figure 1 in Takeshita [78], with units of measurement converted to the ones preferred in this text. The first data series was obtained on August 11th by a team from Osaka University. The second data series was likely obtained by researchers from RIKEN, but I have found no English-language reference to confirm this explicitly.

bone, and three porcelain insulators containing sulfur. When these samples were examined for β-radiation in the laboratory at Kyoto, all showed significant activity, which Shimizu ascribes to activation by neutron capture. Of particular interest is the activation of sulfur, since it requires highly energetic (fast) neutrons [36], which unlike those of low energy would be expected in a nuclear bomb but not in the natural background radiation.

There are strong reasons, however, to reject Shimizu's evidence. Both with his sulfur samples and those reported by investigators from RIKEN [79, p. 216], the activity as a function of distance from the hypocenter is physically implausible. This will be discussed in detail in Section 6.3.1.

Another reason to doubt Shimizu's sulfur activation data is that this line of evidence was not pursued any further. Activation of sulfur (^{32}S) would have been singularly useful to determine the strength and exact location of the detonation, as well as the reach of the fast neutrons produced by it. The activation of sulfur produces radioactive phosphorus (^{32}P), which has a half-life of 14.3 days. Thus, if Shimizu's early high readings had been correct, enough activity should have remained even at 4-6 weeks after the detonation, that is, long enough for the Americans to carry out their own measurements. There is, however, no indication that they ever did so.[7]

Suspicion is also warranted concerning Shimizu's piece of radioactive iron. It is said to have shown and activity of 374 cpm, or approximately 6 Bq. On its own, this is not problematic. However, the sample is said to have been "buried in a collapsed house near the hypocenter", and furthermore to have consisted of a "horseshoe magnet of an integrating Watt-meter." Such instruments are surely much more commonly encountered in physics laboratories than in urban dwellings. Furthermore, if indeed the house containing this instrument had collapsed, how could this sample have been discovered afterwards? Its rather weak radioactivity could not possibly have been detected from above

---

[7]Instead of following Shimizu's lead, his American handlers confiscated all of his written records and then 'lost' them (see Section 1.5.5). As another interesting aside, Shimizu [37] also notes: "Due to physical fatigue and may be to an effect of exposure to nuclear radiations during the field survey in Hiroshima, in the night of the 19th I spat out much bloody sputa, and I was forced to lie on a bed for about three months." Neither fatigue nor the weak radioactivity on the ground in Hiroshima could account for Shimizu's hemoptysis (coughing of blood); however, exposure to mustard gas very well could.

the pile of rubble covering it—particularly if we believe that so soon after the bombing the whole place was brimming with radioactivity.

Among all of Shimizu's samples, the highest activity is reported for a horse bone. This activity is attributed mostly to the activation of phosphor by the capture of slow neutrons. In Chapter 6, it will be shown that collectively the phosphor activation measurements are inconsistent with those pertaining to sulfur activation. Overall, therefore, not one of the findings reported by Shimizu can be taken at face value.

4.3 Conclusion

Once we disqualify Shimizu's findings, two major conclusions emerge. The first one is that, among all measurements on the ground, only those that occurred in the first week have any real power to confirm or refute a nuclear detonation; and their consistently low levels of activity clearly refute it.

The second conclusion is simply that which was already spelled out by Wilson [73], namely, that both the acquisition and the documentation of early radioactivity measurements were wholly inadequate. This inadequacy speaks louder than the evidence itself. If the official story had been true, if the bomb had indeed been the world's very first ^{235}U bomb, such obviously willful negligence would be inexplicable. Fantastic amounts of work and treasure had been poured into the development of this revolutionary weapon; surely those who had accomplished it would also want a detailed record of the outcome and proof of their success. If, on the other hand, the official story were indeed a lie, then the neglect would be entirely understandable, since richer and more detailed evidence would only increase the chances that the fraud might be uncovered in the end.

5 γ-Ray dosimetry by thermoluminescence

> Lest men suspect your tale untrue,
> keep probability in view.
>
> John Gay

This chapter looks at two studies that purport to have measured the γ-radiation released by two atomic bombs. The measurements utilized the thermoluminescence of ceramic materials which allegedly had been exposed to the bomb radiation. While one of the two studies evades specific criticism by presenting only conclusions but no actual measurements, the experimental detail contained in the other study proves it to be fraudulent.

When a fission bomb detonates in the air, radiation will propagate radially in all directions from the *epicenter*, i.e. the site of the detonation. Of all places on the ground, the *hypocenter*, that is, the spot vertically underneath the epicenter, will receive the highest dosage of radiation. With increasing distance from the hypocenter, the dosage will decrease rapidly; and at any given distance, it may be reduced through *shielding* by concrete buildings or other structures.

Both γ-rays and neutrons can in principle be monitored promptly with suitable detectors [36], and the means were already available in 1945. When such direct readings are lacking, as is the case in Hiroshima and Nagasaki, one can still try to determine in hindsight how much neutron and γ-radiation was released in the burst. For γ-rays, this can be done through thermoluminescence measurements on suitable rocks or ceramics that were exposed during the blast; the neutron radiation can be quantified from induced radioactivity. Measurements of this kind are indeed the showpieces among the evidence advanced to prop up the official story; and taken at face value, their findings leave no other conclusion than that some sort of nuclear detonation must indeed have taken place. We will consider both methods and their applications in turn. In this chapter, we will examine two early studies which used thermoluminescence measurements on bricks or tiles to determine the γ-dosages that were released in Hiroshima and Nagasaki [80, 81]. The procedures used by both studies are similar in principle, but they show surprising differences in detail that highlight significant pitfalls of each study (see Table 5.1).

5.1 Calibration of thermoluminescence measurements

As explained in a little more detail in Section 2.8.3, the method involves the observation of light given off by ceramic materials when these are heated up gradually; the intensity of the light thus evoked is proportional to the cumulative amount of γ-radiation which this material was exposed to earlier, and potentially a very long time ago.

A crucial step in this procedure is to establish the relation between the activating γ-ray dose and the resulting thermoluminescence intensity. This relation will be affected by the chemical composition of a particular piece of ceramic, and therefore the measurement must be calibrated empirically for each sample. To this end, both studies use the same clever trick: they first heat the brick or tile in question to obtain an uncalibrated measurement of the thermoluminescence originating from the bomb. This heating run will purge the material of all pent-up thermoluminescence. The deactivated material is then recharged by irradiating it with a known dose of γ-radiation from a laboratory source. From the amount of light released when the sample is heated again, the dose-response ratio can be determined. This value can then be used to calculate the γ-dose that would have caused the thermoluminescence signal which was measured first.

Unless proven otherwise, one must assume that the efficiency of activation may vary with the energy of the impinging γ-particles. To account for this, Hashizume et al. [81] employ a combination of various sources claimed to match the energy spectrum the bomb radiation.[1] In contrast, Higashimura et al. [80] employ only a single ^{60}Co source.

Taken at face value, the calibration procedure which Hashizume et al. [81] adopted would seem superior. There is, however, serious cause

---

[1] The sources used by Hashizume et al. [81] were ^{60}Co, ^{137}Cs, and a linear accelerator producing high-energy X-rays, which differ from γ-rays only in origin but not in nature. The proportions and the X-ray energies are not given, and the assumed bomb γ-spectrum is not detailed either.

Table 5.1: Thermoluminescence measurements on tiles and bricks in Hiroshima and Nagasaki: comparison of assumptions and findings reported by two early studies.

Study	Higashimura et al. [80]	Hashizume et al. [81]
Use of roof tiles from wooden buildings	suitable and used as samples	not usable, since orientation relative to hypocenter unknown
Calibration	irradiation with ^{60}Co	combination of X-rays with γ-rays from ^{60}Co and ^{137}Cs
Glow curve shape	bomb and calibration samples are different	bomb and calibration samples are similar
Thermoluminescence signal at 180°C	not detectable in bomb-exposed tiles	detectable with lifetime of 6.7×10^5 years, used exclusively
Thermoluminescence signal at 330°C	detectable with lifetime of 100 years, used exclusively	not used
Loss of signal due to fire	considered, said to be avoided by sample selection	not mentioned
Loss of signal due to bomb flash	not mentioned	not mentioned
Depth distribution of signal in sample	not mentioned	determined only on a single calibration sample

to doubt their assertions. In one of their experiments, the authors sliced up a brick into layers of 1 cm thickness to determine the depth distribution of thermoluminescence.[2] The result is reproduced here in Figure 5.2A. Now, this depth distribution would depend on the energy spectrum of the activating γ-radiation, since softer (i.e. lower-energy) radiation would exhaust itself closer to the surface, while harder rays would penetrate and cause activation in deeper layers also. Thus, this experiment would be a good way to validate the authors' assumptions about the bomb energy spectrum, and furthermore to observe changes

---

[2]The authors do not detail what, if any, precautions were taken to avoid heating of the brick when it was cut, which might trigger and deplete the thermoluminescence prematurely.

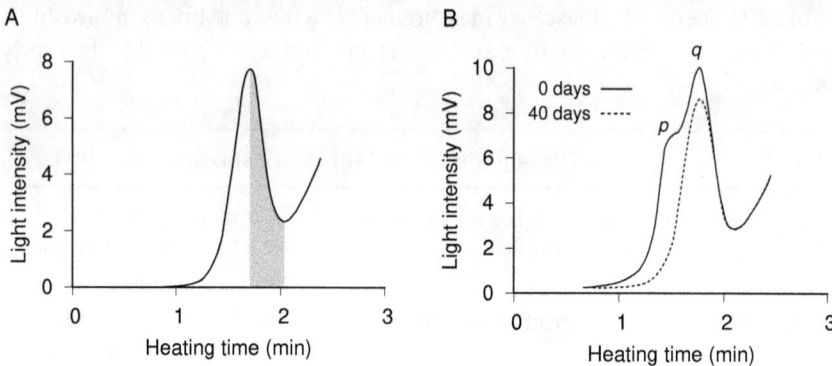

Figure 5.1: Thermoluminescence curves of brick or tile samples, drawn after Figure 6 (A) and Figure 10 (B) in Hashizume et al. [81]. Samples were heated from ambient temperature to 300°C within 3 min. A: Described as 'a typical glow curve of thermoluminescence', which was 'obtained from a sample.' The portion of the signal curve indicated by the shaded area was used to determine the absorbed γ-ray dose. B: Glow curve of an experimentally irradiated sample, showing two overlapping peaks at approximately 1.4 min/140°C (p) and 1.8 min/180°C (q), respectively. 40 days after irradiation, p has vanished, whereas q persists; with this information in hand, Hashizume et al. estimate its lifetime at 670,000 years.

to this spectrum with increasing distance from the hypocenter. It is very strange, therefore, that this experiment was carried out only once, and *only on an experimentally irradiated sample, but never on a native one.* This is just one of several issues that raise the question how this entire study could possibly have survived serious peer review.

5.2 Signal shape and stability

Another flaw in the study by Hashizume is the failure to clearly identify any of the few glow curves they show as that of a native sample rather than of a calibration run.[3] The authors do suggest that native and calibration signals are similar in shape, but they never prove it. The signal shown in their Figure 6 (reproduced here as Figure 5.1A) is referred to as "a typical glow curve from a sample," which is suggestive yet remains ambiguous; all other data shown are described as originating from laboratory activation. Showing some native and

---

[3] On a related note, Higashimura et al. [80] do not show any raw data at all, which considering the novelty of their study is quite unusual.

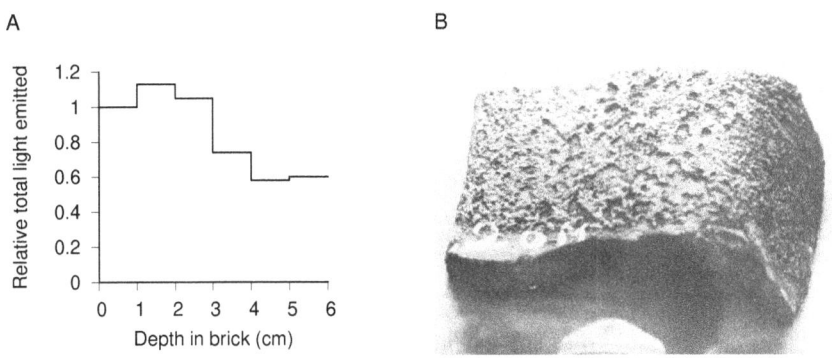

Figure 5.2: Depth profile of thermoluminescence intensity in a laboratory-irradiated brick, and roof tile from Nagasaki with surface damaged by heat. A: The brick was exposed to γ-rays, cut into layers, and the thermoluminescence intensity of each layer was measured separately. Replotted from Figure 7 in Hashizume et al. [81]. B: Bubbled and roughened surface of a roof tile found in Nagasaki. Photograph taken from Ishikawa et al. [8], who assert that the observed effects are due to the flash of light from the bomb.

calibration runs side by side would have greatly helped their case, and it is difficult to imagine that none of our fearless yet imaginary peer reviewers would have demanded it.

Another questionable feature is the assumed stability of the thermoluminescence signal in Hashizume's selected temperature range. While the x axes in Figure 5.1 are labeled in units of time, the rate of heating to the final temperature of 300°C at 3 min would have been fairly linear, and the two overlapping peaks in panel B would be located at approximately 140°C and 180°C, respectively. The temperature at which a given luminescence peak occurs correlates with the *activation energy*, that is, the height of the energy threshold that the trapped electrons in the sample must overcome in order to return to what is ultimately a lower state of energy. This also translates into different stability under ambient conditions; the lower the trigger temperature, the more readily the peak will fade over time even without any heating of the sample.

Hashizume et al. [81] report that their lower-temperature peak (labeled with p in the figure) disappears spontaneously (without heating) within 40 days of experimental irradiation, but claim that the other one (peak q) should be stable with a lifetime of 6.7×10^5 years.[4] Accordingly, they use the right half of this peak to quantify the radiation dose in all their samples (cf. Figure 5.1A). However, such an enormous difference in lifetime for peaks that are separated by only some 40°C seems unlikely. Indeed, a very different assessment is given by Higashimura et al. [80], who report that in their bomb-irradiated samples no peak at 180°C is observed, although it does occur after experimental irradiation with ^{60}Co:

> *Glow curves resulting from bomb radiation in the past and from the ^{60}Co irradiation in the present are different in shape. The glow curve resulting from ^{60}Co irradiation shows ... a distinct peak at about 180° C. On the contrary, the glow curve resulting from bomb radiation has a negligible intensity below 180° C.*

Accordingly, they discard the peak at 180°C altogether and instead evaluate only the signal evoked at a much higher temperature range ($\geq 330°$C), for which they nevertheless much more cautiously claim a lifetime of "longer than 100 years." In summary, between the failure to present the evidence that any of their own bomb-exposed samples exhibit this peak, and the starkly contrasting observations from the earlier study [80], the findings reported by Hashizume et al. [81] cannot be trusted.

5.3 Sample inactivation by heat from the bomb and the fire

If bricks and tiles were to be used for retrospective evaluation of thermoluminescence, it was essential that they be kept at gentle temperatures throughout, from the moment of their activation by the γ-rays from the blast to the laboratory measurement. Premature thermal inactivation could have occurred due to heat either from the bomb itself, or from the subsequent fires. Higashimura et al. [80] state that they used roof tiles which came from areas unaffected by the fire. However, such areas must have been very hard to find. In their book chapter on the extent of the fires in Hiroshima that followed the bomb attack, Kawano et al. [82] state:

---

[4]The lifetime of an exponential decay (as will be assumed with a fading process such as this) is defined as the time within which the original signal decays to a residue of $1/e$ (approximately 0.37). The stated lifetime corresponds to a half-life of 4.64×10^5 years, which is roughly equivalent to 4 successive ice age cycles.

> *Within 30 minutes after the bomb blast, large fires broke out and firestorms started. ... As a result of the firestorms, anything that was burnable was completely destroyed in an approximately 2 km radius from the hypocenter.*

'Anything burnable' should certainly include the wooden buildings whose roof tiles were used for Higashimura's study; all of their samples are said to have been collected within 1 km of the hypocenter.[5] Indeed, Hashizume et al. [81] forgo those roof tiles altogether. Ostensibly, however, this is not because of the direct effect of the fire, which they avoid to discuss altogether, but for a more fastidious reason: since all those wooden houses had been 'destroyed,' it was no longer possible to tell how the roof tile in question had been oriented relative to the impinging γ-rays. This unknown angle would have affected the absorbed dose and thus have been a source of significant yet unaccountable variation. To circumvent this problem, they restrict themselves to flat tiles and bricks from concrete buildings that had been left standing after the attack, and for which the orientation toward the center of the detonation was therefore known. They also emphasize that all their samples had been in a direct line of sight to the center of the detonation, and therefore received an unshielded dose of γ-rays.

How does Hashizume's choice of samples affect the question of thermal inactivation? While many large buildings were left standing after the attack, they nevertheless were also affected by the fire. In the evening of August 8th, that is, two and a half days after the bombing, the physician Michihiko Hachiya noted in his diary [62]:

> *Concrete buildings near the center of the city, still afire on the inside, made eerie silhouettes against the night sky. The glowing ruins and the blazing funeral pyres set me wondering if Pompeii had not looked like this during its last days.*

The tenor of this quote and of the preceding one from Kawano et al. [82] certainly match the impressions conveyed by photographs of the scorched and destroyed city. The pictures in Figure 5.3 show three buildings from which samples were obtained that were allegedly used with success for thermoluminescence measurements. The fires that left

---

[5] Even if those tiles looked undamaged by the fire, they still might have been thermally inactivated, since this will occur at lower temperatures than those required to mar the surface.

5 γ-Ray dosimetry by thermoluminescence

Figure 5.3: Three of many burnt-out buildings that according to various studies [83, 84] yielded pristine tiles or bricks suitable for measurement of γ-ray dosage by thermoluminescence. Top: Hiroshima City Hall; center: Hiroshima Prefectural Industrial Promotion Hall (now commonly called the 'Atomic Bomb Dome'); bottom: Shiroyama elementary school in Nagasaki.

their marks on these buildings broke out some time after the attack, that is, after the bricks and tiles would have had received their dose of γ-rays and been activated for thermoluminescence. Now, maybe we can't be absolutely sure that *every single* brick or tile from such a building would have been thermally discharged in the conflagration; but at the very least, a lot of them must have been, and thus a large proportion of duds would have been among the samples later collected from these buildings for thermoluminescence measurements.[6]

A similar problem arises in connection with the intense flash of light and thermal energy released by the detonation. The heat is said to have etched the surfaces of unshaded granite tombstones, and so reliably and regularly that from the outlines of the shadows thus produced the epicenters of the explosions in both cities could be determined with high accuracy (see for example Hubbell et al. [85] and Figures 13.3 and 13.4). Figure 5.2B shows a a roof tile which was collected at 270 m from the hypocenter in Nagasaki, and whose surface corrosion is portrayed as the direct effect of the thermal flash [8]. If this is true, then several of Hashizume's samples, which were collected at similar or even shorter distances from the hypocenters in both cities, should have shown similar thermal damage to the surface; for as the authors insist, the samples were exposed to the γ-rays without obstruction, and therefore also to the thermal flash.

Considering that such damage only occurs at temperatures substantially higher than those used in their thermoluminescence experiments, it will have occurred to them that thermal inactivation must at the very least be *considered* and measured in control experiments. They already had found a technique that would suit this purpose, namely, the comparison of thermoluminescence in superficial layers to that in deeper ones (see Figure 5.2A). That they do not even *mention* the problem means that their work is unreliable; and so is any such study that does not admit to and convincingly address the problem of thermal

---

[6]These particular buildings are listed in Ichikawa et al. [83] and Egbert and Kerr [84]. Hashizume et al. [81] only give latitudes and longitudes for the locations of their samples; none of these coincide with any of the landmark buildings that one finds depicted and identified in photographs, but one pair of coordinates points to water in a river arm, and another one to a spot of wilderness far from the city.

sample inactivation. So far I have found not one study that convincingly clears this bar.[7]

5.4 Appraisal of reported luminescence data

Higashimura et al. [80] report only the final numbers in terms of γ-dose at different distances from the hypocenter, so the reader is given no opportunity to judge the actual experimental data obtained by these authors. However, the more detailed study by Hashizume et al. [81], while also showing only very few of its raw glow curves, does give the luminescence intensities determined from them (see their Table 2). It also gives the formula used to calculate the γ-ray dose from the luminescence values:

$$\gamma\text{-Dose} = L \times G \times C \times R \qquad (5.1)$$

In this equation, L is the bomb-induced thermoluminescence measured in the first heating run on each sample, whereas G, C, and R are calibration and correction factors. The most important one of these is G, the calibration factor that gives the amount of γ-rays required to induce a certain luminescence response (γ/L), as determined from the second heating run. C is a factor that corrects for the orientation *in situ* of each sample relative to the incident γ-rays; this number varies only from 1.09 to 1.31 and thus has a minor effect on the overall result. R is supposed to correct for fading between the times of activation and of measurement; no value is given for it, but using the very long lifetime which the authors assume for the luminescence peak q (see Table 5.1) its value will be very close to 1.

With this in mind, one surely would expect any major change in the γ-dose to correlate with major changes in L also, which therefore should assume its highest value near the hypocenter, while variations

---

[7]Ichikawa et al. [83], in another experimental study on roof tiles, state that "although the roof tiles were collected with much care to obtain samples which had not suffered from the fire, some samples did not show any thermoluminescence, which probably reflected the fire effect. But since we took only the glow curves of the normal type ... " While this explanation is of course much better than nothing at all, it does not address possible *partial* thermal inactivation. Moreover, this paper explicitly lists several burnt-out or burnt-down buildings among its sampling sites, including Shiroyama school in Nagasaki (see Figure 5.3) and Hiroshima Castle, of which reportedly [86] only the foundation walls had survived the bombing.

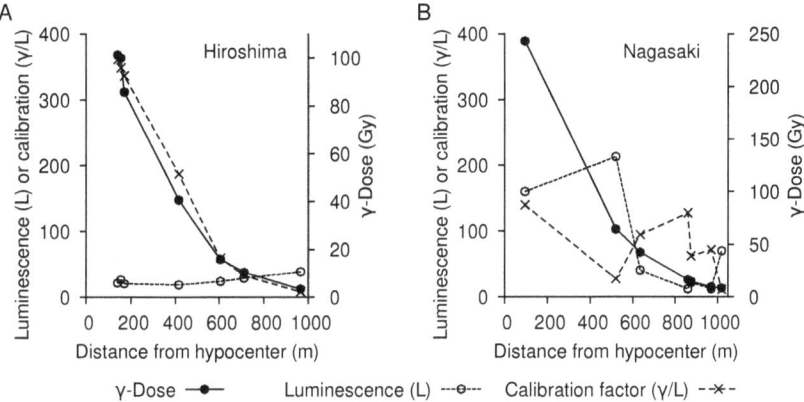

Figure 5.4: Sample thermoluminescence, calibration factors, and γ-dosages as functions of distance from the hypocenters in Hiroshima and Nagasaki. All data are from Table 2 in Hashizume et al. [81]. No units for the luminescence readings and calibration factors are given in [81]; the γ-doses are stated in rad in [81] but have here been converted to Gy.

due to the correction factors should be relatively minor. This is, however, not what we find. Figure 5.4A shows Hashizume's data from Hiroshima. We see that the raw data for L vary only slightly, and in fact reach their highest value at the greatest distance from the hypocenter. Nevertheless, a strong and regular decreasing trend is shown for the γ-dose, which is entirely due to a closely similar trend in the γ/L calibration factors.

After recovering from the surprise, we might wonder if it is *physically* plausible that bricks and tiles, which likely are quite similar in chemical composition, should show such large variation in their sensitivity to activation by γ-rays. This is a valid question, but I will not pursue it and only note that Hashizume et al. do not discuss it either. Instead, I will ask a simpler one: assuming that indeed the calibration factors may physically vary to such a large extent, how *statistically* likely is it that they should do so in this very order, monotonously decreasing with increasing distance from the hypocenter? Since we have seven different values overall, that probability is $1/7! = 1/5040$, or close to 0.0002.

The raw luminescence readings are substantially higher and more variable in samples from Nagasaki than in those from Hiroshima (Figure 5.4B). Remarkably, however, the calibration factors vary exactly the opposite way, going up each time that L goes down, and down each time that L goes up, once more producing a smooth and regular curve for the γ-ray dose as a function of distance from the hypocenter.[8] With again seven values overall and thus six transitions between them, the probability that they all would correspond this way by chance is $1/2^6$ or $1/64$. While this *is* almost a hundred times greater than the probability of the more regular trend in Hiroshima, it is still less than 5%, the threshold below which we conventionally reject random as a valid explanation. Thus, the results from both Hiroshima and Nagasaki independently fail the test of statistical plausibility; that both of them should have turned out this way by chance strains credulity past the breaking point.

5.5 Conclusion

In this chapter, we examined two early and influential thermoluminescence studies that are still widely cited as evidence of γ-radiation from the detonations in Hiroshima and Nagasaki. We saw that in both studies essential precautions and controls are absent. Even more startlingly, in the one study that actually details at least some of its experimental results, the purported evidence of γ-radiation from the bomb is not apparent in the actual measurements of the bomb-induced thermoluminescence, but depends entirely on the stated results of the calibration procedure, whose falsity can be inferred from probabilistic arguments alone.

Since Hashizume et al. [81] obviously fabricated their evidence of γ-radiation, one may ask: why did they falsify the calibration factors rather than the readings of bomb-induced luminescence? The latter would have been more direct and also far more credible. I can't help thinking that they did it for this very reason—they *wanted* to be found out, to let the world know that their report was untruthful, while ostensibly conforming to the official lies and censorship imposed on them. Of course, this is just my own reading, which I cannot prove; readers will judge for themselves.

---

[8]If there is any truth and relevance at all to the raw thermoluminescence readings, then the uniformly low values from Hiroshima may reflect widespread thermal inactivation due to the fire. Nagasaki was not as completely engulfed by fire, and thus more thermoluminescence activity—due to natural background, of course, not to any nuclear detonation—may have been preserved in those brick samples.

There is a number of more recent studies that use the same experimental approach, report largely similar findings, and are equally unconvincing with respect to sample selection. A fairly recent overview of the state of the 'art' has been given by Egbert and Kerr [84], who list two of the burnt-out buildings shown in Figure 5.3 as sampling sites. Remarkably, these authors also suggest that with some samples, particularly from Hiroshima, thermoluminescence activation arose not from direct γ-irradiation during the detonation but rather from radioactive fallout deposited on the samples.

As we will see later, the idea of strong, short-lived fallout has been invoked to account for otherwise inexplicable findings of acute 'radiation' sickness in many people who were not in Hiroshima during the bombing but entered the city shortly afterward (Section 8.7). Egbert and Kerr's thesis may have been invented to prop up this story, which is otherwise entirely without observational foundation.

To advance their argument, the authors propose some highly speculative scenarios to conjure up the requisite high levels of fallout activity, such as neutron activation of sodium chloride in brackish river water, which was then swirled up by the blast wave and deposited on the surfaces of the sample materials in question. To explain why correspondingly high levels of fallout activity were not detected in later direct measurements, they suggest that the deposited fallout was subsequently washed off by the strong rainfalls which lashed both cities during September. However, they neglect to mention the findings of very low activity in early field surveys (see Chapter 4) as well as in soil samples which had been collected and measured only a few days after the Hiroshima bombing (see Section 3.2). These findings conclusively falsify Egbert and Kerr's specious idea of high initial fallout radioactivity.

6 The evidence of neutron radiation

> If it disagrees with experiment, it's wrong.
>
> Richard Feynman

This chapter examines the evidence pertaining to radioactive isotopes whose formation is ascribed to the neutron radiation released by the Hiroshima bomb. It will show that

- the spatial distribution of ^{31}P formed in sulfur samples by the capture of fast neutrons is inconsistent with the activation by a single nuclear detonation at the claimed altitude of 600 m;
- the very small number of samples which have been analyzed for multiple isotopes yield contradictory information regarding the date of activation and the neutron energy spectrum;
- the dosimetry scheme DS86, which drastically lowered the neutron dose estimates for Hiroshima, was at the time of its inception plainly contradicted by the evidence. While some supporting results have since been published, the discrepancies between these 'fresh' data and the older ones have not been convincingly explained.

The purported evidence of neutron radiation is thus replete with inconsistencies and cannot be trusted.

6.1 Neutron dose estimates in the T65D and DS86 dosimetry schemes

We have discussed earlier that a proper nuclear bomb should release both γ- and neutron radiation. The study by Robert Wilson [73] appears to be the earliest attempt to quantify the amounts of both forms of radiation released in Hiroshima and Nagasaki. Noting that he has very little in the way of physical data to work with (see quotation in Section 4.1), he does his best to come up with reasonable estimates, but he cautions that his numbers—particularly those for fast neutrons, which are particularly important with respect to biological effects—are "merely guesses."

Experimental study of this problem began in the late 1950s; this work resulted in the T65D dosimetry scheme [36] (see also Chapter 11). According to T65D, neutron doses had been much higher in Hiroshima, where they accounted for a substantial fraction of the total radiation dose, than in Nagasaki, where γ-radiation had been dominant. This was a consequence of the different bomb designs: the Nagasaki bomb had been enclosed with a large amount of chemical explosives, whose constituent 'light' elements would have stopped neutrons much more effectively than γ-rays. In contrast, the casing of the Hiroshima bomb consisted exclusively of metal elements; it would have attenuated γ-radiation more effectively than the Nagasaki bomb's enclosure, while being more permissive toward neutrons.

6.1.1 Propagation of neutron fluences in observed in bomb tests.
Many of the experimental studies that led to the T65D dosimetry scheme were carried out in conjunction with the bomb tests then ongoing in the United States. To study the reach of the neutrons released in a detonation as well as their *fluence*, that is, the total number of neutrons striking a given area on the ground, suitable detectors were placed at different distances from the detonation. These detectors contained non-radioactive elements able to capture neutrons and thereby become radioactive;[1] from the radioactivity thus induced, the neutron fluence could be inferred. Furthermore, to characterize the energy spectrum of the neutrons, several different precursor elements were employed that preferentially capture neutrons of different energies.

Figure 6.1 depicts some such measurements, which were reported by Auxier [36]. In the figure, the data have been plotted according to Equation 2.11, which corrects the fluence for radial divergence from the epicenter (see Section 2.7.4). We see that all data can be described fairly well with straight lines. Since the y axis is logarithmic, this means that the simple approximation of exponential attenuation along a straight path summarizes the results rather well, even though it does not accurately reflect the way neutrons interact with matter (cf. Section 2.4.4). We do note that the slopes, and therefore the relaxation

---

[1] In some cases, the precursor elements were in fact also radioactive, but the radioactivity of the derived elements formed by neutron capture could be distinguished and measured separately.

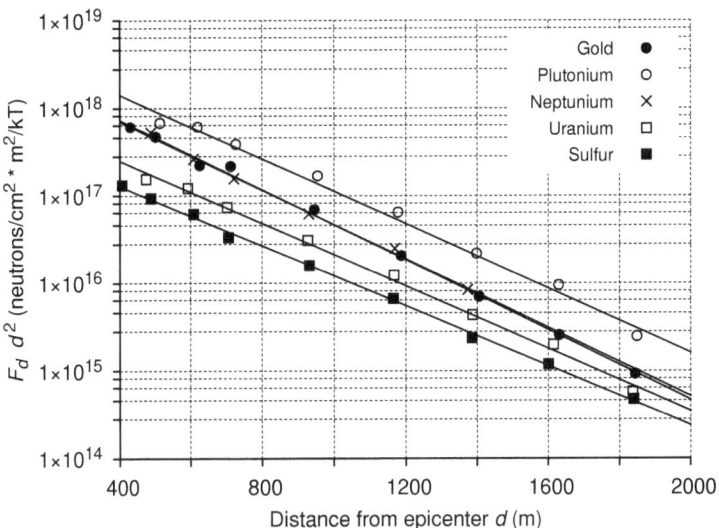

Figure 6.1: Neutron fluence observed in a 'typical bomb test'. Data from Figure 2.2 in Auxier [36, p. 16]. Various detectors were used that contained five different elements which capture neutrons of different energies. Gold captures the slowest neutrons; the threshold energies of the other elements increase in the indicated order. See text for details.

lengths,[2] vary somewhat between elements. The steepest decline, and therefore the shortest relaxation length (218 m) is found with gold, which captures very low-energy (thermal) neutrons, whereas the highest relaxation length (255 m) is observed with sulfur, which also captures the neutrons which are highest in energy (> 2.5 MeV). We note that overall the effect of neutron energy on relaxation length is modest.

The average relaxation length of all five elements shown in the figure is 235 m. However, these measurements were carried out in Nevada, at an altitude of more than 1000 m and presumably in fairly dry air. Both Hiroshima and Nagasaki are at low elevation and very near the sea, with denser and typically more humid air. Both factors will cause more rapid attenuation of neutrons; and this is indeed reflected in the T65D dosimetry scheme, which assumed a neutron relaxation length of 198 m meters for both cities.

---

[2]The relaxation length is defined as the layer thickness of a given medium—in this case, air—that will attenuate a beam of radiation by a factor of $1/e$ (see Section 2.7.3).

At practically important distances from the detonation—that is, on the ground—the T65D dosimetry model assumes a single relaxation length for all neutron energies [36]; in contrast, the neutron propagation calculations given by other authors [87, 88] are better approximated with the use of different relaxation lengths for neutrons of low and high energy, respectively. In the following, we will use either approach as appropriate.

6.1.2 The source spectrum. The range of neutrons traveling through air depends on their kinetic energy. Once they have lost all their initial energy and merely keep bouncing around in thermal equilibrium with the surrounding gas molecules—that is, once they have become *thermalized*—they will quickly be captured by nitrogen atomic nuclei, which will end their independent existence. It may thus be surprising at first glance that slow neutrons reach the ground at all. The explanation is that the slow neutrons observed at e.g. 1200 m did not escape the bomb as such; instead, they escaped as fast neutrons that were progressively slowed down by multiple collisions with atomic nuclei in the air. Thus, only those neutrons that escape the detonation with high energies—according to Auxier [89], this means those 'above the sulfur threshold', which is at 2.5 MeV—will contribute to the neutron dose at practically important distances. To understand the neutron doses on the ground, we must therefore know the distribution of energy among the neutrons emitted by the detonating bomb, often referred to as the *source spectrum*. This is a simple enough concept in theory, but it is very difficult to predict in practice. Glasstone [90] explains the reason:

> *It should be possible, in principle, to calculate the energy spectrum of the neutrons after penetrating the bomb materials. However, since the latter are not completely dispersed when the neutrons are emitted, the neutron spectrum is dependent to a considerable extent on the detailed geometry of the bomb components at an extremely complex stage of the explosion. Because of these and other circumstances, the calculation is virtually impossible and recourse must be had to experiment.*

6.1.3 The T65D dosimetry scheme. In keeping with Glasstone's assessment, the development of the T65D dosimetry scheme did indeed involve a lot of experimentation on this and other questions. Ultimately, however, it was impossible to precisely determine the source spectrum

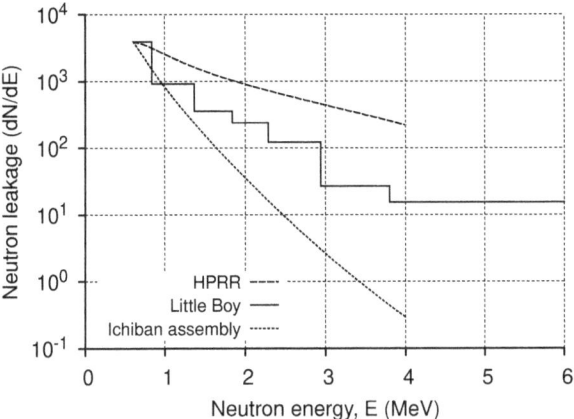

Figure 6.2: Neutron source spectrum of the Hiroshima bomb, according to Loewe and Mendelsohn [87]. The other two spectra, which are arbitrarily normalized to the same value at a neutron energy of 0.6 MeV, represent plausible limiting cases for the bomb spectrum. In the T65D dosimetry scheme, the spectrum of the Hiroshima bomb ('Little Boy') was assumed to resemble that of the HPRR; the 'Little Boy' spectrum shown here is the one proposed by Loewe and Mendelsohn.

of the Hiroshima bomb, since none of the nuclear test detonations performed after the war used a similar bomb design.

Attenuation of neutrons by the bomb casing has two limiting cases, which can be approximated with two surrogate experiments that were in fact carried out in the studies leading up to T65D [36, 91]. The 'Health Physics Research Reactor' (HPRR) was a fast neutron ^{235}U reactor with very little shielding; a neutron spectrum similar to this one would be expected if the bomb casing was already completely dispersed before the bulk of the neutrons was emitted. On the other hand, if the bomb casing still remained intact at this crucial instant, then the spectrum would have been much softer and resembled that of the 'Ichiban assembly', another test reactor which had a casing similar in strength to that of the Hiroshima bomb.

Figure 6.2 shows the experimental spectra obtained with these two devices. Evidently, the contributions of high-energy neutrons—that is, those neutrons that have any chance at all to reach the ground—are quite different. The T65D scheme had assumed that the neutron source spectrum of the Hiroshima bomb resembled that of the HPRR, or in other words, that the neutrons had escaped the detonation largely unimpeded by the bomb casing. This assumption resulted in the high neutron dose estimates in Hiroshima. In fact, up to approximately 800 m from hypocenter, the T65D physical neutron dose exceeded the γ-dose; and if we factor in a neutron relative biological effect (RBE) of 5 (see Section 2.9.2), then neutron radiation would have dominated the biological radiation effects in Hiroshima among all significantly exposed survivors.

6.1.4 The DS86 and DS02 dosimetry schemes. The reign of the neutrons in Hiroshima came to an abrupt end in 1981 with the publication of Loewe and Mendelsohn's paper entitled "Revised dose estimates at Hiroshima and Nagasaki" [92]. It appeared in the journal *Health Physics*, which focuses on the biological and medical aspects of radiation. The paper was entirely devoid of physical detail, which was to follow later; the likely reason for such haste is explained in Section 11.5. Meanwhile, the audience was simply advised that

we have prepared new dose estimates which should be considered trustworthy, in part because ... the corresponding neutron levels have been shown to agree with in situ activation measurements.

A second paper by the same authors [87] presented some physical arguments; however, these were mostly theoretical in nature, and their presentation lacked the detail a reader would need to decide on their validity for himself. Agreement of calculated neutron doses with in situ ^{60}Co activation measurements that had been reported earlier by Hashizume et al. [81] was claimed, but we will see below that the data then available agree better with T65D. Nevertheless, after some further elaboration, Loewe and Mendelsohn's revised dose estimates were officially adopted as the DS86 dosimetry scheme in 1987 [93]. The DS02 scheme, which was announced in 2002 [88] and remains in force today, made only fairly minor changes to DS86; for the purposes of this chapter, the two schemes can be treated as equivalent.

Notwithstanding their demand that the new dose estimates "should be considered trustworthy," Loewe and Mendelsohn were quite aware that these were premature at best. This is readily apparent in the proceedings of a conference on the subject which both Loewe and Mendelsohn attended [89]. Also present was John Auxier, the leading proponent of the T65D dosimetry scheme. The conference took place on September 15th and 16th of 1981, which was one week after Loewe and Mendelsohn had submitted their second paper. At the outset of this conference, Auxier gave an overview of his own very substantial body of work, and he summed up his outlook as follows:

Scientific work either must withstand the hard scrutiny of further work and time or it must be replaced. ... The greatest uncertainty in the T65D curves was taken to be the neutron [source] spectrum for Hiroshima [36]. There have been no significant contributions to the study over the intervening years, and we still await a multidimensional hydrodynamic calculation of the spectrum. In the interim it is clear that further work will either substantiate or modify the T65D values, and, until all evaluations are completed, it would appear premature to change our existing perceptions of the dose-response relationships based on the T65D values.

In other words, Auxier stated that thus far nothing of substance had transpired to invalidate the T65D estimates. In the discussion after his talk, neither Loewe nor Mendelsohn spoke up, and none of the other participants who did raise questions challenged Auxier on this statement either.

Loewe himself gave a presentation at the same conference, which is similar in content to his second paper with Mendelsohn [87]. In it, he accounts for their postulated change to the neutron doses as follows:

The difference between our numbers and the previous numbers is due to two factors. One is the assumed lambda of 198 [meters], when it should be 155. ... This substantial difference accounts for almost all the difference between our doses and the T65D.

This pointed statement suggests that we can decide between T65D and the more recent dosimetry schemes by considering which of the postulated 'assumed lambdas', that is, relaxation lengths, better agrees with measurement. This approach requires that the distance dependency not only of the data but also of the models themselves be well described by a single relaxation length. By using Equation 2.11 to fit dose-distance curves that represent the T65D and the DS86 or DS02 models, we have ascertained that this is the case at distances of up to 1500 m from the hypocenter; beyond this range, there are very few neutron activation measurements anyway. We can therefore use the

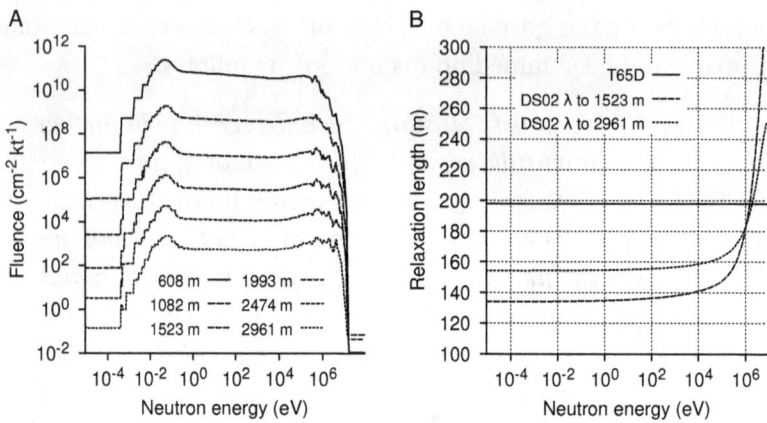

Figure 6.3: Neutron relaxation lengths in the T65D and the DS02 models. A: DS02 calculation of neutron fluence vs. neutron energy. Replot of Figure 6 in Young and Kerr [88, p. 153]. Each curve indicates the fluence prevailing at a specific distance from the epicenter. B: T65D assumes an energy-independent relaxation length of 198 m. In contrast, the relaxation length in DS02 remains at lower values throughout most of the spectrum but rises steeply at neutron energies beyond 10^5 eV. The curves shown here have been fitted to the data in A, using either only the topmost three or all six curves.

relaxation length as a yardstick to compare the various neutron fluence measurements and models.

6.1.5 Energy dependence of relaxation length in T65D and DS02.

While Loewe summed up his revised dosimetry scheme using a single relaxation length of 155 m, the current DS02 model is better described by treating the relaxation length as energy-dependent: while throughout most of the spectrum the relaxation length is similar to that given already by Loewe, at the high end of the spectrum the relaxation length rises steeply (Figure 6.3B). Such high-energy neutrons cause activation of sulfur to ^{32}P and of copper to ^{63}Ni. If the DS02 scheme were correct, measurements of these two isotopes should accordingly indicate relaxation lengths of somewhat above 200 m, while all other isotopes should indicate relaxation lengths up to 155 m. In contrast, with the T65D scheme, all measurements should yield similar relaxation lengths near 200 m. In the following, we will not try to decide which of the two models is better justified theoretically; instead, we will simply compare each model to the available measurements.

Table 6.1: Neutron radiation in Hiroshima: relaxation lengths determined from studies preceding the DS02 report [88]. Values for relaxation length (λ) were determined from tabulated (if available) or graphed data reported in the stated references, using the procedure illustrated in Figure 6.1. Error estimates were used in the fit if available.

Neutron energy	Sample type	Samples	λ (m)	Reference
slow	^{60}Co in construction steel	4	183	[81]
	^{60}Co in construction steel	9	220	[88]
	^{152}Eu in rock and tile	5	203	[94]
	^{152}Eu in rock and tile	14	184	[95]
	^{152}Eu in rock and tile	79	173	[96]
fast	^{32}P in sulfur from insulators	18	2196	[88, p. 645-8]

While measurements of isotopes induced by neutron capture have been reported from both cities, we will limit this discussion to Hiroshima, since here there are more data sets, which also generally contain more individual data points. The perception of greater significance, but also uncertainty concerning the neutron doses released in Hiroshima, already spelled out by Wilson [73], most likely caused more experimental effort to be focused on this city. However, as far as can be ascertained from the limited data, the situation in Nagasaki is quite similar with all types of measurements that will be discussed in the remainder of this chapter.

6.2 Measurements of isotopes induced by low-energy neutrons

Isotopes in this category include ^{60}Co, ^{152}Eu and ^{154}Eu, ^{36}Cl, and ^{41}Ca. While the precursor nuclides of all of these effectively capture thermal neutrons, they can also capture neutrons of higher energy, with somewhat different efficiencies; these finer distinctions will be considered below. For now, it is important that each of these isotopes should exhibit a relaxation length near 200 m according to T65D, but of at most 155 m according to DS02.

The first of these isotopes to be studied was ^{60}Co. Some measurements were carried out already in the 1960s and were cited as evidence in support of the T65D scheme [81].[3] Studies on the other isotopes

---

[3] This paper by Hashizume et al. is the same one which also reported the thermoluminescence data examined in Chapter 5.

began only after Loewe and Mendelsohn's initial announcement [92] of the revised dosimetry scheme that ultimately became DS86, but before the publication of the DS02 report (even though some of the data discussed here have been sourced from the latter report [88]). Several of these studies are summarized in Table 6.1.

For the ^{60}Co and ^{152}Eu studies listed in the table, we can calculate an average relaxation length of 192 m. This clearly agrees much better with the T65D value of 198 m than with the value of 155 m that we should expect with the DS02 dosimetry scheme.

While Table 6.1 does not cover all available ^{60}Co and ^{152}Eu data, similar conclusions can be drawn from several other studies that survey additional measurements using these and other isotopes. In an experimental paper on ^{36}Cl generated by neutron capture in samples of rock and concrete from Hiroshima,[4] Straume et al. [98] also gave an overview of ten other, previously published reports, some of which are included here in Table 6.1. When the data from all those studies are combined, the ratio of measured activity to that predicted by DS86 calculations trends systematically upwards with increasing distance from the epicenter (Figure 6.4). The slope of the trend line which Straume et al. drew across their graph corresponds to a relaxation length of 227 meters.[5]

Thus, overall, the measurements plainly indicate a relaxation length similar to that postulated by the T65D dosimetry scheme. It should be noted that these measurements pertain to three different chemical elements (cobalt, europium, and chlorine). The observed trend therefore cannot be due to the contamination of samples with extrinsic radioactivity, or by the leaching of activity from them, as was claimed at a later time in the case of chlorine (see Section 6.5.1), since such effects should perturb only some elements, but not others.

In light of these findings, it is clear that the abandonment of T65D in favor of DS86/DS02 was a step in the wrong direction. Of course,

---

[4] Since ^{36}Cl has a long half-life and correspondingly low activity, it was measured by mass spectrometry. The same applies to ^{41}Ca, which was measured for example by Rühm et al. [97].

[5] This calculation assumes a relaxation length of 139 m for thermal neutrons in DS86, which matches a graph in the official DS86 report that represents the calculated distance-dependency of neutron-induced ^{152}Eu activity [93, p. 199]. Note the logarithmic y axis in Figure 6.4, which means that the straight trend line is really an exponential function. Its exponent is $(1/139\,\mathrm{m} - 1/\lambda) \times d$, where d is the distance from the epicenter and λ is the 'true' relaxation length.

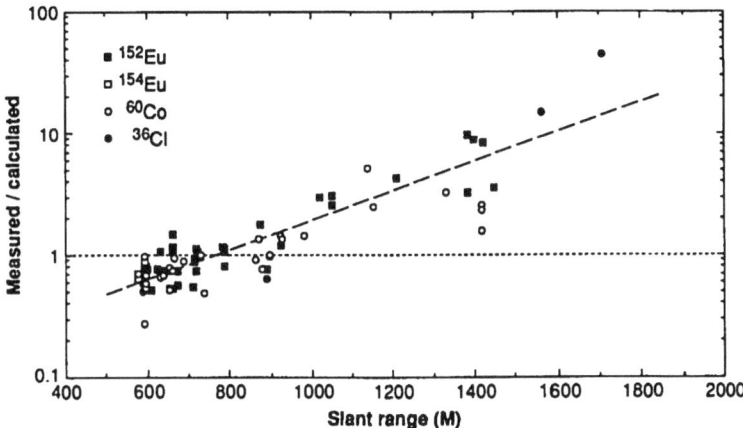

Figure 6.4: Ratio of measured to calculated neutron activation as a function of distance from the epicenter ('slant range'). Plot taken from Figure 1 in Straume et al. [98]. The calculation of the expected neutron activation was performed by those authors according to the then-current DS86 dosimetry scheme. The authors took their data points from ten different studies overall, which used various isotopes as indicated.

a much higher relaxation length that is completely out of tune with either dosimetry scheme is obtained from the sulfur activation studies (see Table 6.1). What might be the matter with those measurements?

6.3 Sulfur activation measurements

While most radioactive isotopes produced by neutron radiation are formed through the capture of slow neutrons, the activation of sulfur (^{32}S) to radioactive phosphorus (^{32}P) is an exception. This reaction involves not only the capture of a neutron, but also the ejection of a proton, so that the overall number of nucleons remains unchanged. As one might expect, this only works with very energy-rich neutrons; the minimum kinetic energy required is approximately 2.5 MeV. Such 'fast' neutrons provide the most direct information on the energy spectrum of the neutrons released by the bomb. They also give a good indication of the fluence to be expected in other segments of the neutron spectrum that contribute significantly to the biological effects of neutron radiation, as do these fast neutrons themselves. Measurements of ^{32}P activity in sulfur samples are thus particularly useful for understanding both the physical and the biological effects of a nuclear detonation. However, unlike isotopes such as ^{60}Co and ^{152}Eu, which have half-lives of several years and therefore can be measured even decades after the event, the half-life of ^{32}P is only 14.3 days, and measurements were therefore possible only in the first few months after the bombing. Thus, one thing that sets the sulfur activation measurements apart from all others is that they were carried out very early on, and moreover exclusively by Japanese research teams.

In Hiroshima, suitable samples were found in the form of porcelain insulators from electric power lines, which contained gram amounts of pure sulfur on the inside.[6] Two Japanese teams reportedly performed measurements on such insulators, but the data collected by a group from Kyoto University were 'lost' when Sakae Shimizu's laboratory notebooks were confiscated and 'mislaid' (see Section 1.5.5). Therefore, the available measurements are mostly those acquired by the other research team, which was from RIKEN and included the investigators Sugimoto and Yamasaki.

6.3.1 The shape-shifting raw data. The earliest mention of the sulfur activation measurements from RIKEN is found in a report by the Manhattan District engineers from 1946 [79, p. 216]. This reference gives locations, distances, and readings in decays per minute (dpm) for exactly nine samples. It is generally assumed that these measurements were obtained using an electroscope, which measures radioactivity cumulatively over time, and which requires calibration with a source of known activity. However, the report also states explicitly that "no additional information concerning these figures was available," so that it is uncertain whether an electroscope was indeed used, and if so, how it was calibrated and for how long each measurement was carried out. Furthermore, this initial report contains no error estimates for any of the measurements.

The same measurements are described again by Yamasaki and Sugimoto in a short appendix to the official DS86 report [93, p. 246]. The number of samples has increased from 9 to 10. Data are again given in dpm and without error estimates. All samples have migrated with respect to the hypocenter; one sample with high activity is now 300 m nearer to the hypocenter, which notably straightens out the dose-distance relationship. Of note, Yamasaki and Sugimoto state that "from

---

[6]Elemental sulfur has both adhesive and insulating properties [99].

these values, the half-value thickness of the atmosphere against the neutrons was found to be 380 m," which corresponds to a relaxation length of 548 m.

Although the DS86 report gives no indication of the fact, this appendix is the literal translation of a Japanese report already published in 1953 [100], and it is unclear whether its authors really prepared it themselves for the occasion or even consented to its inclusion in the DS86 report. The doubt arises from another appendix to the same volume, authored by Hamada [93, p. 272], who claims to have worked out the appropriate error estimates for Sugimoto and Yamasaki's measurements, even though he also states that "the type of Lauritsen electroscope used by Yamasaki and Sugimoto in their sulfur measurements is not yet finally identified." This indicates that those authors were not available for comment, which in turn suggests that their own contribution to the DS86 report was not recent.[7] Surprisingly, Hamada's appendix tabulates actual electroscope measurement times and readings, rather than counts per minute. The total number of measurements has now increased to 11.[8]

The same data are revisited by Young and Kerr [88], who manage to increase the number of samples to 14; two of these samples now yield two separate measurements each, for a total of 16 measurements. Samples have again moved with respect to the hypocenter. Furthermore, the authors supplement the RIKEN data with three measurements reported by Sakae Shimizu from Kyoto, which have somehow been recovered from oblivion, notwithstanding the apparently irretrievable loss of his notebooks (see Table 6.2). The stated values for detection efficiency—the ratio of decays counted to those assumed to have occurred—will depend not only on the sample amounts (which differ between the three samples) but also on many other details of the measurement setup. The detection efficiencies in turn will directly affect the estimates of the

---

[7] Indeed, Dr. Teruichi Harada has informed me that Sugimoto and Yamasaki had died in 1966 and 1981, respectively, which confirms that their contribution could not have been recent.

[8] At the 1981 conference, Loewe made the following statement [89, p. 51]: "I have been unable to get the sulfur data in terms that I can calculate directly (counts per minute in a fixed geometry [which would permit the calculation of decays per minute]). ... I suppose the direct data are available somewhere ... " None of the other experts present pitched in with any further information. It is therefore very surprising to read in [93] that these data have been available as both electrometer readings and as decays per minute all along.

6 The evidence of neutron radiation   112

Table 6.2: The Kyoto sulfur activation measurements. Collated from Table I in [37], Table 1 in [93, p. 267], and Table 5 in [88, p. 648]. 'Range' is the distance from hypocenter; 'Det. Eff.' is detection efficiency, that is, the percentage of all occurring decays that is captured by the instrument; 'Spec. Act.' is specific activity, i.e. the number of decays per minute in one gram of sulfur, at the time of the detonation. The ID of the third sample is given as 510 by [37] but as 518 in the other two references.

		Initial report [37]		Later reports [88, 93]		
Sample ID	Weight (g)	Range (m)	Counts/min	Range (m)	Det. Eff.	Spec. Act.
407	1.5	250	35	550	4.54%	840
411	2.2	350	33	780	3.27%	741
510	2.6	800	23	980	2.80%	518

true specific activities. They were obtained by Monte Carlo simulations; from the information available to him, the reader cannot ascertain whether the claimed uncertainty of the results (15% or less) is realistic.

Considering all of these repeated alterations and 'corrections', the question which version of the data should be deemed 'true' is of course moot. In the following, we will use the version given in the DS02 report [88], not because we consider it credible, but simply because it is the most recent one.

6.3.2 Measurements vs. DS02 calculations. Early on in their report, Young and Kerr claim to have achieved the 'virtually impossible' (cf. quotation in Section 6.1.2) by calculating the radiation doses produced by the Hiroshima bomb from first principles [88, p. 16]:

> *The radiation dose for atomic-bomb survivors is the end product of a series of complex ... calculations ... The first step in this dose reconstruction process is the calculation of the "source term" for the bombs. These calculations, which were done at the Los Alamos National Laboratory (LANL), simulate the explosion of the bombs ... Additional radiation transport calculations are required to evolve these initial distributions from the epicenter of the explosion through the air to the ground.*

We will not attempt to judge the soundness of these calculations as such, but rather focus on comparing them to experiment. To this end, we first note that Young and Kerr's calculated neutron dose-distance curve can be reproduced almost perfectly using the following empirical formula:

$$A = \alpha \times e^{-\frac{s-H}{L}} \qquad (6.1)$$

In this equation, A is the activity expected in this sample; e is Euler's number (2.7183); s is the *slant distance*, that is, the direct distance in meters of the sample from the epicenter; H is the height of the epicenter above ground; L is a length constant; and α is the activity expected at the hypocenter, since at this point $s - H = 0$. For a sample at some ground distance g from the hypocenter, the corresponding slant distance s is given by Pythagoras' theorem:

$$g^2 + H^2 = s^2 \iff s = \sqrt{g^2 + H^2} \qquad (6.2)$$

According to Young and Kerr [88], the height of the epicenter above ground is 600 m,[9] and a fairly good fit of Equation 6.1 to DS02 calculations is indeed obtained when we use this value for H, together with values of 2350 dpm for α and 160 m for L. However, an even better fit results if we simply let a numerical fitting algorithm[10] pick the best values for all three parameters. The result of this procedure is shown in Figure 6.5.

Evidently, our simple equation approximates the DS02 calculation very closely. We can therefore substitute it for the latter in doing our own data analysis. In particular, we can ask whether or not the DS02 calculation given by Young and Kerr [88] is correctly scaled to best fit the measurements. For this purpose, we will keep the shape of the model, which is defined by its H and L parameters, and vary only the pre-exponential scaling factor α so as to best fit the measured sulfur activities. It turns out that this gives an α value of 3233 dpm, which is 42% higher than the one which matches the graph of the DS02 calculation in the report (2278 dpm). What should we make of this finding?

---

[9]You may have noted before that the altitude of the explosion was given as 580 m. This is indeed an oft-quoted value that was determined from the shadows allegedly cast on stones by the flash of the detonation [85]. However, the height of the epicenter has been 'corrected' to 600 m in DS02; more on this below.

[10]All plots shown in this book were prepared using the free software program Gnuplot; numerical fits were carried out either using Gnuplot's built-in fitting routine or LibreOffice's solver tool.

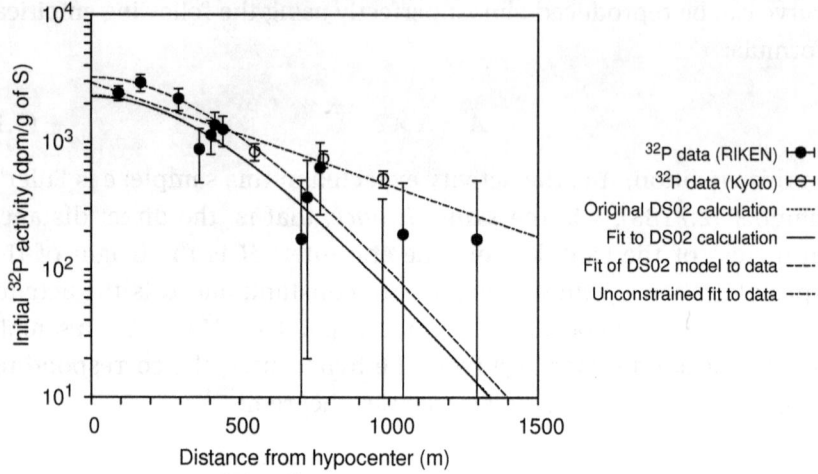

Curve	Fitted parameter values		
	α (dpm)	H (m)	L (m)
Fit do DS02 calculation	2278	681.9	151.25
Fit of DS02 model to data	3233	681.9	151.25
Unconstrained fit to data	2929	0.1	539

Figure 6.5: Measurements and calculations of ^{32}P formation through capture of fast neutrons at Hiroshima. Measurements as tabulated in the DS02 report [88]. The original DS02 calculation, digitized from a graph in the report (p. 654), is almost perfectly congruent with the numerical fit using Equation 6.1 and therefore mostly hidden by it. Fitting of the DS02 model to the experimental data was done by varying only α, whereas in the unconstrained fit the algorithm was allowed to vary all three parameters.

Overall, the sulfur activity on the ground should be proportional to the total neutron fluence, which in turn should be proportional to the 'bomb yield', that is, the energy released in the explosion, conventionally stated in kilotons TNT equivalent. Thus, the most straightforward explanation is that the bomb yield is 42% higher than assumed in the DS02 calculation. That number is 16 kt; if we increase it by 42%, we obtain 22.7 kt. However, Young and Kerr claim that the measurements indicate 18 ± 2 kt as the most likely bomb yield, which they take as confirmation of their calculated value of 16 kt. To accomplish this feat, they employ two tricks:

1. They stipulate that the bomb at the moment of the detonation was tilted against the vertical. Since the bomb had a longitudinal shape with thicker casing at both ends, the assumed tilt caused the neutron fluence on the ground to not be rotationally symmetric. By carefully choosing the angle (15°) and orientation of the tilt, they narrow the gap between calculation and measurement, which according to our analysis is 42%, by about 10%.

2. On page 656 of their report [88], they state that "the sulfur activation measurements of the Riken survey team can be used to make an estimate of the energy yield for the Hiroshima bomb ... The sulfur-activation measurements by the Kyoto survey team were not used ... because of the large uncertainties in the ground distances at which the sulfur samples were collected." As can be seen in Figure 6.5, these latter values trend higher than the ones from RIKEN, and they also have much smaller error bars; thus, their exclusion will significantly lower the weighted average of the sulfur measurements.

The pretext for omitting the Kyoto data is of course not credible—surely the technicians or scientists who collected those samples would have carefully recorded the location of each, and from these the ground distances to the hypocenter could be unambiguously determined. This omission simply amounts to cherry-picking of the evidence, which in real science would be inadmissible.

In the above analysis, we only changed the scale of our DS02-equivalent model, but left its shape unchanged. If we allow the fitting algorithm to adjust all three parameters to best match the measured data, the shape of the resulting curve changes completely. Remarkably, the H parameter vanishes entirely (see table in Figure 6.5), which means that the epicenter drops to the ground and merges with the hypocenter, and the ^{32}P activity becomes a direct exponential function of the distance from this unified center. Thus, if allowed to speak freely, the data flatly reject the DS02 model. Furthermore, while the model that results from our unconstrained fit is even simpler than the one we started with, it is also completely devoid of physical plausibility. If the data agree best with a non-physical model, this suggests of course that they were fabricated.

6.3.3 Burst altitudes and relaxation lengths. We noted above that the DS02 report had raised the burst altitude of the Hiroshima bomb from the previous value of 580 m to 600 m. Its authors justify this as follows [88, p. 29]:

> *Both sets of fast neutron measurements support the elevation of the Hiroshima height of burst to 600 m and the yield to 16 kt.*

The second set of fast neutron measurements referred to in the quote concerns the formation of ^{63}Ni (nickel) in metallic copper, which will be considered in Section 6.5.2; for now, we will stay with the sulfur studies.

Considering the pronounced scatter in the sulfur activation measurements and their very large assumed errors, the claim that such data can serve to define the height of the detonation to within 20 m should raise some eyebrows. To evaluate it more rigorously, we will once more resort to the estimation of relaxation lengths. In Figure 6.6A, the same measurements as in Figure 6.5 have been plotted according to Equation 2.11; following the DS02 report, a detonation height of 600 m has been assumed. In this plot format, the variation in the magnitude of the error estimates assumes grotesque proportions, and accordingly the use or omission of these assumed errors in the fit has a major effect on the result. If we do use the errors, we obtain a λ of 2196 m, as already stated in Table 6.1 above; if we omit them, the result is 508 m. While this number is at least in the triple digits, it is still twice higher than the value of 241 m, which is the best approximation to the official DS02 calculation.

In Figure 6.6B, the assumed height of the detonation has been varied systematically, and for each value the best fit of the relaxation length has been determined. We see that λ decreases with increasing burst height, but realistic values—below, say, 300 m—are attained only at a burst height of 800 m when fitting without measurement errors, or more than 1200 m when using them. Clearly, extorting realistic relaxation lengths and burst heights at the same time from the data is a lost cause.

It will be evident from the above that the use or omission of estimated measurement errors in the analysis is ultimately inconsequential, since either way the results are physically implausible and contradict the claims made in the DS02 report. Nevertheless, considering how strongly these errors affect the outcome of the numerical fits, it should be emphasized again that neither the original report on the RIKEN

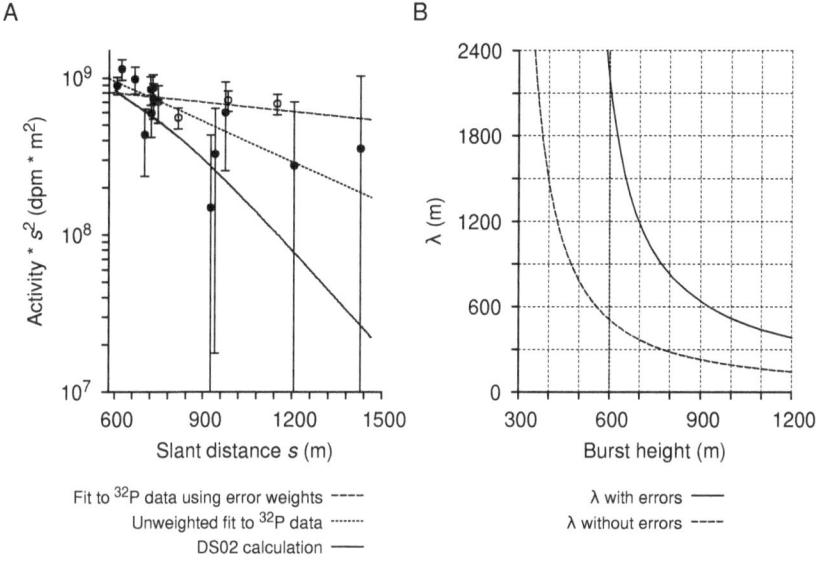

Figure 6.6: Estimation of fast neutron relaxation length λ from measurements of ^{32}P induced in sulfur samples in Hiroshima. A: the same data and DS02 calculations as in Figure 6.5, plotted as a function of the slant distance assuming 600 m as the height of the detonation. The B: Optimal values for λ, assuming different heights of the detonation. At a detonation height of 600 m, λ is 508 m when fitted without error weights and 2196 m when fitted with them.

measurements [79, p. 216] nor that on the Kyoto data [37] actually contain any error estimates. These were divined only at later points in time; and I have not found any justification for the very different magnitude of estimated errors assigned to the data from RIKEN and Kyoto, respectively.

6.3.4 Appraisal of the sulfur activation data. Both Figure 6.5 and Figure 6.6A make it plain that ^{32}P levels in samples taken at distance from the hypocenter at Hiroshima are far too high relative to samples taken near it. This clearly rules out the simultaneous activation *in situ* of all samples by a single nuclear detonation; *they could not have turned out this way even if an atomic bomb had gone off at the purported time and place.* These data must therefore be considered fabrications.

6.4 Comparative cobalt and europium activation studies

In Section 6.2, we already encountered some studies on the activation of these two elements by capture of low-energy neutrons. The predominant stable isotope of cobalt is ^{59}Co, which is converted to ^{60}Co by neutron capture. In contrast, europium contains two stable isotopes in almost equal abundance, ^{151}Eu and ^{153}Eu, which are activated to ^{152}Eu and ^{154}Eu, respectively. The three radioactive isotopes differ in half-life, and the three precursors differ with respect to the efficiency of capture of thermal and *epithermal* neutrons, respectively; the latter ones have kinetic energies exceeding that which remains after thermal equilibration with the surrounding atoms and molecules. Because of these differences, comparing the activities of all three isotopes within the same samples can provide some interesting insights.

6.4.1 Comparing isotopes to estimate the date of activation.

Nakanishi et al. [94] examined rock samples and roof tiles from Hiroshima to determine the total amount ('fluence') of neutron radiation from the bomb. While most samples were analyzed for ^{152}Eu only, the investigators did measure the activities of ^{60}Co and of ^{154}Eu as well on one sample, and they derive estimates of the neutron fluence separately for each isotope. These estimates, together with the half-lives, are listed in Table 6.3.[11] In principle, all three estimates should coincide, but we notice some divergence: the estimated fluence decreases from ^{60}Co on the left to ^{152}Eu on the right. We also note that the half-life changes in the reverse order. Could these two observations be related?

The neutron fluence is calculated from the activity of each isotope at the time of activation, which is presumably the bombing. This value is obtained by correcting a recent measurement for the decay since the time of activation. Since each isotope has its own characteristic half-life, these correction factors will be different, and more importantly the ratios between these factors will vary with time. If we assume too early a date of activation, then all our fluence estimates will be inflated, but those inferred from isotopes with shorter half-lives will be inflated more. Conversely, if we assume too recent a date of activation, then all activities will be underestimated, but those of shorter-lived

---

[11] The half-lives are from an appendix to the official DS86 report [93, p. 310-9], which contains another study by Nakanishi et al. While not the most exact estimates available today, these values are more likely to have been used in [94] for estimating the neutron fluence.

Table 6.3: Neutron fluence estimates obtained from a roof tile sample in Hiroshima by Nakanishi et al. [94]. The roof tile was from Shima Hospital, which stood directly at the hypocenter.

Isotope	^{60}Co	^{154}Eu	^{152}Eu
Fluence (10^{12} cm^{-2})	7.9 ± 0.8	6.4 ± 1.4	6.01 ± 0.42
Half-life (years)	5.2719 ± 0.0011	8.5 ± 0.5	13.2 ± 0.3

isotopes will be *deflated* more. As evident in Table 6.3, the shorter-lived isotopes yield the higher estimates in Nakanishi's study, suggesting that these samples underwent neutron activation only sometime after the bombing.

To find the most likely date of activation, we can project Nakanishi's fluence estimates forward and look for the point in time at which agreement between all three curves is best. This has been done in Figure 6.7A. The curve for each isotope starts with Nakanishi's fluence estimate at the time of the bombing for the respective isotope. The other points on each curve represent the fluence estimates that will result if the assumed date of neutron exposure is changed, but all else is kept constant. All intersections between any two of the three curves occur at or near 3.5 years after the bombing. This is also the point at which the ratio of the standard deviation of all three values to their average attains its minimum. Thus, Nakanishi's fluence estimates suggest that the sample was exposed to neutrons not in August 1945, but approximately 3.5 years thereafter.

6.4.2 Activation by thermal vs. epithermal neutrons. In their initial paper [94], Nakanishi et al. do not spell out exactly how they converted their measurements of isotope activity to estimates of neutron fluence. They do, however, give more detail in a subsequent study that is included as Appendix 5/14 in the official DS86 report [93, p. 310 ff]. The measurements described in this second document pertain to the same three isotopes but to a separate set of samples. The authors assume that not only thermal neutrons may have contributed to the activation, but also epithermal ones, and they estimate the respective contributions of each by comparing the three isotopes' activities.

A little more background is required to understand how this calculation works. Each isotope differs from the two others in its propensity to capture thermal neutrons, which is described by its *thermal cross*

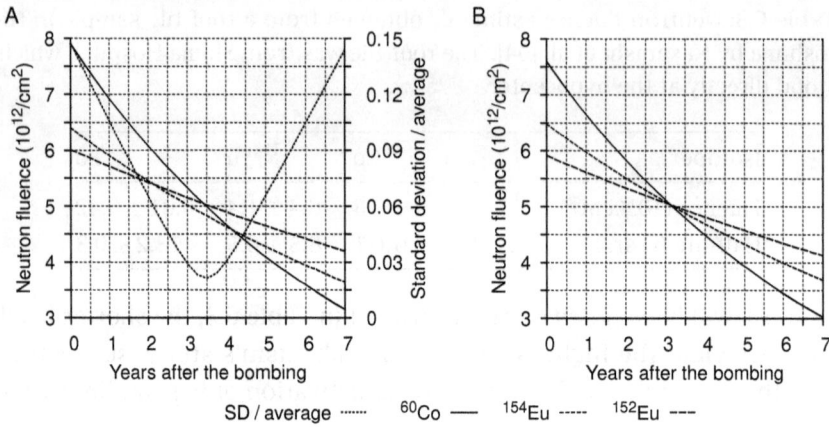

Figure 6.7: Estimating the date of neutron activation by comparing calculated fluences for various isotopes. A: Nakanishi et al. [94] reported neutron fluence estimates from ^{60}Co, ^{152}Eu, and ^{154}Eu. The estimates diverge at the time of the bombing, but they become similar when prorated by 3.5 years, suggesting this as the most likely time of neutron exposure. B: Recalculation of fluence estimates from activities also given in [94]. See text for details.

section, and also to capture epithermal ones, for which the authors provide a *resonance integral* (Table 6.4).[12] The ratio of these two parameters is again different with each isotope; with ^{152}Eu, the thermal cross section exceeds the resonance integral, whereas the reverse is true of the other two isotopes. Therefore, at a given total neutron fluence, a high contribution of epithermal neutrons will boost the activities of ^{60}Co and particularly of ^{154}Eu, whereas exposure to thermal neutrons only will favor formation of ^{152}Eu. It follows that we must also get the contributions of thermal and epithermal neutrons right in order to satisfy the requirement that all fluence estimates coincide at the time of activation.

With two isotopes only, we could only determine one unknown parameter, which means we would need to fix either the time of activation or the fraction of epithermal neutrons. However, with a third isotope available, we can numerically fit the fractional contribution of epithermal neutrons that makes the three fluence estimates the most similar

---

[12]While the use of single numbers to specify the values of resonance integrals seems common practice, it appears to require an assumption about the shape of the epithermal part of the neutron energy spectrum. Nakanishi et al. are not explicit on this point, however.

Table 6.4: Nuclear data and measurements used to calculate the timing of neutron activation. Measurements from [94]; half-lives from Wikipedia, other nuclear data from Table 1 in [93, p. 312]. Epithermal neutron fraction and neutron fluences were obtained by numerical fitting and correspond to the graph in Figure 6.7B.

Isotope	Eu-152	Eu-154	Co-60
Activity measured (Bq/kg of sample)	28.2	1.32	4.22
Element content (mg/kg of sample)	1.38	1.38	23
Half-life (years)	13.537	8.593	5.2714
Thermal cross section (10^{-24} cm^2)	5,900	320	37.2
Resonance integral (10^{-24} cm^2)	3,700	1,635	75.5
Precursor isotope			
Abundance (fraction)	0.479	0.521	1
Bulk atomic weight	152	152	59
Years since bombing: 32.107			
Epithermal neutron fraction: 4.02%			
Neutron fluence at time of bombing (10^{12} cm^{-2})	5.910	6.479	7.589

at *any* point in time; and the result should indicate the most likely date of activation. With Nakanishi's initial sample, it turns out that this is slightly above 3 years after the detonation (Figure 6.7B). Moreover, the epithermal fraction that produces this agreement is rather low (4%). The resulting fluence estimates for the individual isotopes are close to those given in the original study, suggesting that Nakanishi et al. [94] had determined a similarly low contribution of epithermal neutrons. In fact, if we instruct the fitting algorithm explicitly to match Nakanishi's fluence estimates as closely as possible, it returns an epithermal fraction of 5%.

The second study by Nakanishi et al. [93, p. 310-9] measured all three isotopes on two samples. If we apply the same analysis to those samples, the results are quite different: the time of activation is within 0.5 years of the bombing, and the epithermal neutron fraction is greater than 20%. The latter number agrees with a graphical analysis contained in the original report.

Another study that we may draw into this comparison is one by Rühm et al. [97], who examined the abundance of all three isotopes, as well as two additional ones (^{36}Cl and ^{41}Ca), in a tombstone from a graveyard near the hypocenter. They conclude that the soft neutron spectrum assumed by DS86 cannot explain the collective findings. They test various hypothetical neutron spectra, all of which are 'harder' than the one assumed by DS86. They obtain the best fit to their collective data with no thermal neutrons at all—or, rather, with a *negative* contribution of thermal neutrons, which is of course physically impossible. We therefore can take 100% as their best estimate of the epithermal neutron contribution. It is noteworthy that both ^{36}Cl and ^{41}Ca are rather long-lived isotopes;[13] thus, their abundance would not be affected by any inaccuracies in the date of activation. The observed deviations from expected values—^{36}Cl was found lower, and ^{41}Ca higher than expected based on DS86—can therefore be ascribed unambiguously to the neutron energy spectrum.

The findings from all three studies are compared in Table 6.5. Evidently, once more nothing really fits together. All samples were collected at or near the hypocenter and should have been exposed to the same neutron energies, or at least similar ones—yet, the contribution of epithermal neutrons varies from almost nothing (4%) to 100%. Nor does the sample composition explain this variation—neither the two roof tiles nor the two granite samples resemble each other. The most similar results are obtained with the two samples characterized in Nakanishi's second study, even though they are of different composition and come from different locations. In summary, both the very wide spread of the epithermal neutron fraction and the delayed activation of the single sample from Nakanishi's first study [94] indicate that these four samples were not activated by the same neutron source at the same time.

6.5 New and improved measurements: everything finally falls into place

The discrepancy documented in Section 6.2 between DS86 calculations and the observed range of neutrons was cause for considerable puzzlement, and throughout the 1990s much ink was spilled on attempts to reconcile the recalcitrant data to the officially sanctioned theory, all ultimately unsuccessful.[14] It was clear, therefore, that one had

---

[13] The half-life of ^{41}Ca is approximately 100,000 years, and that of ^{36}Cl 300,000 years.

[14] In a particularly imaginative study, Hoshi et al. [101] proposed that the neutrons had escaped the bomb not through the intact casing or through some sort of evenly

Table 6.5: Comparison of three neutron activation studies using multiple isotopes. Fractions of epithermal neutrons and the approximate date of activation relative to the bombing were determined as described in the text.

Sample	Epithermal neutrons (%)	Activated at (y)	Ref.
Roof tile (Shima hospital)	4	+3.125	[94]
Roof tile (Shima hospital)	21	−0.25	[93]
Granite (Motoyasu bridge)	26	+0.5	[93]
Granite (tombstone)	100	n/a	[97]

to give way. In regular science, that would of course have been the theory; for, as famous physicist and Manhattan Project participant Richard Feynman so pithily explained, "if it disagrees with experiment, it's wrong." However, as should by now be clear, we are not dealing here with pedestrian, workaday science—something greater and more precious than mere scientific truth was at stake, and therefore the experimental data had to relent. Accordingly, new and improved data were presented in the experimental chapters of the DS02 report [88].

6.5.1 Revised thermal neutron measurements. Isotopes that are induced mostly by thermal neutrons include ^{36}Cl, ^{60}Co, and ^{152}Eu. With all of these, a systematic deviation from DS86 had originally been observed; the data agreed closely with T65D instead (see Section 6.2), even though this was not explicitly acknowledged in the corresponding literature. To prop up the revised dosimetry schemes, more compliant data were therefore needed. The earlier measurements on ^{36}Cl were disavowed in the DS02 report and declared tainted by surface contamination. However, the amount of ^{36}Cl attributed to 'background' with new samples in the revised study [88, p. 502] (1.24×10^{-13} ^{36}Cl/Cl) is almost identical to that which had already been interpreted as background in the original one [98], so that it remains unclear exactly why those earlier data should now be considered invalid. In fact, the DS02 report simply supplants the earlier measurements, which had been performed on concrete samples, with new ones obtained on granite, for which it claims close agreement of distance-dependent neutron

---

fluidized and distended state of it, but rather through a fractured casing with a discrete circumferential crack exactly 3 cm wide. They also take the liberty of elevating the height of the detonation by 90 m. Yet, even these two tricks in combination only reduce but do not remove the systematic deviation of calculations from the measured data.

6 The evidence of neutron radiation 124

fluence with DS02 calculations. Similarly, for ^{60}Co, some new data sets are rounded up that display better agreement with DS02 calculations than earlier measurements, but no clear explanation is offered for the difference between these new results [88, p. 456 ff] and the old ones.

While some of the authors of the original report on ^{36}Cl [98] readily cooperated in the disavowal of their own previous results, the researchers who had contributed most of the earlier ^{152}Eu data, Nakinishi and Shizuma [95, 96], were not so obliging but asserted that their original measurements had been accurate and were reproducible [88, p. 482 ff]. It therefore became necessary to throw them under the bus. To do so, several samples, purportedly a subset of those measured earlier by Shizuma et al. [96], were sent out to four different laboratories, which proceeded to measure them again. The new results agree closely with DS02 calculations. The discrepancy is tentatively ascribed to a failure of the earlier study [96] to properly account for background; however, a close reading of that study shows that background and limits of detection sensitivity had been given the required attention. Shizuma et al. were, of course, excluded from this splendid effort, which was described in the DS02 report [88, p. 578ff] and also in a separate publication [102]. As far as the reader is concerned, this is a case of one person's word against another's, which to adjudicate he lacks the means.

In summary, the DS02 report introduces new measurements of thermal neutron activation that agree with its own calculations of distance-dependent neutron fluence. With all three isotopes—^{36}Cl, ^{60}Co, and ^{152}Eu—the calculations are well approximated using Equation 2.11 with a relaxation length of 136 m, which agrees with the analysis in Figure 6.3 (cf. the lowermost curve in panel B). No substantial explanation is given as to why earlier measurements for all of these isotopes had agreed with T65D rather than with DS02. Moreover, all of the new data introduced in DS02 pertain to single isotopes only; there are no simultaneous measurements of multiple isotopes on the same samples, which, while being more informative, are more apt to reveal embarrassing problems and inconsistencies.

6.5.2 New measurements of fast neutrons. An interesting development documented in the DS02 report is the detection by mass spectrometry of a long-lived nickel isotope, ^{63}Ni, which is formed from

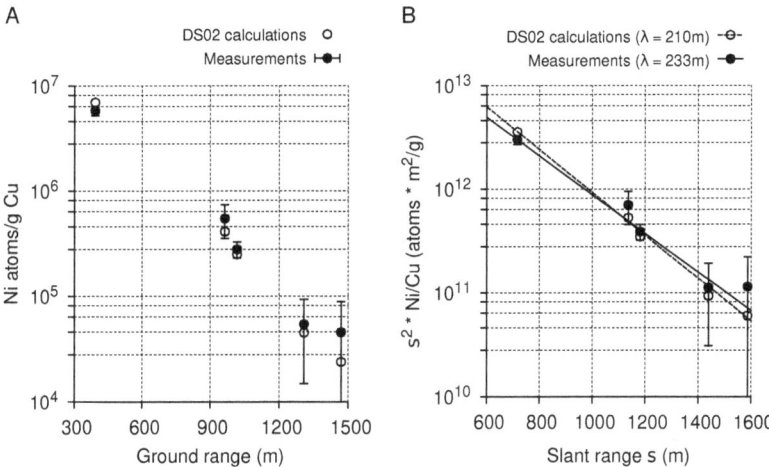

Figure 6.8: Measurements of fast neutron fluence at Hiroshima by ^{63}Ni induced in metallic copper samples. A: Replot of Figure 2 from page 677 in the DS02 report [88]. B: analysis of data in A according to Equation 2.11. The λ values are determined from the slopes of the fitted lines. Slant ranges were calculated from ground ranges according to Equation 6.2, using a detonation height of 600 m.

copper (^{63}Cu) by capture of a fast neutron and concomitant ejection of a proton. The only other isotope to detect fast neutrons measured thus far had been ^{32}P induced in sulfur, which is very short-lived (see Section 6.3); therefore, the advent of this method marked a major technical breakthrough.

Samples of metallic copper from five different sites in Hiroshima were recovered. All samples are said to have been in a direct line of sight to the detonation and should therefore give us an accurate picture of distance-dependent neutron fluence, undistorted by variations of radiation shielding between samples. As Figure 6.8 shows, the five samples, which span a considerable range of distance from the hypocenter, indeed follow a fairly regular trend. We notice, however, that the experimental relaxation length is somewhat higher than the calculated value. We can make both equal by increasing the height of the detonation from 600 m to 692 m (with concomitant changes to the assumed bomb yield also). While this result is certainly in better agreement with the official story than the numbers inferred from the sulfur activation data (see Section 6.3), it hardly supports the decision taken in the DS02 report to anoint 600 m as the 'true' height of the detonation.

6.6 The generational model of fakery

While the reader might at this point feel understandably bewildered by the many incongruent findings presented in this chapter, we maintain that these do in fact follow a recognizable pattern. To show this, we will divide the evidence into three generations.

6.6.1 Evidence faked very shortly after the bombings. Most important in this generation are the sulfur activation measurements discussed in Section 6.3. When tasked with producing these data, the experimenters most likely did not have the benefit of an elaborate, accepted theory that would fix the location of the epicenter, the source spectrum of the neutrons, and their attenuation by the atmosphere. Thus, they lacked the necessary guidance in selecting the proper parameters while exposing their fake samples to neutron radiation in the laboratory. Despite their best intentions, therefore, they produced flawed data that even after numerous 'corrections' and the contrivance of very large measurement errors fit neither the T65D nor the DS02 dosimetry scheme.

We noted in Section 6.3.1 that Yamasaki and Sugimoto's report on sulfur activation had originally been published in Japanese in 1953 [100]. The same volume contains another report by the same authors on measurements of ^{32}P in human bones [103]. While the measured isotope is the same in both cases, within bones it is produced from ^{31}P through a straightforward capture of a thermal neutron. For these measurements, the authors obtain a half-thickness of atmospheric attenuation of 90 m, corresponding to a relaxation length of 130 m. Considering that these are apparently the only data that both precede and support the DS86 and DS02 reports, it is rather peculiar that neither report includes them. Most likely, the authors of both reports felt unequal to the task of explaining away the discrepancy between a relaxation length of 548 m for fast neutrons (^{32}P in sulfur, see Section 6.3.1) but only 130 m for thermal neutrons, as determined by the same investigators, using the same methods and equipment; and they therefore once more resorted to cherry-picking the evidence.

6.6.2 Evidence faked with the benefit of early dosimetry models. It is difficult to say when exactly the samples for these measurements were produced, but the findings discussed in Section 6.4.1 suggest that at least some of this was going on as early as three years after the war. By this time, it should have been possible to develop a frame of reference that would include estimates of the bomb yield, location of the epicenter, and range of neutron transport through the air. The pronounced variation in the neutron energy spectrum that is evident from Table 6.5 suggests that this aspect had not been sorted out. Alternatively, it could be that the possible study of more than one isotope in the same sample was not anticipated when these samples were fabricated. Measurements of single isotopes on each sample only—a practice restored to prominence in the DS02 report, notwithstanding greatly increased analytical capabilities—could not have detected anything amiss with the neutron spectrum or with the date of activation. In this case, there would have been no need to match the neutron spectra of the laboratory sources to each other or to that of the imaginary bomb.

As we had seen in Section 6.2, the relaxation lengths inferred from the various measurements of this period are in reasonable agreement with the T65D dosimetry model. It may well be that a considerable amount of evidence supporting T65D was generated, and that the so-called 'DS86 neutron discrepancy' arose simply from the continued use of this stockpiled evidence after the introduction of the DS86 scheme.

6.6.3 Evidence faked to prop up the current low neutron dose estimates. The measurements which support the current estimates are limited in number and scope, but they appear to match both the low- and the high-energy part of the neutron spectrum (cf. Figure 6.3). Their very belated appearance in the literature—the 'DS86 neutron discrepancy' was allowed to fester for more than a decade, without any contrary evidence being presented—suggests that these samples were prepared only a short time before the publication of the DS02 report [88].

6.7 Conclusion

This chapter has shown that the evidence of neutron radiation cannot withstand close scrutiny; incongruent findings and questionable data manipulations abound. In this regard, it resembles the previously discussed evidence of nuclear fallout and of γ-radiation. Thus, no firm ground exists anywhere in the entire arena of physical studies adduced to prove that the nuclear detonations really happened. With this in mind, we will now turn our attention to the medical side of the evidence.

7 Sulfur mustard and napalm

> I suffer badly from phlegm and from coughs and colds a lot. That all started [when] one of the shells disturbed the residue of mustard gas that had been lying there for months.
>
> Cecil Withers, British World War 1 veteran [104]

This chapter describes the chemical properties and biological effects of sulfur mustard, drawing on case reports from its uses in warfare, particularly in World War I. The chapter touches only briefly on the 'nuclear' bombings; its main purpose is to provide background for the discussion of clinical observations in the bombing victims in subsequent chapters.

The chapter concludes with an overview of the technical and medical aspects of napalm and its use in warfare.

Sulfur mustard is a synthetic poison that gained notoriety as the 'king of battle gases' in World War I, in which it caused more casualties than all other poisonous gases combined, even though it was first used only in 1917. Other battle gases like chlorine and phosgene had been used for longer, but their effectiveness had diminished because of protective measures, in particular gas masks. Sulfur mustard bypassed this protection because it attacks the skin, its fumes easily penetrating clothes and sticking to them. By damaging the deeper layers of the epidermis, it causes the formation of blisters, which may become confluent and cause the skin to peel off in large sheets. Agents of this kind are called *vesicants*; the term derives from the Latin word *vesica* (blister). Victims that are not protected by gas masks will also inhale the gas and suffer damage to the airways; in addition, sulfur mustard may be swallowed and then attack the intestinal tract.

The second most important vesicant is lewisite; it, too, was developed during World War I, but apparently was not deployed. In World War II, both agents were stockpiled by several of the participants, but

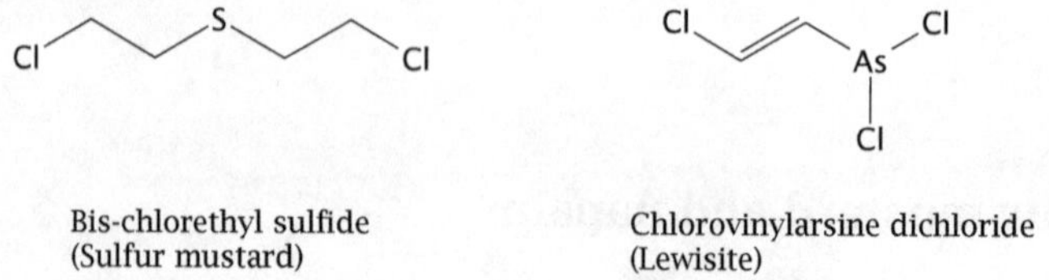

Bis-chlorethyl sulfide
(Sulfur mustard)

Chlorovinylarsine dichloride
(Lewisite)

Figure 7.1: Structures of sulfur mustard and of lewisite

the only acknowledged use was by Japan in its Chinese campaign. According to Infield [105, p. 187], the U.S. had filled mustard gas into various types of aerial bombs, which were otherwise used for incendiaries; thus, sulfur mustard would have been ready and available for aerial attacks. In the 1980s, sulfur mustard was again used by Iraq in its war on Iran, and its most recent use reportedly occurred in the Syrian civil war [106].

While sulfur mustard and lewisite differ in chemical composition (Figure 7.1), their acute toxic manifestations are similar [21].[1] For reasons detailed below, we consider sulfur mustard the most likely vesicant to have been used in Hiroshima and Nagasaki, and we will therefore focus on this agent.

7.1 Physicochemical properties

Sulfur mustard has a boiling point of 217°C [35] and a melting point of 14°C; for deployment at cooler temperatures, the melting point can be lowered by mixing the poison with organic solvents. In its pure form, liquid sulfur mustard is oily and poorly water miscible, which slows down its hydrolysis (decomposition by reaction with water). Slow decomposition, a tendency to penetrate porous materials such as wood or bricks, and its high boiling point allow it to persist in the environment for potentially long periods of time. This is illustrated by these words of British World War I veteran Cecil Withers, quoted from Fitzgerald [104]:

> *I suffer badly from phlegm and from coughs and colds a lot. That all started when the British were shelling hard at the last Battle of*

---

[1]Most sources name sulfur mustard as the poison released in the disaster at Bari, but Maynard [107] in his Master's thesis suggests that it was in fact lewisite. While he presents some intriguing circumstantial evidence, this question is peripheral to the main theme of this book and will not be pursued.

the Somme. One of the shells disturbed the residue of mustard gas that had been lying there for months. They talk about secondary smoking ... I got secondary gas.

In contrast to sulfur mustard, lewisite has a low boiling point (77°C) and thus is much more volatile; it is therefore likely to dissipate much more readily. We know that the noxious agent used in Hiroshima persisted for weeks [16, 34]; this is the first reason to suspect the use of sulfur mustard rather than lewisite. Another reason is the foul smell, which in Hiroshima was noted by many [15, 16]. Apparently, this smell arises mostly from contaminants in the technical product, which are numerous [108]; the pure product has only a faint smell [109, p. 32]. Lewisite, in contrast, is said to smell only slightly of geraniums [110].

7.2 Mode of action and toxicokinetics

The molecular structures of sulfur mustard and of lewisite are shown in Figure 7.1. Evidently, they are quite different; in particular, the two chloroethyl groups of the mustard molecule, which mediate its reaction with DNA (see below) are lacking in lewisite. This suggests that their reactions with molecules within the cells will be different, too, even though the consequences may be similar.

7.2.1 Reaction with DNA. The reaction of sulfur mustard with DNA begins with the formation of an episulfonium ion (Figure 7.2). This three-membered ring is highly unstable and may react with any nucleophiles within the cell; but, for the same reasons as with ionizing radiation (Section 2.11), the most consequential target molecule is DNA. Any of the four bases found in DNA[2] may react, but the most reactive one is guanine, and in particular the specific nitrogen (N7) in the imidazole ring shown in the Figure. Importantly, sulfur mustard is a *bivalent* molecule; both of the two chloroethyl ($-CH_2-CH_2-Cl$) groups attached to the central sulfur atom can react in the same manner. This may cause the formation of a cross-link between two bases on opposite strands of the DNA molecule; and downstream of such cross-links, both strands may break,[3] resulting in the same kind of lesion also observed

---

[2]These bases are the purine derivatives adenine and guanine, as well as the pyrimidine derivatives cytosine and thymine. Within RNA, uracil replaces thymine.

[3]This has been demonstrated with nitrogen mustard [52], which reacts with DNA in the same manner as does sulfur mustard.

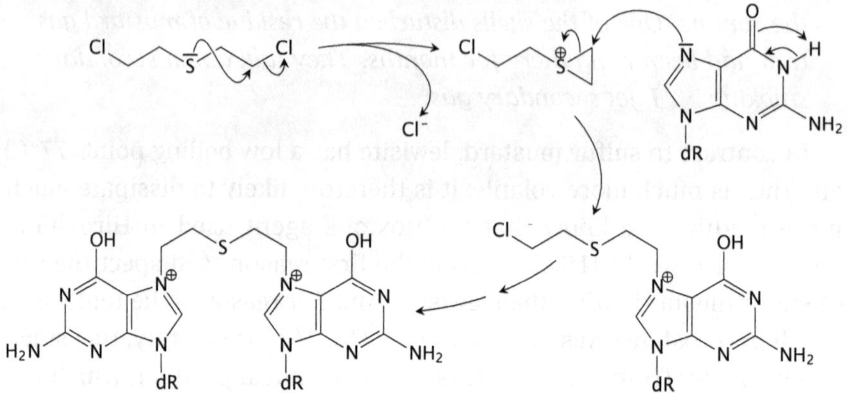

Figure 7.2: Cross-linking of guanine bases in DNA by sulfur mustard. dR represents deoxyribose. The first step consists in the formation of an episulfonium ion; this three-membered ring is highly reactive and readily attacked by the N7 of guanine or by other nucleophiles such as glutathione. Capture of the second guanine involves the same steps as shown explicitly for the first one.

with ionizing radiation. An important role of such cross-links in the biological effect of sulfur mustard is supported by the early finding that similar compounds in which one of the two reactive groups is missing have much lower toxicity [109, p. 35].

The similarity of the mutagenic DNA lesions caused by ionizing radiation and by sulfur mustard explains that the two noxious agents produce similar biological effects both in the short term, such as bone marrow damage and epilation, and in the long term, such as leukemia and cancer. The reactivity of lewisite toward DNA has received surprisingly little attention; unlike sulfur mustard, however, lewisite has no clearly documented mutagenic or carcinogenic potential [21, 111]. The significantly increased incidence of leukemia and of some solid tumors among survivors of the Hiroshima and Nagasaki bombings [112, 113] thus further supports the thesis that sulfur mustard rather than lewisite was used in the attacks on both cities.

7.2.2 Depletion of glutathione. While reaction with DNA mediates most of the damage at low concentrations of sulfur mustard, reactions with other nucleophiles provide an alternate mechanism of toxicity at higher levels. A particularly important molecule is glutathione, which has a key role in scavenging various kinds of toxic compounds inside the cell. If glutathione is depleted by its reaction with sulfur mustard, this will impair the cell's ability to neutralize *reactive oxygen species* (ROS), which arise as the main products or as side products of many metabolic processes; the unscavenged ROS may then cause cytotoxic effects [114].

One biochemical pathway that involves ROS is the formation of skin pigment (melanin); and the melanocytes (pigmented cells) of the skin, which carry out this pathway, are more susceptible to sulfur mustard toxicity than are the non-pigmented keratinocytes [115]. Accordingly, levels of exposure that kill the melanocytes yet permit the keratinocytes to regenerate may cause skin depigmentation. On the other hand, lower levels of sulfur mustard that permit both keratinocytes and melanocytes to regenerate may result in hyperpigmented skin areas. The latter are often seen delineating the depigmented ones.

Glutathione reacts with sulfur mustard via its sulfhydryl (-SH) group, which makes an excellent nucleophile for attacking the episulfonium intermediate shown in Figure 7.2. Although the chemistry is different, sulfhydryl groups also react strongly with lewisite; this suggests that the similarity of the early manifestations on skin and mucous membranes is indeed due to this mechanism. Experimental data on the reaction products formed by lewisite *in vivo* are, however, very sparse [21, 111].

7.2.3 Systemic uptake and distribution. Sulfur mustard is taken up through skin contact, inhalation, and ingestion. Soldiers exposed to sulfur mustard in World War I, as well as the workers in the factories producing the poison, were often protected by gas masks; aware of the danger, they would mostly have avoided ingestion of contaminated food or water. In contrast, the unprotected and unaware victims in Hiroshima and Nagasaki most likely took up significant amounts by all three routes.

When applied experimentally to the skin of experimental animals, 80% of the compound will typically evaporate, but the other 20% will be taken up. Approximately 80% of that latter fraction, or 16% of the total, will indeed reach the blood circulation and then the inner organs, while the remainder (4% of the total) will react and remain within the skin itself [116]. The fraction taken up into the system distributes between different organs. While the relative abundances found in different organs vary somewhat between studies that use different methods of detection—chemical [117], radioactive tracers [118, 119], or DNA damage [120]—it is apparent that organs with strong blood flow receive and retain the highest amounts. These organs include the brain, the lungs, the spleen, and the kidneys.

As noted earlier, sulfur mustard is poorly water-miscible. Such substances are called *hydrophobic* or *lipophilic*, and they tend to accumulate in tissues which a high content of of *lipids*, i.e. fat-like substances. The brain is not only strongly perfused, but also particularly rich in lipids in the form of *myelin*, which enwraps many nerve fibers, endowing them with low membrane capacitance and high speed of conduction. It is therefore understandable that Batal et al. [120] found the highest abundance of DNA adducts in the brain, slightly ahead of the lungs. However, since cell proliferation in the brain is generally very slow, this organ is not very sensitive to the consequences of DNA damage by sulfur mustard; this parallels its relatively low susceptibility to radiation.

With the passage of time, sulfur mustard will redistribute from the brain and other highly perfused organs into the tissue with the highest fat content—fat tissue. This was demonstrated by Drasch et al. [117], who examined the body of an Iranian soldier who had succumbed to sulfur mustard poisoning one week after exposure. It is notable that the sulfur mustard observed after this time was still in its native, unreacted form. Slow redistribution, via the bloodstream, from fat tissue to other organs would likely give rise to protracted DNA and cell damage over time; this may contribute to the oft-noted slow recovery of sulfur mustard victims, and also to the delayed onset of 'radiation sickness' in patients from Hiroshima and Nagasaki (Section 8.8).

Yue et al. [121] compared the abundance of DNA adducts in several major organs after experimentally exposing rats to sulfur mustard. When normalized to the total amount of DNA in each tissue, the highest content was found in bone marrow, followed by the brain, pancreas, lungs, and spleen. The high susceptibility of the bone marrow to sulfur mustard is a long-established fact [122], as is that of the gonads. Nevertheless, we note that high levels are reported consistently in some organs—brain, lungs, and kidneys—that are among the least susceptible to ionizing radiation.

7.2.4 Metabolism. The reactive nature of sulfur mustard makes it amenable to several pathways of metabolic conversion and inactivation. We already mentioned the reaction with glutathione; this reaction is facilitated by the enzyme glutathione-*S*-transferase, which is particularly abundant in the epithelial cells of the liver and the small intestine. Glutathione conjugation is an effective detoxification pathway for drugs and xenobiotics; as long as glutathione is not depleted by large amounts of substrate—such as, for example, sulfur mustard in the skin—this reaction is beneficial.

Sulfur mustard is also susceptible to hydrolysis, which occurs in two steps and results in its inactivation (Figure 7.3A).[4] Another important reaction is oxidation, which occurs extensively *in vivo* [123]. The enzymes responsible have apparently not been characterized. Until such evidence becomes available, both cytochrome P450 and peroxidase enzymes are plausible candidates. The first oxidation intermediate is the sulfoxide, which has low toxic activity (Figure 7.3B); however, a second oxidation will give the sulfone, which can eliminate HCl and thereby turn into divinyl sulfone, a highly reactive and mutagenic compound [124]. In this context, it is noteworthy that a high level of peroxidase activity occurs in the thyroid gland. Thyroid peroxidase is known to mediate sulfoxidation of structurally similar thioether compounds [125], and conversion of sulfur mustard to divinyl sulfone in the thyroid gland might expose this organ to increased carcinogenic activity. Thyroid cancer has been observed in Iranian sulfur mustard victims [126], and its incidence is also significantly increased in Hiroshima and Nagasaki survivors [127].

7.3 Clinical and pathological manifestations

From its biochemical mode of action, it is clear that sulfur mustard is not selective for any organ or cell type. Therefore, the severity of damage to any particular organ is largely governed by the extent of its exposure. Directly exposed are usually the skin, the eyes, and the airways and lungs. The fraction of the poison that is taken up systemically will preferentially affect organs that are strongly perfused, such as the lungs, the brain, the spleen, the kidneys, as well as the adrenal and

---

[4]Hydrolysis will also occur in the environment; however, since sulfur mustard is poorly water-miscible, this process will be slow.

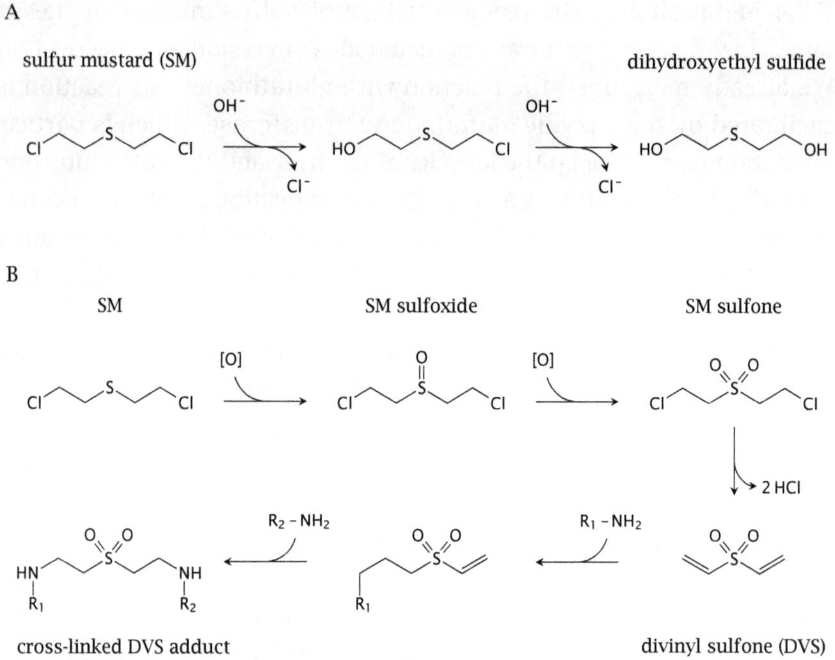

7 Sulfur mustard and napalm

Figure 7.3: Metabolism of sulfur mustard. A: Hydrolysis. Substitution of both chlorine atoms with hydroxyl groups abolishes the molecule's reactivity and toxicity. B: Oxidative metabolism. This pathway is most likely catalyzed by peroxidase or cytochrome P450 enzymes. Stepwise oxidation of the sulfur atom gives first the sulfoxide and then the sulfone, which can eliminate HCl to yield divinyl sulfone. The latter, like native sulfur mustard, has two reactive groups and is highly mutagenic.

thyroid glands. In organs exposed to high doses, glutathione depletion is more likely to cause damage in the short term; in those subjected to lower doses, the tendency to respond to DNA damage with apoptosis (programmed cell death) is a crucial determinant. The latter category includes in particular the gonads, the bone marrow, and the lymphatic tissues.

7.3.1 Blood circulation. Most organs will become exposed to sulfur mustard through the blood circulation; and since the blood levels are evidently high enough to cause severe damage in many of these organs, we can also expect toxicity to the blood circulation itself.

In experimental animals exposed to sulfur mustard, the larger blood vessels (arteries and veins) were observed to lose tone and become dilated; the affected organs appeared *congested*, i.e. more strongly filled with blood than usual. The smallest blood vessels (the capillaries) became leaky; plasma fluid and proteins were lost from the bloodstream, as sometimes were blood cells, and caused the surrounding tissues to swell up [28]. Such findings explain the clinical picture of hypovolemic shock and general edema in severely exposed victims [128] and also in experimental animals [17].[5] Leakiness of the microcirculation is also apparent from the loss of plasma proteins in the urine; and acidity of the urine indicates metabolic acidosis, which is a hallmark of severe circulatory shock [109, p. 228].[6] The poisoned victims will initially look pale, as perfusion of the skin is largely shut off in favor of the vital organs. In later stages, they will appear swollen and cyanotic. The loss of plasma fluid should also trigger intense thirst; this is documented in cases of severe mustard gas poisoning [109, p. 228], and it is also observed in other diseases that cause generalized leakiness of the microcirculation, or *capillary leak syndrome* [131]. Even with intensive care readily available, this condition is often fatal [132], and such an outcome will of course be even more likely under field conditions.

The proteins contained in the extravasated plasma fluid include coagulation factors and fibrinogen, which will become activated and may solidify. Particularly in the lungs, this can result in the formation of fibrin 'casts' that obstruct the lumen of the bronchi and bronchioli, which has been observed both in autopsies of human victims [28, 109] and in experimental animals [133].

7.3.2 Airways and lungs. In mustard gas victims not protected by gas masks, the airways and lungs are prominently affected. The inhaled sulfur mustard will condense on the mucous membranes and attack the epithelial cells within them. The necrotic (dead) cell layers may

---

[5]The hydrostatic pressure in the capillaries always exceeds that within the surrounding tissue. Normally, this pressure gradient is balanced by the osmotic effect of the large quantity of protein contained in the blood plasma. Once the capillary walls become leaky toward the plasma proteins, however, this balancing mechanism breaks down, and plasma seeps freely into the tissues. Any fluid added through drinking or infusion will do likewise and amplify the edema.

[6]Shock, in the pathophysiological sense, is the failure of the circulation due to lack of blood volume, to loss of vascular tone, vascular leakage, or to failure of the heart.

Sulfur mustard has been reported to inhibit cholinesterase, which cleaves acetylcholine, an endogenous mediator that promotes vasodilation [129]. This may contribute to the loss of vascular tone in victims. Acetylcholine receptors in the skin have also been implicated in the causation of blistering [130].

remain in place, held together by extravasated and coagulated fibrin, as so-called *pseudomembranes* [134], or they may desquamate in a manner similar to the epidermis of the skin. Either way, the victims will experience hoarseness and pain in the throat and chest, and they will have difficulty breathing and swallowing.

The bronchi may become obstructed by fibrin cast formation (see above) or by clots forming from blood spilling out of damaged blood vessels [133]. Coagulation can also be activated within the lung's blood vessels themselves; the clots formed in place will then block the further flow of blood through the lungs [135]. Since partially obstructed bronchi tend to let more air in than out, air will become trapped in the peripheral lung tissue, a condition known as *emphysema* [28]. Distended zones of lung tissue will then compress adjacent ones and disrupt their ventilation. Such collapsed areas of lung tissue are referred to as *atelectases*; they may also be caused directly by complete occlusion of the bronchi that ventilate them. Elevated pressure and structural injury may induce the trapped air to leave its regular confines and enter the interstitial space of the connective tissue; this is referred to as *interstitial emphysema*.

If the patient survives this initial stage, the injured lung tissue will be susceptible to infections, and thus foci of bronchopneumonia will develop. Overall, lungs damaged by sulfur mustard will exhibit general circulatory congestion and a varied pattern of bronchial obstruction, hemorrhage, and inflammation.

7.3.3 Eyes. Affliction of the eyes is usually early and painful (Figure 7.4), but also transient. The lesions to the exposed parts of the eyeball, the cornea and the conjunctiva, are similar in principle to those found on the epidermis and mucous membranes, with necrosis and desquamation; however, they are mitigated by the prompt and steady rinsing action of the tear fluid.

The corneal epithelium, when damaged, will initially appear turbid and then erode; this causes impaired vision, pain and reflexive blepharospasm. In combination, these symptoms will create a subjective perception of blindness; Alexander [22] reports that some of his patients at Bari believed themselves permanently blinded until their eyes were forced open to prove to them that they could still see. The deeper layers of the cornea, and the remainder of the eyeball, may escape

Figure 7.4: Ocular symptoms of mustard gas exposure, A: Eyelid edema and blepharospasm in a sulfur mustard victim one day after exposure, which occurred in 2016 in Syria. Skin desquamation with secretion and blisters are also seen. Reproduced from Kilic et al. [106] with permission by the corresponding author (Mesut Ortatatli). B: British soldiers in World War I, transiently blinded by exposure to sulfur mustard. Photograph by Second Lieutenant T. L. Aitken; Imperial War Museum, London.

undamaged. The eroded epithelium will regenerate from the periphery toward the center. In most cases, the loss of vision is reversible within days or a few weeks.

While the above covers the consequences of external exposure, it is also necessary to consider the possible effects on the eyes of sulfur mustard transported in the bloodstream. While the literature offers no pertinent experimental evidence on sulfur mustard itself, some studies have been reported on various functionally similar compounds, including nitrogen mustard and busulfan, which are or were used in the treatment of cancers and leukemias. Patients thus treated may develop symptoms in parts of the eyeball not usually affected by superficial exposure. *Uveitis*, that is, inflammation of the iris and adjacent soft tissue structures, and edema of the retina have been described in patients receiving cancer treatment with nitrogen mustard [136]. Cataract, which afflicts the lens, has been induced with nitrogen mustard and busulfan in experimental animals [137, 138]. Similar effects are likely to occur after systemic uptake of sulfur mustard. In addition, we can expect bleeding in the retina and other places in patients with generalized purpura due to bone marrow suppression (see Section 8.2.1).

7.3.4 Skin. While skin blisters are a prominent feature of mustard gas lesions, the spectrum ranges from mere erythema over desquamation and blisters to deeper necroses of all layers of the skin and the underlying soft tissues. The severity will vary not only with the amount of sulfur mustard applied, but also with the texture of the skin and its humidity; the palms of the hand have thicker skin and are less susceptible, whereas areas covered by tender and humid skin such as the armpits and genitals are more so.[7] Severe lesions may be surrounded by a halo of less severely afflicted areas. When such lesions heal, the more lightly affected peripheral areas tend to become hyperpigmented (Figure 7.5), whereas the more severely affected ones will show depigmentation. The underlying reason was discussed in Section 7.2.2 above.

---

[7]Among the four acute radiation sickness patients described in the ICRC report mentioned in Section 1.5.2 [32], two had burns around the mouth. They may have been wearing face masks in the days following the bombing, as described by Burchett [16]; the humidity trapped under these would then have softened the skin and thus amplified the local effect of mustard gas.

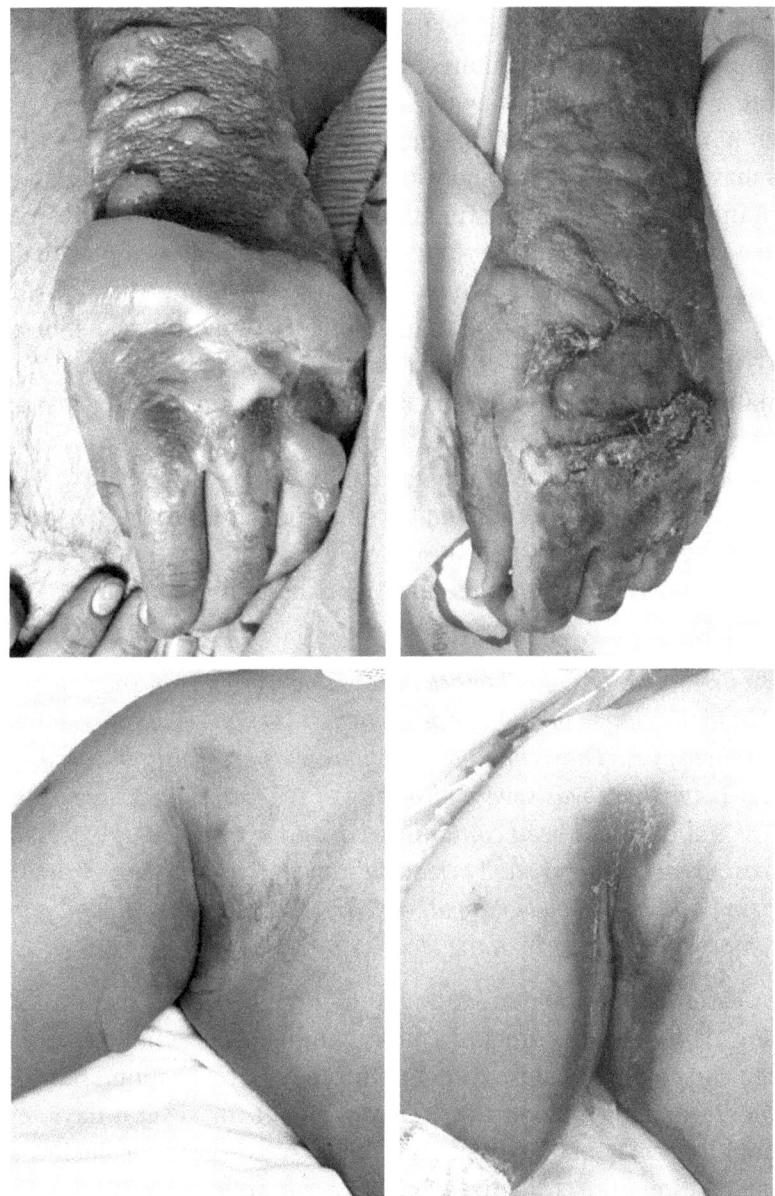

Figure 7.5: Skin lesions in mustard gas victims. Top: large blister in an early lesion, and beginning wound healing after partial removal of dead tissue at a later stage. Bottom: axillary lesion, surrounded initially by erythema and later on by hyperpigmentation. After 11 days (left), necrotic skin is still adherent; it is sloughed off several days later (right). Reproduced from Kilic et al. [106] with permission by the corresponding author (Mesut Ortatatli).

The skin may be exposed by being splashed directly with liquid sulfur mustard, but also by indirect contact with contaminated weapons or other objects, as well as by the fumes, which easily penetrate clothes, even in multiple layers. While mustard splashed on exposed skin areas may be rapidly wiped and washed off before doing much damage, contaminated clothes may function as a reservoir of the poison and cause more severe damage to the skin underneath. Examples of skin lesions observed underneath clothing are shown in Figure 7.6. Similarly, Alexander [22] reports that, among the mustard gas victims at Bari, those who stripped off their contaminated clothes on their own initiative fared much better than those who kept them on for the night after the disaster. Such apparent negligence can be understood if we consider that the onset of mustard skin lesions is typically delayed by several hours; once the pain becomes perceptible, the poison has already been taken up, and the damage is done. On the time course of the clinical manifestations, the American military physician Harry Gilchrist notes [139, p. 44]:

> *At first the troops didn't notice the gas and were not uncomfortable, but in the course of an hour or so, there was marked inflammation of their eyes. They vomited, and there was erythema of the skin. ... Later there was severe blistering of the skin, especially where the uniform had been contaminated, and by the time the gassed cases reached the casualty clearing station, the men were virtually blind and had to be led about, each man holding on to the man in front with an orderly in the lead.*[8]

A careful experimental study on the time course of mustard skin lesions [140] also documents a slow, gradual progression. They early stage consists in a massive edema through extravasation, indicating capillary damage. Blood flow remains intact for several days, even though necrosis of the tissue is underway; vascular occlusion and sequestration of necrotic tissue finally occur after some 10 days. Such a time course resembles clinical observations.

7.3.5 Digestive tract. The earliest and most common gastrointestinal symptom is vomiting. Unless it is bloody, however, vomiting need not be due to direct action of the poison on the digestive organs, but may

---

[8] Cf. Figure 7.4.

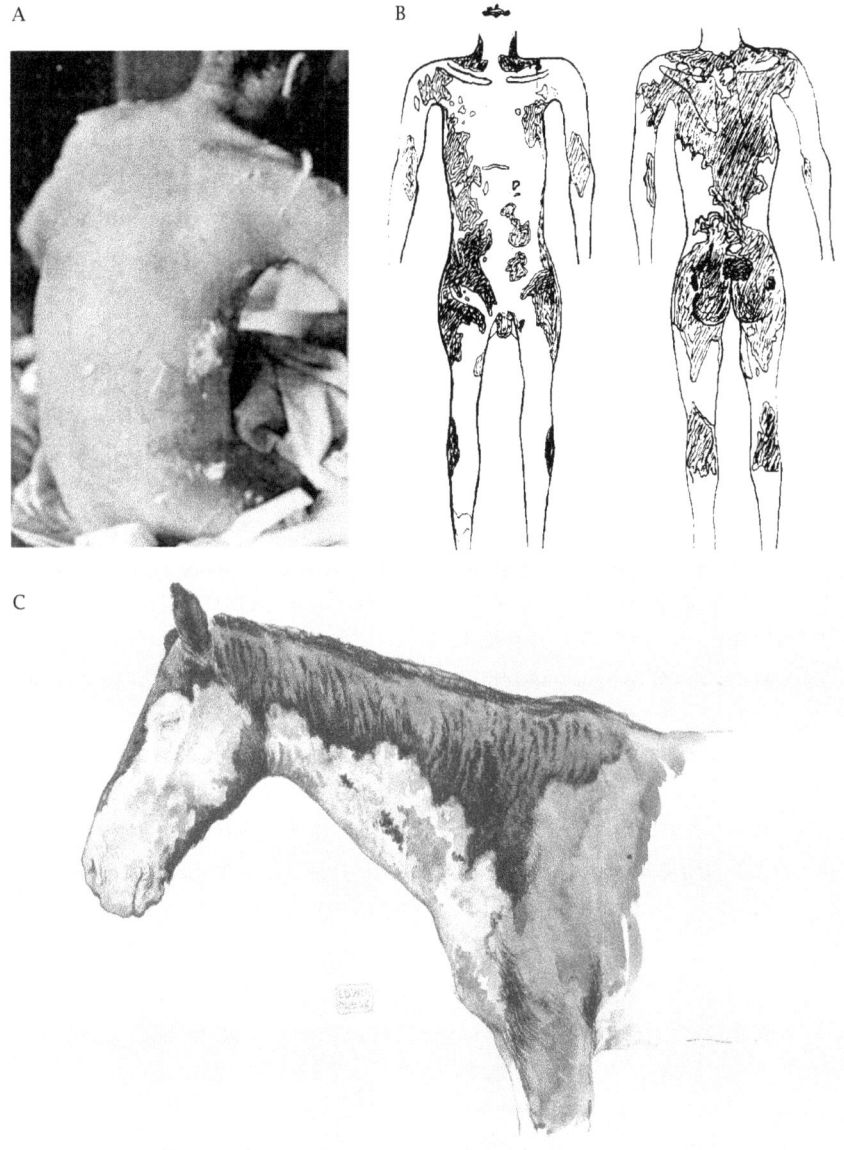

Figure 7.6: Clothes or hair do not protect from mustard gas. A: Fraying and desquamating skin in an accidentally poisoned mustard factory worker. B: Distribution of lesions in another affected worker. A and B adapted from [109]. C: Skin lesions in a warhorse exposed to mustard gas in World War I. Sketch by Edwin Noble (Imperial War Museum, London).

instead result from its stimulating effect on the *area postrema* in the brainstem, which triggers vomiting in response to various chemical agents. A more specific indication of damage to the intestinal organs themselves is diarrhea, which in severe cases may also be bloody.

Warthin and Weller [109] relate that physicians who had been treating cases of mustard poisoning in World War I disagreed as to whether diarrhea constitutes an early and typical symptom of mustard gas poisoning. Two cases described in detail by Heitzmann [28] developed diarrhea only about 10 days after the exposure; on the other hand, Warthin and Weller [109, p. 75] describe an acute case with diarrhea setting in promptly, together with vomiting, and they also report rapid onset in experimental animals injected with the poison (pg. 91). Dacre and Goldman [17], too, cite a number of experimental animal studies and human case reports that list early diarrhea as a typical symptom of mustard gas poisoning.

If and when diarrhea occurs in a given case of mustard gas poisoning may simply depend on the dosage. The digestive tract may receive sulfur mustard both by ingestion and through the bloodstream. In the first case, one would expect higher local levels and earlier onset of symptoms, whereas in the latter case levels in the GI tract may be lower and the onset of manifest symptoms delayed, as is the case with the bone marrow.

Autopsy reports paint a somewhat variable picture, with edema, focal or regional necroses, pseudomembranes, hemorrhages within the mucous membranes or spilling out into the lumen, and secondary infections. Overall, the pathological features are rather similar to those observed in the respiratory tract.

7.3.6 Bone marrow, spleen, and gonads. These organs host cell types which are highly susceptible to radiation, and which likewise are highly susceptible to the genotoxic effect of sulfur mustard. In many cases, it is indeed the bone marrow toxicity that causes the patient's demise, through either uncontrollable bleeding due to lack of thrombocytes, or unmanageable infections due to the lack of leukocytes. Accordingly, in the autopsies of such patients, one finds a barren bone marrow, absent sperm cell production, and depletion of lymphocytes in the spleen. None of these observations distinguish organ damage by sulfur mustard from that caused by radiation.

7.3.7 Kidneys, liver, and brain. In most cases, these organs show signs of damage to the vascular system rather than to the organ-specific epithelial or nerve cells. The blood vessels are congested, occasionally bleeding into the tissues has occurred; in the liver, there may be some signs of fatty degeneration, and in the kidneys protein may have seeped out of the blood vessels, into the urine-conducting and -processing conduits (the *tubuli*; [28]). These changes, while not overly dramatic, are not expected in patients exposed to doses of radiation that do not kill on very short notice (1-2 days).

7.4 Napalm

The name "napalm" denotes gasoline-based incendiaries that have been rendered viscous and sticky using a variety of suitable additives. When filled into bomb shells and ignited by a detonating charge, usually with the help of white phosphorus, napalm will disperse in large burning gobs, which will adhere to the surfaces they strike. Since gasoline has a very high heat of combustion, the burning clumps of napalm will very effectively ignite flammable targets, and they will do extensive damage to non-flammable ones—including, of course, the human body.

One thickening additive that was found to be both cheap and effective is a combination of naphthenic acid with a mixture of fatty acids produced from coconut oil. The word "napalm" combines the names of naphthenic acid and of palmitic acid, the latter being one component of the coconut-derived mixture. These acids were converted to their aluminum salts, or soaps, before being combined with the gasoline.[9] According to Björnerstedt et al. [141], this 'proper' napalm is particularly suitable for flamethrowers, whereas polymeric thickeners have been widely used when filling incendiary bombs.

While napalm strikes its human victims with severe injury and often death, the medical literature on its effects is astonishingly sparse. As of this writing (in 2019), a simple search for "napalm" on PubMed retrieves 29 articles, of which only 7 (seven) are written in English, and none

---

[9]The aluminum contained in these soaps should become oxidized in the fire and be left behind on the ground. A reaction with soil minerals might produce certain variants of garnet, in particular $Fe_3Al_2(SiO_4)_3$ or $Mn_3Al_2(SiO_4)_3$, which could account for, or contribute to, the 'pink carpet' which de Seversky had observed in Hiroshima and also in other firebombed cities (see Section 1.1).

of these provides much useful detail.[10] The most substantial medical articles, albeit also low in number, have been contributed by military physicians from the former Soviet Union, which aided its allies North Korea and North Vietnam in the treatment of napalm victims during the respective wars [142-144]. Prominent findings reported by these physicians include:

1. napalm burns tend to be very deep (3rd and 4th degree);[11]
2. in the acute stage, loss of consciousness and circulatory shock are frequent;
3. burns that affect the face or areas near it often damage the airways and lungs, leading to hypoxia and sometimes asphyxiation;
4. burns to the face will often involve the eyes, with scarring of the eyelids causing secondary damage to the corneas;
5. more than 35% of the North Korean soldiers who had been hit by napalm died on the spot;
6. slightly more than half of all Korean survivors developed keloids, that is, hypertrophic, prominent, swollen scars.

According to Dolinin [143], the U.S. used approximately 200 tons of napalm per day during the Korean war, whereas during the Vietnam war daily production—presumably similar to daily use—amounted to about 700 tons. Much of it was, of course, used against civilians. Only occasionally has the American and international public been confronted with the resulting horrors; awareness seems to be limited to the iconic 'Napalm Girl' Kim Phuc (see Figure 9.5). It is quite difficult to find images of any other Vietnamese napalm victims, but some are shown in William Pepper's 1967 article "The Children of Vietnam" [145] in *Ramparts* magazine, which as of this writing is available online. Several of these victims are very severely disfigured. Images of acknowledged Japanese napalm victims—other than scorched and shriveled corpses left behind by the Tokyo bombing of March 1945—seem likewise to have been purged from the public record.

---

[10]For comparison, a search for "mustard gas" (with quotes) returns 1935 hits.
[11]The classification of burns by severity is explained in Section 9.1.2.

8 Statistical observations on acute 'radiation' sickness in Hiroshima and Nagasaki

> It is ... difficult to explain the complete absence of radiation effects in ... people who were theoretically exposed to lethal dosages of radiation.
>
> Ashley Oughterson and Shields Warren [146]

The standard narrative of the atomic bombings implies that a) all those exposed near the hypocenter with light or no shielding received lethal doses of radiation, b) those exposed at 2 km or more from the hypocenter should have been safe from acute radiation sickness (ARS), and c) radiation intensities high enough to cause ARS prevailed only for a few seconds during the detonations themselves. This story fails to account for the following observations:

- there is a substantial number of survivors who were exposed near the hypocenter, either in the open or protected only by wooden houses;
- there are victims of ARS at distances which should have been safe;
- in Hiroshima, multiple cases of ARS, some with lethal outcome, were recorded among those who were not in the city during the bombing but entered it shortly afterwards;
- in survivors, a history of ARS correlates very poorly with official radiation dose estimates; one third of the survivors in the highest dose group did not report even a single characteristic symptom of ARS.

The observed distribution of ARS in time and space thus clearly contradicts the claimed causation by radiation released in a single strong pulse.

8 Statistical observations on acute 'radiation' sickness

8.1 Physical assumptions

Before delving into the data themselves, we will note some assumptions which concern physical conditions and methods, and which will guide the interpretation of the medical data.

8.1.1 Radiation doses from fallout and induced radioactivity are negligible. As discussed earlier (Section 2.5), the most important forms of radiation from a fission bomb are the γ-rays and neutrons released during the blast itself. In contrast, residual radioactivity on the ground due to fallout and to neutron capture should be minor; while it might pose some health risk in those exposed to it for long periods of time, residual radioactivity should not cause or contribute to acute radiation sickness. Cullings et al. [30] put it succinctly:

> *The radiation doses were truly acute, being received almost completely in a matter of seconds; furthermore, every person in each city received the dose at the same time ... The situation regarding residual radiation was most recently reviewed in the DS86 Final Report.[1] As that report makes clear, doses from residual radiation are generally believed to be small.*

Note that the authors arrived at this conclusion when starting from orthodox tenets regarding the inner workings and the explosive yields of the nuclear bombs. Thus, we don't need to assume that no nuclear detonations ever happened in order to dismiss fallout and neutron-induced radiation as possible causes of ARS; we are not making a circular argument.[2]

8.1.2 Biology trumps physics in the detection of lethal radiation. All physical dosimeters and radiation counters are subject to measurement errors; but no frayed cable, leaky battery, or distracted operator can prevent the lethal effect of radiation on a human being.

---

[1] See Roesch [93].

[2] A low level of exposure to fallout is supported by measurements of the fission product ^{90}Sr in exhumed bones of Hiroshima bombing victims [147]. Some ^{90}Sr was indeed detected in these samples, but the average levels were lower than in bones from Japanese who were exposed to the global fallout in later years; this agrees with the detectable but relatively low levels of local fallout near Hiroshima (Chapter 3).

The lethal dose of radiation for humans is approximately 8 Sv; with γ-radiation, this is the same as 8 Gy.[3] The only possible way to survive such a dose is through a bone marrow transplant, which of course was not available to the bombing victims. Indeed, total body irradiation with a lethal dose of γ-rays is one of two methods used to condition leukemia patients for a bone marrow transplant. Once a patient receives some 10 Gy of γ-rays as a single dose, his bone marrow *will* die—as will, hopefully, all of his leukemic cells, for that is the real purpose of the procedure; and so will *he*, unless transplanted with the bone marrow of a healthy donor immediately afterwards. Irradiation could not serve this purpose if it were anything but deadly every single time.

If a human being does not die, it did not receive a lethal dose; there can be no false-negative reading. Thus, if a physical measurement or calculation indicates that lethal radiation prevailed at a certain time and place, but a human who was present then and there survived, then this biological outcome categorically falsifies the physical statement.

False-*positive* findings of sickness and death due to radiation can, of course, be produced with 'radiomimetic' compounds such as sulfur mustard; and accordingly the second conditioning method for bone marrow transplant is the use of drugs exactly of this kind.[4]

8.2 Manifestations of acute radiation sickness

The seriousness of acute radiation sickness depends, above all, on the dose of the radiation received. Other important considerations are whether that dose is delivered all at once or in multiple sessions, and whether it is applied to the whole body or only to some part of it. In a nuclear detonation, irradiation should usually affect the whole body evenly, and accordingly all doses stated in the following should

---

[3] A benchmark that is easier to determine accurately than the 'always lethal dose' is the LD_{50}, that is, the dose that will be lethal to 50% of all individuals in a sufficiently large sample. The human LD_{50} has never been accurately determined; there simply are no adequate data. Under these circumstances, the best available substitute is the LD_{50} experimentally determined with rhesus monkeys (see Section 11.3 and [148]).

[4] One early agent used for this purpose was nitrogen mustard, which acts in exactly the same manner as does sulfur mustard. Nowadays, drugs are more commonly used than radiation.

be taken as whole-body doses.[5] Also important are type and particle energy of the radiation; this is discussed in Section 2.9.2.

The sensitivity to radiation differs greatly between tissues and cell types in the body, and therefore different organs will respond at different threshold doses. Three sub-syndromes that concern different target organs can be distinguished.

8.2.1 The hematopoetic syndrome. This syndrome is caused by damage to bone marrow stem cells, which are among the most radiosensitive cell types.[6] It becomes manifest at doses above 1.5-2 Sv, and no patients who received more than 5-6 Sv will survive it if intensive medical care is unavailable. All types of blood cells are descended from bone marrow stem cells, and thus all of them will fail to be renewed in hematopoetic syndrome (HS for short). However, the consequences are most dramatic with the white blood cells and with thrombocytes, since these are short-lived (see Figure 8.4). In contrast, mature red blood cells have a life span of 120 days; they can sustain the patient even when their regeneration ceases for several weeks, and they will thus not limit his lifespan in the acute phase of HS.

When leukocytes fail, the patients will suffer from infections; when platelets are depleted, bleeding will occur spontaneously or after minor trauma. Numerous scattered hemorrhagic spots will arise which are most readily observed beneath the skin or the mucous membranes of the oral cavity, but which equally affect the inner organs; and in severe cases, the patient may bleed to death internally. This condition is referred to as *purpura*, and the characteristic hemorrhagic spots are called *petechiae*.

As long as some bone marrow stem cells survive, blood cell formation will eventually resume; if levels of white blood cells and of platelets fall dangerously low, they may be transiently substituted by transfusion. If all stem cells were wiped out, then only a transplant of bone marrow from a compatible donor can possibly save the patient.

---

[5]Local cancer radiotherapy often uses doses which are much higher than the ones stated here, and which would be lethal if applied to the whole body.

[6]The cells of the bone marrow are shielded to some degree from natural radiation by the mineral of the surrounding bone matrix. Did natural selection hide them there because they were sensitive, or did they evolve to be sensitive because they were shielded?

Radiation doses similar to those that damage the bone marrow will also damage the hair follicles. In this case, too, loss of function may be transient or permanent; higher doses will cause greater loss of hair, and permanent hair loss may occur at doses similar to those that irreversibly destroy the bone marrow. Thus, hair loss provides a useful proxy for estimating the extent of damage to the bone marrow.

8.2.2 The gastrointestinal syndrome. At doses of 6 Sv and above, damage to the intestines will give rise to diarrhea and often outright intestinal bleeding. The breakdown of the gut barrier will facilitate infections, which will be made worse by the depletion of white blood cells. Loss of fluid and electrolytes will further aggravate the situation. Intensive care with antibiotics and replacement of fluids and electrolytes, in addition to treatment of the hematopoetic syndrome, may rescue patients with doses up to 10-12 Sv, but at dosages higher than this the prognosis of gastrointestinal syndrome becomes hopeless. Of course, none of these therapeutic measures were available in Hiroshima and Nagasaki; under those conditions, practically all patients with manifest gastrointestinal syndrome should have died.

8.2.3 The cerebrovascular syndrome. At very high doses—the threshold doses given in the literature vary considerably, reflecting the paucity of clearly documented cases; but a widely cited IAEA report states 20 Gy [149]—radiation will kill within 1-2 days by direct action on the central nervous system. It is believed that damage primarily affects the small blood vessels in the brain; inhibited perfusion then causes various manifestations of brain dysfunction, most conspicuously coma.

Hall and Giaccia [150, p. 218] point out that, even though neurological symptoms may initially dominate the clinical picture, the damage to the vascular system is likely general. This matches their case descriptions of two workers who developed cerebrovascular syndrome after receiving extremely high doses of irradiation by accident, and who also suffered general circulatory shock, to which they succumbed within two days after the exposure.

8.2.4 Prodromal and latent stages. The hematopoetic and gastrointestinal syndromes described above take days or weeks to become fully manifest; and, for reasons explained in Section 2.11, the delay will be longer with lower radiation doses. Minutes to hours after exposure, however, there will be some early signs, less severe and less characteristic. Most common at this *prodromal* stage are vomiting and mild headache; diarrhea and fever indicate higher doses and presage later manifestation of gastrointestinal syndrome. In all but the most severe cases, these prodromal signs subside, and the patients will enter a *latent* stage showing few clinical symptoms or none at all. During this time, however, cell proliferation within the bone marrow and, at higher doses, within the intestine drops off, and the specific syndromes manifest themselves once the initially surviving maturing or fully mature cells in these organs expire.

8.3 Acute radiation doses in Hiroshima and Nagasaki

The tenet that, in Hiroshima and Nagasaki, doses sufficient to cause acute radiation sickness could have been inflicted only during the blast itself (see Section 8.1.1) gives rise to a number of testable predictions, which we will examine in the following.

8.3.1 Radiation dose as a function of distance from the hypocenter. Since there were no instruments in place to measure the radiation doses when the detonations occurred, we have to make do with approximations based on indirect methods and calculations. The officially endorsed dose estimates have seen some fairly considerable changes over time. Figure 8.1 depicts the biologically effective or equivalent doses for both Hiroshima and Nagasaki, based on current estimates of γ-ray and neutron intensities [30]. In this graph, the biological dose was calculated by applying an experimentally determined dose-dependent relative biological efficiency (RBE) function for neutron radiation [48] to the neutron component of Cullings' radiation levels.

8.3.2 Shielding from radiation by buildings. The dose estimates in Figure 8.1 apply to persons who were directly in the path of the radiation, without any sort of solid matter between them and the point of the detonation up in the air (the epicenter). However, many people were indoors at the time of the bombing, and some of those who found themselves outdoors were shaded from the detonation by some intervening structure.

Traditional Japanese houses were simple buildings with one or two stories, constructed mainly from wood, sometimes with thatched roofs but usually with tiled ones. This was the predominant type of building in both Hiroshima and in Nagasaki, although in the latter city the

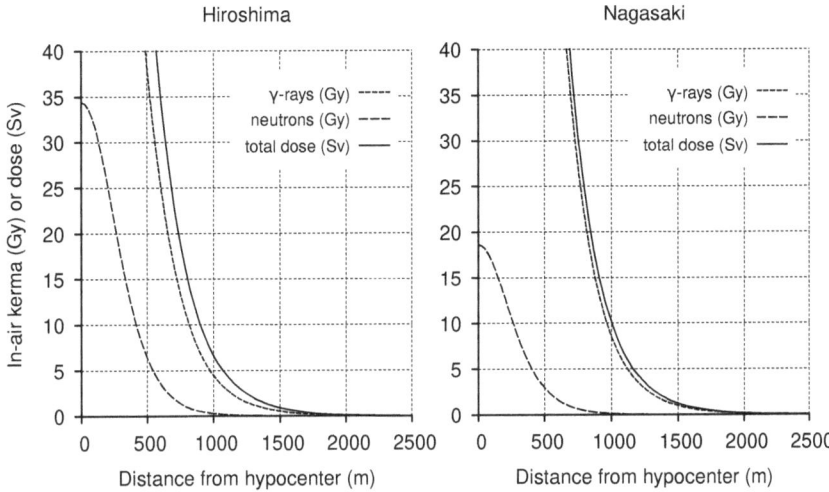

Figure 8.1: Estimated radiation doses at Hiroshima and Nagasaki, as a function of distance from the hypocenter. The in-air kerma for γ-rays and neutrons was taken from Cullings et al. [30]. To calculate the total dose, the dose-dependent relative biological effect of neutrons was estimated according to Sasaki et al. [48] (see text for details).

proportion of concrete buildings is said to have been somewhat higher. The penetration of γ-rays and fast neutrons into such traditionally constructed buildings was studied quite thoroughly in the 1950s and 60s, as documented by Auxier [36] and Arakawa [151]. According to these measurements, γ-ray doses inside such buildings would have been ≥ 60%, and neutron doses ≥ 40% of those in the open. Thus, these buildings would have given only very limited protection from bomb radiation. In contrast, buildings constructed from concrete could have provided effective shielding, particularly within rooms facing away from the detonation.

8.3.3 Threshold distances for radiation doses. Considering the almost complete lack of medical care available to the bombing victims, we can assume that survival of more than 6 Sv would have been impossible; according to the estimate shown in Figure 8.1, this threshold is reached or exceeded in both cities at distances up to 1000 m. Accordingly, there should have been no possibility of surviving an unshielded exposure within 1000 m in either Hiroshima or Nagasaki. Within 500 m, unshielded doses should invariably have caused cerebrovascular syndrome, the most severe and rapidly deadly form of ARS; and this should apply not only to persons without shielding, but also to those shielded by no more than a traditional wooden house. On the other hand, beyond 1500 m in both cities, the unshielded dose drops to a level below which no serious manifestations of acute radiation sickness are to be expected.

8.3.4 Predicted distance distribution of ARS. From the foregoing observations, we can conclude that the statistics on ARS in Hiroshima and Nagasaki should exhibit a highly regular pattern, with the following characteristics:

1. within 500 m, all of those exposed without shielding or inside traditional wooden houses should have suffered cerebrovascular syndrome, and none of them should have survived beyond 2-3 days;
2. between 0.5 and 1 km, ARS should have occurred in all persons exposed inside wooden houses or without shielding; and in the latter group, there should be no survivors;
3. between 1 km and 1.5 km, a very large proportion of victims who were exposed with light shielding or in the open should have suffered ARS, ranging from mild and transient to violent and deadly;
4. at most a few light cases of ARS should have occurred among those exposed beyond 1.5 km, regardless of shielding;
5. absolutely no ARS cases whatsoever should have occurred beyond a distance of 2 km.

Note that these threshold distance values are based on current dose estimates. Early estimates were substantially higher [151, 152]. If we assume that those earlier numbers were in fact correct, then a similar pattern should still emerge, but with each of the boundaries stated in the list above approximately 500 m further out.

8.4 Observed distance distribution of ARS in Hiroshima

We will now compare observed occurrences of ARS and of survival to predicted ones. The two key sources for this purpose are Oughterson et al. [33] and Sutou [34]. Both studies report statistics on several thousand individuals. The first one was compiled by the 'Joint Commission for the Investigation of the Effects of the Atomic Bomb in Japan', a group of American and Japanese physicians convened at the initiative

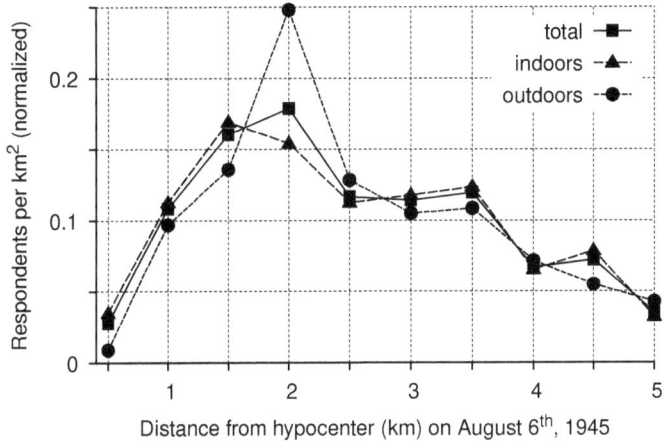

Figure 8.2: Location of survivors of the Hiroshima bombing by shielding and distance from the hypocenter. A survey in 1957 [34] canvassed all persons then living within 7 km of the hypocenter. The number of respondents who reported having been within a given distance on the day of the bombing is normalized in this graph to the size of the circular area in question. The low density of respondents who had been within 500 m of the hypocenter most likely reflects low survival rates. In contrast, the decreasing trend beyond a distance of 2 km may simply be due to lower population density in the suburbs. Data from Tables 1-4 in [34].

of Ashley W. Oughterson, a professor of surgery at Yale who at the time was serving as a colonel in the U.S. military. This commission only arrived at Hiroshima and Nagasaki in October 1945, but it did acquire and organize data previously collected by Japanese physicians; and the statistical evaluation of these earlier Japanese data constitutes the main substance of the commission's report. Most of the figures tabulated in [33] pertain to patients still alive and in medical care at 20 days after the bombings; recorded are slightly below 7000 survivors in each of the two cities.[7]

---

[7] For vivid accounts of the pitiful conditions these patients were suffering at the time, see for example the book by Swiss ICRC physician Junod [153], as well as the short film *Hiroshima-Nagasaki 1945* [154].

The second study was carried out in 1957 by Dr. Gensaku Oho,[8] a physician from Hiroshima, who enlisted the help of student volunteers to canvas the resident population of Hiroshima. The main purpose of this study was to determine the occurrence of radiation sickness among persons who had not been exposed to the bombings themselves, but who had entered the area close to the hypocenter only afterwards. The more recent paper by Sutou [34], which is used here, is a partial translation of and commentary on Oho's earlier study.

8.4.1 Survival of persons exposed within 500 m of the hypocenter.
The first prediction is that no one should have survived beyond a few days who was exposed, with light shielding or without it, within 500 m of the hypocenter. This prediction is falsified by the following findings:

1. Twelve of Oho's respondents in 1957 reported having been exposed within 0.5 km of the hypocenter. Of these, one had been exposed outdoors, whereas eleven had been indoors; presumably, at least some among this number had been inside wooden buildings.
2. Keller [10] lists eight patients at Osaka University Hospital as having been exposed inside wooden buildings within no more than 500 m, and among them four had been within 50 m. He further states that of all patients in his survey five succumbed, and that the average day of death among these five was 26 days after the bombing. Therefore, at least three patients exposed within 500 m the hypocenter were still alive some four weeks after the bombing. Even the patients who did succumb within four weeks had survived long enough to be transported to Osaka, and therefore must have lived longer than compatible with cerebrovascular syndrome, which they invariably should have suffered.

This number of confirmed survivors is certainly very small, which means that the inferno in the city center must have been every bit as deadly as eyewitness testimony indicates [14, 156] (see also Figure 8.2). Nevertheless, if we accept that there are any survivors at all, *then this finding alone disproves the story of the nuclear detonation, and no amount of physical studies can possibly salvage it*—remember that

---

[8]The last name is transcribed as 'Obo' by [34] and [155] and as 'O-ho' in some other sources. Not knowing which spelling is the most appropriate, I adopted the one which I saw used most widely.

Table 8.1: Prevalence of specific symptoms of acute radiation sickness—epilation and/or purpura (E/P)—among patients in Hiroshima who were still alive 20 days after the bombing, by distance from hypocenter and type of shielding. The columns labeled with † give the numbers of patients known to have died later. 'Japanese' buildings are understood to be of traditional, wooden construction. Excerpted from Tables 59H and 68H in [33].

Distance (km)	Outdoors, unshielded			Inside Japanese building		
	Alive at 20 d	E/P (%)	†	Alive at 20 d	E/P (%)	†
0–1.0	105	88.6	22	410	85.9	120
1.1–1.5	249	42.6	9	560	38.6	19
1.6–2.0	689	14.2	4	754	10.1	3
2.1–2.5	590	6.8	1	731	4.7	0
2.6–3.0	192	7.8	0	390	2.6	0
3.1–4.0	159	3.8	0	325	1.2	0
4.1–5.0	68	2.9	0	127	0.8	0

no false-negative measurements are possible with our *Homo sapiens* reference dosimeter.

8.4.2 Survival and incidence of ARS among patients exposed within 1 km of the hypocenter. Oughterson et al. [33] do not separate exposure within 0.5 km from that within 1 km, presumably because they considered the numbers in the former group too low. However, beginning with 1 km, they group patients by distance intervals of 0.5 km, and they carefully subdivide each group according to different types of shielding. Table 8.1 contains a selection of these data, on which we can make the following observations:

1. On the twentieth day, 88.6% of patients exposed within 1 km and in the open have developed specific symptoms of radiation sickness, which means that 11.4% have not. Similar proportions are found with those who were exposed while inside Japanese style houses.

   With doses as high as those predicted for this range, the latency period of ARS should last at most 8-18 days [31]. Therefore, the observation of patients who on the 20th day still show no signs of manifest ARS deviates from expectation.

2. Of the 105 patients exposed in the open and still alive on the 20th day, only 22 are known to have died later on. Oughterson et al. [33] quite sensibly state:

It is probable that other unreported deaths occurred in this group of people, and some may have died as a result of radiation after the end of the survey in Japan.

However, they also show (in their Table 58) that death rates steadily declined as time went on. Out of a total of 6663 patients recorded in Hiroshima as being alive on the 20th day, 254 or 4% are reported to have died subsequently. 137 of these deaths occurred between days 20 and 29, whereas only two occurred between days 70 and 79, and another five occurred between day 80 and the unspecified end date of the survey. Considering this time course, it is highly likely that most of the 83 patients who had been exposed in the open within 1 km, and who had survived the entire time period of the study, also remained alive thereafter—in marked contrast to the expectation that they should all have perished.[9]

In summary, while the proportion of ARS sufferers in this group is large, it is not as large as predicted. Even more difficult to explain is the number of those who experienced ARS yet survived it.

8.4.3 Incidence of ARS at >1 km from the hypocenter. Above, we stated that a large proportion of persons within 1-1.5 km should suffer from ARS. In patients exposed without shielding or with light shielding only, the proportion listed in Table 8.1 is close to 40%. While this is low, we must allow that in some cases the symptoms may not yet have been manifest on the survey's reference date, for at dosages below 4 Gy the latency period may exceed 20 days [31]. In contrast, the mortality is again implausibly low. The ARS cases observed beyond 2 km from the hypocenter—at frequencies below 10% and decreasing with distance, but not quite dropping to zero even between 4 and 5 km—differ from expectation unequivocally; they are not explained even by the highest published estimates of acute radiation doses.

The above findings were confirmed by Oho, who documented cases of ARS among survivors who had been at ≥ 2 and even ≥ 3 km from the hypocenter during the detonation. Importantly, this applied even to

---

[9]Indeed, some such survivors were still encountered in the survey carried out by the Atomic Bomb Casualty Commission (ABCC) during the 1950s (see Section 11.2).

some survivors who had stayed away from the hypocenter for several weeks after the bombing [34].

8.5 Observed distance distribution of ARS in Nagasaki

The observations made above for Hiroshima mostly apply to Nagasaki as well (see Table 68N in [33]); however, some findings are quantitatively more pronounced. Symptoms of and death due to ARS are less frequent within 1 km than in Hiroshima, even though radiation doses are supposed to have been higher (see Figure 8.1): among survivors exposed in the open or shielded only by a wooden house, less than 60% exhibit epilation or purpura. Among survivors exposed between 1.5-2.5 km, a greater percentage than at Hiroshima shows symptoms of ARS. On the other hand, beyond 4 km from the hypocenter, that percentage does indeed drop to zero in Nagasaki, whereas it remains positive even at this distance in Hiroshima.

8.6 ARS symptoms in people shielded by concrete buildings

Concrete buildings will afford substantial protection from both γ-rays and neutron radiation, and we should therefore expect a lower number of ARS victims among those inside these buildings than in those inside wooden buildings or in the open. This is indeed observed; within 1 km from the hypocenter, the incidence of ARS is approximately 25% lower inside heavy buildings than outside, both in Hiroshima and Nagasaki (Oughterson et al. [33], Tables 68H and 68N). Yet, ARS inside heavy buildings in Hiroshima remains more prevalent than it is in the open in Nagasaki, even though the radiation dose is said to have been higher in Nagasaki.

More detailed statistics on this question are reported by Oughterson and Warren [146], who in their Table 3.7 show findings from three individual concrete buildings in Hiroshima, all of which were situated between 700 and 900 meters from the hypocenter. In each building, some people were protected by multiple walls or floors, such that the total shielding was equivalent to ≥ 154 inches (or 394 cm) of water (see Table 8.2). The stated radiation dose *outside* the buildings was up to 80 Gy, which amounts to approximately ten times the lethal dose. However, after passing through this much shielding, it should have been attenuated to a mere 4 mGy. This corresponds to just ²⁄₃ of the

Table 8.2: Attenuation of γ-rays and fast neutrons by different materials. Numbers are estimates of the layer thickness that would have reduced initial radiation doses in Hiroshima by 90%. Data for γ-rays from Ishikawa et al. [8, p. 72]; value for fast neutrons and concrete calculated from numbers given by Yılmaz et al. [157].

Material	Layer effecting 90% attenuation (cm)	
	γ-rays	fast neutrons
Iron	9-13	
Concrete	30-45	26-28
Wood	125-175	
Water	65-92	
Soil	45-65	

typical annual dose of a U.S. citizen and will, of course, not produce any acute symptoms at all.

Nevertheless, Oughterson and Warren report cases of ARS—some of them lethal—among persons thus protected. They propose that these may be due to neutrons, apparently assuming that neutrons are less effectively shielded by concrete than are γ-rays. However, this is now known to be incorrect (see Table 8.2); and moreover, as already noted, the estimated neutron dose at Hiroshima was very substantially reduced in the decades after their book was published [49].

As a second *deus ex machina*, the authors suggest that the bomb's γ-radiation may have been of much higher particle energy, and therefore more penetrating, than is generally assumed. However, they do not offer a physical basis for this hypothesis, nor do they pursue its wider implications for the physical and medical dosimetry of the entire event, which would have been substantial. Such lack of thoroughness suggests that the authors themselves do not take their own proposal seriously. When commenting on the reverse scenario—the wondrous survival of some individuals exposed to strong γ-radiation—the authors dispense with any special pleading and blankly state (p. 63):

> *It is equally difficult to explain the complete absence of radiation effects in a number of people who were theoretically exposed to lethal dosages of radiation.*

We note that Oughterson and Warren acknowledge the dilemma of ARS occurring among those beyond the reach of the bomb's radiation, while failing to appear in some of those exposed to a 'theoretically lethal' dose. Adjusting dose estimates will not solve this dilemma: increasing doses may avoid the Scylla of death despite protection, but it will wreck the ship on the Charybdis of inexplicable survival; assuming lower doses to explain miraculous survival will make the deaths of shielded victims all the more incomprehensible.

8.7 ARS in people who were outside Hiroshima at the time of the bombing

The occurrence of ARS symptoms in persons who were outside Hiroshima on the day of the bombing, but who entered the zone within 1 km of the hypocenter afterwards, is a crucial piece of evidence. While anecdotal reports are found in many sources [12, 14, 16, 32, 62], the only statistical survey on this question is the one by Gensaku Oho; and it is telling that we owe this crucial study to the personal initiative of this energetic doctor from Hiroshima and his student volunteers, rather than to the official institutions created and maintained for such investigations by the governments of the United States and of Japan.

Oho's most important findings are summarized in Figure 8.3. Many people entering the area within 1 km of the hypocenter report symptoms of ARS; the percentage of people thus affected exceeds 50% among those who stayed for more than 2 days. Additional tables and figures presented by Sutou [34] clearly document that the same effect is also present among those who were in Hiroshima during the bombing: while of course many in this group suffered ARS regardless of their whereabouts in the aftermath, the incidence is higher among those who also came near the hypocenter in that period.[10]

Findings such as those reported by Oho can, of course, not be explained with the radiation released during the detonation. There are three ways of dealing with this problem:

---

[10]The text in reference [34] states distances from the 'epicenter'; however, in direct correspondence, the author confirmed that the intended meaning is 'the ground site right under the detonation', for which the term 'hypocenter' is conventionally used.

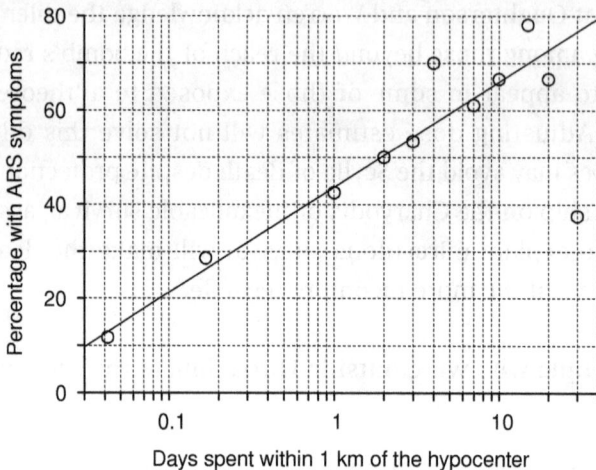

Figure 8.3: Symptoms of ARS in 525 persons who were outside Hiroshima during the bombing, but who came within 1 km of the hypocenter in the aftermath, as a function of time spent in that area. Data from Table 7 in [34]. The regression line was fitted with weighting for sample size. Symptoms of ARS include fever, diarrhea, bloody stools, bleeding from the mucous membranes, loss of hair, and generalized weakness.

1. The findings are ascribed to fallout or residual radiation, which are assumed to have been much greater than conventional or official estimates [34, 158, 159].
2. The findings are declared to 'warrant further analysis' and then studiously ignored [36, p. 90].
3. The findings are ignored without ceremony. If you guessed that this is the most common approach, you are indeed correct.

The last two alternatives require no further comment. Regarding the first one, it was shown earlier that real fallout must have been lower, not higher than the official estimates, and there is no basis whatsoever for higher estimates of neutron-induced radioactivity.[11]

The thesis of this book—namely, that sulfur mustard, not radiation was the cause of 'ARS'—provides a ready explanation for cases of the

---

[11] It is remarkable how two mutually exclusive narratives—harmful radiation released in the blast only, and major contribution from fallout or induced radiation—have co-existed peacefully for many decades in the literature. In this field of 'research', hard questions are never answered, but dodged and deferred forever—if need be, as in this case, through the use of Orwellian doublethink.

disease among late entrants to the city. Sulfur mustard is known to linger, and its persistent stench was noted by Burchett four weeks after the bombing [16]. Wind-driven mustard fumes would explain why those located downwind from the hypocenter suffered more ARS [158] and were at greater risk of developing cancer [160, 161]. While Yamada and Jones [158] ascribe the surplus incidence of ARS in this group to high β-radiation from isotopes contained in the black rain, the very low levels of ^{137}Cs in extant black rain samples [6] clearly disprove their explanation.[12]

8.8 Late-onset ARS

In patients who suffered ARS due to exposure only after the bombing, the symptoms should develop with some delay; and this is indeed reflected in the statistics reported by Oughterson et al. [33].

Characteristic symptoms of ARS hematopoetic syndrome (see Section 8.2.1) are purpura, caused by the failure of the blood platelets, and oropharyngeal ulcers due to bacterial and fungal infections, which are brought on by the lack of granulocytes. In patients who exhibit these symptoms after exposure to a single dose of irradiation, they become manifest between days 8 and 28, with shorter latency at higher doses [149]. Figure 8.4 shows that this is also true of most Hiroshima bombing victims; however, in about 25%, the initial manifestation is delayed until the fifth week or later.[13] For illustration, the figure also shows the time course of platelet and granulocyte counts in patients exposed to irradiation after the reactor meltdown at Chernobyl. Both cell counts reach their lowest point before the 28th day, which explains that symptoms will be manifest by this time.

---

[12] The wind is said to have blown toward the west at Hiroshima [160]. Yamada and Jones [158] do not specify where in the city their black rain victims had been located. However, Masuda in [162] gives a detailed map, constructed from statements obtained from many survivors, which indicates that the black rain was most intense in the northwest.

While Peterson et al. [160] find cancer incidence increased in the west, Gilbert and Ohara [163] find acute radiation disease most abundant in the north, but below average in the west. ARS requires high doses, whereas cancer may be caused in a large enough population by lower doses also; therefore, the observed discrepancy suggests a fairly uneven distribution of the mustard gas.

[13] It is also interesting to note that oropharyngeal lesions are manifest in a considerable number of Hiroshima bombing victims in within the first week, and even on the first day. It seems likely that these very early lesions are due to direct, local action of inhaled or ingested sulfur mustard rather than to hematopoetic syndrome.

8 Statistical observations on acute 'radiation' sickness

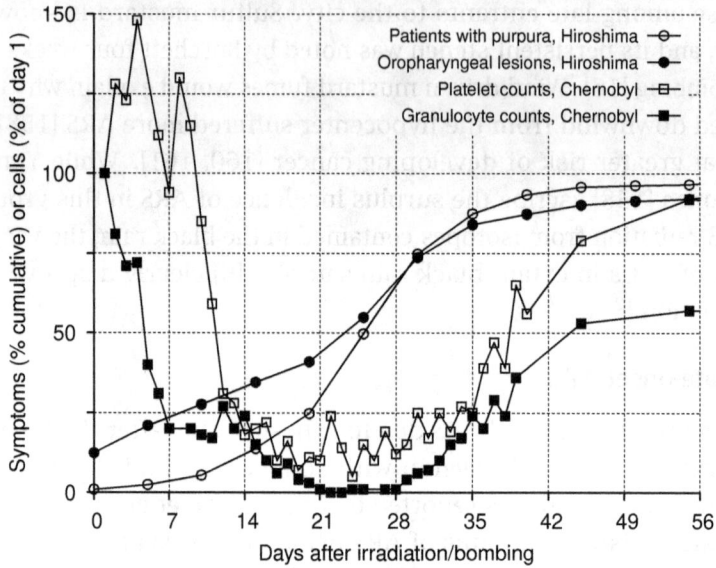

Figure 8.4: Time of onset of purpura and oropharyngeal lesions in Hiroshima bombing victims, and blood cell counts in accidentally irradiated patients. Data for onset of purpura (bleeding) and oropharyngeal lesions in Hiroshima victims from Table 17H in Oughterson et al. [33]; 100% is the total of all patients that exhibited the symptom at any time during the observation period. Platelet and granulocyte counts (from Fliedner et al. [164]) represent median values of 11 patients who were exposed to whole body irradiation at Chernobyl. Values are relative to those on day 1, which were in the normal range for both cell types.

Anecdotal evidence confirms the occurrence of late cases. For example, in his posthumously[14] published book *First into Nagasaki* [166], the American journalist George Weller notes on September 22nd:

> *New cases of atomic bomb poisoning with an approximate fifty percent death rate are still appearing at Nagasaki's hospital six weeks after the blow fell ... Whereas formerly twenty patients a day with dwindling hair and their bone marrow affected were coming to Japanese hospitals, the rate is now fallen to about ten.*

---

[14]MacArthur had declared both Hiroshima and Nagasaki out of bounds for civilians, but, just like Burchett sneaked into Hiroshima [16, 165], Weller stole into Nagasaki. Unlike Burchett, however, Weller still dutifully filed his reports with MacArthur's censors, who promptly prohibited their publication. Weller did retain a copy, which was found in his estate by his son, who edited and finally published it in 2007.

The decreasing, yet still ongoing observation of new cases agrees with the data in Figure 8.4. While from this limited information we cannot be sure whether the death rate in new cases was indeed falling, this would be plausible in real ARS [149] and similarly also in mustard gas poisoning. What is *not* plausible in true ARS, however, is the repeated occurrence of new cases, particularly ones with fatal outcome, as late as six weeks after the exposure. These patients must have taken in the poison some time after the bombings, probably in a cumulative fashion, just like some of the subjects surveyed by Oho [34].[15]

8.9 ARS symptoms and official radiation dose estimates

You may have seen studies on atomic bomb survivors that correlate some biological outcome such as cancer with individual radiation doses. The question of dosimetry will be discussed in Chapter 11, which also shows a graph which correlates the incidence of ARS symptoms radiation doses (Figure 11.1B on page 224). The correlation is obviously very poor, and the dose-response curve is wildly implausible biologically, as can be seen by comparison with proper data shown in Figure 11.1A.

The data set from which Figure 11.1B was constructed contains radiation doses at higher resolution than depicted in the figure. If we plot a histogram of the number of people grouped by the individual dose values in the file, we see that the dataset contains no cases with estimated doses above 6 Gy (Figure 8.5 A). However, the number of people with an assigned dose of exactly 6.000 Gy greatly exceeds that of any other individual dose value above 3 Gy; in fact, only below 1 Gy do we find dose values with higher head counts than 6 Gy exactly. This peculiar pattern strongly suggests that all raw dose estimates higher than 6 Gy were simply truncated at that value; probably because they were deemed unsurvivable, and quite possibly under the impression of the rhesus monkey experiments shown in Figure 11.1A. It should go without saying that such sausage-making does not qualify as science. Furthermore, whether truncated or not, in this highest of all dose

---

[15] Poison in the air was noticeable for several weeks after the bombings also at Nagasaki. Tatsuichiro Akizuki, a Nagasaki physician, vividly describes how a heavy rainstorm pelted yet cleansed the city on September 2nd and 3rd [167, p.135]: "I looked up at the sky and shouted: 'Don't punish them this way—it is too much! Haven't you done enough?' ... The 4 September turned out to be a fine, cool, autumn day. ... 'Something has happened!' I said to Miss Murai. 'I feel there's a change in the air—I'm sure of it.' ... 'That's it!' I said to myself. The poison has been washed away!'"

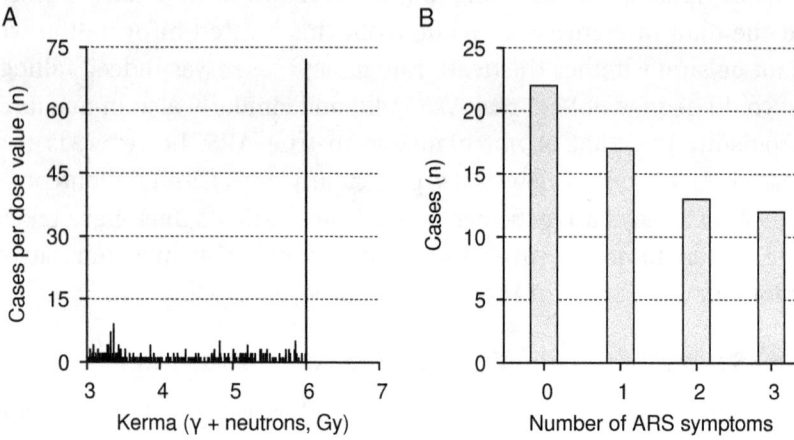

Figure 8.5: Numbers of survivors grouped by dose values (A), and incidence of ARS symptoms among those assigned an estimated dose of 6 Gy (B). In RERF's dataset [168], one or more symptoms were given as 'not reported' for 8 out of the 72 survivors with exactly 6.000 Gy; these subjects are included in A but excluded in B.

groups, the number of individuals with 0 or only one symptom of ARS exceeds that with two or more symptoms (Figure 8.5B). The 22 individuals without any symptoms clearly count among Warren's and Oughterson's mystery patients with 'complete absence of radiation effects' in spite of exposure to 'theoretically lethal' doses of radiation.

The findings presented in this section reinforce our previous observation that the distribution of ARS does not fit the official story of the bomb and its radiation. We will revisit the question of purported radiation doses and biological effects in Chapters 11 and 12.

8.10 Diarrhea as an early symptom of ARS

Before leaving this topic, one recurrent motif in the reports on 'radiation sickness' from Hiroshima and Nagasaki should be noted: the widespread and early occurrence of diarrhea, often bloody, among the patients. A graphic account is given by Michihiko Hachiya [62]. The author, a head physician who had been injured in the bombing and admitted as a patient to his own hospital, wrote in his diary on August 7th:

> *Everything was in disorder. And to make matters worse was the vomiting and diarrhea. Patients who could not walk urinated and defecated where they lay. Those who could walk would feel their way to the exits and relieve themselves there. Persons entering or leaving the hospital could not avoid stepping in the filth, so closely was it spread. The front entrance became covered with feces overnight, and nothing could be done for there were no bed pans and, even if there had been, no one to carry them to the patients.*
>
> *Disposing of the dead was a minor problem, but to clean the rooms and corridors of urine, feces, and vomitus was impossible.*

Such events would suggest an outbreak of some virulent enteric pathogen, which is indeed common in disaster situations; and Hachiya and his staff initially assumed this to be the case. Also on August 7th, Hachiya writes:

> *Dr. Hanaoka ... brought word that there were many who not only had diarrhea but bloody stools and that some had had as many as forty to fifty stools during the previous night.[16] This convinced me that we were dealing with bacillary dysentery and had no choice but to isolate those who were infected.*
>
> *Dr. Koyama, as deputy director, was given the responsibility of setting up an isolation ward.*

However, already on August 13th, he notes:

> *My conjecture that deaths were due to the effects of a germ bomb causing dysentery I had to discard because diarrhea and bloody stools were decreasing.*

Hachiya's conclusions are confirmed by the data given in Oughterson et al. [33], which show that both bloody and non-bloody diarrhea are strongly correlated with other ARS symptoms, and also that case numbers were highest early on and then declined (Figure 8.6), even though the hygienic conditions remained about as bad as can be imagined.

Diarrhea can indeed occur in real radiation sickness. However, it commonly occurs very early on only in patients who have received a dose of 6 Sv or greater [149]. Under the conditions then prevailing in

---

[16] Such cases are unlikely to have survived more than a few days, and they will therefore be missing from Oughterson's statistics.

8 Statistical observations on acute 'radiation' sickness

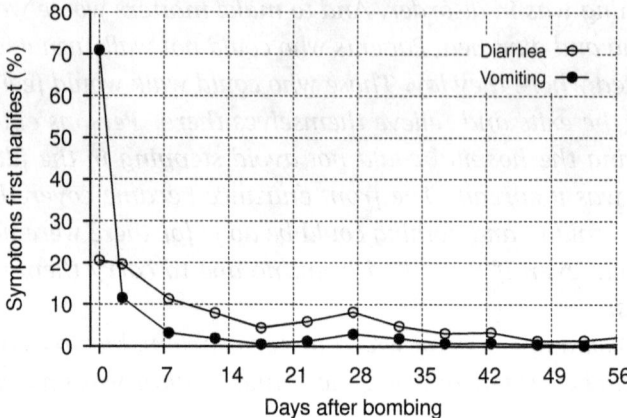

Figure 8.6: Time of onset of diarrhea and vomiting in Hiroshima bombing victims still alive 20 days after the bombing. Data from Table 17H in [33]. The first data point in each series represents the day of the bombing.

Hiroshima and Nagasaki, patients hit with such a high dose would not have survived. Yet, the data listed by Oughterson et al. [33] pertain to patients who were alive 20 days after the bombing, and 96% of whom remained alive when the study concluded several months later (see Section 8.4.2), which means that they were not lethally irradiated. Thus, the timing of diarrhea observed in Hiroshima also indicates that the reported radiation sickness was not actually caused by radiation. On the other hand, early onset diarrhea has been described in multiple reports on mustard gas exposure of humans and of experimental animals (see Section 7.3.5).

8.11 The curse of the pharaohs

Many of the data presented in this chapter were drawn from the report of the Joint Commission [33], and we saw that these data contain clear evidence against nuclear detonations as the cause of ARS in Hiroshima and Nagasaki. We thus might wonder what the commission's members, most of whom were physicians, were really thinking while they assembled their data. The only first-hand account by any of them which I have found is that by the pathologist Averill Liebow [77]. The author offers many interesting glimpses into the conditions of the work, but he does not betray any doubt or puzzlement concerning its scientific findings. However, writing originally in 1965, Liebow notes:

It is true that few who took part are left to tell ... Indeed it is as though some curse, like that which the superstitious say fell upon Lord Carnarvon and his men when they violated the tomb of Pharaoh Tut-ankh-amen, has been visited upon those who pried into the ravaged heart of Hiroshima. Only three of the seven American medical officers live. Drs. Oughterson and Tsuzuki, the chief organizers for the two countries, have died; so too, while still young, have Drs. Calvin Koch, Jack D. Rosenbaum, and Milton R. Kramer. May this record do honor to these able and devoted men.

Liebow's analogy surely is intriguing. We will, however, leave it for others to pursue, lest we be accused of superstition.

9 Skin burns in survivors

> This boy, age nineteen, sustained burns ... secondary to the explosion of an incendiary bomb. These lesions are entirely comparable to those seen in atomic bomb survivors.
>
> Melvin Block and Masao Tsuzuki [169]

The literature ascribes most of the burns observed in survivors of the 'atomic' bombings to the flash of the detonations. It will be shown here that this interpretation meets with numerous difficulties:

- In Hiroshima, the incidence of severe burns was greatest at a distance of between 2 and 2.5 km from the hypocenter. At this range, the intensity of the flash should have been only $1/8$ of that at a distance of 1 km.
- Many 'flash burns' occurred in skin areas covered by clothes, and in some cases even underneath clothes that remained intact after the 'flash'.
- The outlines of hypertrophic scars (keloids) left behind by the burns are often discontinuous and completely irregular—partial shielding by clothes cannot explain such patterns.
- Proper flash burns should be manifest immediately. While this is indeed true for some of the observed burns—presumably those caused by napalm—others became manifest only after a significant delay, which is typical of the chemical burns caused by mustard gas.

Overall, therefore, the evidence clearly rejects the traditionally accepted interpretation of survivors' burns as 'flash burns'. In contrast, the observations are well explained by the combined effects of napalm and mustard gas.

Disfiguring scars of the skin have a prominent place in Hiroshima and Nagasaki lore. These lesions are mostly ascribed to the 'flash burns' caused by light from the 'ball of fire,' which is said to have formed during the first second of the nuclear detonation [90]. One might wonder why, among the various physical effects accompanying a nuclear detonation, only the flash of light is considered in this context. Can we rule out ionizing radiation as a possible cause of skin burns?

When animals are experimentally irradiated with γ-, X-, or neutron rays at doses that are lethal due to their effect on the bone marrow or other sensitive organs, the skin nevertheless shows little evidence of injury [26, p. 44 ff.]. Thus, if someone survives a nuclear detonation by 20 days or beyond, as is the case with the group of victims surveyed by the Joint Commission [33], we can infer that any major skin burns could not have been caused by γ- or neutron rays from the bomb. Preferential damage to the skin can indeed be brought about by β-rays (see [26] and Section 2.7.1). Radionuclides in the fallout must have given off some β-radiation, but only at levels too low to cause acute injury.[1] Thus, the only mechanism that remains for the causation of skin burns by nuclear bombs is indeed thermal radiation.

It is worth noting that a nuclear detonation releasing a flash of light as intense as purportedly occurred in the bombings should indeed have caused flash burns. This is confirmed by experimental studies, some of which are discussed in Section 9.6. However, as we will see in this chapter, many features of the observed burns show that they cannot have been caused in this manner; the evidence points instead to napalm and to mustard gas as the true causes of many of these burns.

9.1 Classification of skin burns

Before we dig into the evidence, a few words about terminology are in order. Skin burns can be classified according to the cause and, independently, according to severity.

9.1.1 Causes of burns. These include contact (hot objects or liquids, napalm), chemicals (sulfuric acid, mustard gas), and thermal radiation. Although all of the major causes that we will consider here—flash burns, napalm, and mustard gas—fit into this classification, they all differ from more commonplace causes encountered in everyday life.

---

[1] Yamada and Jones [158] report 'obvious' effects of alleged high β-doses in a relatively small group of Hiroshima victims who had been exposed to black rain. However, these authors don't report skin burns, but instead base their claim on epilation and mucosal symptoms; and they disregard that these victims also exhibited purpura, which is a clear sign of bone marrow damage and could only have been caused by more penetrating forms of radiation.

Mustard gas burns develop more slowly than those with some widely used caustic chemicals, such as strong acids (sulfuric or hydrochloric acid) or bases (lye). The delayed onset of its effect makes mustard gas particularly treacherous. This is illustrated by the casualties of the Bari incident (Section 1.4.5): the victims did not perceive any pain shortly after exposure, and many neglected to change their contaminated clothes before the night, only to awake to severe skin burns on the morning after [22].

Napalm burns may be classified as contact burns. However, in this case the combustible material is designed to stick together in sizable chunks that adhere to target surfaces [141], which means that the amount of heat transferred to those surfaces will be unusually high. Thus, compared to conventional contact burns, napalm burns tend to be particularly severe [142, 170].

Nuclear flash burns are a special case of burns caused by thermal radiation. Here, the energy is delivered in a particularly brief and intense pulse, which means that the heat absorbed by the skin has no time to dissipate toward the tissues beneath, but instead causes very high temperatures within a thin superficial layer. Investigators have found ways to emulate such high intensity flashes; the results of some such studies are detailed in Section 9.6.

9.1.2 Severity of burns. Burn severity is expressed in degrees:

- first degree burns show irritation and erythema (reddening), but no damage to the anatomical skin structure;
- in a second degree burn, a superficial layer of the skin detaches to form a blister. Usually, the skin underneath can regrow from deep-set patches within hair follicles or sweat glands and heal quickly, with minor scarring or without it;
- a third degree burn destroys the entire depth of the skin. The wound is closed by new skin growing inwards from the periphery, and a scar will form;
- a fourth degree burn includes significant injury to tissues beneath the skin.

All manifest burns should be painful to some degree. Volunteers who received experimental first or second degree flash burns uniformly reported instantaneous pain (see Section 9.6). Third and fourth degree burns will destroy the nerve endings of the skin together with the skin itself, which may alter pain quality and intensity; however, as long as the victims remain conscious, they should still perceive some sort of pain, originating from pain receptors in the most superficial layer of tissue that remains viable. With chemical burns, however, pain will often not be perceived in the instant of contact with the chemical, but only after the chemical has penetrated the skin and a damaging chemical reaction has had time to occur. As noted above, with mustard gas in particular the manifestation of visible lesions and the perception of pain tend to be delayed.

9.2 Statistical observations on burns in Hiroshima and Nagasaki

9.2.1 Flash burns vs. flame burns. When the survivors studied in each city by the Joint Commission (see Section 8.4) were grouped by distance from the hypocenter, the highest incidence of burns of any kind in any of the groups was 47.3% (see Tables 8H and 8N in [33]). Up to 1.4% of all victims were diagnosed with only flame burns, and up to 32.6% with only flash burns. Up to 7.3% were listed with both flame and flash burns, while the cause of the burns was stated as unknown in 9% of all cases. Thus, the majority of burns were considered flash burns, but the presence of some putative flame burns must be kept in mind.

9.2.2 Observed incidence of burns by distance from the hypocenter. Figure 9.1A shows the intensity of the thermal radiation as a function of distance from the hypocenters.[2] Within 1 km of the hypocenter, these intensities would have exceeded anything that has been tried in experiments on human volunteers or animals (see Section 9.6); however, we can extrapolate that such doses should cause burns of at least the third degree. Overall, considering the postulated intensities and the experimental findings, we should expect the following features in the distribution of flash burns about the hypocenter:

- the number and severity of flash burns should have been greatest near the hypocenter. With increasing distance from it, both incidence and severity should have decreased;
- within 1 km of the hypocenter, most flash burns should have been of third or fourth degree. Lower degrees should only have occurred

---

[2]The table in the reference contains, for each city, two slightly different estimates for different assumed atmospheric visibilities, of which Figure 9.1A shows the averages.

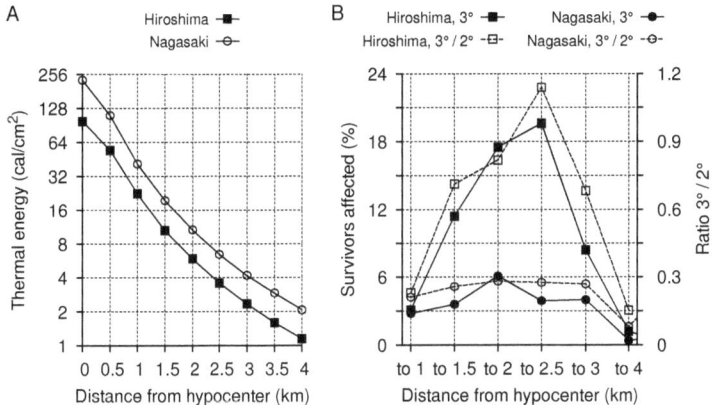

Figure 9.1: Radiant heat and incidence of burns as functions of distance from the hypocenters at Hiroshima and Nagasaki. A: radiant heat (calories per cm^2) vs. distance from hypocenter. Data from Ishikawa et al. [8]. B: Incidence of third degree burns in victims remaining alive after 20 days, by distance from the hypocenter, and ratio of incidence of third degree burns to that of second degree burns. Patients who had both second and third degree burns were counted only in the latter category. Data from Tables 9H and 9N in [33].

with attenuation by at least two layers of clothing or some equivalent partial protection;

- burns should have been more severe in Nagasaki than in Hiroshima, or at least not less so.

Figure 9.1B shows that none of these expectations corresponds to observation. The incidence of third degree burns grows from the hypocenter towards a maximum at 2 or 2.5 km, respectively. In Hiroshima at least, this increase is so pronounced that it cannot plausibly be explained by the statistical noise from flame burns.[3] To judge burn severity, we can look at the ratio of third degree burns to second degree burns. In Hiroshima, this ratio also increases substantially between 1 and 2.5 km. In Nagasaki, neither trend is very pronounced, but both the incidence of third degree burns and the burn severity are strikingly

---

[3] If we ascribe all third degree burns to patients with flash burns only within 1 km, but the minimum possible number between 2 and 2.5 km, then the incidence of third degree burns in patients with flash burn only drops to 22.3% within 1 km and remains at 22.1% between 2 and 2.5 km. Thus, even this extreme scenario fails to show the expected decrease in burn severity.

9 Skin burns in survivors

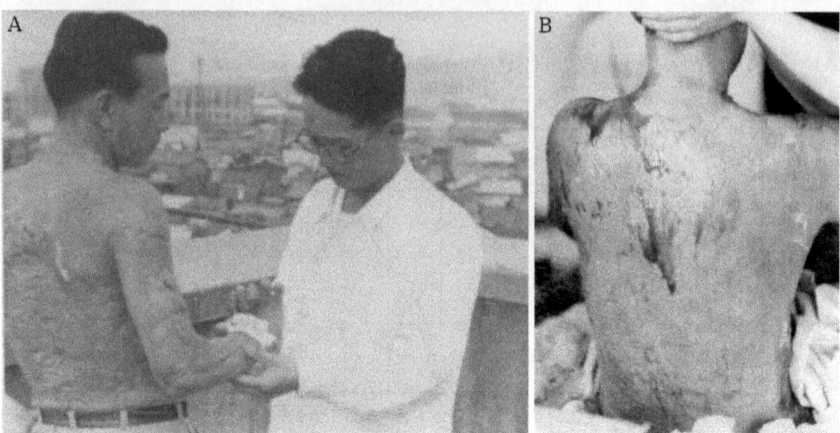

Figure 9.2: Burns of the skin limited to areas that had been covered with clothing. A: keloids subsequent to 'flash burn' in a bombing victim receiving treatment at Hiroshima's Red Cross Hospital, several years after the bombing [171]. The physician pictured is Dr. Terufumi Sasaki, who is portrayed in John Hersey's book *Hiroshima* [7]. B: chemical burn in an American mustard gas factory worker [109].

lower than in Hiroshima, even though the bomb yield, and therefore the thermal radiation, are said to have been greater in Nagasaki.

9.2.3 Flash burns in skin areas covered by clothes. Clothes should afford partial protection from flash burns (see Section 9.6). Since dark clothes will absorb heat more readily than white or light ones, we might expect flash burns in covered areas to be more common with dark clothes. The numbers stated in Table 13 in [33] support such a relationship: those wearing colored clothes more often had burns in covered areas in addition to uncovered ones.[4] With neither white nor colored clothes, though, should we expect any burns to occur in the covered areas *only*, without any burns in the exposed skin. However, the scars left by just such a burn are seen in Figure 9.2A. The scars cover almost the entire upper body and the arms of the victim, but none are visible above the collar line. A strikingly similar distribution is observed in panel B, which shows a victim of mustard gas exposure;

---

[4]This is a rare example of an observation that is indeed most readily explained by the orthodox story of nuclear detonations, which I urge its believers to duly celebrate. However, these burns are not grouped by distance from the hypocenter; colors may have differed between inner city and surrounding districts. The number of layers of clothes in either group is also unknown.

we note only some dark pigmentation, but no deep lesions on the back of the neck.[5] For further examples of the same effect in alleged nuclear flash burns, see [77, 169, 172]. Moreover, Oughterson et al. [33] state in their Table 13 that 5.4% of all burn victims in Hiroshima, and 9% of those in Nagasaki, had burns in the clothed area only.

Whatever the color or thickness of the clothes, they would have to be burned away by the radiant heat first in order to reach the skin underneath. Nevertheless, some burns apparently occurred underneath the intact clothing. Eyewitness Mr. Hashimoto relates giving first aid to a girl with burns on her backside, as quoted by Hachiya [62]:

> *I ... began painting [with mercurochrome] the wounds of a girl dressed in* monpe *[pants] ... Her wounds were mostly on her buttocks and these I found hard to bandage, for when she stood up the bandage slipped off. ... Finally, I gave up and in desperation pulled down her monpe, and after repainting her wounds, pulled up her monpe and put the bandages on right over them.*

From this account, it is quite clear that this girl still *had* her pants, yet had suffered burns underneath them, in a location that is commonly affected by sulfur mustard, as moist skin areas generally are (see [109] and Figure 7.6).

Finally, while I have not seen any experimental studies on the subject, I surmise that the layer of sturdy hair that covers the skin of a horse should provide substantial protection from flash burns. Nevertheless, there are multiple reports of horses having suffered burns as well, for example this one by eyewitness Akihiro Takahashi [156, p. 193]:

> *... a horse, only raw flesh, lying dead with its head in a cistern.*

While we cannot be sure about the cause of such burns in every single instance, a plausible one is mustard gas, which should penetrate hair and fur just as readily as it penetrates clothing. Mustard gas lesions in horses were indeed noted in World War I (see Figure 7.6).

---

[5]The mustard-exposed patient in the picture was initially treated with oil-based unguents ('the grease method'), causing gangrenous infection; he improved after his treatment was switched to aqueous disinfectants. Father Arrupe, a Jesuit priest and physician who treated a number of burned patients in Hiroshima, thought that the oil treatment administered by Japanese physicians promoted infections and subsequent keloids [171]. Keloid often follows napalm burns [142]; its likelihood in mustard gas burns I was unable to ascertain. In any case, while both napalm and mustard gas might cause burns restricted to clothed areas, this is implausible with flashes of light.

9 Skin burns in survivors 178

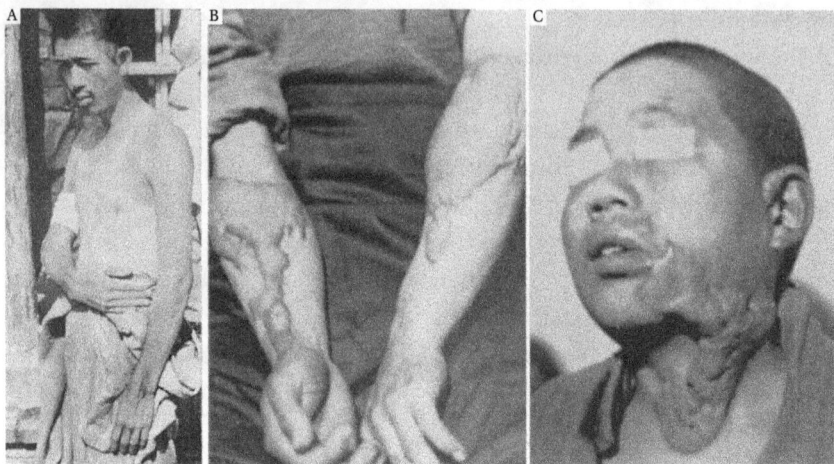

Figure 9.3: Skin lesions in Hiroshima bombing victims ascribed to 'flash burn'. A: general erythema and local hyperpigmentation of exposed skin in a man exposed at 2.4 km from the hypocenter; photographed on October 11th 1945. Taken from Oughterson and Warren [146, p. 147]. B and C: keloids (hypertrophic scar tissue) in two patients exposed at 1.3 and 1.7 km, respectively, from the hypocenter. Taken from Block and Tsuzuki [169].

Overall, therefore, the manifestations of burns in covered skin observed in Hiroshima and Nagasaki do not fit the pattern expected of true flash burns.

9.2.4 Irregular shapes of flash burns. Much like a sunburn, a flash burn should affect the exposed areas of skin quite evenly. Figure 9.3A shows the expected distribution; however, part of the skin shows fresh erythema, even though this picture was taken only on October 11th, that is, more than two months after the bombing. While experimental flash burns of low or moderate severity indeed initially manifest as erythema, they progress within days either to heal without defect, or to first shed the damaged skin and then heal, possibly with some degree of scarring (see Section 9.6). Thus, the erythema visible on October 11th could not have been caused by the bombing on August 6th. We can speculate, but cannot prove, that this fresh sunburn was staged and photographed as a welcome present for the Joint Commission that arrived in Hiroshima on the following day.

Panels B and C of Figure 9.3 show keloid or hypertrophic scar tissue formed in lesions ascribed to flash burns.[6] The lesions have highly irregular shapes that cannot plausibly be explained with any sort of partial cover by clothing or shielding. Nevertheless, such irregular shapes are typical of 'flash burn' illustrations in both general and medical references; the more regular pattern shown in panel A is the exception.[7]

The irregular shape was noted by early observers. Shigetoshi Wakaki, a Japanese military officer who was involved in weapons research and development, and who entered Hiroshima shortly after the bombing, notes [173, p. 88]:

The greater the distance from the centre, the greater the proportion of those who had freckle burns.[8] This made it difficult to explain the burns simply by radiant heat ... at least some part of the cause was something other than radiant heat.

Additional evidence to prove that the lesions could not possibly have been caused in the claimed manner will be introduced in Section 10.2. For now, we will dismiss the idea of nuclear flash burns and turn to the more interesting question of what the *real* causes of the observed burns may have been.

9.3 Fast and slow burns

If one surveys multiple eyewitness reports, a dichotomy emerges between burns that became manifest immediately after the bombing and those that developed more slowly. We will here quote one illustra-

---

[6] There is some difference of opinion on whether or not keloids are the same as hypertrophic scars. The reference from which these pictures were taken [169] lumps them together; in the present context, we have no need to settle this question.

[7] The reference from which the photograph in panel A is taken [146] claims it to show 'pigmentation', but pigmentation is pronounced only on the wrists, whereas on most of the arms it is suggestive of a sun tan. (The original picture in [146] is colored and shows both tanned and sun-burnt skin areas.) Much of the visibly colored skin is red, not brown; and the authors, both ivy league professors of medicine, were surely aware that humans don't produce red skin pigment.

[8] I have not seen the term 'freckle burns' used anywhere else; it seems possible that 'patchy burns' might have been a more apt translation. In any case, it is clear that Wakaki's unusual term refers to some kind of irregular, discontinuous burned area.

I should add that Wakaki nevertheless managed to satisfy himself that the story of the nuclear bombing, which was given out in military circles very early on, is indeed true overall, even though he questions it in many details.

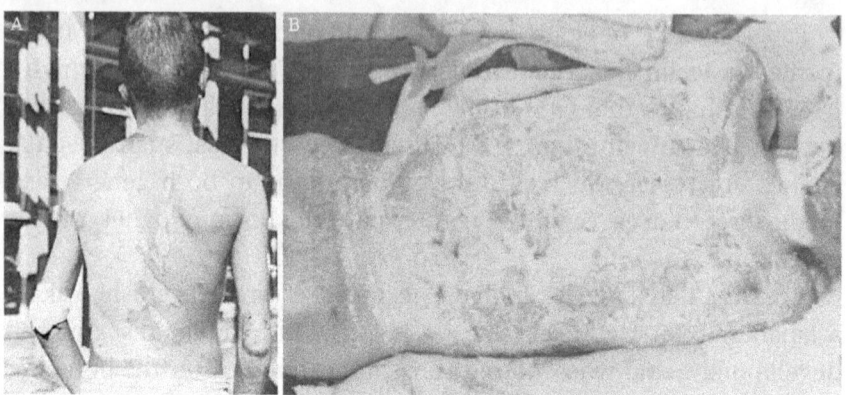

Figure 9.4: Two cases of 'nuclear flash burn' from Nagasaki. Photographs from [146], taken in October. A: This man was wearing a khaki uniform when exposed in the open at 0.5 miles from the hypocenter. (He should have died of radiation sickness within days.). The pattern of hypo- and hyperpigmentation on his back suggests second degree burns, perhaps due to mustard gas, while the thick scar tissue on his right elbow suggests a more severe burn, possibly by napalm. B: Extensive burns in a man 1.2 miles from the hypocenter. The details given in [146] suggest that this man is Sumiteru Taniguchi (see text).

tive example for each. Sumiteru Taniguchi of Nagasaki [156, p. 113] suffered burns immediately:

> *The wind from the blast, coming from behind, hurled me and my bicycle to the ground ... I think two or three minutes passed before the earth stopped trembling and I heaved myself up. ... The skin of my left arm had peeled from the upper arm to the tips of my fingers and was hanging in strips. When I felt my back and buttocks, I found that the skin there had been burned to a pulp and that only the front part of the clothes I had been wearing remained.*

The burns to Taniguchi's backside were indeed extensive (see Figure 9.4 B), and he had to lie with his face down for more than a year until the wounds finally began to heal, ultimately with severe scarring and keloid formation.

An instance of delayed skin injury in a bombing victim is described by the physician Michihiko Hachiya [62]. In his diary, he notes between August 6th and August 8th:

(6th) *I opened my eyes; Dr. Sasada was feeling my pulse. What had happened? ... I must have fainted.*

(7th) *Dr. Sasada, who had looked after me yesterday, lay on my left. I had thought he escaped injury, but now I could see that he was badly burned. His arms and hands were bandaged and his childish face obscured by swelling ...*

(8th) *Dr. Sasada's face was more swollen this morning than yesterday, and blood-stained pus oozed from his bandaged arms and hands. I felt a wave of pity when I thought how he had used those hands to help me two days ago.*

Further on in his diary, Hachiya reports how Dr. Sasada later develops symptoms of bone marrow suppression, but ultimately recovers. From Hachiya's description, it is apparent that Sasada's hands were injured not in the bombing itself; he could not have felt Hachiya's (presumably faint and rapid) pulse with wounded, bandaged hands. His burns sprung up only after he had tended to many victims who, like Hachiya himself, had been more severely injured outright.[9]

Mr. Taniguchi's immediately manifest burns and tattered clothes strongly suggest that he was hit directly with some sort of incendiary, most likely napalm. In contrast, the most straightforward explanation for Dr. Sasada's delayed burns is that, by touching the skin and clothes of his patients who had been contaminated with sulfur mustard, he was himself exposed to toxic quantities of it. His swollen face and subsequent symptoms of bone marrow suppression are likewise suggestive of mustard gas exposure.

The limited available data do not permit us to estimate the relative abundance of each type of burn; we will therefore merely discuss qualitatively the evidence which leads us to attribute them to napalm and to mustard gas, respectively.

9.4 Evidence of napalm burns

According to his description of his own travails on August 6th, Hachiya himself, like Mr. Taniguchi, was most likely burned by napalm, possibly

---

[9] On August 14th, Hachiya notes in his diary statement by another colleague, Dr. Hinoi, to the effect that "Dr. Sasada's hands were badly burned and he remembers them catching on fire. He remembered nothing else though." This is obviously at variance with Hachiya's own recollection.

9 Skin burns in survivors

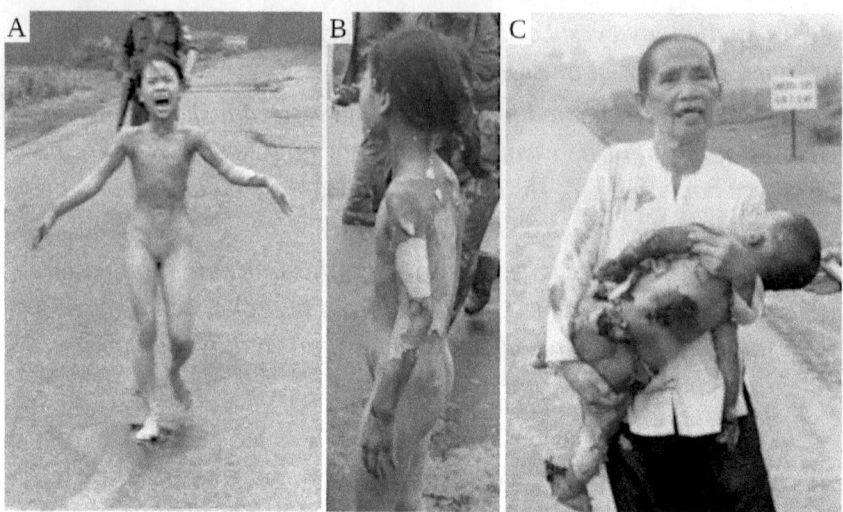

Figure 9.5: Victims of the napalm attack at Trang Bang, South Vietnam, on June 8th 1972. A: Minutes after the bombing, a girl in the nude (Kim Phuc) is running toward a group of photographers. B: She has severe burns, whose full extent is apparent only from behind. C: Kim's grandmother is carrying her grandchild Danh, Kim's cousin, who is extensively burned and will die within the hour. Scorched skin is peeling from his foot and backside.

with some additional mustard lesions as well. As he struggles towards the hospital, bereft of his clothes, he observes:

> *Others moved as though in pain, like scarecrows, their arms held out from their bodies with forearms and hands dangling. These people puzzled me until I suddenly realized that they had been burned and were holding their arms out to prevent the painful friction of raw surfaces rubbing together. A naked woman carrying a naked baby came into view. I averted my gaze. Perhaps they had been in the bath. But then I saw a naked man, and it occurred to me that, like myself, some strange thing had deprived them of their clothes.*

Have we seen something like this anywhere else? Considering the widespread use of napalm—large amounts were dropped on Japan, and even larger ones on Korea and Vietnam—generally accessible information on napalm is extremely scarce (see Section 7.4). However, there is one very widely known picture of a napalm victim: Kim Phuc, a Vietnamese girl who in 1972 suffered burns when her village in South

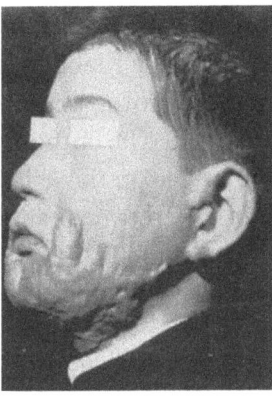

Figure 9.6: Splash burn to the face and neck caused by napalm and gasoline. This picture appears as Figure 7 in Block and Tsuzuki [169].

Vietnam was attacked by the country's own air force (the village had been infiltrated by the Vietcong). This picture (Figure 9.5A) shows her running in the nude, in the 'scarecrow' posture also described by Hachiya. The real extent of her burns is only visible from another angle (Figure 9.5B), which also reveals the immediate peeling of the skin. Peeling and flapping skin are likewise apparent in Kim's even more severely burned cousin Danh (Figure 9.5C). While the little boy died within an hour of the attack, Kim survived. Even with expert surgical treatment, however, her burn wounds turned into extensive scars that resemble the keloids shown in Figure 9.3.

The pronounced tendency of 'nuclear flash burns' to heal with keloid formation has often been noted; Harada [174] cites figures of > 70% for burns and > 20% for injuries from a reference in Japanese. The same is true of napalm burns. According to the Russian physician Plaksin [142], keloid formation was observed in 52.7% of all patients in a series of 1026 Korean napalm burn patients. The author ascribes this to the high amount of heat transferred from the burning napalm to the adjacent tissues.

While pictures of victims with 'nuclear flash burns' abound, those of napalm burns from conventionally firebombed Japanese cities such as Tokyo are surprisingly hard to find, even though survivors with napalm burns should have been common enough. I have only found one such picture, which is shown here as Figure 9.6. According to the source

[169],[10] the victim was burned in an incendiary bombing raid on Tokyo when burning napalm hit a nearby fuel barrel, causing it to explode. The effect of burning gasoline on the skin would have been similar to that of burning napalm itself. The authors state explicitly that his lesions were 'entirely comparable' to those in atomic bomb survivors, and also that they saw more than twenty similarly afflicted bombing victims from Tokyo. In all likelihood, at least some of those patients had been struck by napalm directly rather than by burning gasoline.

In summary, the evidence strongly suggests that those of the burns in Hiroshima and Nagasaki that were manifest immediately, accompanied by burning and stripping of clothes, and followed by keloid formation, were caused by napalm. While rare, explicit accounts of exposure to napalm or a similar substance can indeed be found. John Toland [76, p. 803] relates this experience of a boy in Nagasaki:

> *Hajime Iwanaga, who would be fourteen the next day, was bathing in the Urakami River near the torpedo factory. He ... exuberantly ducked his face in the water as the pika[11] flashed. Seconds later he emerged into a blinding world. Something warm clung to his left shoulder. It was yellowish. Mystified, he touched it and saw skin come off. He splashed toward the bank as the sky darkened ominously, and was reaching for his clothes when two dark-green spheres, the size of baseballs, streaked at him. One struck his shirt, set it afire, and disintegrated.*

Those green spheres carried fire, but did apparently not cause any harm through kinetic impact, which means that they consisted of some soft, incendiary material, much like napalm. The material on the shoulder may have been a chunk of napalm, too, that was extinguished

---

[10] The senior author of this study is the very same Dr. Masao Tsuzuki who had a run-in with American censors when giving voice to the widespread perception of poison gas at Hiroshima (see Section 1.4.4). When Tsuzuki published this study on flash burns, censorship was still in force, which may have influenced his restrained commentary on the great similarity of gasoline or napalm burns and nuclear flash burns.

Block and Tsuzuki state that 54.4% of all 'flash burn' patients had developed keloids, which is close to Plaksin's figure of 52.7% in Korean napalm victims.

[11] Hachiya [62] explains the term 'pika' as follows: "*Pika* means a glitter, sparkle. or bright flash of light, like a flash of lightning. *Don* means a boom! or loud sound. ... Those who remember the flash only speak of the '*pika*'; those who were far enough from the hypocenter to experience both speak of the '*pikadon*.'"

when the boy dived underwater. For comparison, here is Kim Phuc's recollection:

> *Her first memory of the engulfing fires was the sight of flames licking her left arm, where there was an ugly, brownish-black gob. She tried to brush it off, only to scream out at the pain of the burn that had now spread to the inside of her other hand.*

In both cases, the size and texture of the lumps of incendiary material described are consistent with those of napalm [141].

9.5 Chemical burns by mustard gas

In Section 1.4, we noted the similarity of skin lesions described by John Hersey in victims of the Hiroshima bombing to those observed by Alexander [22] in the mustard gas casualties at Bari. Eyewitness testimony from Hiroshima and Nagasaki further suggests that chemical burns to the skin by mustard gas were common. Kiyoko Sato, a girl from Hiroshima, had been evacuated to the countryside and returned to the city about a week after the bombing. Upon arrival, she finds her mother just a few moments after she has died [156, p. 55]:

> *If I had only walked a little faster, I would have been in time! I was distressed that I had not been able to see her alive and cried loudly. My mother's face was covered in blisters and had swollen to twice its normal size, and her hair had fallen out. She was unrecognizable as the mother I had known so well.*

A boy from Nagasaki, Yoshiro Yamawaki, walked across the city in search of his father on the day after the bombing, together with his twin brother [175]:

> *There were many dead bodies amongst the debris littering the roads. The faces, arms and legs of the dead had become swollen and discolored, causing them to look like black rubber dolls. As we stepped on the bodies with our shoes, the skin would come peeling off like that of an over-ripe peach, exposing the white fat underneath.*

Neither witness mentions any scorching of the dead bodies in question, and both descriptions match the known appearance of mustard gas burns.[12] We already noted above instances of burns becoming manifest only on the next day or occurring under clothing that remained intact; neither incendiaries nor flash burn can account for these observations. Having already considered the evidence that points to mustard gas as the cause of 'radiation disease', we now see that the expected skin lesions were prevalent also.

9.6 Appendix: experimental flash burns to the skin

The light intensities assumed to have been released by the bombings in Hiroshima and Nagasaki are shown in Figure 9.1 A. The surface temperature of the 'ball of light' at its most luminous stage should be in the range of 5000-7000 °K [90], which is similar to that of the sun. Therefore, the supposed atomic flash can be likened to a brief, intense pulse of sunlight, with similar proportions of ultraviolet, visible, and infrared light.

A number of experimental studies on animals and on human volunteers have attempted to model the flash burns produced by nuclear bombs. In a study on dogs [176], a thermal dose of 8 cal/cm² was applied to 20% of the body surface. Figure 9.1A shows that this intensity is well within the range of intensities expected near the hypocenter. Mortality was relatively low (2 dogs out of 30) and due to septicemia. The wounds appeared different from those caused by contact burns:

> *Following a flash burn of the magnitude given in this study, an eschar is formed on the burned surface. ... This initial eschar persists throughout ... Healing of the flash wound was usually complete by four weeks with the eschar acting as a protective dressing for epithelization from deep hair follicles and wound edges.*

These results suggest that peeling of the skin might not occur in nuclear flash burns. However, blistering lesions were observed in an experimental study on human volunteers [177]. At sufficiently high doses, a superficial skin layer came off one or two days after the irradiation and left behind a red, moist wound, which does resemble the observations of peeling skin in the bombing victims. This study

---

[12] Strictly speaking, the skin peeling off after a mustard burn would expose not the subcutaneous fat (as stated by the boy) but rather the layer of connective tissue above it (the dermis).

reports several more pertinent observations that we can compare with those made in those victims:

- A dose of 2 cal/cm² produced only a transient erythema, which typically subsided within half an hour. This represents a first degree burn.
- With doses of 3.9 cal/cm² and above, erythema of the lesion itself was immediate, and it persisted until it gave way to blisters, whereas the vicinity of the lesion showed delayed and transient erythema. Thus, any lesions of at least second degree are visible in some form immediately and throughout.
- The maximal dose given—4.8 cal/cm²—produced at least second degree burns in all volunteers, and third degree burns in some.
- While for obvious reasons the experimental flash burns were small (1.25 cm in diameter), it nevertheless was evident that the entire light-exposed area was evenly burned.
- The volunteers reported immediate pain, which was described as sharp or stinging and increased with the intensity of the flash.

Clothes should offer some protection against flash burns, although it is conceivable that at very high intensity the clothing might burn up, and enough heat might be left over to damage the skin underneath. A study by Mixter [178] used an animal model (pigs) to compare the doses required to set burns in nude skin to those required with skin areas covered by one or by two layers of fabric, respectively. With nude skin, the doses determined by Mixter are similar to those that had been determined in humans by Evans et al. [177].

While Mixter's data on the effect of clothing show some scatter, a reasonable approximation is that each layer of fabric raises the energy threshold for a burn by a factor of 2.5. Thus, burns beneath two layers of fabric—which can be assumed to have been present in most victims at least around the hips—would require about 6 times more energy than on exposed skin.

10 Early clinical and pathological findings in the bombing victims

> The use of poison gas is forbidden, but wasn't this suffering worse than poison gas?
>
> Yasuko Ise, high school student from Hiroshima [14]

In this chapter, we will scrutinize both eyewitness testimony and the medical literature in order to understand the symptoms observed in the bombing victims immediately or shortly after the event. Key observations include:

- early fatalities suffered acute lung damage, sometimes with secondary effects such as ocular compartment syndrome. These manifestations are compatible with mustard gas inhalation, but they have not been reported in accidental cases of extremely high and rapidly fatal irradiation;
- the medical literature on the bombing victims reports not a single case of acute retinal burns, which should have been common among those who reported having looked a the 'nuclear flash';
- pathological reports on internal organs in early fatalities, while scarce, nevertheless point to mustard gas rather than radiation as the underlying cause.

Overall, these findings reinforce the conclusions reached in the preceding chapters on acute radiation sickness and on skin burns.

Chapter 8 discussed the acute medical effects of the bombings from a quantitative, statistical point of view. In this chapter, we will look at them in more qualitative detail. The evidence available for this purpose is limited. In the hours and days following the bombings, chaos reigned, and none of those who died during this time received adequate diagnosis and treatment. Their sufferings and symptoms are described only in the scattered testimony of eyewitnesses, both laypersons and medical doctors, who were anguished as much by the apocalyptic scenes around them as by their inability to help.[1]

Important sources for this chapter include the recollections by two Japanese physicians. We already mentioned the diary by Michihiko Hachiya [62] from Hiroshima, a detailed account by an experienced, perceptive, and compassionate observer; this document should be read by anyone interested in the humanitarian dimension of the disaster. From Nagasaki, there is the report by Tatsuichiro Akizuki [167], a more junior physician, who unlike Hachiya was not himself incapacitated in the attack[2] and therefore was able to give more detailed observations on the victims immediately after the bombing.[3] The reports by Oughterson and colleagues [33, 146] will again be used. The one by Oughterson and Warren [146] includes a chapter by Liebow et al. on the autopsy material collected mostly by Japanese pathologists, which was published independently as a journal article elsewhere [42].

In addition to the above books and reports, which were all written by physicians or medical scientists, important detail can be found in eyewitness accounts by non-specialists. The compilations of such testimony by Osada [14] and by Sekimori [156] are particularly valuable.

10.1 Clinical picture in early fatalities

10.1.1 Symptoms apparent immediately after the bombing.
On the day of the Nagasaki bombing, Dr. Tatsuichiro Akizuki was on duty at his hospital in the Urakami district, 1800 m from the hypocenter. The building was damaged and partly destroyed by fire, but all of the staff and the patients quickly escaped and initially survived.

---

[1] Even though Japan had capitulated on August 15th—9 days after the bombing of Hiroshima, and 6 days after that of Nagasaki—the U.S. did not send any physicians or medical supplies at all to either city until September, and even then gave only meager support [153]. The purely investigative Joint Commission arrived only on October 12 h [77]. This prolonged failure to assist and to investigate seems to have been deliberate.

[2] At some later time, Akizuki did experience symptoms of ARS such as fatigue and loss of hair; admirably, however, he stayed with and cared for the patients under his watch throughout the entire time.

[3] Another physician's report from Nagasaki is that by Raisuke Shirabe, a professor of surgery at Nagasaki medical school [179]. While this chapter does not cite specific examples from this source, Shirabe describes multiple cases of acute burns, consistent with napalm, and also several victims without visible burns whose clinical course is consistent with mustard gas poisoning.

The attack had occurred at 11 a.m.; shortly afterwards, the first victims from outside began to arrive, seeking help:

About ten minutes after the explosion, a big man, half-naked, holding his head between his hands, came into the yard towards me ... 'Got hurt, sir,' he groaned; he shivered as if he were cold. 'I'm hurt.'

I stared at him, at the strange-looking man. Then I saw it was Mr. Zenjiro Tsujiomoto, a market gardener and a friendly neighbor to me and the hospital. I wondered what had happened to the robust Zenjiro. 'What's the matter with you, Tsujimoto?' I asked him, holding him in my arms.

'In the pumpkin field over there—getting pumpkins for the patients—got hurt...' he said, speaking brokenly and breathing feebly. It was all he could do to keep standing. Yet it didn't occur to me that he had been seriously injured.

'Come along now,' I said, 'You are perfectly all right. I assure you. Where's your shirt? Lie down and rest somewhere where it's cool. I'll be with you in a moment.'

His head and his face were whitish; his hair was singed. It was because his eyelashes had been scorched away that he seemed so bleary-eyed. He was half-naked because his shirt had been burned from his back in a single flash. ...

Another person who looked just like him wandered into the yard. ... 'Help me,' he said, groaning, half-naked, holding his head between his hands. He sat down, exhausted. 'Water ... Water ...' he whispered.

As time passed, more and more people in similar plight came up to the hospital—ten minutes, twenty minutes, an hour after the explosion. All were of the same appearance, sounded the same. 'I'm hurt, hurt! I'm burning! Water!' ... Half-naked or stark naked, they walked with strange, slow steps, groaning from deep inside themselves ... they looked whitish. ... One victim who managed to reach the hospital asked 'Is this a hospital?' before suddenly collapsing on the ground. ...

'Water, water' they cried. They went instinctively down to the banks of the stream [below the hospital], because their bodies had been scorched and their throats were parched and inflamed; they

were thirsty. I didn't realize then that these were the symptoms of 'flash burn.'

Thus far, Akizuki has described victims whom he had encountered within one hour or so of the attack. At this early stage, we can make the following observations:

- Akizuki does not immediately recognize his 'strange-looking' neighbor, which suggests that his features are already somewhat distorted. They will be much more so later in the day.
- He notices some signs of immediate burns—singed hair and eyelashes, as well as nudity (see Section 9.4).
- Akizuki does not describe any other outward signs of injury; instead, he reassures his suffering neighbor that he is alright.
- The victims speak hoarsely; their throats are 'parched and inflamed,' and they are thirsty; their breath is labored.
- The victims are pale and weak, and some collapse.
- The victims are holding their heads between their hands, suggesting that they have a severe headache.

10.1.2 Symptoms apparent after several hours. While the above observations capture the early stage of the injuries, the victims' aspect is strikingly transformed later on. Here is Akizuki's description:

In the afternoon a change was noticeable in the appearance of the injured people who came up to the hospital. The crowd of ghosts which had looked whitish in the morning were now burned black. Their hair was burnt; their skin, which was charred and blackened, blistered and peeled. Such were those who now came toiling up to the hospital yard and fell there weakly.

These victims might have come from another district of the city, further away from the hospital but closer to the hypocenter, where they might have suffered more severe immediate burns. However, a similar change is also apparent in the victims who had arrived earlier. While on his way to help an injured colleague, he again encounters some of them:

When I reached the little river, I came across an astonishing scene. Half-naked or nearly naked people were crouching at the water's edge. All looked alike, without distinction of sex or age; long hair was the only clue to the female sex. On one side their bodies had been grilled and were highly inflamed. The procession of white ghosts which had passed me some time before had gathered here on the bank of the stream, seeking water to relieve the terrible thirst and the scorching pain of their bodies. Crowds of these victims lined the stream.

'Oh, how it hurts! I'm hurting—burning!' said Mr. Tsujimoto, groaning. His face, which had been whitish, when I saw him earlier, was now darker, blackened; his lips were swollen. His wife sat not far away, her face and body also blackened, moaning insensibly.

It is clear that, in this group of patients at least, overt symptoms have become manifest with a delay of several hours. They are now obvious even in the wife of Mr. Tsujimoto, whom Akizuki had not even mentioned as being afflicted earlier on.[4] Still later in the day, Akizuki describes both Mr. and Mrs. Tsujimoto as 'cinder-burnt.' While Mrs. Tsujiomoto will live for a few more days, her husband expires the same night:

At about midnight, Mr Tsujimoto's condition suddenly worsened. ... By degrees, Mr. Tsujimoto's breathing became harsher. I could not feel any pulse. ... Suddenly Mr. Tsujimoto went into a violent fit of convulsions; his eyes bulged. 'His last moment has come!' said someone.

Labored breathing in the bombing victims is confirmed by another eyewitness from Nagasaki, Akira Nagasaka [156, p. 74]:

A woman, probably in her mid-thirties, was lying on the ground, her hair wild, her clothes in tatters, her face red with blood. She was putting all the strength that remained in her to raise her head and murmur, "Water, water."

When I had gathered my wits about me, I scooped some dirty water out of a nearby ditch and gave it to her. She drank it as if it were the most delicious thing ever to pass her lips, but most of it merely trickled down her chin onto her breast. "More, please,"

---

[4]While Akizuki's statement that 'on one side their bodies had been grilled' might suggest some sort of real flash burn, he later also notes that some of the patients had burned faces and backs, for which he gamely asserts some contortionist explanation. This echoes Oughterson and Warren [146], who twist the protagonists of their case descriptions into the most unnatural poses for the same reason.

she begged, but she could do no more than gasp for breath when I brought it, having no strength left to drink.

The testimony from Hiroshima is, if anything, even more gruesome.[5] Eyewitness Kosaku Okabe [156, p. 35] was not near the hypocenter for the bombing, but he came upon the scene in downtown Hiroshima several hours afterwards:

Wherever a puddle of water had collected from burst water pipes, people had gathered like ants around a honey pot. Many had died where they lay at the water's edge, their strength gone. Others had clambered over the dead bodies to get at the water, only to die in the same way, their bodies piling one on top of another.

Okabe also describes the aspect of the victims:

Most people had been wearing light summer shirts that morning. But most of the dead were bare chested, and many were completely naked, perhaps because their clothes had been burned off them. The parts of the body that had been exposed to the flash had suffered great burns, and the skin was turning purple and trailing from the body in strips.

In every case, the eyeballs of the dead were either protruding from their sockets or hanging out completely. Blood had gushed from the mouth, ears, and nose. The tongue had swelled to the size of a golf ball and had pushed its way out of the mouth, gripped tightly by the teeth. The whole anatomy seemed to have been destroyed. Most bodies were bloated, and it was often impossible to tell whether they were male or female.

The grisly, apocalyptic picture painted by Okabe's testimony might seem exaggerated, but each detail is confirmed by other eyewitnesses [14, 156, 180]. While the victims described by Okabe are already dead, another witness depicts the scene when some of them are still alive. Hachiya [62] relates the observations told him on August 6th by one of his visitors, Mr. Hashimoto, who was already mentioned in the

---

[5]We noted earlier that the incidence of both radiation sickness and burns in victims near the hypocenter was lower in Nagasaki than in Hiroshima, even though the bomb yield in Nagasaki is said to have been higher (see Chapters 8 and 9). It seems likely that less mustard gas, and perhaps also less napalm, was used in the second bombing than in the first.

preceding chapter. Like Okabe, Hashimoto entered the inner city after the bombing:

When I reached the Misasa railway bridge ... I encountered a dead man. I saw many others in the water tanks fighting for breath. The sight was horrible.

Mr. Hashimoto also describes the days following the bombing:

During those days, wherever you went, there were so many dead lying around it was impossible to walk without encountering them—swollen, discolored bodies with froth oozing from their noses and mouths.

Overall, the testimony given by several independent witnesses from the two cities is remarkably consistent. We therefore can't dismiss it, but instead must try to understand what exactly could have caused such terrible injury and disfigurement.

10.1.3 Pathophysiological interpretation of early symptoms. Before identifying the causes, we must take a step back and consider what the clinical signs observed in these victims tell us about the underlying pathophysiology.

Skin burns. A key observation here is that in some victims at least, such as the Tsujimotos, burns of the skin were manifest only after some hours, as is typical with mustard gas. The blackened aspect of the skin in such cases was most likely caused by intense cyanosis rather than 'scorching,' which should have been apparent immediately (see for example Figure 9.5C). It is quite likely, of course, that some victims suffered both immediate (napalm) and delayed burns.

Circulatory shock and capillary leak syndrome. The initial paleness reported by Akizuki in patients who arrived on foot at his clinic suggests beginning circulatory shock. At a more advanced stage of shock, paleness may give way to cyanosis; this is observed by Akizuki in some of the initially pale patients at a later time, and it is also described by Okabe in the victims that he encounters several hours after the Hiroshima bombing.

Shock may be accompanied by capillary leak syndrome, which causes intense thirst and, after intake of large volumes of water, extreme edema (Figure 10.1). All of these symptoms were described in the bombing victims.

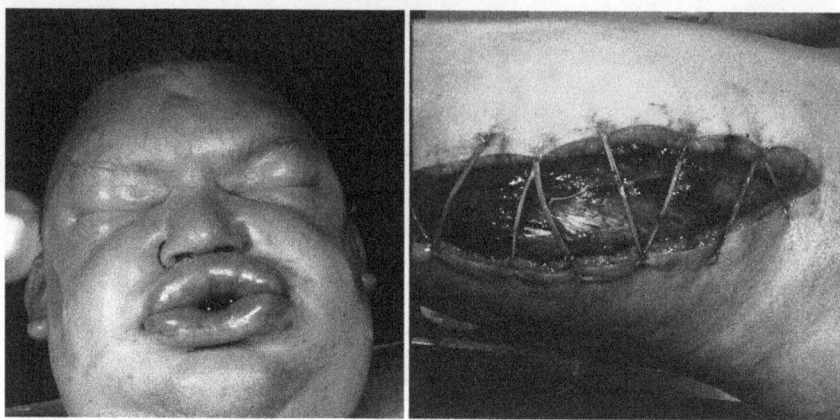

Figure 10.1: Patient with capillary leak syndrome (deceased; [181]). Left: the face is cyanotic and extremely swollen. Right: swelling of a limb has led to fascial compartment syndrome, in which nerves and blood vessels are compressed by the edematous muscle tissue within a tightly confined space. Transient incision of the fascia (a sheet of firm connective tissue) that encloses the compartment was carried out to relieve the compression.

A related observation is the acute headache, which is suggested by Akizuki's description of patients holding their heads between their hands. Headaches are caused by vascular distension in the meninges; the simultaneous occurrence with shock suggest that the latter was likely caused in part by the loss of vascular tone.

Injury to the lungs and airways. Acute respiratory distress is described in early fatalities, but both Hachiya and Akizuki also report labored breathing in the patients they examine in the subsequent days and weeks. Immediate affliction of the upper airways can be surmised from Akizuki's observation of hoarseness in the victims he meets shortly after the bombing.

The froth oozing from mouths and noses noted by the sharp-eyed Mr. Hashimoto in the dead bombing victims indicates severe pulmonary edema, while outright bleeding from the mouth and nose, described by Okabe, suggests injury to blood vessels in the mucous membranes of the airways, and possibly to larger vessels inside the chest.

Also pertinent is Dr. Masao Tsuzuki's remark on the 'suffocating pain' experienced by those who inhaled the gas which 'permeated immediately after the explosion of the atomic bomb' (see Section 1.4.4).

Overall, it is plain that some noxious agent released at Hiroshima and Nagasaki attacked the lungs and airways.

Traumatic asphyxia and orbital compartment syndrome. With the assumptions of capillary leak syndrome and injury to the lungs and airways, we can account for the thirst, the general edema, the respiratory distress, the cyanosis, as well as the blood and froth spilling from the mouth and nose. The peeling skin is, at this point of the exposition, no longer a mystery. That leaves the bleeding from the ears and the eyeballs protruding or even hanging out. How can we fit these into the picture?

The protruding eyeballs are a telltale sign of *orbital compartment syndrome*. The eye socket (Latin: *orbita*) is a confined space, and if some irregular process such as edema or hemorrhage claims some of that space, then the eyeball is displaced outwards. One contributing factor would have been the capillary leak syndrome, but there most likely was another one—*traumatic asphyxia*, also known as *Perthes syndrome*. Most commonly, traumatic asphyxia is triggered by compression of the thorax, but it can also occur with other causes of disrupted respiration, including severe asthma attacks [182]. It arises when pressure to the chest or injury to the lungs prevents blood pumped by the right heart from entering the lungs. The blood therefore backs up into the right heart and from there into the large veins that supply it, particularly those within the head. Blood vessels become distended, the blood stagnating within them becomes desaturated of oxygen, its color turning dark, and plasma fluid leaks into the tissues; the patient's face turns purple and swollen. Bursting blood vessels may cause bleeding from all cranial orifices, including the ears. Bleeding could likewise have occurred behind the eyeballs; in fact, the convulsions and bulging eyeballs in the dying Mr. Tsujimoto suggest some such event. Since severe lung damage was present in the bombing victims, we can conclude that the preconditions for traumatic asphyxia were met.

While traumatic asphyxia and ocular compartment syndrome are both rare in normal life, there is indeed at least one clinical case report that describes them in combination [183]. As it turns out, the severely injured patient in this case also developed capillary leak syndrome. The authors state that capillary leakage preceded the orbital compartment syndrome, and they consider it a contributing cause of the latter.

Based on the foregoing, it stands to reason that the combination of lung and vascular injury present in the bombing victims could also account for the development of orbital compartment syndrome.[6] We can thus reduce the overall clinical picture to three fundamental pathophysiological effects:

1. injury to the lungs and airways;
2. injury to the vasculature, leading to capillary leak syndrome and shock;
3. injury to the skin, causing it to peel.

10.1.4 Causal attribution. What could have caused these three effects? The easy part of the answer is that neither 'flash burn' nor ionizing radiation can account for this entire clinical picture. As discussed in Section 9.6, flash burns should have been visible in some form immediately, but Akizuki fails to notice them in several patients whom he encounters shortly after the bombing. Without very severe exterior burns, there simply is no mechanism by which a flash of light could produce acute respiratory distress.

As regards ionizing radiation, here is the case description of a patient who received approximately five times a lethal dose of it [150, p. 218]:

In a nuclear criticality accident at Los Alamos in 1958, one worker received a total body dose of mixed neutron and γ-radiation estimated to be between 39 and 49 Gy. Parts of his body may have received as much as 120 Gy. This person went into a state of shock immediately and was unconscious within a few minutes. After 8 hours, no lymphocytes were found in the circulating blood, and there was virtually a complete urinary shutdown despite the administration of large amounts of fluids. The patient died 35 hours after the accident.

This patient received a dose of radiation about as high as it could have been near the hypocenter in Hiroshima. He promptly developed cerebrovascular syndrome and also general circulatory shock, and he

---

[6]According to Fred and Chandler [182] and Dwek [184], lasting ocular injury, suggestive of damage by increased pressure within the eye sockets, is common in traumatic asphyxia even without manifest capillary leak syndrome. Dwek explains exophthalmia (protruding eyeballs) in such patients with hematoma in the eye socket, but with the limited diagnostic means available in his day, distinguishing hematoma from edema behind the eyeball would have been difficult.

quickly died of it—without intensive care, he probably would have died on the same day, as did many of the victims in Hiroshima and Nagasaki. However, no mention is made of facial or general cyanosis, respiratory distress, peeling skin, or dangling eyes. Since he lost consciousness so quickly, he would not have had time enough to find a puddle and drink enough water to swell up to any great extent. Thus, apart from shock and rapid death, his clinical picture bears no resemblance to that described in the victims at Hiroshima and Nagasaki.

Animal experiments reported by Bloom et al. [26] showed the lungs to have relatively low susceptibility to radiation; lethal whole-body doses of X-rays or neutrons produced little or no evidence of lung tissue damage when compared to controls.[7] The skin, too, showed very minor effects at such doses. While these findings do of course not rule out lung or skin damage with supra-lethal irradiation, they exclude *preferential* damage to these organs, which is evident in the Hiroshima and Nagasaki victims.

The more difficult and interesting part of the answer concerns how we actually *can* account for the clinical picture. Since we already have evidence that napalm and mustard gas were used, we will examine if they can explain it.

Napalm. Mr. Tsujimoto, the patient most thoroughly described by Akizuki (Section 10.1.1), has lost his shirt in the bombing, and his hair and eyelashes are singed. Even though he does not present any obvious burns at the time, this does suggest some possible exposure to napalm, albeit probably not through a major direct hit.

According to Björnerstedt et al. [141], the fire from a sufficiently large napalm bomb will inflict harm through radiating heat even at some distance. Moreover, conventional burns can cause smoke inhalation

---

[7]While Bloom [26] was published only in 1948, the experiments described in the book were carried out mostly before 1945. From the great variety of radionuclides they used, it is clear that Bloom and colleagues must have had high-priority access to novel isotopes as these became available through ongoing research in Fermi's laboratory. Considering that the reports by Bloom and by Oughterson and Warren [146] were both prepared under the auspices of the Atomic Energy Commission, it is peculiar that Oughterson and Warren do not cite Bloom. Even more bizarrely, Bloom's 800 page volume does not even mention the atomic bombings, at least not within its otherwise very extensive index. Thus, no connection is ever made between Bloom's experimental work and the clinical or pathological observations in Hiroshima and Nagasaki. Bloom does briefly note that in some experiments mustard gas was tested in parallel with radiation but gives no details on the conclusions drawn from such studies.

injury, which can result in acute respiratory distress with rapid deadly outcome [185]. Severe burns will also cause circulatory shock; and with napalm, this may occur even when only some 10% of the total body surface have been burned [143]. Thus, napalm could in principle set off the pathophysiological cascade that would produce all of the symptoms seen in the early fatalities, and this may well have happened in some of them.

It is doubtful, however, that napalm was the only cause in Mr. Tsujimoto's case. Smoke inhalation injury tends to occur with fires indoors, since here the smoke accumulates in a confined space; Mr. Tsujimoto, however, reported having been hurt while harvesting pumpkins in the field. Conceivably, one might also suffer smoke inhalation injury outdoors, if surrounded and trapped by fire; but it seems unlikely that one could escape such an inferno without also receiving significant burns to the skin. According to Dolinin [143], asphyxia occurs in approximately 5% of napalm victims, particularly in those with manifest burns to the face. Overall, napalm seems unlikely as the cause of respiratory distress in Mr. Tsujimoto, or in the other victims with similar early symptoms. We thus should consider the possible role of mustard gas.

Mustard gas. I should note upfront that the literature does not report any clinical cases of mustard gas poisoning which exhibit the complete picture described in Section 10.1.2. While capillary leak syndrome and extensive damage to the skin and lungs are documented (see Chapter 7), I have not found a single case report on traumatic asphyxia caused by mustard gas. Nevertheless, I propose that exactly this did occur at Hiroshima and Nagasaki. My reason is that the bombing victims must have sustained much graver acute lung injury than any earlier victims—their sufferings, even though caused by poison gas, were indeed 'worse than poison gas'. In World War I, mustard gas was introduced only after other poison gases had been, so that the soldiers who encountered it were already equipped with gas masks. Likewise, gas masks had also been worn by the poisoned mustard gas factory workers described by Warthin and Weller [109]. In contrast, the victims at Hiroshima and Nagasaki had no warning and no protection, and they must have inhaled the gas in far greater amounts than those earlier victims.

As a consequence of such high doses to the lungs, the airways would have become clogged by swelling mucous membranes, fibrin plugs, and blood clots (see Section 7.3.2). Air becoming trapped behind such obstacles—acute emphysema—would have raised the pressure inside the chest and compressed the pulmonary veins, thus preventing the flow of blood returning from the body and the head. Additionally, clots would have formed within the lungs' blood vessels themselves, further impeding the flow of blood back into the lungs. In the most severely poisoned victims, the acute obstruction of the airways and the lung circulation would have been incomparably worse than in any asthma attack.[8]

Pulmonary effects similar to those just described for mustard gas have also been documented for smoke inhalation injury [187], which is common in napalm burn victims.

Possible use of other lung poisons. While in my estimation mustard gas can account for the acute lung toxicity which occurred among early fatalities, the use of other lung poisons cannot be ruled out. Both chlorine and phosgene were used in World War 1 and caused acute and severe lung damage among their victims [109, 139]. Another plausible candidate is lewisite, which is known to have been produced and tested by the U.S. during World War II [21], and whose acute effects resemble those of sulfur mustard but arise more rapidly, probably due to its greater volatility [35].

Our final, somewhat surprising candidate is cadmium. Apart from napalm, the Americans also employed a second incendiary in their firebombing raids, namely magnesium-thermate bombs. One variant of this bomb type, the AN-M50TA2, contained a 'secret toxic agent' [188, p. 429] which was later identified as cadmium [189].[9] The high

---

[8]The most similar scenario may have occurred in Iranian soldiers subject to Iraqi mustard gas attacks. Freitag et al. [186], who report on some Iranian veterans with severe chronic bronchopulmonary damage, also state that "many soldiers died immediately on the battle field, probably due to acute chemical-induced pulmonary edema." The surviving victims reported that "they first noticed a bitter taste and a garlic-like smell immediately after the exposure to the poison gas. Minutes to hours later, dizziness, headaches, and shortness of breath were common complaints." The authors raise the possibility that lung poisons other than sulfur mustard may have been used, but I have not found this corroborated in other sources.

[9]Reference [189] is the only source in which I have found this information. I deem this source credible for two reasons. Firstly, it closely matches [188] in all other details given on the various types of the M50 bomb. Secondly, it was compiled as part of an environmental survey in a U.S. Army weapons dump; the authors thus surely had a need to know the identity of the 'secret toxic agent'. The document containing this information may have been made publicly visible by mistake.

temperature produced by the burning thermate and magnesium should vaporize the cadmium. The medical literature reports several cases of acute lung toxicity due to inhalation of cadmium vapors, sometimes fatal [190, 191]. A reference text on drugs and poisons [192, p. 1767] notes diarrhea among the symptoms of acute poisoning; as noted in Section 8.10, acute diarrhea was common also among the bombing victims. Thus, *if* AN-M50TA2 bombs were indeed used, then it stands to reason that vaporized cadmium released from them would have contributed to acute toxicity among the victims. However, as will be discussed in Section 13.2.5, I have not found any clear indications that this weapon was indeed employed in the 'nuclear' bombings.

Chapter 7 already explained why lewisite is unlikely to have been used *instead* of mustard gas rather than in addition to it. The reasons given there apply to the other poisons discussed in this section also.

10.1.5 Conclusion. In summary, therefore, I propose that napalm and mustard gas, alone or in combination, can account for the full clinical picture observed in the early fatalities, while radiation cannot. Mustard gas was very likely the dominant cause in those victims who initially appeared to be free of burns, such as Mr. Tsujimoto, but napalm may well have contributed significantly in many other victims. The use of other poisons is possible but cannot be demonstrated based on the limited evidence available.

10.2 Acute retinal burns: the dog that didn't bark

When exposed to a nuclear detonation, the eyes may be harmed both by the flash of light and by ionizing radiation. The latter most commonly causes *cataract*, that is, increased opacity of the lens, which typically becomes manifest with a delay of several months or years. An increased incidence of cataract has indeed been repeatedly described in survivors from Hiroshima and Nagasaki; this will be considered in Section 12.3.2. Here, we will focus on the acute lesions that were observed very shortly after the bombing, as well as those that were not observed but should have been.

We have seen earlier that most of the skin burns observed in Hiroshima and Nagasaki were ascribed to the flash of light from the detonation. This raises the question how the same flash would have affected the eyes. The intuitive expectation is that it should have significantly harmed them. Dr. Oughterson thought so, too, according to the ophthalmologist John Flick [193]:

"They say this explosion gives off the light of ten-thousand suns!" he [Oughterson] said to me. "If this be true there should be something for you to do."

While the 'ten-thousand suns' estimate is as vague as it is dramatic—does it refer to overall intensity at some specific distance, or to the maximal brightness of the fireball?—ocular lesions caused by nuclear detonations have indeed been described in both humans and animals.

10.2.1 Retinal burns observed in humans after later bomb tests. Probably all of us have been warned against looking at a solar eclipse with unprotected eyes. Doing so may cause circumscribed burns to the retina, which will leave behind a permanent defect in the field of vision (a *scotoma*). The same would be expected in people who happen to look at a nuclear flash, and indeed Rose et al. [194] have reported on six American soldiers who developed just such burns after looking at the fireballs of later nuclear tests, from distances of up to ten miles. The authors also explain why retinal burns may occur at such large distance from the detonations; the reason is illustrated in Figure 10.2. While the light intensity at the pupil decreases with the square of the distance, this effect is exactly compensated by the diminishing size of the retinal image. The brightness of the latter decreases only in proportion to the haziness of the air, which thus becomes the limiting factor.[10]

The size of the pupil also limits the light intensity at the retina, of course; that is, after all, its purpose. Since the pupil is wider at night than during the day, it follows that retinal burns will occur at greater distances by night. Rose et al. [194] do not provide any details on the time of day or the magnitude of the detonations that occasioned their clinical cases, which means that we cannot directly apply their findings to the conditions at Hiroshima and Nagasaki.

The quantitative aspects of retinal burns are somewhat more explicitly addressed by Byrnes et al. [195]. These authors present studies on 700 rabbits, which were exposed to the flashes of nuclear detonations

---

[10] Another limitation would be the less than perfect optical precision of the eye's refractive elements (cornea and lens), but within a few kilometers from the detonation this should not matter much, at least in those without, or with properly corrected, near- or farsightedness.

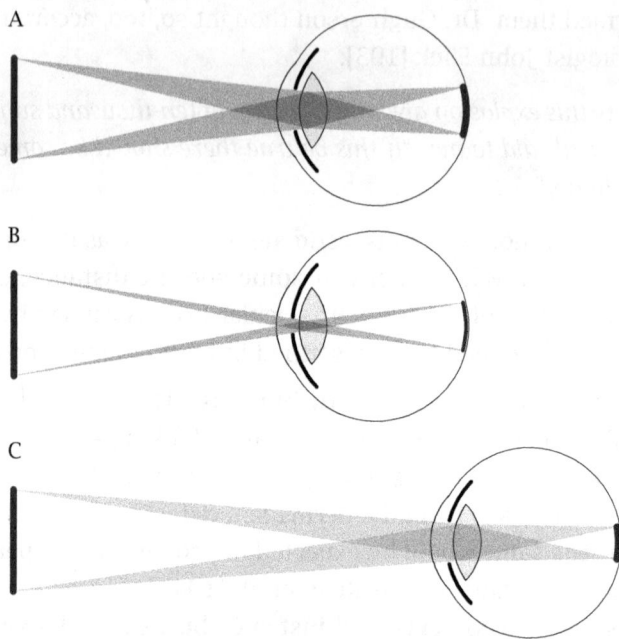

Figure 10.2: Effects of pupil diameter and of object distance on retinal images. A: All light that originates from the same point on the object and falls onto the aperture (pupil) is focused onto the same point on the retina; this creates an inverted image of the object. B: If the pupil narrows, the size of the retinal image remains unchanged, but its intensity is reduced. C: If, relative to A, the pupil diameter stays the same but the object distance increases, then the light that falls onto the pupil is 'spread thin', but this is exactly compensated by the reduced size of the image—the intensity of the retinal image stays the same.

at night, at distances of up to 42 miles. At all distances, the retinas suffered discrete burns, which with increasing distance decreased in size and in the degree of tissue destruction. Within eight miles of the detonations, the authors describe a 'volcano-like' appearance of the lesions,[11] with prominent edges and a deep central hole, the bottom of which they made out to be the *sclera*, that is, the eyeball's sturdy outer layer of connective tissue. The rabbit eye lesions appear similar to those in Rose's human patients (Figure 10.3).

---

[11]The volcano-like appearance agrees with the mechanism of injury proposed by Byrnes et al. [195] and Vos [196], namely, a local steam explosion within the retina, caused by the very rapid absorption of energy, which allows no time for heat dissipation.

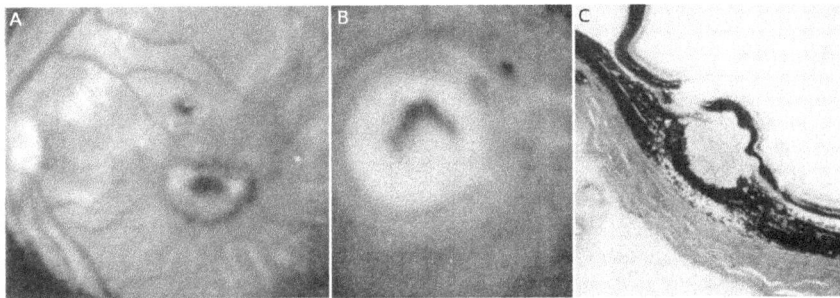

Figure 10.3: Nuclear flash burns of the retina in a human and in a rabbit. A: retinal burn in a soldier exposed 2 miles from the detonation, photographed 6 weeks after the event [194]. B: Early stage of retinal lesion in rabbit. C: Histological section through rabbit retinal lesion. The band of gray tissue is the sclera; the dark layer comprises the choroid and the retina. The retina is bulged and ruptured. B and C from Byrnes et al. [195].

Byrnes et al. [195] do not state the magnitudes of the detonations that burned those rabbit retinas. They do, however, apply the findings from their rabbit studies to provide explicit estimates for the range at which a 'typical' 20 kt fission bomb—as described theoretically in Glasstone [90], and as purportedly used in Hiroshima and Nagasaki—should cause retinal burns in humans, by day or by night, and under various conditions of visibility. They conclude that the range would be up to 40 miles by night, and some 10-20% less by day. However, they do not spell out all of the assumptions that went into these estimates, and it is not clear to me why the difference in range between day and night would be so small. Their assumed decrease of the pupil aperture from 8 mm by night to 4 mm by day will reduce the energy reaching the retina by a factor of 4; according to my own calculations, this should reduce the range by day to approximately half that by night, giving a maximum range a bit below the atmospheric visibility. Of note, the largest distance among Rose's case reports [194] is 10 miles.

10.2.2 Retinal doses of thermal radiation at Hiroshima and Nagasaki.
To gain a firmer footing, we can estimate the heat dose to the retina at Hiroshima and Nagasaki from the thermal radiation which purportedly prevailed on the outside (see Figure 9.1A), the geometrical constraints of ocular vision (see Figure 10.2), and the transmittance of the translucent parts of the eyeball. Following Byrnes et al. [195], the latter will be taken to be 0.4. We will assume a pupil diameter of 2 mm, which corresponds

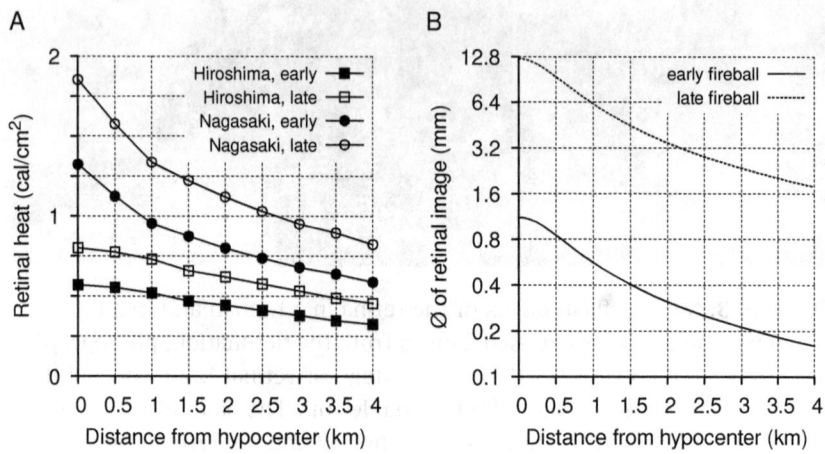

Figure 10.4: Thermal energy density (A) and diameter (B) of retinal images of the Hiroshima and Nagasaki nuclear bombs. 'Early' and 'late' in A refer to the stage of the fireball. See text for details.

to full adaptation to bright sunlight—the bombings occurred on bright, sunny summer mornings—and a distance from the pupil to the retina of 24 mm.

According to Glasstone [90], the fireball has two distinct stages of high luminosity. The 'early fireball' exists at 1 ms after the detonation. It lasts only a very short time, during which a comparatively small cumulative amount of radiation is released; however, its small diameter of only 27 m means that this amount will be focused onto a small retinal image, where the intensity may still reach harmful levels. The late fireball is larger (200-300 m across) and also much longer-lived—up to 3 seconds, but most of the energy is released within the first second. It thus reaches a higher energy density across a larger retinal image. We will consider both stages of the fireball in our calculation.

The results are depicted in Figure 10.4. For interpreting them, with need to know the thermal energy which, if transferred to the retina as a very brief flash, will produce a retinal burn. Byrnes et al. [195] estimate this value to be 0.1 cal/cm^2, and they also state that in a separate series of experiments, which is not described in detail in the cited study (and which I have not found published elsewhere), burns were indeed induced with an only slightly higher energy (0.14 cal/cm^2). All data points in Figure 10.4A exceed that threshold.

What are the roles of early and late fireball, respectively, in the generation of retinal burns? On the short time scale of the early fireball (1 ms), no protective lid reflex will be triggered, so that anyone with the flash in their field of vision will receive at least this dose of energy in full. On the other hand, the longer duration of the late fireball means that some of the energy may be shut out by lid reflexes. The question therefore arises to what extent the late fireball contributes to the formation of retinal burns. The sizes of the burns observed by Rose et al. [194], when compared to the predicted ones in Figure 10.4B, suggest that the late fireball does contribute significantly; but since those authors do not tell us how similar those nuclear detonations were in size to the 'typical' 20 kt bomb—if they were larger, then maybe so were the early fireballs—we cannot be quite sure. In any event, even in the most stringent scenario—pupils adapted to a bright sky before the flash, and considering the early fireball only—the retinal doses of thermal radiation still exceed the burn threshold. Overall, therefore, both theoretical considerations and previous evidence [194, 195] indicate that retinal burns should have been very common in both Hiroshima and Nagasaki.

10.2.3 Flick's eye exams in bombing victims. The ophthalmologist John Flick arrived in Japan in early September and spent several weeks examining a large number of patients in both Hiroshima and Nagasaki. His report [193] is the most comprehensive and detailed of its kind. He writes:

At the end of the second day I had examined approximately 300 patients. I had found the usual traumatic lesions one sees in wartime but none of the corneal or lenticular syndromes I had expected to find. There were few ophthalmias among the sick and those found were of the nonspecific kind due to infection. Knowing the high degree of radioresistance of the tissues of the posterior segment I had paid little attention to ophthalmoscopic studies.[12]

---

[12]Flick notes that, on arrival, "we learned that the death rate was 100 per day among those survivors and felt that any studies made would have to be instituted quickly." This must also have occurred to other medical officers; nevertheless, Oughterson's 'Joint Commission' arrived only a full month later in October. Liebow [77] suggests that this was due to problems with weather and logistics, but these did not stop Flick, nor several other advance teams with non-medical tasks such as, it would seem, painting 'atomic bomb shadows' (see Section 13.5).

10 Early clinical and pathological findings

The posterior segment of the eyeball includes the retina, and its examination uses an ophthalmoscope. Thus, Flick's remark suggests that he was initially focused on the effects of ionizing radiation more than on those of the flash of light.[13] Nevertheless, a short while later, he does make a thorough study of the retinal symptoms in survivors. This is prompted by his observation of retinal bleeding in two patients with hematopoetic syndrome (see Section 8.2.1):

> *On the third day I was examining two moribund Japanese soldiers with bloody diarrhea, bleeding from the gums, covered from head to foot with petechiae. Their white [blood cell] counts were 2,000 and 900. I examined their eyegrounds. Both had extensive hemorrhagic and exudative lesions of the retina. It seemed entirely consistent with the rest of the picture ... these characteristic fundus [retinal] lesions were one of the most reliable criteria of radiation sickness.*

In his paper, Flick individually summarizes and also tabulates several dozen of his cases. Of the retinal lesions he describes, he attributes not a single one to 'flash burn', nor do any of the lesions shown as illustrations exhibit the striking volcano crater aspect evident in Figure 10.3.

The dearth of clinical cases of retinal flash burn in Hiroshima and Nagasaki is acknowledged by Rose et al. [194] and Byrnes et al. [195]. Both papers do, however, cite one report which purportedly describes one actual case. From Rose et al.:

> *The literature reveals no report of such a burn except for a single case of bilateral central scotoma incurred in the Hiroshima atomic explosion.*

The clinical picture described in the reference given by Rose and by Byrnes, however—Oyama and Sasaki [197]—is not at all characteristic.[14]

---

[13] The cornea has comparatively low susceptibility to ionizing radiation, and lenticular lesions tend to become manifest with delay; it is therefore not clear to me why Flick was initially concentrating on these.

[14] Both Rose and Byrnes cite this reference second-hand ('cited in Cogan ...') and apparently never read it. I obtained the Japanese original and had it translated by a native speaker (T. Harada). It is not a full clinical case report, but only a short abstract one page long. In translation, its title reads *A case of corneal burns by the atomic bomb*. The text describes a patient who suffered burns to the face (probably by napalm), followed by scars as well as corneal lesions; only a single concluding

Thus, the medical literature documents not a single case of retinal flash burns in Hiroshima or Nagasaki.

10.2.4 Pathological findings in the eyes of deceased victims. Flick shows some histopathological pictures of retinas from deceased patients, which exhibit the sequelae of hemorrhages but again have no similarity with flash burn lesions [193]. Likewise, Liebow, who surveys the autopsy materials he had commandeered from Japanese pathologists while serving on the Joint Commission, mentions hemorrhage as the only type of retinal lesion [42].

Schlaegel has reported a study on autopsy materials from a series of patients at Nagasaki who had died from 'radiation sickness' approximately four weeks after the bombings [198]. He finds a variety of lesions, mostly to the anterior eye (see Section 10.3); however, he does not describe or discuss any cases of retinal flash burn. The same is true of another, shorter report by Wilder [199]. Overall, I have found not a single study that provided any evidence of retinal burns in autopsy materials from Hiroshima or Nagasaki.

10.2.5 Anecdotal reports of retinal flash burns. In contrast to the medical literature, both Akizuki and Hachiya suggest that some sort of retinal burns indeed occurred. In early September, Akizuki is visited in his hospital by an American military physician, who proceeds to examine the eyes of his patients [167, p. 131]:

> He seemed to be an eye specialist, for he began eventually to examine the patients eyes with an ophthalmoscope ... The American remarked: "Most of them have had the optic nerves of their retinas damaged by the A-bomb's flash, and their eyesight has been impaired. They may even lose it altogether."

Similarly, in his diary entry from August 23rd, Hachiya recounts a conversation with his hospital's ophthalmologist, Dr. Koyama:

> I asked Dr. Koyama what his findings had been in patients with eye injuries. "Those who were watching the plane had their eye grounds burned," he replied. "The flash of light apparently went

---

sentence notes that *degenerative* retinal lesions—not retinal burns—'were also seen.' While the visual deficit (scotoma) in a true retinal burn should have been manifest immediately, it was noted by this patient only with some delay, suggesting that it arose from the scarring of the corneas; this is a well-known late effect of facial napalm burns [143].

through the pupils and left them with a blind area in the central portion of their visual fields. Most of the eye-ground burns are third degree, so cure is impossible."

On the next day, Hachiya muses about his own condition:

I recalled Dr. Koyama's account of patients who had been blinded by looking directly at the pika. *Their blindness was understandable because their eye nerves had been scorched. My exposure was indirect. I had seen only the flash, but the heat rays had not reached me so the "mirrors" in my eyes were not injured.*

Hachiya's distinction between exposure to the flash and the thermal rays is fictitious, however—'thermal rays' may comprise both visible light ('the flash') and infrared light, but with a nuclear fireball visible light should account for the greater share. Moreover, both visible and infrared light travel in a straight line; one cannot suffer one but be spared the other.

It is noteworthy that Oyama and Sasaki published their short abstract [197] while employed in the same hospital as Hachiya and Koyama. Presumably, the authors would have had access to the patients examined by Koyama, or at least to their files. In this hospital, a significant number of autopsies were carried out in the weeks after the bombing by Hiroshima medical school pathologist Dr. Tamagawa. His autopsy samples were later appropriated by Liebow, who makes no mention of retinal burns (see Section 10.2.4).

That neither clinical files nor autopsies from Koyama's own hospital furnished more than Oyama and Sasaki's single case, which morphed into a 'retinal flash burn' only in the skilled hands of later American authors, strongly suggests that Koyama's diagnosis was premature.[15] The cases he observed may have been similar to those which Flick attributed to thrombocytopenia rather than to flash burns, and which would indeed have healed in those patients who survived their ARS in the end. In my view, therefore, the anecdotal reports are lacking in substance and cannot stand up to the uniformly negative evidence

---

[15] Dr. Teruichi Harada pointed out to me that Dr. Oyama and Dr. Koyama share the same first name, and that the two last names are most likely different English transliterations of the same Japanese last name, whose pronunciation would be more accurately reflected by "Koyama." This would imply that Dr. Koyama himself changed his mind regarding the nature of the retinal lesions he had reported to Hachiya.

from the proper medical literature; they are discussed here only for completeness' sake.

10.3 Other acute eye lesions

Many witnesses describe a 'blinding flash', but do not report having been unable to see afterwards. A very bright flash that stays below the burn threshold can indeed transiently suppress our vision; many will have experienced this when exposed to a photographer's flash.[16] In bright daylight, this effect will last a few minutes at most; however, some victims appear to have been blinded for longer periods of time. On August 7th, Hachiya notes in his diary:

> *I heard footsteps, and a man appeared at the door, outlined in the flickering darkness. His elbows were out and his hands down, like the burned people I had seen on my way to the hospital. As he came nearer, I could see his face—or what had been his face because this face had been melted away by the fire. The man was blind and had lost his way.*

Like the case described by Oyama and Sasaki (see Section 10.2.3), this one may have been caused by napalm, but the loss of vision is more acute. Hachiya does not report on the subsequent clinical course in this case. Likewise, he reports once only on another one:

> *"Has he been fed?" I asked Miss Kado. "Don't worry, Doctor," replied Miss Kado. "There are plenty of potato leaves in the garden, so I don't think he'll be hungry."*
>
> *The patient we were talking about was a horse who had been burned and blinded by the fire. Whoever saw him first did not have the heart to turn him away, so he was put in the garden under our window.*

Flick [193] describes a single case of transient blindness which lasted for several days, and which was followed by symptoms suggestive of moderately severe 'radiation sickness':

---

[16] If you have not, you can experience it second hand by watching Hitchcock's famous movie *Rear Window*, in which James Stewart's character, a wheelchair-bound photographer, tries without success to ward off an attacker by repeatedly blinding him with camera flashes.

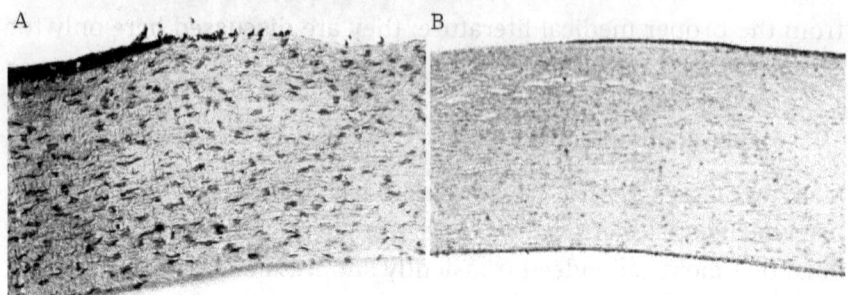

Figure 10.5: Denuded corneal epithelium. A: corneal denudation in a rabbit eye experimentally exposed to mustard gas [109]. B: corneal denudation, with regeneration underway, in a Nagasaki bombing victim [198].

> *Furuta, a young Nagasaki woman, aged 18 years, was in Ohashi in a wooden house. She states that at the time of the explosion she was blinded and could not see for three days. From August 15th to 18th she had fever up to 40°C. At this time the cuts she had began to be infected. Fever recurred, September 4th to 14th, up to 40°C, and there was soreness of the gums and tonsillitis.*

The combination of symptoms in this case strongly suggests a causation by sulfur mustard (see Section 7.3.3 and 7.3.6). More severe exposure of the eyes to mustard gas can result in the loss of the epithelial cell layers which cover the cornea [109, p. 97]. A similar lesion was described by Schlaegel [198] in one deceased Nagasaki victim (see Figure 10.5). Schlaegel himself ascribes it to ultraviolet rays; however, if UV rays from the flash had indeed been to blame, then the concomitant and much more intense visible light should have caused severe retinal burns as well. Schlaegel also summarizes some clinical observations, related to him by Japanese colleagues, which are entirely consistent with the typical clinical course of mustard gas lesions:

> *Conjunctivitis and superficial keratitis [inflammation of the cornea] were found in many of the patients, but the effects disappeared in about a month.*

On August 24th Hachiya describes another case of blindness in a patient who has been suffering of 'radiation sickness':

> *Mr. Sakai died, complaining of shortness of breath and blindness.*

The most likely explanation in this case seems retinal bleeding, as described and explained by Flick (see Section 10.2.3). Overall, therefore, clinical and pathological findings on acute eye lesions don't provide any specific evidence of eye damage by ionizing radiation or by intense light, while some findings are suggestive of causation by mustard gas or napalm, respectively.

10.4 Lungs

10.4.1 Emphysema and atelectasis in early fatalities. As noted before in Section 10.1.4, the lungs have low radiosensitivity, and they should not have been significantly affected by radiation in any victims that survived the bombing for more than a day. Nevertheless, in the relatively limited number of autopsies that were performed on victims who died within the first one or two weeks, emphysema (distension of lung tissue) was commonly found: Table 8.25 in Ishikawa et al. [8] notes emphysema in 5 patients out of 12 who died between August 9th and 15th, and whose bodies were dissected by the Japanese pathologist Yamashina.

In their loot of Japanese autopsy materials, Liebow et al. [42] also observe emphysema, as well as atelectasis, which is the opposite of emphysema—namely, lung tissue that is devoid of air because it has been cut off from ventilation. They find both in the majority of the limited number of early fatalities they survey. On page 856, they note:

The foci of pulmonary emphysema and atelectasis without hemorrhage observed in some of the early casualties (Fig. 20) are difficult to interpret. These were found frequently at death in patients who had not been exposed to blast.

Liebow's Figure 20 (referred to in the quote) is shown here as Figure 10.6. The deceased patient is a thirteen years old boy, who is said to have died on the third day; thus, the lesions are truly acute and indicate some sort of obstruction of bronchioles (small bronchi).[17]

The difficulty which Liebow and colleagues perceived with interpreting their findings is readily dispelled if we consider causes other than

---

[17]If large bronchi rather than small ones had been occluded, correspondingly large segments of air-filled tissue should been cut off from ventilation, and we should not see the alternation of inflated and deflated alveoli across distances as short as evident in this picture.

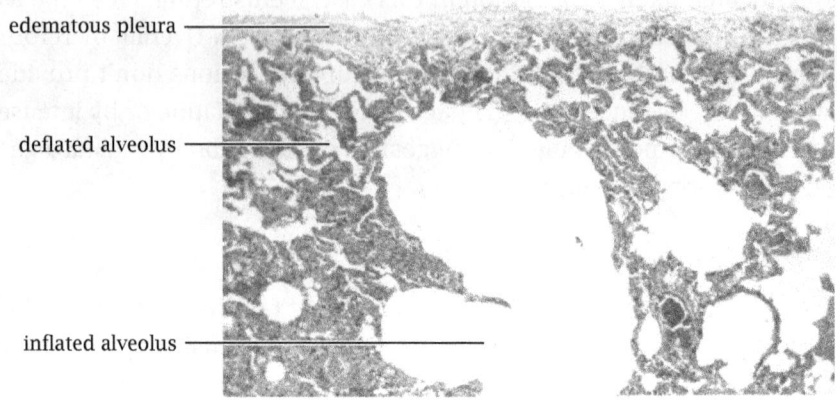

Figure 10.6: Lung emphysema (excessive inflation) and atelectasis (excessive deflation) in an early fatality from Hiroshima. Photograph from Liebow et al. [42], annotations by this author.

atomic bombs. The book *The residual effects of warfare gases* discusses the effects of mustard gas on the lungs and observes [139, p. 92]:

> *Emphysema was frequently found in combination with bronchitis. It usually appeared immediately after gassing and was compensatory in character, due to the extensive atelectasis found following gassing with mustard.*

The atelectasis, in turn, is understood to arise from bronchial obstruction. Thus, what we have here is a milder expression of the pathological changes in the lung which we invoked in Section 10.1.4 to account for the clinical picture in immediate fatalities on the day of the bombing.

10.4.2 Focal and confluent hemorrhage, inflammation, and necrosis of the lungs in later fatalities. The largest group of patients whose autopsy materials were surveyed by Liebow et al. were those who had succumbed within weeks 3 to 6 after the bombing. In slightly more than half of these cases, the authors found a varied picture with edema, hemorrhage, necrosis, and infection. These processes were focused on the bronchioles (small bronchi) but tended to expand and become confluent (see Figure 10.7).

With respect to this group of patients, Liebow et al. don't express any puzzlement as to the causation; presumably, they ascribe their findings to the bone marrow suppression, which would pave the way

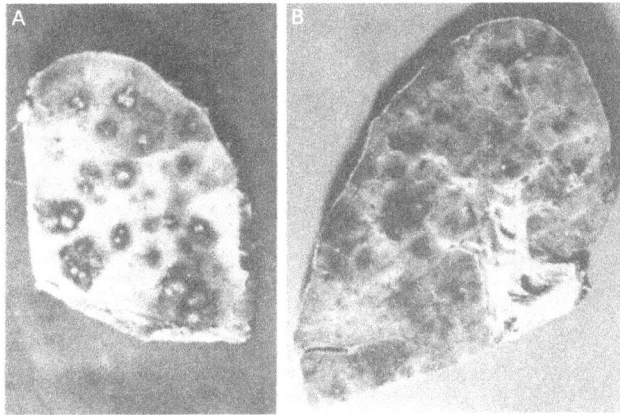

Figure 10.7: Focal necrosis, inflammation, and hemorrhage in the lungs of bombing victims. Photographs taken from Figures 17 (A) and 19 (B) in [42].

for infections and also for the hemorrhage. This is indeed most likely an important contributing factor, and it would be equally well explained by radiation and mustard gas. We may note that the lesions remain centered on the bronchi, which suggests primary damage to them; this would be expected with mustard gas, yet not impossible in its absence. The same combination of findings was reported in a series of autopsies of German mustard gas victims (from the final months of World War I) by Heitzmann [28]. In summing up his findings, Heitzmann describes the appearance of the lungs as *bunt*, that is, checkered, which seems an apt description of the lungs shown in Figure 10.7. On the other hand, high-dose irradiation alone did not cause any of these changes in animal lungs [26, p. 704 ff]. Overall, while Liebow's findings *suggest* causation by mustard gas rather than by radiation, the time elapsed between trauma and death means that this evidence is more ambiguous than the atelectasis and emphysema at the very early stage.

10.5 Neck organs

In most of the cases surveyed by Liebow et al. [42], death occurred in or after the third week. Therefore, as with the lung pathology in the preceding section, it can be difficult to distinguish primary damage from secondary effects of bone marrow suppression, which facilitates severe infection in these locations and would by the third week have reached its peak. In some of their cases, however, they do describe and depict injury that is predominantly necrotic—that is, due to direct damage by either radiation or mustard—rather than infectious. This is particularly clear in their single reported case of early death, a young man of 19 years who died on the tenth day and who is listed in their records as 'K-98'. Concerning this case, the authors note:

> In the records of the necropsies of 2 individuals, K-98 (group I) and K-109 (group II), who were recently dead, the skin was said to have "peeled" easily revealing a pink raw surface beneath. The tongue, pharynx, and esophagus of one of these patients, K-98, showed remarkable changes in the epithelium with sloughing over large areas.

Later on, they remark that "the changes in the tissues of K-98 undoubtedly represent radiation effects." Of course, these findings represent *anything but* radiation effects, since all of the epithelial tissues in question are quite radioresistant and thus should not have been destroyed by radiation more severely than any others; and it is hard to believe that Liebow and particularly his co-author Warren, who had been studying these matters for many years, would not have known this. Instead, both the peeling skin and the necrotic mucous membranes of the pharynx and esophagus are perfectly typical of mustard gas exposure. The authors also note that bone marrow damage has already set in, which rounds out the picture.

10.6 Gastrointestinal tract

The experimental studies reported by Bloom [26] indicated that among the intestines the duodenum (i.e., the uppermost part of the small intestine) is the most susceptible to both radiation and sulfur mustard. However, it is likely that in their studies on mustard gas they applied the poison by intraperitoneal or intravenous injection, so that the gastrointestinal tract would have been affected by way of the bloodstream, causing an equable exposure of all segments.

We had already seen in Section 8.10 that early and violent diarrhea was common among the bombing victims. The most likely explanation is that they had ingested food or water contaminated with mustard gas. In such a case, we might expect that the toxic effect will be most pronounced in those bowel segments within which the ingested food and fluids dwell and stagnate the longest. Within the small intestine, this is the lowermost part, whose emptying into the large intestine is controlled and delayed by the ileocecal valve [200]. It is interesting, therefore, that Liebow et al. [42] note:

In the small intestine also there were foci of necrosis, usually discrete. They were most numerous in the region of the ileocecal valve where there was almost always involvement.

The authors show several pictures of necrotic ileocecal valves and adjoining segments of small and large intestine, in which exposure to ingested mustard would have been prolonged by generally slow transport of bowel content. Likewise, the stomach is strongly affected, although from the descriptions of these lesions it is again difficult to distinguish direct effects from those facilitated by bone marrow failure.

An interesting episode of gastrointestinal affliction is related by Hachiya [62]. Having recovered from his initial illness and injury after several weeks, he leaves his hospital to visit friends in downtown Hiroshima. On his return, he suffers violent diarrhea, initially watery but later bloody. On the next day (September 24th), he muses:

I wondered if I had inhaled the 'bad gas' people spoke about, during my wanderings in the ruins yesterday?[18] *The next time the amount was less, but mucus was present and tenesmus greater.*

Considering that his symptoms are gastrointestinal rather than respiratory, it seems more likely that he has ingested rather than inhaled the poison. On September 29th, he notes:

I passed a plug of mucus about ten centimeters long and cylindrical in shape, with surface markings like a casting of intestinal mucosa. I was not a little startled to see this, and on examining it closely was convinced I had had a mucous enteritis rather than radiation sickness.

Even though Hachiya refers to it as mucus, the plug must have consisted of some firmer material, since mucus would be too soft to retain a specific three-dimensional shape during passage through the

---

[18] Overall, however, Hachiya makes it clear that he does not subscribe to the poison gas theory. On August 12th, he notes: "That a poison gas or deadly germ had been loosed in Hiroshima, I had finally dismissed, but these rumors were disturbing. ... If a poison gas had been used, it should have killed everyone. Whatever killed these people, therefore, could not have been a poison gas."

anal sphincter. Indeed, his description evokes the fibrin casts that form within bronchi whose blood vessels leak blood plasma into the luminal space after having been scoured by sulfur mustard (see Section 7.3.2).

10.7 Other organs

Most of the other organs affected in the bombing victims were exposed via the bloodstream rather than directly. In many of these, such as the bone marrow, spleen, and gonads, the pathological findings will indeed be similar between mustard gas and radiation, with severe depletion of the respective organ-specific cell types. Predictably, these are the organs that Liebow et al. [42] like to dwell on. In the early reports by the Japanese pathologist Yamashina (listed by Ishikawa et al. [8] in their in Table 8.25)—which were completed before Japan's capitulation, and thus before Liebow and his colleagues could lay their hands on the autopsy materials—the liver is more prominently afflicted than one would expect with radiation, based on the mostly negative findings from experiments that exposed animals to high radiation doses [26, p. 541 ff]. Yamashina's observations—congestion, cloudiness, fatty liver—are compatible with findings reported in mustard gas poisoning [17] but are not specific for this condition. Overall, a more detailed examination of further organs appears unlikely to add significant weight to the evidence in our case and will therefore be omitted.

11 The radiation dose estimates used in studies on survivors

> Garbage in, garbage out.
>
> Wilf Hey

This chapter describes how individual radiation dose estimates were produced for each survivor of the 'atomic' bombs, and it then examines the correlation of these estimates with biological outcomes. We will see that

- serious efforts to determine radiation doses began belatedly, after a prolonged period of general neglect and strict censorship of medical research;
- the T65D dosimetry scheme, published in the 1960s, provided individual dose estimates, which were based on radiation measurements during later bomb tests, in combination with each survivor's distance from the hypocenter and extent of shielding against radiation by his environment. These dose estimates correlate very poorly with biological outcomes, in particular acute radiation sickness and somatic chromosome aberrations;
- the DS86 dosimetry scheme brought major changes to global and individual dose estimates, but it did not reduce the discrepancies between individual dose estimates and biological outcomes.

The collective findings show that the genotoxic effects in individual bombing victims do not correspond closely to their personalized dose estimates. The pervasive use of these flawed estimates in survivor studies has marred not only those studies themselves, but also radiation biology and medicine in general.

11.1 The Atomic Bomb Casualty Commission (ABCC)

After the 'Joint Commission' (see Section 8.4) had ended its investigations in late 1945, nothing much happened for a while in the way of systematic medical studies on the bombing survivors. In 1947, the Atomic Bomb Casualty Commission (ABCC) was set up. While minimally staffed and equipped in its early stages [201], it had grown considerably by 1950, when its staff exceeded 1,000 members, most of whom were Japanese [202]. However, it was slow to produce, or at least to publish, any data on the medical condition of the survivors. A first report on the blood cell counts of 924 bombing survivors in Hiroshima, and a matched control group from the neighboring city of Kure, appeared only in 1949; the study noticed only minor residual effects in highly exposed bombing victims [203]. During this early era, Japanese scientists and physicians were subject to strict censorship, and almost none of their work was allowed to be published, with many manuscripts disappearing without a trace and often without even so much as a negative decision [15, 41].

Thus prevented from spreading their wings, the physicians at ABCC appear to have simply confined themselves to their daily routine work. Accordingly, the most important initial findings were first reported by independent workers. As noted in Section 8.7, the crucial finding of widespread radiation sickness among late entrants to the inner city was made by an astute and energetic physician from Hiroshima with no affiliation to the ABCC. The same applies to the initial observation of leukemia in bombing survivors [204]:

> The first intimation that leukemia was elevated among the survivors arose through the perceptiveness of a young Japanese physician, Takuso Yamawaki. As early as 1949, he believed that he was seeing more cases of leukemia in his clinical practice than he expected, and he sought the advice of hematologists at the Atomic Bomb Casualty Commission, who confirmed his diagnoses. This finding, the first evidence of a possible increase in any cancer among the survivors, immediately prompted an effort to confirm and extend what apparently was being seen. The task was made difficult, however, by the absence of individual dose estimates, the lack of a systematic case-finding mechanism, and uncertainties about the size of the population at risk.

The concluding sentence of the quote illuminates what the ABCC had or had not accomplished until 1949. While some surveillance studies on at least the most severely affected survivors were underway in the early 1950s, these were criticized in 1955 by an outside review panel for their lack of focus and of proper control groups, as well as for high participant attrition [205]. This panel, known as the Francis committee, also noted the lack of individual radiation dose estimates: nobody at ABCC was quite certain how much radiation had been received by any of the patients or study subjects they were dealing with. This uncertainty led to the following absurd argument among four ABCC geneticists, who were surveying possible genetic effects of radiation in children then being born to mothers who had survived the bombings [41, p. 201f.]:

When a survivor said she had been distant from the hypocenter, but reported experiencing severe radiation sickness, she could conceivably be placed in one of two different categories ... Morton felt that reported distance was more reliable than reported symptoms ... Neel took the opposite position ... McDonald sided with Morton, Schull sided with Neel, and the debate raged on for some weeks, with much anecdotal evidence proffered by both sides.

It seems to have escaped the combatants' notice that they were in fact all agreed on the same principle: the data should be bent out of shape to fit the same preconceived notion, namely, that radiation sickness could only have occurred near the hypocenter. Their argument merely concerned the technical question of *which way* to bend the data.[1]

11.2 Establishment of individual dose estimates

The Francis committee's recommendations finally led to the design and implementation of two large-scale, long-term surveillance programs that are still ongoing, namely, the 'Life Span Study' and the 'Adult

---

[1] In fairness to the four scientists, it must be noted that they did not falsify the data in their published study [206]. They avoided this by simply dropping the distance as a criterion altogether for the subjects who had reported radiation sickness; only those with no such history were grouped by distance, whereas those with the disease were all lumped together into a single group. They did, however, not state their reason for doing so, namely, the difference between expected and observed spatial distribution of ARS symptoms.

Health Study'. In support of these studies, a major effort was also undertaken to determine the individual doses of radiation that each of the enrolled study subjects would have received in the bombings. As described by Jablon et al. [207] and in more detail by Auxier [36], various true-to-scale, open-air physical experiments were carried out, often in conjunction with ongoing nuclear bomb tests, in order to determine the in-air doses of γ- and neutron radiation that would have prevailed at various distances from the hypocenters in Hiroshima and Nagasaki, as well as the shielding characteristics of traditional Japanese buildings.

The results of these measurements were then used to derive the individual radiation doses by taking into account the specifics of location and shielding for each survivor, as gathered from detailed interviews. The interviews presented their own difficulties, because the mystery survivors from near the hypocenters put in another appearance; but these were resolutely dealt with by the undaunted investigators. Seymour Jablon, an American statistician with the ABCC, recounts [208]:

> *Although some persons report being in the open at close distances, the stories must be considered as mistaken, since the intensity of blast and heat effects at near distances were such as to make survival impossible ... Survivors who stoutly aver such experiences may be sincere in their statements; however, there is a possibility of post concussion amnesia with a resulting erroneous story. ... The fact that so few survivors do not remember the details of the event may be taken to imply that those survivors who are amnesic for the explosion have substituted for their actual experiences a satisfactory surrogate.*

In other words, survivors who had been very near the hypocenter and should have died, but hadn't, and who furthermore had not noticed the large explosion that should have killed them, but hadn't, were declared 'amnesic' forthwith. Based on this 'diagnosis', their entire recollection was then discarded as an elaborate fantasy. This crafty and robust approach allowed the interviewers to prevail over all contrary evidence.

The initial set of dose estimates thus obtained became known as 'Tentative 65 Doses' (T65D). The T65D system was used from the late 1960s [209] until the publication of Loewe and Mendelsohn's revised estimates in the early 1980s; these were subsequently endorsed as the 'Dosimetry Scheme 1986' (DS86; see Section 11.5). A further, fairly minor modification occurred in 2002 (DS02). Ever since their inception, these dose estimates have been used by the ABCC and by its successor organization, the 'Radiation Effects Research Foundation' (RERF), as the frame of reference for interpreting any and all medical observations on the survivors in Hiroshima and Nagasaki. The studies published by this institution have greatly influenced the scientific literature on radiation biology and medicine (see for example [210, 211]). However, can the dose estimates used in these studies be trusted?

11.3 Correlation of radiation dose estimates with ARS symptoms

Figure 11.1A shows some proper radiation dose-response curves, which were obtained in rhesus monkeys exposed to mixed γ- and neutron radiation during a series of bomb tests, as well as in mice experimentally exposed to X-rays. While the mice can tolerate higher radiation doses than the monkeys,[2] both curves exhibit a very steep, clearcut transition from very low levels of response—in this case, mortality—to very high ones; doses that cause almost complete mortality exceed those which cause virtually none by a factor of no more than 2. The results obtained with rhesus monkeys, in particular, are more than merely illustrative, since these monkeys are physiologically similar to humans and thus provide the best available animal model for estimating human radiosensitivity.[3]

With acute radiation sickness in humans, we should expect dose-response curves shifted to the left relative to the rhesus monkey curve in Figure 11.1A, yet they should be similar in shape. Characteristic symptoms such as bleeding, epilation, and oropharyngeal ulcers should be rare below 2 Gy but regularly present beyond twice that dose [149]. This is, however, not at all what we see in Figure 11.1B. The dose estimates and associated symptom frequencies shown in this graph

---

[2]The difference might arise at least in part from the neutron component of the radiation received by the monkeys, but not the mice. Indeed, according to Carsten [148], the LD_{50} of mice is only slightly above that of rhesus monkeys.

[3]Both humans and rhesus monkeys are primates and share some metabolic traits likely to affect susceptibility to radiation. They require ascorbic acid as a vitamin, while also degrading adenine and guanine to uric acid. Radiation effects are mediated by radicals (Section 2.11); both ascorbic acid (vitamin C) and uric acid can scavenge radicals and thus mitigate radiation effects.

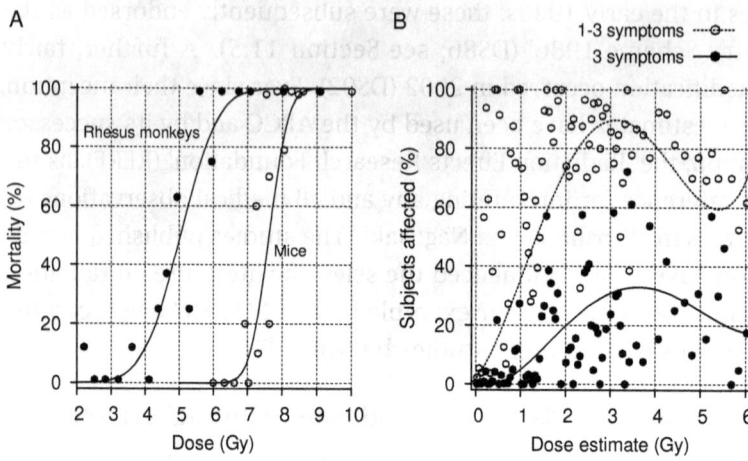

Figure 11.1: Mortality due to experimental irradiation in mice and rhesus monkeys, and incidence of ARS symptoms vs. estimated radiation doses in A-bomb survivors. A: Mortality in rhesus monkeys exposed during a series of bomb tests [212] and in mice subjected to single doses of 250 kV X-rays [213]. Trend lines are fits to a cumulative Gaussian distribution. B: Incidence of ARS symptoms in A-bomb survivors. The three symptoms reported in the data set [168] are epilation, bleeding, and oropharyngeal lesions. Doses have been grouped such that each data point comprises at least 10 subjects. Trend lines are fourth order polynomial fits, weighted for sample size.

were obtained from a dataset published by RERF;[4] adjoining dose ranges were here merged as needed so that each data point in the graph is drawn from a sample of at least 10 subjects (but some data points, particularly at or near 0 Gy, represent many more individuals). The incidence of symptoms scatters widely across almost the entire dose range; it reaches high levels in some dose groups well below 2 Gy, while

---

[4]This data set [168] was released in 2000 and includes 75,991 survivors (51,390 from Hiroshima and 24,601 from Nagasaki). For 71,776 survivors, the dataset states unambiguously whether each of the three ARS symptoms or flash burns were present; the graphs shown here are drawn from this subset.

RERF stipulates that each work which includes any of their data contain the following statement: "This report makes use of data obtained from the Radiation Effects Research Foundation (RERF) in Hiroshima, Japan. RERF is a private foundation funded equally by the Japanese Ministry of Health, Labour and Welfare and the U.S. Department of Energy through the U.S. National Academy of Sciences." Furthermore, I am to say that "the conclusions in this report [the one which you are reading] are those of the authors and do not necessarily reflect the scientific judgment of RERF or its funding agencies." We can safely assume that RERF's disclaimer applies in our case.

failing to reach saturation even as the dose approaches a presumably fatal level (6 Gy). Clearly, the estimated dose is a very poor predictor of the biological outcome.

11.4 Dose estimates and somatic chromosome aberrations

Another biological end point that we can compare to estimated radiation doses are chromosome aberrations in somatic cells. Many readers will be familiar with the concept of inherited chromosomal aberrations. One example is Down syndrome, which is caused by an extra (third) copy of chromosome 21; others are Turner syndrome (one of two X chromosomes is missing in women) or Klinefelter syndrome (an extra X chromosome is present in men).

11.4.1 Biological background. While some specific chromosome aberrations give rise to genetic diseases, most aberrations are not heritable, since they will be lethal in early embryonic development. However, they may persist when introduced not into the germline cells but instead into somatic (body) cells of adults or also of children. In the context of radiation damage, chromosomal aberrations begin with DNA double strand breaks in one or more chromosomes, followed by faulty rejoining of the fragments. Even though most such breaks will be resealed properly by DNA repair enzymes, the abundance of chromosome aberrations after irradiation is remarkably high. Furthermore, with proper experimental precautions, a fairly regular relationship can be observed between the radiation dose and the frequency of chromosome aberrations; this can be used for the approximate determination of radiation doses received for example in nuclear accidents [214, 215].

Chromosomes are observable, in their picture-book crossed-pair-of-sausages form, only during cell division (mitosis), and more specifically only during its *metaphase*, that is, the stage immediately before the two chromatids (the individual sausages) of each chromosome are pulled apart to join the separate nuclei of the incipient daughter cells. For most of the lifetime of the daughter cells, each chromatid will remain single, and it is for the most part at this stage that radiation will produce the characteristic lesions. Any lesions that are not properly repaired will then be copied into a new second chromatid shortly before the next mitosis, which explains why aberrations are typically visible in both chromatids at that stage.

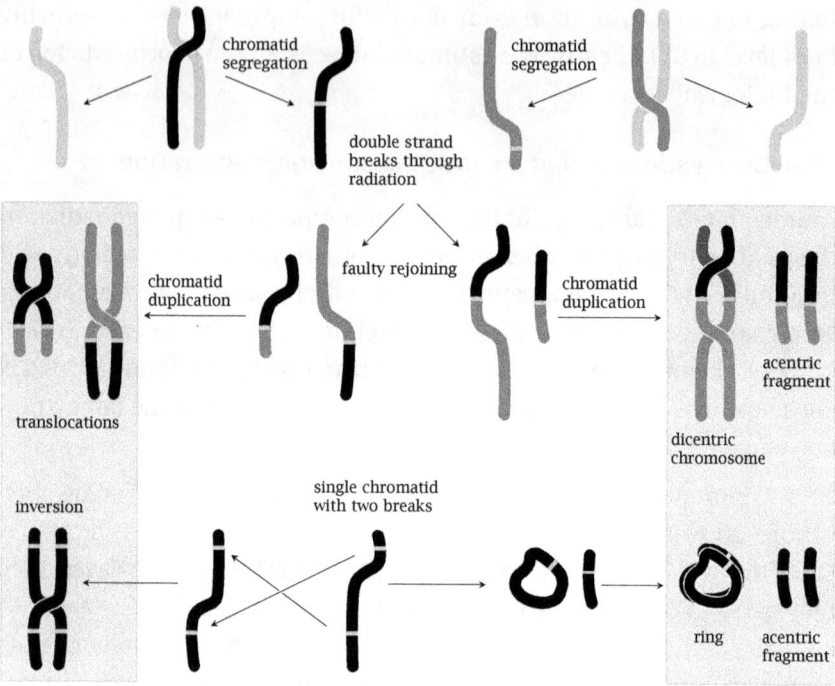

Figure 11.2: Induction of chromosome aberrations by DNA damage. Top and center: if two chromatids which belong to different chromosomes undergo double strand breaks at the same time, then faulty rejoining may produce translocations, dicentric chromosomes, and acentric fragments. Bottom: two simultaneous double strand breaks in a single chromatid may produce an inversion or a ring and an acentric fragment. Inversions and translocations tend to be stably transmitted during mitosis; rings as well as dicentric and acentric forms tend to be lost from one or both daughter cells during mitosis.

A crucial part of each chromosome is its *centromer*, which is where the two chromatids are joined together, and also where the *mitotic spindle*—the apparatus of structural and motile proteins that will pull the two chromatids apart—attaches. For chromatid separation and segregation into the two daughter nuclei to work reliably, each chromosome must have exactly one centromer. This is the case with all intact chromosomes, but it may not be so with the aberrant ones which form downstream of radiation damage (Figure 11.2). Aberrant forms with zero or two centromers may go missing from one or both daughter nuclei during cell division. They can therefore be reliably counted only in cells that enter their very first mitosis after the radiation exposure.

In diagnostic practice, chromosome aberrations are observed and counted in *lymphocytes*, a particular type of white blood cells (leukocytes) that are crucial for producing antibodies, for killing virus-infected cells, and for other functions of the specific immune system. Lymphocytes have a typical life span of four to five years. Unless stimulated by the presence of their specific cognate antigens—for example, lymphocyte A may recognize and be activated by measles virus, while lymphocyte B might react to tetanus vaccine—they tend to be dormant, i.e. to not undergo any cell divisions. When they are isolated from a blood sample, they can be artificially induced to divide using certain non-specific *mitogens*. In these artificially induced and synchronized mitoses, we can expect to find both stable and unstable chromosome aberrations at high frequency, as long as both irradiation and examination occur within the time frame of the regular lymphocyte lifespan. However, as the pool of irradiated, dormant lymphocytes is replaced after several years with newly formed cells, the unstable chromosome aberrations tend to diminish [216]; and furthermore, we must expect the rate of lymphocyte attrition, and therefore of loss of unstable aberrations, to vary among individuals.

The techniques for quantifying chromosome aberrations were developed around 1960, that is, a considerable time after the bombings of Hiroshima and Nagasaki; and the first such studies on the survivors appeared in the 1960s [217-219]. Nevertheless, these early studies relied mostly on unstable aberrations, which are more conspicuous (see Figure 11.2) and thus easier to observe and count experimentally. Because of the inherent variability that must be assumed in these data, we will not discuss them in detail; instead, we will focus on later studies that quantified stable aberrations [220-222].

After the passage of sufficient time, as was the case with the A-bomb survivors, the genetic makeup of the peripheral blood lymphocytes should resemble that of the bone marrow stem cells, from which all lymphocytes are ultimately descended, and which will self-renew throughout life. Once such a state has been reached, we would expect most of the observed aberrations to be of stable varieties, and furthermore that the aberration frequency in a given individual should be constant over time. Long-term surveillance of several accidentally irradiated subjects suggests that the frequency is indeed stable [215, 216, 223]. However, some stable chromosome translocations may affect the proliferation rate of the cells that contain them, which would then increase or decrease the abundance of these particular cell clones. In special cases, proliferation may be increased to the point of inducing leukemia; in particular, chronic myeloic leukemia is typically caused by the so-called *Philadelphia chromosome*, which arises through a translocation between chromosomes 9 and 22 that creates a growth-promoting aberrant gene at one of the two faulty fusion sites.

One more point should be noted before we delve into the data: any and all of the above radiation effects can also be observed with DNA-alkylating agents, including nitrogen mustard [224] and also sulfur mustard. The latter has been shown in former workers of a Japanese poison gas factory [225].[5]

11.4.2 Stable chromosome aberrations observed in survivors. Figure 11.3 summarizes the chromosome aberration study by Otake [220]. Shown here are the frequencies of cells with any aberrations, but the data in Table 2 of the reference indicate that 85-90% of these aberrations are in fact stable translocations. This agrees with the length of time that has passed between the irradiation and the measurement—most unstable aberrations should by then have been washed out by successive rounds of cell division.

Panels A and C in the figure show estimated radiation doses and frequencies of cells with one or more aberrations for individual subjects from Hiroshima and Nagasaki. As seen before with the symptoms of radiation sickness (Figure 11.1),[6] the most obvious and dominant feature of this graph is the very high degree of scatter—throughout most of the dose range, the frequency of cells with aberrations can be anything from 0 to 20% or more.[7] This means, of course, that the

---

[5]This factory was located on Okunoshima, a small island only some 50 kilometers from, of all places, Hiroshima.

[6]It would be most interesting to see a correlation of chromosome aberrations to ARS symptoms, that is, to have empirical data on both the x and the y axis. I have not found such a study, however; a senior RERF researcher, when asked, could not locate any such data either.

[7]Data were expanded from Figures 1 and 2 in [220], which give case numbers for each combination of dose interval and aberrant cell frequency. Coinciding data points have been slightly offset horizontally and vertically to try to render them all visible. A large number of subjects with estimated doses of exactly 0 Gy has been omitted, but the distribution of aberrant cells was similar to the lowest dose group shown (0-0.009 Gy).

In panels A and C, the y axis is truncated at 35%; according to another study [226], the highest values approach 50% and occur near the middle of the estimated dose

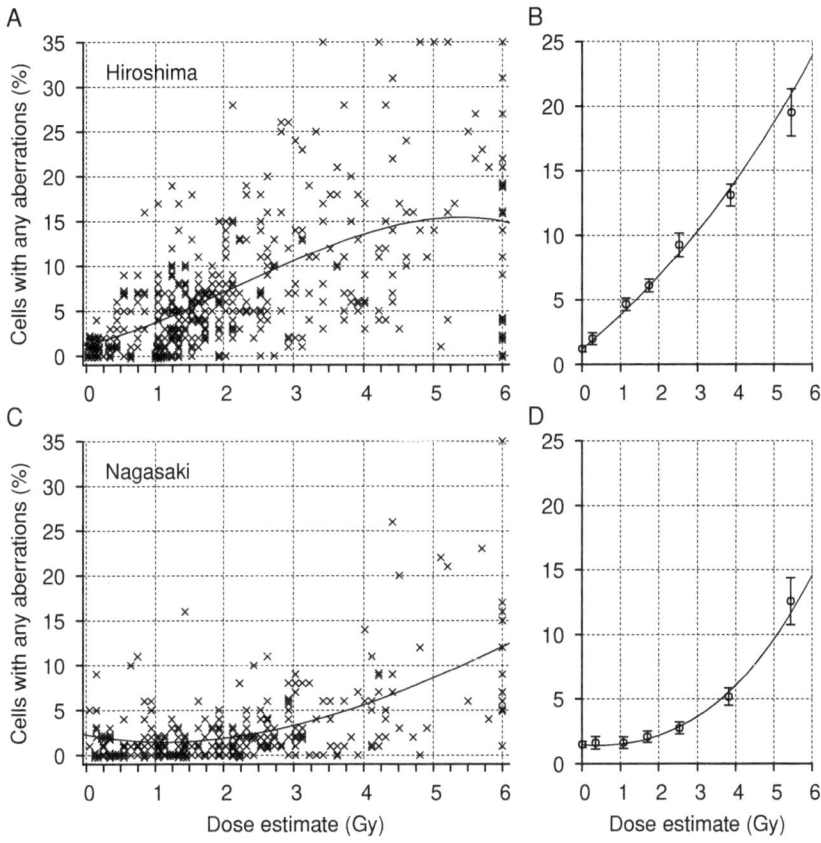

Figure 11.3: Chromosome aberrations in peripheral blood lymphocytes observed in A-bomb survivors. A, C: Aberrant cells observed in individual survivors from Hiroshima and Nagasaki, plotted against T65D radiation dose estimates [220]. Trend lines are third-order polynomial fits; both have R^2 values close to 0.34. B, D: The same data as in A and C, respectively, after passage through the RERF ~~sausage factory~~ statistics department (replots of Figure 3 in Otake [220]). The author refers to his error bars as '95% confidence intervals'.

assigned dose estimates have almost no predictive value—if at a given dose any extent of chromosome damage can occur, *then of course any extent of any other biological effect can occur as well*. We have already seen this with acute radiation sickness, and we will in Chapter 12 see the same effect with fetal malformations also.

---

range. Also note the 'traffic congestion' at the right end of the x range—it turns out that estimated doses higher than 6 Gy were truncated to that value, presumably because in reality such doses would have been unsurvivable. See also Section 8.9.

Before we leave Otake's study, we should take a look at the inferences that he was able to draw from the data shown in Figure 11.3A and C. In preparation for this exercise, the author

> chose dose intervals so as to present as smooth a curve as practicable based upon the frequency of aberrant cells in the two cities and the sample size in each dose interval.

For each of these groups, he then calculated a '95% confidence interval'. Considering that these intervals often don't overlap between adjacent dose groups (see Figure 11.3B and D), and accordingly that about half of the individual data points shown in panels A and C are *not* comprised within them, he can only mean that we should be 95% confident in his *averages*. These are, of course, about as useful for predicting individual aberration frequencies as is the annual average temperature in Oklahoma City when it comes to packing one's suitcase for a journey to the place.[8]

Otake next uses his averages to choose between several quantitative models of the relationship between dose estimates and chromosome aberrations. Taking into consideration that, according to the T65D dose estimates then in force, Hiroshima received significant neutron radiation, whereas Nagasaki did not, he infers from the two dose-response curves shown in Figure 11.3B that the frequency of aberrations is linear with respect to the neutron dose, but varies with the third power of the γ-dose. Furthermore, he derives estimates, again complete with 'confidence intervals', for the relative biological effectiveness of (RBE) neutrons as compared to γ-rays.

While the linear relationship with neutrons and other particles with high linear energy transfer agrees with conventional wisdom,[9] most other pertinent studies assert that low LET radiation (γ-rays) acts in proportion to the square of the dose or to a linear-quadratic combination. Regardless of what the truth of the matter may be, it seems an extraordinary proposition to decide such subtle differences based on data that scatter as widely as those in Figure 11.3A and C. The matter was soon forgotten, however, because shortly after the publication of

---

[8]Darrell Huff, who pioneered the didactic use of temperatures in Oklahoma City in his book *How to lie with statistics* [227], gives the average as 60°F (15.6°C) and the difference between annual highs and lows as 130°F (71.5°C).

[9]The concept of linear energy transfer is explained in Section 2.7.2.

Otake's study Loewe and Mendelsohn's 'new and improved' dosimetry scheme largely did away with the neutron contribution in Hiroshima altogether (see Section 11.5).

Even though Otake's conclusions are unconvincing, his study does at least give us a glimpse of the actual experimental data. This is the exception in the works released by RERF; for example, a study published under RERF's auspices by Awa [221] presents only a summary graph similar to Figure 11.3B above, without even hinting at the variability of the underlying data. Awa was, however, very much aware of the problem, as is evident from the following conversation, recorded a few years ago at an internal RERF history forum [228]:

> *Awa: We found several unbelievable cases while examining the relationship between dose estimates and chromosome aberration frequencies. They included proximally exposed survivors with no chromosome aberrations and distally exposed survivors with chromosome aberrations. We called them DCs (discrepancy cases), cases with a discrepancy from prediction. I assume those cases included individuals who wanted to hide the fact that they had been exposed to A-bomb radiation for marriage or various other reasons.*
>
> *Teramoto [interviewer]: Was there a dispute between the Departments of Statistics and Genetics over the interpretation of this discrepancy?*
>
> *Awa: Yes, and each group refused to yield.*
>
> *Teramoto: By that time, the biennial blood sample collection from AHS [Adult Health Study] participants had already begun. I assume researchers examined samples collected from the same subjects on multiple occasions and concluded that the argument of your group was correct.*
>
> *Awa: Yes. We examined each sample many times, in some cases as many as 10 times, and determined that no individual variation was involved.*

Awa's suggestion that false assertions of low exposure stemmed from concern over marriage prospects is intriguing—might *high* exposure have been claimed untruthfully by those keen to *avoid* marriage? More seriously, though, the debate over these discordant cases is of

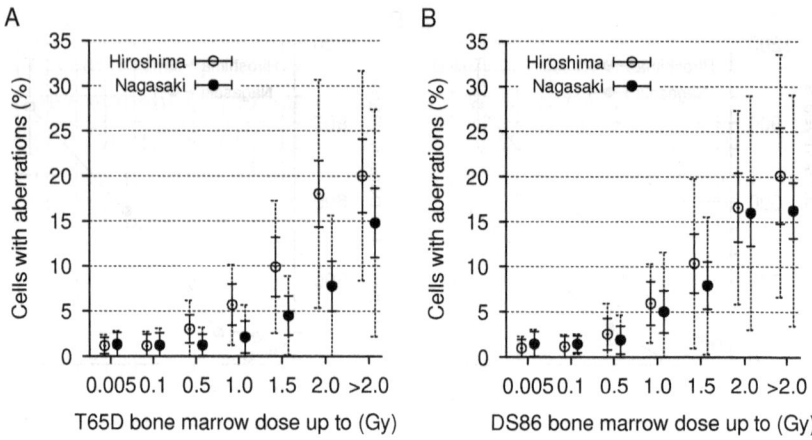

Figure 11.5: Chromosome aberrations in bombing survivors vs. T65D and DS86 dose estimates. A: T65D; B: DS86. Data points are observed averages; observed standard deviations are indicated by dotted lines, expected ones by solid lines. Replotted from Figure 3 in [226].

this end, the authors reproduce a leukemia incidence graph published previously by Rossi and Mays [229], shown here as Figure 11.4A, and then transmogrify it by replacing the T65D doses used by those authors with their own new and improved dose estimates (Figure 11.4B). In one fell swoop, both of the circumstances that had aroused attention have disappeared: the difference in dose-response between the two cities has vanished, and the neutron component in Hiroshima has been reduced to a marginal role.

Considering that Loewe and Mendelsohn were able to present such precise dose calculations as early as 1981, it is peculiar that the new DS86 dosimetry scheme could be unveiled to the public only in 1987, when the full report was finally published by RERF [93]. While the physicists continued to argue over its validity for many years and in fact never settled their dispute conclusively, a survey of the biomedical literature after 1981 indicates that the ploy was a success: this audience bought the new dose estimates sight unseen, and their previously lively interest quickly died down.

One issue that DS86 did nothing to resolve is the excessive variability of biological effects at any given estimated dose. This is illustrated for chromosome aberrations in Figure 11.5. As with the leukemia incidence, the DS86 scheme largely does away with the difference between the two cities. However, at bone marrow doses greater than 0.1 Gy, the observed standard deviation in the number of cells with aberrations is 2-3 times greater than the theoretical expectation with both dosimetry schemes. At high doses the observed standard deviation spans almost the entire range; and considering that with a Gaussian distribution nearly $1/3$ of all observed values fall *outside* of a single standard deviation, the variability is obviously similar to that depicted in Figure 11.3. Thus, regardless of which dosimetry scheme we employ, we can expect the same kinds of systematic errors and distortions in the resulting dose-response curves.

11.6 Conclusion

The import of this chapter is simple: the official radiation dose estimates, regardless of the flavor of the day—T65D, DS86, or the but slightly modified DS02, which was not here discussed in detail—do not reliably capture and predict the biological effects of radiation in the survivors of the bombings. This failure is of course expected if indeed there *was* no nuclear detonation and no radiation, save for the trifling amount of radioactivity contained in the dispersed reactor waste. Application of these fictional dose estimates to real biological outcomes will produce spurious and distorted radiation dose-response curves; it will systematically overestimate sensitivity at low doses but underestimate the effect of high doses. The error is less obvious with cancer and leukemia, which are themselves stochastic occurrences, than with deterministic radiation effects such as chromosome aberrations and acute radiation sickness. Spurious correlations can also be expected with disruptions of fetal development; this will be examined in the following chapter.

12 Disease in long-term survivors

> Radiation [is] unlikely to be responsible for high cancer rates among distal Hiroshima A-bomb survivors.
>
> Eric Grant and colleagues, RERF [230]

This chapter will look at late manifestations of genotoxic exposure among the survivors, in particular birth defects, cancer, and cataract. The key observations are as follows:

- The low observed rate of malignant disease in prenatally exposed survivors, while surprising, can be readily reconciled with exposure to either radiation or chemical genotoxic agents.
- The most common birth defect in prenatally exposed survivors is microcephaly, often accompanied by mental retardation. The latter is strongly correlated with a history of acute radiation sickness in mothers, but very poorly with radiation dose estimates.
- Cancer incidence is significantly increased even in those survivors with very low estimated radiation exposure, and also in those who entered the inner city of Hiroshima shortly after the bombing.
- Cataract may be caused by radiation, but also by genotoxic chemicals such as sulfur mustard. Its incidence is greatest near the hypocenter; however, increased rates also occur at distances which should have been beyond the reach of radiation doses sufficient to cause cataract.

While late disease manifestations are thus not qualitatively characteristic, their spatial and temporal distribution further strengthens the case against radiation as the causative agent.

In Chapter 11, we already saw that systematic studies on diseases in long-term survivors got underway very belatedly, and also that these studies have suffered, and continue to suffer, from being burdened with fictitious estimated doses of imaginary radiation. As we will see below, many of the more useful studies are those which predate these dose estimates, and which therefore use more tangible points of reference such as symptoms of acute radiation sickness or distance from the hypocenter.

12.1 Malformations and malignant disease in prenatally exposed survivors

The numbers of prenatally exposed survivors in Hiroshima and Nagasaki are not large, but they have been the subject of some interesting and surprising findings. It turns out, however, that none of these findings provide substantial proof for or against the thesis of this book; instead, we will here argue that the observations are compatible with either radiation or mustard gas as the causative agent. This section thus will not advance the main case of the book beyond corroborating yet again that radiation dose estimates are unreliable (see Section 12.1.4). Readers interested only in the evidence relevant to the main thesis may skip ahead to Section 12.2.

Among the effects of genotoxicity considered here, malformations are deterministic, whereas malignant disease—cancer and leukemia—is stochastic (Section 2.11.4); we should therefore expect a steep dose effect curve with the former and a shallow one with the latter. However, the susceptibility to radiation/genotoxicity of the embryo and fetus changes very substantially with time, being highest in the first trimester of the pregnancy; thus, if we lump all prenatally exposed survivors together regardless of the gestational age at exposure, we can expect the dose-effect curve to be somewhat broader than with acute radiation sickness or mortality in adults.

12.1.1 Experimental studies on teratogenesis induced by radiation and by alkylating agents. The literature in this field is rather large; we will here only consider some selected studies. A classical study by Russell and Russell [231] examined the effects of high doses of radiation (1-4 Gy) on the development of mouse embryos, focusing on malformations of the skeletal system. Between the 6th and the 12th day of gestation, malformations were readily induced by doses of 2 Gy and centered on the bones of the trunk and the skull. Irradiation with higher doses also induced malformations in the limbs, and it extended the susceptible period beyond the 12th to the 14th gestational day.

Most experimental teratogenesis studies have been carried out with mice and rats. While these two species have similar developmental

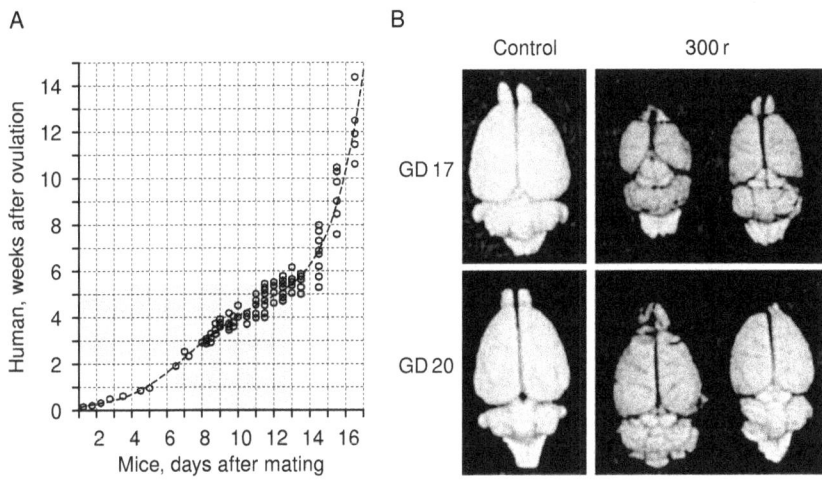

Figure 12.1: Time correlation of mouse and human embryonic development, and time-dependent effect of prenatal irradiation on brain growth in rats. A: Intrauterine development of mouse and man. Data points replotted from Otis and Brent [232]. Each point represents a specific organ development milestone. Highlighted in gray is the phase most susceptible to radiation-induced malformations in the mouse [231] and its equivalent in humans, estimated from the fit polynomial (dashed line). B: Reduced brain size in rats after irradiation with an X-ray dose of 300 r (approximately 3 Gy) on gestational days (GD) 17 and 20, respectively. Adapted from Hicks [233].

schedules, the human embryo develops much more slowly; however, the developmental time tables of human and rodent embryos can nevertheless be correlated by comparing the dates at which specific developmental end points are attained (Figure 12.1A). The slope of that relation is not uniform, since, in contrast to mice and rats, whose entire pregnancy lasts only about three weeks, humans have a lengthy period of fetal growth which follows the relatively short few weeks of organ development in the embryonic stage. The organ that develops the latest and the longest is the brain, which remains susceptible to irradiation into the early fetal period. This can also be observed in rats, which show a substantial reduction in brain size after irradiation on gestational day 17, and a lesser one even on day 20, which is just two days before the end of pregnancy (Figure 12.1B). Comparison with panel A of the figure suggests that human embryos or fetuses should be susceptible to radiation-induced microcephaly at least until the 15th week, but probably beyond. This correlates well with clinical observations on children who were prenatally exposed to high doses of radiation when their mothers underwent treatment—usually for cancer—during pregnancy [234]. Among these cases, microcephaly and mental retardation occurred up to the 20th week.

The radiation doses used by Russell and Russell [231] amount to one quarter to one half of the LD_{50} in adult mice (see Figure 11.1). Remarkably similar findings were reported by Sanjarmoosavi et al. [235], who used sulfur mustard in rats. These authors gave an LD_{50} of sulfur mustard of 4.4 mg/kg, and they injected pregnant rats with either 0.75 mg/kg or 1.5 mg/kg between gestational day 11 and 14. The lower dose sufficed to induce various malformations on day 11, but no later; the higher dose evoked a similar response until day 13 but failed to do so on the 14th day. Thus, with both radiation and sulfur mustard, there is a time-dependent and fairly high threshold dose for teratogenic effects.

The prenatal effects of radiation and of DNA-alkylating agents were directly compared by Murphy et al. [236]. As Figure 12.2 shows, the ratios of teratogenic to toxic doses were found to be similar between X-rays and nitrogen mustard, which in turn is similar to sulfur mustard in structure and reactivity. In both cases, teratogenic doses are only slightly below the fetal LD_{50} and a little less than one third of the maternal LD_{50}. Considering that the treatment in question was applied on gestational day 12, and that the teratogenic efficacy diminishes as pregnancy progresses, the minimal teratogenic dose might actually surpass the fetal LD_{50} in later stages.

In view of the experimental and clinical evidence discussed so far, we might expect the following observations in prenatally exposed victims and survivors in Hiroshima and Nagasaki:

1. malformations or stunted organ development should be observed mostly in those exposed between the 6th and the 20th pregnancy week;
2. the most commonly affected organ should be the brain;
3. severe malformations in the children should correlate with maternal toxicity (acute radiation sickness);
4. the incidence of outright fetal death may reach or exceed that of severe malformations.

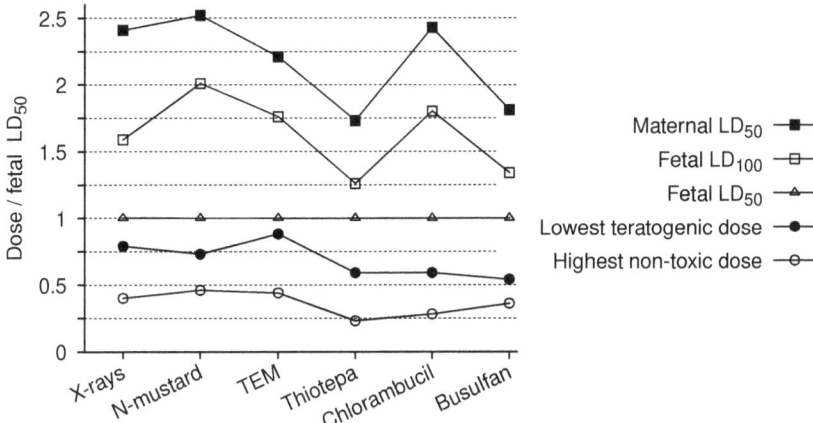

Figure 12.2: Embryotoxic effects of X-rays and of alkylating agents. Pregnant rats were exposed on the 12th day of pregnancy to varying doses of either X-rays or one of several alkylating agents, including nitrogen mustard (N-mustard; TEM is triethylene melamine). All dose effects are given relative to the fetal LD$_{50}$ of the agent in question (which thereby becomes equal to 1). Replotted from Figure 2 in Murphy et al. [236].

In the next section, we will see that the pregnancy outcomes observed among the bombing victims correspond closely to these empirically based expectations.

12.1.2 Correlation of mental retardation with maternal ARS and with fetal and infant mortality. The most frequently observed somatic aberration was indeed microcephaly, commonly defined as a head circumference that is two or more standard deviations below the average. When evaluating microcephalic survivors for mental retardation, early studies applied very stringent criteria [237]:

Mental retardation was diagnosed only if the subject was unable to perform simple calculations, to carry on a simple conversation, to care for himself, or if he was completely unmanageable, or had been institutionalized.

It seems likely that some of the microcephalic children whose condition was not quite so bad as this had some degree of mental impairment nevertheless.

The first published reports on microcephaly with mental retardation are that by Yamazaki et al. [240], who described cases from Nagasaki,

12 Disease in long-term survivors

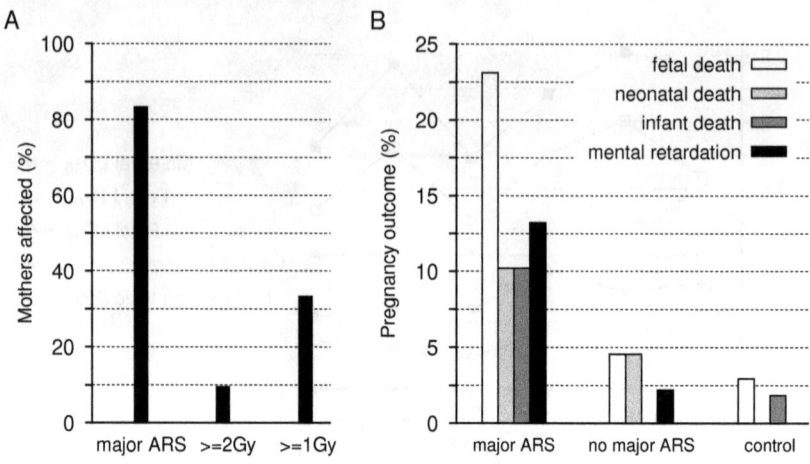

Figure 12.3: Mental retardation in children exposed in utero at Hiroshima and Nagasaki. A: Correlation of mental retardation among prenatally exposed children with clinical ARS and with radiation dose estimates. 83.3% of mentally retarded children were born to mothers with 'major' ARS symptoms, but only 9.5% to mothers with estimated doses that would cause characteristic ARS symptoms (≥ 2 Gy; Otake and Schull [238]). Data for ARS from Miller [239] for Hiroshima and from Yamazaki et al. [240] for Nagasaki. B: Pregnancy outcomes in Nagasaki. Mothers in the control group had been at > 4 km from the hypocenter; all others had been within 2 km. Adapted from Figure 1 in [240].

and those by Plummer [241] and Miller [239], who reported on cases from Hiroshima. Between these three studies, there are 18 children with microcephaly and mental retardation who have no other reported likely cause of retardation (e.g. Down syndrome), and for whose mothers it is known whether or not they had suffered ARS in the aftermath of the bombings (information on maternal ARS is lacking in one additional case). As it turns out, 15 out of 18 mothers had indeed suffered 'major' ARS symptoms, that is, one or more of epilation and purpura, and in the case of Yamazaki et al. also oropharyngeal lesions. Miller also lists several abnormalities other than microcephaly, but aside from Down syndrome, of which there are two cases, all of these occur only as single instances.

The only authors to explicitly correlate adverse pregnancy outcomes other than mental retardation with maternal ARS are Yamazaki et al. [240]. Even though their case numbers are small—their entire sample of mothers with major ARS graphed in Figure 12.3B comprised only 30 subjects—the findings are clear enough: like mental retardation, fetal, neonatal, and infant death (the latter being defined as occurring within the first year) are strongly correlated with maternal ARS. Oughterson et al. [33] give abortion rates for their samples of close to 7,000 survivors from each city. Within 1,500 m of the hypocenter, the proportion of pregnancies ending in abortion approaches 40% in Hiroshima; in Nagasaki, this value is exceeded even if all those within 3,000 m are included.[1] The total number of abortions in Oughterson's entire sample is 45, which exceeds that of mentally retarded children found in later studies on survivors.

In summary, fetal or infant death and mental retardation in surviving children are all strongly associated with acute radiation sickness in the mothers and, therefore, with exposure to a high level of radiation or chemical genotoxicity.

12.1.3 Mental retardation and time of exposure. A later study by Wood et al. [242] reports 30 prenatally exposed victims with mental retardation. Nine of these 30 cases are ambiguous, since the children have additional conditions—chromosome aberrations, or histories of brain infections or perinatal complications—that might well account for the observed mental deficit. The number of 21 cases without such ambiguity is slightly higher than the 18 such cases reported in earlier studies (see above). Figure 12.4 shows the putative week of gestation at the exposure for each of Wood's 30 cases, as well as the mother's distance from the hypocenter.[2] With the exception of one earlier, ambiguous case, mental retardation begins with the 6th week of gestation. The average gestational age of all cases is 14 weeks when the ambiguous cases are omitted, and 15 weeks when they are included. Some cases arise after the 20th week; the single very late case, exposed beyond 3000 m from the hypocenter, was likely not caused by the bombing.

We had seen earlier that symptoms of ARS were observed in some late entrants to the city center in Hiroshima (Section 8.7); major ARS

---

[1] It is noteworthy that the number of abortions is one metric that paints a grimmer picture for Nagasaki than for Hiroshima; in most others, Hiroshima appears to have been hit the harder.

[2] Wood et al. [242] do not state the incidence of ARS in the mothers, but most cases must have been the same ones as in the earlier studies, which reported a high correlation.

symptoms were apparent in some individuals who first entered the inner city up to two weeks after the bombing. Moreover, we had noted that such delayed exposure could account for cases of ARS that became manifest unusually late (see Section 8.8). If postponed exposure could induce mental retardation in unborn children also, we might expect that the *apparent* gestational age of these children—namely, that at the time of the bombing, rather than at the actual exposure—should be reduced in keeping with the time delay of exposure. However, no such trend is apparent in Figure 12.4 among those who had been more than 3000 m removed from the hypocenter during the bombing, and who would be the most likely to have been exposed only afterwards. On the other hand, out of the five cases in this group that are unambiguous, four still cluster around the 15th pregnancy week, suggesting that they, too, were caused by exposure during the bombing or only a short time thereafter.

Overall, we can conclude that the timing of mental retardation induced by prenatal exposure agrees well with expectations based on experimental studies and on prior observations on the children of mothers who had received radiation treatment during pregnancy.

12.1.4 Mental retardation and radiation dose estimates. Considering that both experimental studies and observations on the bombing victims clearly indicate that mental retardation results only with high levels of exposure, it is of considerable interest to compare this clinical outcome to estimated radiation doses. If the dose estimates were realistic, most mothers of retarded children should have high dose estimates; this is, however, not observed. According to Otake and Schull [238], only about 10% of the mothers have estimated doses of ≥ 2 Gy, and only about 32% reach or exceed 1 Gy (Figure 12.3).[3] Another oddity of Otake and Schull's study is the discrepancy between the two cities—27% of those exposed to 0.5-1 Gy in Hiroshima, but 0% of those so exposed in Nagasaki, were mentally retarded. (The numbers are close to 37% for expecting mothers exposed at > 1 Gy in both cities.)[4]

---

[3] In calculating these percentages, only mothers with estimated doses of greater than zero were considered. Including mentally retarded children whose mothers received an estimated dose of 0 Gy exactly would decrease these percentages further.

[4] Otake and Schull also maintain that mental retardation was caused only between the 8th the 15th gestational week. The do note that "a few discrepancies exist" as to the gestational ages given by Wood et al. [242] and those in the ABCC's files, which they

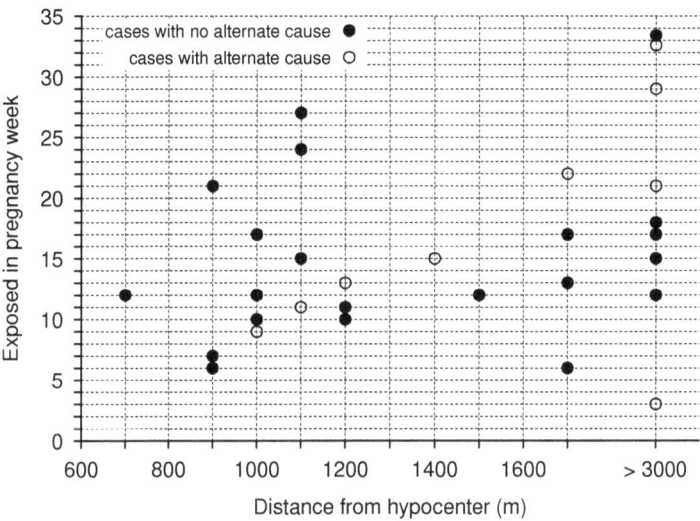

Figure 12.4: Microcephaly and mental retardation in children who were exposed *in utero*: time of exposure vs. distance from hypocenter. Data from table in appendix to Wood et al. [242] and combined for Hiroshima and Nagasaki. The category '> 3000' also includes children born to mothers who where out of town during the bombings.

Blot [243] as well as Miller and Mulvihill [244] report that microcephaly, with or without accompanying mental retardation, is significantly increased already at estimated doses below 0.2 Gy, and very strongly at levels between 0.2 and 0.3 Gy. Considering the evidence from animal experiments, this simply is not plausible.[5] Overall, the poor correlation between dose estimates and clinical outcomes that we noted with ARS in Section 11.3 also applies to microcephaly with mental retardation in prenatally exposed children.

12.1.5 Cancer and leukemia in prenatally exposed survivors.

A major discovery in radiation biology and medicine, and one which was initially greeted with much skepticism, was that prenatal exposure to even the small doses of radiation which are used in X-ray diagnostics

---

prefer. The time distribution one obtains using Wood's data (see Figure 12.4) agree better with the findings discussed in Section 12.1.1 than do Otake's, however.

[5] In animal experiments, radiation doses as low as these *did* induce intrauterine death or CNS malformations when applied to the very early embryo [245], but this resulted in anencephaly or exencephaly rather than microcephaly. Such grave defects would lead to death before or immediately after birth; some such cases may indeed have occurred among the fetal or neonatal deaths in Hiroshima and Nagasaki.

will cause a measurable increase in the incidence of childhood cancer and leukemia. First reported in 1956 by Stewart et al. [246],[6] this finding was later confirmed in two independent large-scale studies in the UK [247] and the U.S. [248]. While the exact magnitude of the risk remains under debate, it is generally believed to be at least as high as in the first decade after birth, which is the most sensitive period of extra-uterine life [249].

Against this background, it is certainly surprising to learn that only one case of cancer, and no cases of leukemia, occurred during the first ten years among the prenatally exposed in Hiroshima and Nagasaki [250, 251], even though a considerable number of leukemias did occur among those who had been exposed as young children. Using the then current estimate of the cancer risk per dose of radiation [247] and the survivors' estimated radiation doses, Jablon and Kato [250] calculated that approximately 37 of those prenatally exposed should have been afflicted by cancer or leukemia, and they suggested that the cancer risk of prenatal radiation exposure must be far lower than assumed.

A lot of ink has since been spilled over the question whether the discrepancy between observed and expected incidences is statistically robust. Since Jablon and Kato's expected cancer rate is based on the very same estimated radiation doses which were already shown to be unreliable (see above and Chapter 11), there is no point in joining that argument. Rather than explaining away Jablon and Kato's findings, as some have tried, with statistical contortions, we will consider instead if they can be properly understood in a scientific context.

We might start from the assumption that the toxic principle was not radiation, but rather a chemical poison. Drugs and poisons which are present in the maternal circulation differ considerably in their ability to traverse the placenta and reach the unborn child. This is well illustrated in an experimental study by Calsteren et al. [252]: among six different anticancer drugs examined, the fetal plasma levels ranged from 0% to 57% of the maternal ones. Thus, in principle, the embryo and fetus may be protected from a drug or poison that harms the mother, while no such protection is possible with γ- or neutron radiation. However, this line of reasoning fails with the poison used in Hiroshima and Nagasaki,

---

[6]The X-ray doses used in diagnostic imaging at the time were considerably higher than those in use today, yet nevertheless far lower than those required then and now in therapeutic irradiation.

since the observed teratogenic effect (see Section 12.1.2) indicates efficient traversal of the placenta. Evidently, the poison affected the unborn children to a similar extent as radiation would have, yet it induced only a very small number of malignancies.[7] Thus, we clearly must reexamine the assumption of high prenatal susceptibility to cancer induction by radiation or other mutagenic stimuli.

Anderson et al. [254] reviewed a number of experimental studies that compare the effects of X- or γ-rays and of various chemical carcinogens before and after birth. The chemicals were not similar to sulfur mustard, and they might undergo metabolic activation or inactivation before and after birth to different degrees; therefore, we will here only consider the radiation studies from that review. Among these, the majority find greater carcinogenic potential after birth than before, but exceptions are observed. In a particularly comprehensive study by Sasaki [255], mice were irradiated at various times before or after birth, then allowed to live out their lives until their natural death, and finally autopsied. Interestingly, the most sensitive time for cancer induction was tissue-dependent; among 9 different types of tumors, 7 were induced by radiation more readily after birth than before it, whereas the reverse was true for the other two.

Cancers and leukemias are very often accompanied (and sometimes caused) by chromosome aberrations. We had seen in Section 11.4.1 that somatic chromosome aberrations can persist for a very long time. Interestingly, however, they may be eliminated rather quickly after fetal exposure to alkylating agents [256] or to radiation [257]; this apparently applies to lymphocytes but not epithelial cells [258]. Low rates of chromosome aberrations were also observed in the lymphocytes of prenatally exposed bombing survivors, even if their mothers had high rates of persistent aberrations [259]. Lymphatic leukemia—that is, leukemia originating from precursor cells of lymphocytes—is the single most common childhood malignancy in general, and it also was the most common one among children postnatally exposed in Hiroshima and Nagasaki. The mechanism by which the fetus eliminates chromosome anomalies from lymphocytes, and presumably also from

---

[7]This assessment pertains to the first ten or fifteen years after the exposure, which is the appropriate length of time when comparison is made to studies such as Stewart and Kneale [247]. Long-term follow up of prenatally exposed survivors has found significantly increased cancer rates in adulthood, however [253].

their precursor cells, remains to be elucidated; but the effect as such is clear enough, and it may well account for Jablon and Kato's remarkable observation that childhood leukemias were absent from prenatally exposed bombing survivors.

Surprising as this evidence may be, it does not distinguish radiation from radiomimetic compounds such as sulfur mustard as the genotoxic agent used in Hiroshima and Nagasaki. It also does not rule out the induction of childhood cancers—in small numbers, and thus detectable only in samples much larger than those of the bombing survivors—by medical X-ray exposure. In this context, the collective evidence simply indicates that we should not linearly extrapolate from low doses to very high ones or vice versa.

12.2 Cancer and leukemia

The literature on the incidence of cancers and leukemias among the bombing survivors in Hiroshima and Nagasaki is quite large. Many of the reported findings fit equally well with either radiation or radiomimetic chemicals as the underlying cause. We will here not attempt to review the entire field; instead, we will focus on a small number of studies that do provide some clues as to the true cause of these cases.

12.2.1 Correlation of death due to cancer and leukemia with acute radiation sickness and burns. While many early studies correlated cancer incidence to distance from the hypocenter, virtually all recent ones use radiation dose estimates as the explanatory variable. As we have seen, however, the radiation dose estimates are fairly loosely correlated with biological outcomes such as acute radiation sickness and somatic chromosome aberrations (Sections 11.3-11.5). Therefore, we might ask if those biological outcomes themselves might be more suitable as predictors of cancer risk than the radiation dose estimates.

Chromosome aberrations have apparently been studied only in a fairly limited number of survivors, and moreover there seems to be no dataset that would allow one to correlate them to cancer incidence. However, the fairly large data set which we used in Section 11.3 to correlate radiation doses with acute radiation sickness [168] also contains cancer and leukemia mortality data. We can therefore examine to what degree ARS symptoms predict cancer risk.

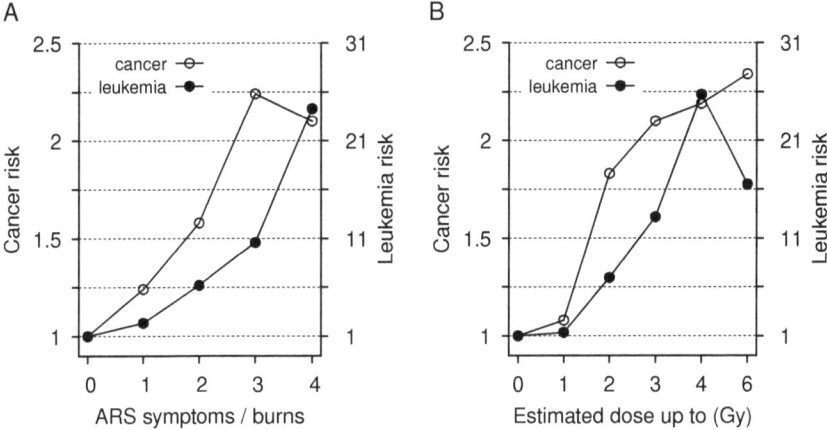

Figure 12.5: Risk of death due to cancer and leukemia vs. number of clinical symptoms (A) and radiation dose estimates (B). Symptoms comprise three proper signs of ARS (epilation, bleeding, and oropharyngeal lesions), and burns are counted here as a fourth symptom. Risks are relative to zero symptoms (A) or zero Gy (B). Data from [168]; in both A and B, only subjects with unambiguous information for all three ARS symptoms and for burns were included (these account for > 90% of the total).

The result is depicted in Figure 12.5A. The risk of both cancer and leukemia clearly increases with the number of ARS symptoms. Interestingly, burns, when present, also increase the cancer risk, even though their specific contribution to the total risk is somewhat lower than that of each single ARS symptom. Figure 12.5B shows the correlation of cancer and leukemia risk with radiation dose estimates, as determined from the same data set. Considering our earlier observation that these estimates are not very good at predicting ARS symptoms, the high degree of correlation evident in this figure may be surprising. We will examine this question in the next section; for now, we will focus on ARS symptoms and burns.

Given that ARS symptoms are caused by the genotoxic effects of radiation or of radiomimetic chemicals, their correlation with the risk of cancer and leukemia is expected. In contrast, the association of cancer risk with burns is surprising. A trivial explanation of this correlation might be that burns are simply a secondary indicator of exposure to radiation or to poison. Burns are indeed highly correlated with ARS and with radiation dose estimates (not shown). However, even if we consider only those survivors who have no ARS symptoms and/or have dose

Table 12.1: Association of death due to cancer or leukemia with burns in subjects without symptoms of ARS ('no ARS'), those with estimated radiation doses below 5 mGy ('no radiation'), or those who meet both conditions ('neither'). The column labeled 'Cancer' comprises both cancer and leukemia. Incidence is the number of cancer or leukemia deaths per 1000 person-years; risk is the ratio of incidence of those with burns to those without in each sample. 'Age' is the average age of survivors at the bombing. Data from [168]; only subjects with unambiguous information for all three ARS symptoms and for burns were included (these account for > 90% of the total).

Sample	Burns	Subjects	Person-years	Age	Cancer	Incidence	Risk
no ARS	−	63,072	1,850,801	27.8	4,729	2.56	
	+	4,059	117,960	29.2	385	3.26	**1.28**
no radiation	−	31,580	927,705	27.9	2,285	2.46	
	+	908	25,783	31.0	90	3.49	**1.42**
neither	−	31,138	914,522	27.8	2,253	2.46	
	+	835	23,660	30.8	84	3.55	**1.44**

estimates of less than 5 mGy, some risk associated specifically with burns remains (Table 12.1).[8] Among survivors without ARS, the cancer mortality observed with burns but minimal radiation dose is exceeded by those without burns only at estimated doses of 1 Gy and beyond. Thus, burns as the only documented indicator of exposure appear to carry an increased cancer risk. Note, however, that survivors with burns are older by about three years on average than those without; this age difference may contribute to their increased risk of cancer.

While thermal burns might occasionally cause skin cancer in the long term, the great majority of cancers in this statistic concerns internal organs; thus, the commonly imputed trauma mechanism ('flash burn') does not explain the documented cancer risk, which therefore provides yet another piece of evidence against the official story of the nuclear

---

[8]In some of the very high dose categories, as well as in those with all three ARS symptoms present, the relative cancer risk associated with burns is actually below 1. In these groups, mortality in the acute phase must have been high; significant incremental acute mortality due to burns would have biased the group of survivors toward lower doses to interior organs, and therefore toward a lower cancer risk. Conversely, reduced survival of burns due to concomitant ARS may have contributed to the reduced incidence of burns near the hypocenter in Hiroshima (Figure 9.1).

detonation. More interesting than this conclusion, though, are the implications for the alternate scenario developed in this book.

We had noted in Section 9.4 that studies on napalm injury are extremely scarce in the medical literature, and I am not aware of any statistics on cancer incidence in napalm victims. However, as with other thermal burns, it is not biologically plausible that napalm burns should increase the cancer risk of interior organs. In contrast, an elevated general risk of cancer would be expected after exposure to genotoxic agents such as sulfur mustard. Thus, the cancer risk associated with burns strengthens our previous conclusion that a substantial fraction of the reported burns were indeed chemical burns due to mustard gas (see Section 9.5).

12.2.2 Cancer rates at low radiation doses. We saw before that estimated radiation doses don't predict ARS symptoms particularly well (Figure 11.1), but on the other hand that the cancer risk indeed correlates with radiation doses (Figure 12.5B). Can we reconcile these two observations?

As noted in Section 2.11.4, ARS is a deterministic radiation effect, whereas cancer is a stochastic one. Thus, with cancer, all we can ask is whether the incidence in *large* samples increases with the radiation dose, which is indeed the case. On the other hand, with acute radiation sickness, such a correlation of averages is not enough; instead, the presence or absence of ARS in small samples or even every single survivor should exhibit a plausible relationship to the estimated dose; there should be at most a very small number of outliers, which might arise for example from clerical errors in dose assignment or clinical history-taking. As we had seen before, this is clearly not observed.

If we consider an arbitrary dose interval—say, from 2 to 3 Gy—we can assert that, in the calculation of the cancer incidence in this dose range, spillover from the adjacent dose ranges on both sides will at least partially cancel out: subjects who were assigned to this interval but really received a dose above 3 Gy will contribute some surplus cancer cases, which will be balanced by lower cancer case numbers among those subjects included in the interval that really received below 2 Gy. However, such mutual compensation will not occur at the edges of the entire dose range. While the upper edge is but sparsely populated, the sample size near the lower edge is very large. Thus, the cancer incidence

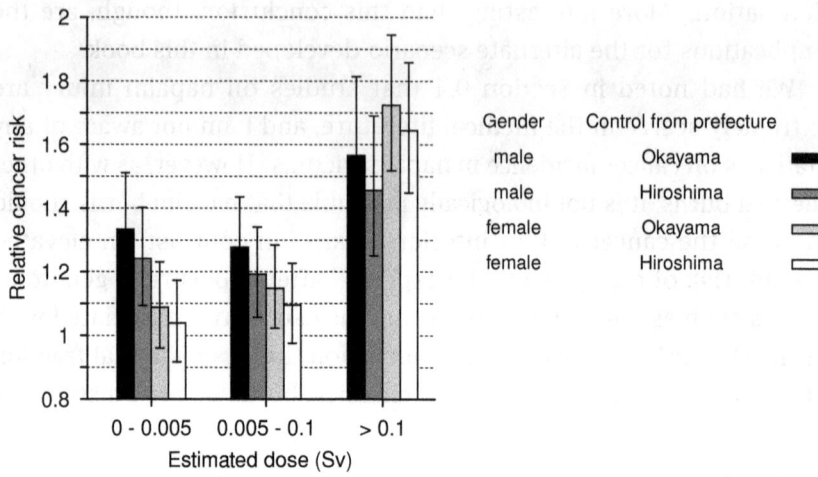

Figure 12.6: Cancer risk of Hiroshima bombing survivors compared to control groups from outside the city. Data from Tables 1 and 2 in Watanabe et al. [262]. Bombing survivors are grouped by estimated radiation dose. Control groups are the entire populations of Hiroshima prefecture, which includes Hiroshima city, and of the adjoining Okayama prefecture. Error bars are 95% confidence intervals.

at the low end of the dose range should tell us something about the accuracy of dose assignment. If estimated doses were accurate, then the cancer incidence among survivors with very low estimates should be essentially the same as in unexposed control subjects; on the other hand, if a significant number of survivors with low estimates really received higher doses, then there should be surplus cancer incidence within this group.

Readers will be familiar with the general idea of control groups, and they will appreciate that control groups should, as far as possible, be unexposed to the agent or stimulus under study. They may therefore be surprised to learn that ABCC/RERF's long-term studies have used, and continue to use, control groups from within the two cities, consisting of survivors who were deemed to have been outside the reach of bomb radiation. The practice has been criticized vigorously and repeatedly [159, 260, 261], but RERF has not paid heed to these well-founded objections.

When one compares the exposed to the exposed, there is of course no chance—and no risk—to discover anything amiss. There exists, however, one study that has compared the cancer risks of Hiroshima survivors with low estimated doses to a *proper* control group from outside the city. In this study [262], the cancer incidence in subjects from Hiroshima was matched to that in two different control groups, namely, the entire population of Hiroshima prefecture and that of the adjoining Okayama prefecture. The former contains the city of Hiroshima, which accounts for a sizable minority of its entire population; however, within the population of Okayama prefecture, the number of bombing survivors should be negligible.

The results of the study are summarized in Figure 12.6. In the comparison of Hiroshima survivors with both control groups, precautions were taken to correct for differences in gender and age, both of which will have a strong effect on cancer incidence. The survivors were divided into three dose groups; the lowest dose group, with estimated doses of 0-5 mSv, is the very same one which RERF routinely misuses as 'negative controls'. The cancer risk relative to the two control populations is clearly and significantly increased in men, and slightly but not significantly in women.

The upper bound (0.1 Sv) of the second dose range is still fairly low; it is thus not too surprising that the cancer risk changes little relative to the lowest dose group, but in women the risk trends slightly higher. A very large and unambiguous increase in cancer risk, which is now greater in women than in men, is seen in the highest dose group. In each case, the risk is higher relative to Okayama prefecture than to Hiroshima prefecture. The most straightforward explanation for this difference is that the Hiroshima prefecture control group only 'dilutes' the bombing survivors, but does not entirely exclude them. The population of Okayama prefecture can be considered unaffected by this problem, and it therefore constitutes the more appropriate control group.

The difference in cancer risk between men and women, particularly in the lowest dose group, is interesting. Watanabe et al. [262] comment as follows:

> *Confounding factors, such as smoking and drinking alcohol, may also affect the distribution, but there were also more males than females involved in the rescue efforts subsequent to the bombing,*

and these males may therefore have been active in areas with residual radiation.

Could the elevated cancer risk in the survivors indeed be due to heavier drinking or smoking among survivors than control subjects? Smoking promotes cancer of the lungs more strongly than that of any other organ; however, among the male survivors in every dose category, the relative excess risk of lung cancer was *below* the average of all cancers (but it was above the average excess cancer risk among women in the middle and high dose groups). Similarly, alcohol should have preferentially increased the relative excess risk of gastric cancer, but this number was indeed below the total relative excess cancer risk in both genders and within all dose groups. Thus, at least in men, whose overall excess cancer risk in the low and middle dose category is most in need of an explanation, there is no indication at all that smoking or drinking is the cause.

This leaves us with the second proposed interpretation—namely, that men preferably participated in rescue and recovery after the bombing, during which they were exposed to residual radiation. Watanabe et al. adopt this view:

> *It cannot be denied that even survivors in the very low [dose] category may have been subject to additional radioactive fallout and may have breathed in or swallowed induced radioactive substances in the vicinity of the hypocenter.*

The assumption that excess morbidity in men was caused by prolonged exposure near the hypocenter agrees with anecdotal evidence: multiple child survivors quoted by Osada [14] relate that their fathers stayed behind in Hiroshima, sometimes falling ill from ARS, while mothers and children found refuge outside the city. If delayed exposure were indeed a major factor, the risk in male survivors should be age-dependent, since boys younger than 12 years or so were likely not called up to join in the rescue effort, and they should thus have a lower cancer risk than those who were 16 years or older. Watanabe's study does not, however, break down the cancer risk by age.[9]

---

[9]The subjects included by Watanabe et al. [262] were between 0 and 34 years old in 1945. Within this group, the fraction of males too young to join the cleanup effort would have been quite substantial, and accordingly the cancer risk in those who were old enough to participate would be even higher than apparent in the published statistic.

Reacting to Watanabe's findings, scientists from RERF issued a papal bull entitled "Radiation unlikely to be responsible for high cancer rates among distal Hiroshima A-bomb survivors" [230] that dismisses them as 'implausible', insisting that (1) the risk should really have been higher in women than in men, and (2) that Watanabe's observed risk was altogether too large. Their first assertion was based on RERF's own studies, which, as we have already discussed, relied on phony dose estimates and improper control groups. The second claim was supported by the conventional wisdom that bomb radiation was short-lived, and fallout was small—thus, there was no possible source of radiation, and Watanabe's findings must therefore be spurious. What better explanation did RERF have to offer? You guessed it—smoking.

While we agree with RERF that there is indeed no plausible source of residual radiation which could account for the substantially increased cancer risk among the male survivors in the low-dose group, we certainly don't accept their conclusion that Watanabe's findings must therefore be spurious. Instead, we will next examine Watanabe's suggestion of an increased cancer risk among those who joined the cleanup effort in the inner city.

12.2.3 Cancer and leukemia in early entrants to Hiroshima. If staying behind in the city after the bombing increased the risk of cancer, then some increased risk should also be observed in those who entered the city only after the bombing. This is indeed the case. A review by Watanabe [155] documents a strikingly increased risk of leukemia in those who entered the city within the first three days of the bombing, relative to those who entered the city subsequently (Table 12.2). Entry between days 4 and 7 still seems to carry a slightly elevated risk when compared to later entry, but this difference is not statistically significant.

The same author also reported an increased incidence of thyroid cancer among those who entered Hiroshima within 7 days of the bombing, and who were diagnosed between 1951 and 1968 in the surgical department of Hiroshima University Hospital [155, p. 519]. The incidence of thyroid cancer in this group was similar to that among the directly exposed. However, the overall number of cases in this sample of early entrants was small (9), which limits the statistical power of this study.

12 Disease in long-term survivors

Table 12.2: Incidence of leukemia in early entrants to Hiroshima. Data from Table 21 in [155]. The difference in incidence between those who entered within the first three days after the bombing and either of the other groups is statistically significant ($p = 0.0008$). For the difference between the second and the third group, $p = 0.24$.

	Time of entry (days)		
	≤ 3	4–7	8–14
Population	25,799	11,001	7,326
Number of cases	62	9	4
Incidence/10^5/year	8.90	3.03	2.02

Watanabe summarizes one additional Japanese study on thyroid cancer with similar findings. Furthermore, he reports that bronchial carcinoma, too, was notably increased among early entrants, but as with thyroid carcinoma the overall number of observed cases was low. Watanabe also surveys cancers of several other organs, but here he does not consider early entrants separately from the directly exposed.

A more recent study on cancer in early entrants was reported by Matsuura et al. [263]. This investigation included almost 50,000 subjects who entered the city of Hiroshima in the first 20 days after the bombing; and out of these, 36,000 entered it already between August 6th and 8th. The authors define 'the city' as 'the region within about 2 km of the hypocenter'. Their most important results are summarized in Figure 12.7.

Before discussing the significance of this study, one word about its methodology is in order. The authors used a Cox proportional hazard model, which might more intuitively be called a 'risk factor model': if multiple determinants affect the risk, it is assumed that each can be represented by a constant risk factor, to be determined by a global numerical fit, and that the overall risk for a given individual can then be obtained by multiplying all the specific risk factors that apply to it. For example, the data in Figure 12.7 include some individuals who were exposed directly at > 2 km from the hypocenter and also came to within < 2 km of it during the first 3 days. The cancer risk of these subjects would be estimated by multiplying the two corresponding risk factors, both of which are close to 1.2. Other influences such as sex and age

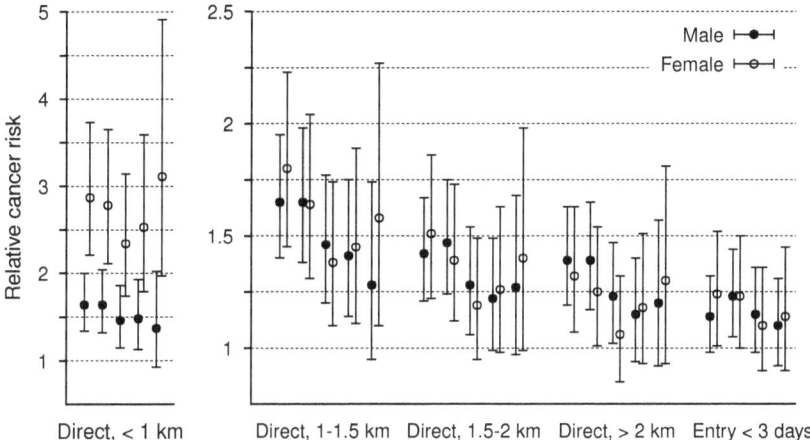

Figure 12.7: Cancer risk in subjects directly exposed to the Hiroshima bombing and in early entrants to the city. Data from Table 5 in Matsuura et al. [263]. Directly exposed subjects are grouped by distance from the hypocenter; a fifth group includes those who came within 2 km of the hypocenter between August 6th and August 8th. In each group, the five values (with 95% confidence intervals) represent the death rates for observation periods beginning on January 1st of 1968, 1971, 1974, 1977, and 1980, respectively. A risk of 1.0 applies to early entry after 3 days.

can be accounted and corrected for by assigning them their own risk factors.

Matsuura et al. focused on the years 1968-1982, because complete records were available to them for those years. Figure 12.7 shows the relative risk of death due to cancer in five sub-populations, defined by different starting dates that ranged from January 1968 to January 1980. With each group, the period of observation, during which cancer deaths were counted, began with the respective starting date and ended on December 31st of 1982. They defined these groups as follows:

> *Each sub-population included subjects who had already been recognized as survivors before the defined starting date and excluded those who had died or had not been recognized as survivors before this starting date. For example, an individual who had been recognized as a survivor before January 1, 1968, and had lived in Hiroshima Prefecture until December 31, 1982, was included in all the sub-populations.*

We find that the highest relative cancer risk occurs among those survivors who were within 1 km of the hypocenter at the time of the bombing. While this would be expected, there is a surprise—the risk is almost twice higher in women than in men. Given that in all other exposure groups the risk is similar between both genders, I cannot think of a plausible explanation for the large gender difference in this one exposure group.

The group—or, strictly speaking, the risk factor—we are most interested in is that of entry within 3 days of the bombing into the inner city. This risk hovers near 1.2 for each of the five starting dates reported by the authors. The lower bound of the 95% confidence interval[10] dips slightly below 1.0 for most data points, which means that the elevated risk is not statistically significant at the corresponding level. To put this into perspective, we must consider the following points:

1. In all five exposure groups, the confidence intervals are smaller with observation periods that started earlier, and therefore lasted longer. This is of course expected, since the numbers of cancer deaths counted will be higher in this case. Had suitable data been available for the period of time before 1968, the increased risk among the early entrants would very likely have been statistically significant also.

2. Matsuura et al. include among the early entrants all survivors who came within 2 km of the hypocenter. Most other studies on early entry, for example Sutou [34], use a smaller radius; the large radius used here will tend to 'dilute' the cancer risk.

3. The comparison group are those who entered later than 3 days after the bombing, presumably for want of a control group without any history of exposure at all. Had a proper control group been available, the incremental cancer risk in early entrants would likely have been greater.

The authors report that, within the limited data available for this study, statistical significance is attained when the period of early entry is limited to only the 6th of August; the incremental risk due to entry on

---

[10] Assuming that the 95% confidence intervals given by the authors are two-sided, with equal chances of the true risk factors falling above or below them, the inclusion of the value of 1.0 means within a confidence interval means that the upward deviation of the risk is not significant at $p < 0.025$.

this day is clearly higher than with the three subsequent days. Overall, we concur with Matsuura et al. [263] that their findings demonstrate a moderate but definite incremental risk of cancer in those who came within a radius of 2 km of the hypocenter very shortly after the Hiroshima bombing. This corresponds with similar findings pertaining to acute radiation sickness, which were discussed earlier in Section 8.7. To explain their finding, Matsuura et al. suggest that early entrants were exposed to fallout or induced radioactivity:

There has been little research regarding internal exposure due to intake of food and water contaminated by radiation ... it is important to determine conclusively whether the differences among entrants in mortality risk are due to residual radiation.

The elevated cancer risk evident in those with low dose estimates (Section 12.2.2) as well as in early entrants indicates indeed that a resident carcinogenic agent was present in the city for some time after the bombing; but for the various reasons detailed before, we maintain that this agent was sulfur mustard rather than radioactivity.

12.2.4 Distribution of cancer risk about the hypocenter. With a proper nuclear bomb, the intensity of radiation should have been highest at the hypocenter and then decreased outward from it in a regular, rotationally symmetrical fashion. The same should therefore be expected of the cancer risk. However, two studies on this question have not found this rotational symmetry at Hiroshima [160, 161]. Figure 12.8 illustrates the findings from one of them. The contour lines of equal relative tumor risk are not round, and the distribution of the risk appears centered some 300 m to the west of the hypocenter. At an angle of 178° and a distance of 2 km, the cancer risk equals that at 62° but only 1.2 km out. This may have been due to the wind, which on the day of the bombing is said to have blown in a westerly direction [160], or possibly also to the limited aiming accuracy of the bombing.

12.2.5 Incidence of cancer in specific organs. To further examine whether radiation or mustard gas is the more likely cause of cancer among the bombing victims, we might ask whether the distribution of malignancies among different organs is similar between survivors and known radiation exposures. This turns out to be unprofitable, however, since one cannot find suitable groups for comparison.

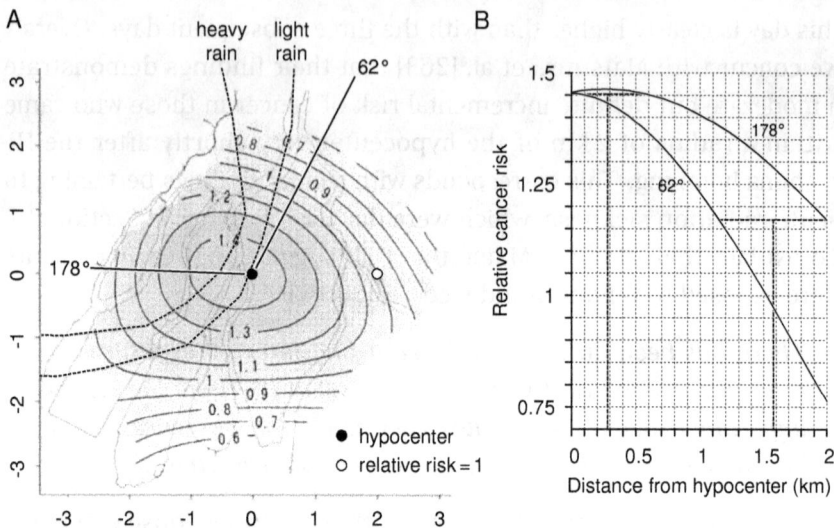

Figure 12.8: Distribution of cancer risk about the hypocenter in Hiroshima. A: Contour map of relative risk. Along the lines at angles 178° and 62°, the highest and lowest relative risk, respectively, were observed at any given distance from the hypocenter. Numbers on both axes are distances from the hypocenter in km. B: Relative risk as a function of distance from the hypocenter at the angles of minimal risk and maximal risk. With the latter, the risk initially increases. The horizontal dashed help lines connect points of equal risk on both curves; from their midpoints, we can estimate that the 'hypocenter of risk' deviates from the one of the alleged detonation by approximately 300 m. Map in A and data in B from Tonda et al. [161].

Most uses of medical irradiation, both diagnostic and therapeutic, are limited to certain body parts. This uneven exposure makes comparison of cancer incidence between organs largely meaningless. Total body irradiation has been used as a conditioning procedure for bone marrow transplants. However, in the apparently only large group of such patients to have been surveyed for secondary malignancies [264], conditioning by irradiation had always been used in combination with cytotoxic drugs, which will also contribute to the risk. Moreover, the underlying disease, as well as immunological complications after the bone marrow transplant procedure, may further skew the organ distribution of secondary cancer. Whole-body exposure to high doses of radiation only, without any confounding treatment, has occurred in some nuclear accidents, but case numbers are far too small for any sort of meaningful statistics.

Readers interested in the question of organ-specific radiation-induced cancer risk may consult two older studies by the United Nations [265] and the National Academy of Sciences [210], which cover it in greater detail than more recent reports issued by the same organizations. We will here forgo a systematic discussion of every organ and instead only give two examples to illustrate that the evidence is indeed inconclusive.

Lung cancer. Considering the prominent affliction of the lungs and airways in bombing victims who were killed outright or made acutely ill, we might expect the incidence of lung cancer to be more prominently elevated among survivors than that of other cancers. There are indeed some studies to suggest that this is the case; for example, Ishikawa et al. [8, p. 286] summarize an early study from Hiroshima that finds the relative risk of lung cancer to be higher than that of the four other organs listed (breast, stomach, ovary, and cervix uteri). However, case numbers in this study are very small. As noted above, the study by Watanabe et al. [262] found the relative excess risk of lung cancer to be lower than the average of all cancers in men, while it was somewhat above the average in two out of three dose groups in women. Thus, there is no strong evidence of a preferential affliction of the lungs.

If indeed the lungs are *not* preferentially afflicted by cancer, should we consider this evidence *against* the use of sulfur mustard in the bombings? Lung cancer rates were indeed very greatly increased among former workers of the Okunoshima mustard gas factory [266]. However, most of these workers had been exposed to the poison continuously for more than five years, and some for more than ten, whereas the bombing survivors suffered only a single acute exposure. More suitable for comparison are veterans who were exposed to the gas in battle. Studies on British [267] and Iranian [268] veterans found only slightly and non-significantly increased rates of lung cancer among them. Overall, therefore, the available data don't provide conclusive evidence for or against the use of sulfur mustard in the bombings.[11]

---

[11] One interesting observation related by Watanabe [155] is the distribution of histological types. He summarizes several studies that found a relatively high proportion of undifferentiated and squamous cell carcinomas among Hiroshima survivors. These are also the most common types among mustard gas factory workers [266].

Thyroid cancer. Among the bombing survivors, the highest relative risk of any solid cancer pertains to the thyroid; it is only exceeded by the risk of leukemia. Parker et al. [127] reported a relative risk of 9.4 in men and 5.0 in women, respectively, but each value has a very large associated 95% confidence interval. Schmitz-Feuerhake [260] suggested that this high cancer incidence was caused by uptake of ^{131}I, a short-lived radioactive iodine isotope that is formed by ^{235}U or ^{239}Pu fission, and which indeed produced thyroid cancer in the general population near Chernobyl after the reactor meltdown in that city [269, 270]. This explanation would, of course, require significant exposure to fallout from the nuclear detonation, which is ruled out by the findings presented in Chapter 3.

Thyroid cancer is also readily induced by radiation from sources other than incorporated radioactive iodine [265, p. 226]. On the other hand, in Section 7.2.4, we suggested that metabolic activation of sulfur mustard in the thyroid gland might cause preferential carcinogenesis in this organ. Zojaji et al. [126] reported two cases of thyroid cancer among 43 Iranian veterans who had been exposed to the poison.

Overall, therefore, the high incidence of thyroid cancer seems compatible with both nuclear radiation and sulfur mustard as the underlying cause. These two examples may suffice to illustrate that this line of inquiry holds little promise for the purpose of this study.

12.3 Long-term disease other than cancer

With these diseases, the situation is similar as noted above with cancers of specific organs: the available information is mostly of low resolution and on the whole does not provide unequivocal evidence for or against the thesis of this book. We will again only discuss selected examples.

12.3.1 Cardiovascular and respiratory disease.
The functions of the heart and of the lungs are closely linked, and disease in one will often affect the other also. If pulmonary gas exchange and blood flow are restricted by some chronic lung disease, the right heart, which pumps the blood into the lungs, will show characteristic signs of strain and may eventually give out. Disease of the left heart, which receives blood from the lungs and pumps it into the general circulation, will cause blood to back up into the lungs. This can result in acute lung edema; a lesser degree of lung edema will promote pneumonia. From these

considerations, we can draw the following conclusions: (1) a diagnosis of pneumonia or heart failure on a death certificate does not tell us whether the organ in question really was the primary focus of disease; and (2) broad diagnostic categories such as 'cardiovascular disease' or 'non-cancer lung disease' do not provide sufficient information to reason about disease mechanisms.

As it turns out, most of the information contained in long-term studies on survivors is precisely of this fragmentary sort. We can only say that the incidence of 'cardiovascular disease' and of 'non-cancer lung disease' are somewhat elevated in the bombing survivors; should readers still put stock in the radiation dose estimates, they will be pleased that numbers for the excess risk per Gray are readily available [271–274]. Cardiovascular disease was also found more prevalent among American radiologists [275] and in Iranian veterans exposed to mustard gas [276]. The latter study catalogs a number of specific diagnostic findings, from which it concludes:

Induction of cardiomyopathy, reduction in left ventricular ejection fraction and loosening of right ventricle appear to be the most important latent complications of sulphur mustard exposure.

This statement suggests both direct toxic action on the heart and indirect effects of lung disease. The diagnosis and treatment of some Iranian veterans with particularly severe chronic obstructive lung disease is described by Freitag et al. [186]. The latter study also well illustrates that a small number of competently and thoroughly documented disease cases can be much more instructive than large-scale statistics that employ very broad and generic categories. Unfortunately, no individual case descriptions of cardiovascular or pulmonary disease among the Japanese bombing survivors are available.

The thesis of this book implies that lung damage similar in nature and in severity to Freitag's cases should also have occurred in the 'nuclear' bombings. With the poor level of medical care available to the survivors, it seems likely that many such cases would have taken a fatal course even before 1950, that is, during the time period for which not even retrospective health statistics are available. Overall, therefore, we can only state that the very limited information on these victims appears compatible with either radiation or mustard gas as the primary causative agent.

12.3.2 Cataract. Cataract is a clouding of the normally transparent lens of the eye. It can occur spontaneously, mostly in old age, but it can also arise in response to specific pathogenic stimuli. The most common one of these is the elevated blood glucose level in diabetic patients; a similar disease mechanism operates in galactosemia, which is a rare disease. Both ionizing radiation [277] and cytotoxic anticancer drugs [138, 278] can produce cataract as well. The previously cited study on American World War II veterans who were misused as guinea pigs for studies on sulfur mustard and lewisite states that 50 out of 257 respondents of a health survey report cataracts or other eye problems; the exact proportion of cataracts within this number is not stated [21, p. 384-5].

Radiation cataract has been the subject of numerous experimental and clinical studies. In assessing them, we need to be clear about what exactly constitutes cataract. While in common usage the diagnosis implies that lens obfuscation is so severe as to cause manifest impairment of visual acuity, most statistical and experimental studies count as cataract any turbidities that can be observed using opthalmological instruments, even if vision is not affected.

The dose-response relationship assumed for radiation cataract has seen some revisions over time. Merriam and Focht [279], who examined a series of 73 patients, found a threshold dose for single exposure of 200 r (approximately 2 Gy); if radiation was administered in multiple sessions, the threshold dose was higher. A complicating factor is that cataract, once initiated, can slowly progress over time, so that the degree of severity and the threshold dose will be influenced by the time span of observation. The cited study had an average follow-up period of 8 years after irradiation.

A study on patients who had received radiation therapy as infants, and who were examined 30-45 years after this treatment, was reported by Wilde and Sjöstrand [280]. These authors found minor but consistently observable turbidities in eyes exposed to as little as 0.1 Gy. They ascribe this very low threshold to a higher sensitivity of the infant's lens. They do report a fairly clear and uniform progression of cataract severity with radiation dose.

Since radiation cataracts were expected in atomic bomb survivors, they were frequently examined for this condition. Flick [193] was looking for it as early as 1945, although he was soon persuaded by

Table 12.3: Cataract incidence in Hiroshima survivors by distance from the hypocenter. Data from Table 3 in [282].

Distance (km)	Examined cases	Cataracts	
		n	%
Under 2	159	87	54.7
2-3	126	25	19.8
3-4	126	4	3.2
over 4	25	1	4.0
Total[a]	436 (435)	117 (116)	

[a]Numbers in brackets are given in the original [282].

the evidence to shift his focus to retinal hemorrhages instead (see Section 10.2.3). A small series of clinically manifest cases was reported by Cogan et al. [281]. While several large-scale studies report fairly high incidences of cataract, only a small fraction of these patients have clinically deteriorated vision.

As expected, more recent studies use radiation dose estimates as the explanatory variable, and they find an increased risk of clinically manifest cataract requiring surgery at doses below 0.5 Gy [283]. This does not agree with clinical studies that evaluate actual radiation and is most likely due to erroneous dose assignment.[12] An older study that predates the radiation dose estimates and therefore uses distance from the hypocenter as its covariate is that by Kandori and Masuda [282]. The results of this study, which reports on survivors from Hiroshima only, are shown in Table 12.3. As expected, the incidence of cataract decreases with distance from the hypocenter. However, an appreciably increased number is found beyond a distance of 2 km, at which radiation doses should have been too low for inducing cataract in all but the youngest subjects (but the authors do not state that all of those affected beyond 2 km had been young). This pattern of incidence falling off more slowly than presumed radiation dose resembles that found earlier with acute radiation sickness (see Section 8.4).

---

[12]Another study with some very bumpy dose-response curves is Minamoto et al. [284]. These authors also find a substantially higher risk of cataract at equal dose in Nagasaki than in Hiroshima. The most plausible explanation for the collective oddities in this report is of course that the dose estimates are wrong.

12.4 Conclusion

The diseases considered in this chapter add to the evidence against the nuclear bombings more due to their temporal and spatial distribution than by virtue of their specific clinical manifestations, on which there simply is too little information in the published literature. It seems likely that such information is kept under lock and key in the archives at RERF.

With this chapter we finish our inquiry into the medical observations in Hiroshima and Nagasaki. We conclude that even on their own, without recourse to the physical studies discussed in the first part of this book, the medical arguments alone suffice to unambiguously reject the story of the atomic bombs. At the same time, they provide strong support for mustard gas and napalm as essential components of the massacre.

13 How was it done?

> When using our forces, we must appear inactive; when we are near, we must make the enemy believe that we are far away ...
>
> Sun Tzu

This chapter develops a hypothetical scenario for the conventional attacks that accounts for the perception by most witnesses of a flash and by fewer witnesses of a 'bang'. In this scenario, the flash was created with photoflash bombs, while the 'bangs' were local events caused by detonation in the air of high explosives, which possibly were contained in bombs that resembled the purported Nagasaki bomb ('Fat Man') in size and shape. Also exploded in the air were bombs filled with napalm and with mustard gas, which then rained down on the city.

Furthermore, the chapter makes the case that the Japanese authorities were not surprised or deceived by the 'atomic' bombings but rather colluded both in staging them and in obfuscating their true nature. It is also discussed how special effects like 'atomic shadows', censorship, and propaganda were used to implant and maintain the myth of the atomic bombings.

One striking aspect of the 'nuclear' bombings is certainly the great success of the deception; it appears that all survivors believed, or eventually came to believe, that they had indeed witnessed real nuclear detonations. Even Dr. Masao Tsuzuki, who realized that some poisonous gas had been dispersed, tried to fit this observation into the story of the atomic bombs.

The deception had two elements: firstly, a make-believe nuclear detonation, and secondly, the concealment of the dispersal of conventional incendiaries and of mustard gas. In this chapter, we will examine how the bombings were carried out, and how the deception was achieved.

13 How was it done?

13.1 The make-believe nuclear detonation

13.1.1 The flash.
Many eyewitnesses likened the event to a very large photographer's flash (see for example the quote in Section 13.1.4). Nakatani [1] has proposed that the flash was produced using photoflash bombs, possibly of the AN-M46 type, which was 8 in by 48 in in size [285]. The regular purpose of such bombs was to illuminate, at night, a large target area, so that it could be photographed from high altitude. A flash of such power should make an impression even at daytime. Whether this particular model was indeed used or another one, and whether only one or several such bombs were used in each city seems difficult to ascertain from the available evidence. However, statements such as that of Mr. Tanimoto, who according to Hersey [7] described the light as 'a sheet of sun' which 'traveled from east to west' (see quote in Section 1.3) suggest a rather sustained display of white light, as does this quote by a Dutch prisoner of war, who experienced the Nagasaki bombing while working in a shipyard within the city [286, p. 728]:

> *I saw an indescribably strong, white light that might be comparable to the light at the end of a welding torch, but it lasted much longer, incredibly long.*[1]

Quite possibly, therefore, multiple photoflash bombs were employed in each bombing.

13.1.2 The bang.
We noted earlier that many eyewitnesses saw a flash but heard no detonation, and also that those near the hypocenter were less likely to hear a bang than those further from it. Moreover, there is no clear correlation of damage intensity with distance from the hypocenter. Similar degrees of destruction were observed by engineer Shigetoshi Wakaki [173], who experienced the bombing at Hatsukaichi, a town situated 13 km from the hypocenter, and by Fathers Arrupe [171] and Siemes [287] at the Jesuit convent in Nagatsuka, which is located only some 4 km from the alleged center of the detonation. According to these witnesses, damage to buildings in both areas was mostly limited to blown-out windows and doors.

The only plausible explanation for this pattern is that there was not one large detonation but several smaller ones whose effects were limited and local. Both Wakaki and the Jesuits looked around for some

---

[1] Translated from Dutch by Hans Vogel.

focus of impact (e.g. a blast crater) on the ground, but none of them found it. Wakaki, himself an explosives expert whose job was to develop ordnance for the Japanese army, specifically comments [173, p. 59 f]:

Judging from the blast and assuming the bomb weighed one ton, it cannot be too far—perhaps about 100 metres to the centre of the explosion, I thought to myself as I ran. Yet no matter how far I ran the amount of window glass damage was about the same and I seemed to be getting no nearer the centre of the explosion. Another strange thing was that although the window panes of the upper storeys were damaged, the ground floor panes were not. The contrast was very striking.

The absence of a clear focus of the detonation on the ground suggests that the detonation had been an air burst. Furthermore, the preferential damage to windows in the upper floors suggests that the altitude of that burst had not been very great, so that at some distance from it the lower floors of the houses were shielded from the shock wave by the adjacent rows of buildings.

While damage to buildings in the Nagatsuka and Hatsukaichi areas was limited, the local air bursts seem to have had greater impact in other parts of the city. The Jesuits owned a second building inside the city, some 1.3 km from the hypocenter; and Father Siemes reports that in its vicinity this building alone was left standing. He ascribes this to the reinforcements made to its structure by his confrère Father Gropper at some earlier time. The typical state of repair of traditional Japanese buildings is described by de Seversky as follows [5]:

One must see to believe the flimsiness of average Japanese wooden structures, many of them termite-eaten and dry-rotted for generations. To make things worse they are top-heavy with thick tile roofs, used to protect them from sparks, should neighboring houses catch fire. Sometimes houses tumble down without apparent reason, expiring, as it were, of sheer old age. I nearly crumbled one myself in Nagasaki when I accidentally kicked a wall with my artificial leg.

The immediate or protracted collapse of many wooden houses induced by the 'bang' agrees with numerous eyewitness accounts. In the foreword to his collection of such testimony from Hiroshima schoolchildren, Arata Osada summed it up as follows [14]:

> *The astounding number of casualties was chiefly caused by the complete surprise of the attack, the large number of buildings that collapsed and the rapid spread of fires from the embers of charcoal fires used to prepare breakfast—plus, of course, the devastation caused by secondary heat radiation near the blast center.*

While we agree with Osada that stoves within collapsed houses were not the only fire starters, we maintain that the second major cause was not heat radiation but napalm, as will be discussed shortly. For now, we should consider what sort of weapon might have been used in these air bursts. While local in their effects, their reach nevertheless seems to have exceeded that of regular explosives.

Thermobaric weapons. While a conventional explosive combines fuel and oxidizer in the same material—and often, as with trinitrotoluene (TNT), in the same molecule—a thermobaric weapon consists mostly of fuel only, which is first dispersed into a cloud using a relatively small initial detonation. A second detonation then ignites the resulting mixture of air (which provides the oxygen) and dispersed fuel. Such weapons had been under development towards the end of World War II in Germany. It is not out of the question that the U.S. made use of these results, or that they had independently pursued their own development of such weapons in secret.

Of note, finely powdered magnesium and aluminum are apparently suitable as fuel for such weapons; the ignition of dispersed magnesium or aluminum might offer an alternate explanation for the flash. Thus, thermobaric weapons might plausibly account for both the 'flash' and the 'bang'; Occam's razor may therefore suggest them as the preferred explanation. One large thermobaric weapon would not, however, account easily for the apparently uneven pattern of 'bangs' experienced in the cities.

The 'Pumpkin' bomb. A special Air Force bomb group (the 509th) had been created that was to carry out the 'nuclear' bombings. In the months leading up to the event, this bomb group was stationed on Tinian, an island in the Northern Marianas. According to Leslie Groves, the leader of the 'Manhattan Project', this group used for training purposes a special type of conventional bomb that mimicked the future Nagasaki bomb [40, p. 285]:

> Because they had been modified to carry the atomic bomb, the B-29's of the 509th Group could not easily carry standard conventional bombs. They could, however, deliver bombs having the same shape as the Fat Man, and such a bomb had been developed and produced to provide training and experience to the crews. Known as the Pumpkin, this bomb contained 5,500 pounds of explosives, and was designed for blast effect only, with a proximity fuse that would permit its use for an air burst.

According to Hansen et al. [4, p. I-143],

> the wartime FAT MAN implosion bomb was almost 11 feet long, five feet in diameter, and weighed about 10,000 lbs.

Assuming that the Pumpkin replicated also the weight of the 'Fat Man', Hansen's number leaves some 4,500 lbs of weight for the casing. The shock wave produced by detonating this much explosive in such a heavy and presumably sturdy casing should indeed have been considerable. But why was it necessary to employ this much explosive just to practice the drop of an atomic bomb? Wouldn't it have been much cheaper, and therefore more conducive to training, to simply use a dud? Groves has the answer [40, p. 285]:

> Although it was primarily a training device, we had always recognized that it could have tactical uses; now as part of the group's security cover, we let it leak out on Tinian that its mission was the delivery of Pumpkins in battle. ...
>
> The Pumpkins began to arrive at the end of June. Reaction [sic] to these bombs were mixed. The members of the 509th who, with a few exceptions, still did not know the real reason for their training, were somewhat disappointed that they had spent so much time in practicing to deliver this fairly modest weapon. ...
>
> To familiarize the plane crews with the general areas of the targets and to ensure more certain navigation and target recognition, the cities selected for the Pumpkin missions were in the general vicinities of, but outside, the atomic targets. The bombings were carried out at the same high altitudes.

In this context, we must note that the 509th Bomb Group received a very considerable number of B-29 planes modified to carry Pumpkins or nuclear bombs. According to Groves [40, p. 256 ff], General Arnold, the head of the Air Force, promised Groves the delivery of 42 such planes overall.[2] The number of modified planes could hardly have been much smaller, if indeed Groves 'cover story'—namely, that dropping Pumpkins was the real purpose of the entire bomb group—should have appeared credible.[3] The question then arises how many modified planes would truly have been required to prepare adequately for the atomic bombings. In his book, Groves himself states that the minimum number was one. Of course, a certain level of redundancy would have been advisable. While we might accept a number of three or even five such planes as appropriate, a number of up to 42 surely is excessive. We therefore conclude that these planes had indeed been modified explicitly for the delivery of Pumpkin bombs.

In light of the foregoing, we propose that the air bursts which occurred as part of the 'nuclear' bombings were created using Pumpkin bombs, of which several were used in each bombing. This accounts for the circumstance that many witnesses report hearing loud bangs—and, to a man, all of these witnesses were under the impression that the bomb had detonated in their own vicinity—whereas many others did not. Furthermore, it explains why similar degrees of destruction were observed at very different distances from the hypocenter. Depending on their state of repair and on their proximity to the nearest detonating Pumpkin, wooden houses were damaged or collapsed entirely, with fire resulting in many cases.

13.1.3 The parachutes. Many eyewitnesses report having seen multiple parachutes that were dropped above each city shortly before the flashes and bangs occurred. It is unclear, however, whether these

---

[2] While Groves suggests that the first batch of 14 such planes was 'not in the best working condition' and the following second and third batch of 14 planes each were merely 'replacements', he does not state that the first batch was actually mothballed. Norris [288, p. 11] states that the 509th Group had 'several dozen' such modified planes.

[3] Intriguingly, Groves makes no mention of any conventional replica of the Hiroshima bomb ('Little Boy') being delivered to Tinian. The much slimmer shape of this bomb would of course not have accommodated nearly as much conventional explosive as the 'Fat Man'.

parachutes carried any of the devices used to produce the illusion of atomic detonations.

Wakaki, the weapons engineer, personally participated in the disassembly of the cargo attached to three parachutes and reports that it contained no explosives but only physical instruments and radio transmitters for monitoring the supposed nuclear blast [173, p. 95 ff]. On the other hand, Father Siemes suggests that some parachutes may have carried bombs [287]:

> A few maintained that they saw the planes drop a parachute which had carried something that exploded at a height of 1,000 meters.

Bombs carried by parachutes are also mentioned in the first Japanese radio broadcast on record [289, p. 242]:

> A small number of B-29s penetrated into Hiroshima city little after eight A.M. yesterday morning and dropped a small number of bombs. As a result, a considerable number of homes were reduced to ashes and fires broke out in various parts of the city.
>
> To this new type of bomb are attached parachutes, and it appears as if these new bombs exploded in the air. Investigations are now being made with regard to the effectiveness of this bomb, which should not be regarded as slight.

As noted above, the Pumpkin bombs were large and heavy; they should therefore have been quite conspicuous and also required rather large parachutes. Witness testimony mentions neither large cargo nor large parachutes. Thus, if indeed any bombs were carried by parachutes, these would have been of a different type; possibly the photoflash bombs, which is indeed suggested by some witness reports. Here is one such report [14, p. 127]:

> All of a sudden, something white like a parachute fell out from the plane. Five or six seconds later, everything turned yellow. It was like I'd looked right at the sun. Then there was a big sound a second or two later and everything went dark.

Even if the parachutes did not themselves carry the photoflash bombs, they would certainly have held the attention of most spectators and caused them to look at least in the general direction of the flash. This would have enhanced the impression of the flash on those onlookers. At the same time, the falling parachutes would also have diverted attention from the other planes that were needed to carry out the attack—to deliver the pumpkins, but also the bombs filled with napalm and mustard gas, which we will consider shortly.

13.1.4 The 'beautiful cloud'. The most detailed description of the Hiroshima cloud is given by Ogura [12, p. 15 f]. The author, a professor of history at Hiroshima University, is at the time some 4 km east of the city center but walking towards it:

> *I came to the east side of Shin'ozu Bridge. I stopped there for a minute, and just as I looked toward the sea and noticed the way the waves were sparkling, I saw, or rather felt, an enormous bluish white flash of light, as when a photographer lights a dish of magnesium. Off to my right, the sky split open over the city of Hiroshima. I instinctively flung myself face down onto the ground.*
>
> *I lay there without moving. Then I raised my head and looked up over the city. To the west, in the sky that had been blue a minute before, I saw a mass of white clouds—or was it smoke? Whichever it was, it had taken shape in an instant. Then a halo of sparkling lights, a little bit like the ring that forms around the moon as a sign of rain, appeared near the cloud mass and expanded like a rainbow. The outer edges of the white cloud mass rolled down and curled inward toward the center while the entire shape ballooned out to the sides.*
>
> *Immediately another mountain of clouds, accompanied by a huge column of red flame like lava from a volcano that had erupted in midair, formed under the first cloud mass. I don't know how to describe it. A massive cloud column defying all description appeared, boiling violently and seething upward. It was so big it blotted out much of the blue sky. Then the top of it began to spill down, like the breakup of some vast thundercloud, and the whole thing started to seep out and spread to the sides. The first cloud mass set down a foot like a huge waterspout, suddenly growing into the form of a monstrous mushroom. The two immense masses of clouds, one above the other, then rapidly formed into a single vast column of vapor, reaching all the way to the ground. Its shape was constantly changing and its colors were kaleidoscopic. Here and there it glittered with some small explosion.*

While other individual witness accounts are less detailed, they collectively confirm Ogura's description. For example, eyewitness Hiroshi Shibayama recounts [156, p. 97 f]:

Suddenly I heard the sharp crack of an explosion. ... The wall of the factory collapsed in a pile of dust. What had happened? Without thinking I turned around to look in the direction of the explosion. The Nishioka boy cried out, "How beautiful!" Rising rapidly into the cobalt blue sky was a towering mass of cloud—deep red, yellow, white, blue, purple, all the colors swirling violently. Unaware of its import, I was fascinated by its beauty.

This mesmerizing display of colors is of course not accounted for by an atomic detonation; it rather suggests that some colored smoke bombs were used. Indeed, some such smoke bombs seem to have reached the ground [156, p. 136 f]:

I noticed what seemed to be a multicolored parachute floating in the sky to the east above Gokoku Shrine. ... My ten-month-old son, inside the house, began to cry as if burned. I had just turned to see to him when a sudden shock from behind propelled me into the room. Tottering, I threw myself down on the baby. ...

It was a little while before I looked down at him. I was amazed to see blood streaming from his forehead. ... I thought that a bomb must have exploded. As I gathered up the baby and searched for the first-aid kit, the air of the room became heavy with purple smoke. My first thought was poison gas. Afraid of being trapped inside, I took the baby downstairs and out into the street. Then the house collapsed and began to burn.

Purple smoke is also described by Brigadier General Thomas Farrell, who was Groves' deputy in the 'Manhattan Project' and reported to him after overseeing the Hiroshima attack [40, p. 323]:

Sound—None appreciable observed.
Flash—Not so blinding as New Mexico test because of bright sunlight. First there was a ball of fire changing in a few seconds to purple clouds and flames boiling and swirling upward.

Groves also quotes a description, allegedly composed by Farrell himself, on the previous test explosion at Alamogordo. That detonation

13 How was it done?

was described as considerably more colorful. The same could be said of Farrell's prose itself:

> *The whole country was lighted by a searing light with the intensity many times that of the midday sun. It was golden, purple, violet, gray and blue. It lighted every peak, crevasse and ridge of the nearby mountain range with a clarity and beauty that cannot be described but must be seen to be imagined: It was that beauty the great poets dream about but describe most poorly and inadequately.*

Another important element in Ogura's testimony is his mention of 'lava from a volcano that had erupted in midair'. This is echoed for example in the testimony of British POW Thomas Jones, who observes the Nagasaki cloud from a distance [166, p. 69]:

> *Following the explosion I saw a beautiful pure white cloud, which changed to red inside and commenced expanding. I thought it was a bomb raining red hot stuff down like a volcano.*

We will revisit this aspect and its significance below (Section 13.2.2).

13.1.5 The black rain. A conspicuous part of standard Hiroshima lore is the 'black rain', which came down a short while after the bombing. It fell predominantly to the north and north west of the hypocenter, in an area that stretched approximately 30 km in east-west and 40 km in north-south direction [162, p. 125 ff]. In parts of the affected area, more than 100 mm (4 inches) of precipitation were observed.[4]

The black rain is said to have picked up radioactive matter in the air and deposited it as fallout on the ground. However, as we noted in Chapter 3, the level of activity shows unexpectedly large variation between samples of a similar nature and origin (see Figure 3.4B).[5] Such pronounced inhomogeneity suggests that the fallout was indeed not deposited by the rain. How else could the fallout have been dispersed? It may simply have been dropped from airplanes. Masamoto Nasu in his book *Children of the Paper Crane* [290] relates the experiences of

---

[4]The black rain area stated by [162] is considerably larger than in older reports (see map in Figure 3.1).

[5]Figure 3.4B also shows rather large variation in the ratio of plutonium to cesium. Quite possibly, several batches of nuclear waste were dispersed which contained both radioactive elements in different proportions.

the Sasaki family[6] as they seek safety from the approaching fire on a boat near Misasa Bridge, 1.5 km north of the hypocenter:

After a while, the pleading voices faded. Some had drowned, many had been roasted by flame and heat. Fujiko and the other occupants silently continued to bail water out of the boat. A little after 9:00 A.M, they heard the drone of a B-29 in the dark sky. Somewhat later came a patter as drops of a black, oily liquid splattered them. "The B-sans are covering us with oil so we'll burn better," someone murmured.

A similar quote can be found in Ogura's book [12, p. 76 f]:

Mr. Yamaoka said, "When the black rain started to fall … "
"Eh?" I couldn't help exclaiming. Two of the others also looked at him with surprise. "I was in Yokogawa when it fell," the third man said. "I was terrified. I thought it was some kind of incendiary bomb that sprayed oil."

We note that in both cases the black drops are described as oily. There is of course no reason why rain—be it spontaneous or prompted by cloud seeding[7] or a nuclear detonation—should produce oily rather than watery precipitation. Therefore, this testimony strongly suggests that some of the 'black rain' was indeed artificially dispersed. If this oily fraction contained the radioactivity, the inhomogeneous distribution of the fallout could be readily explained.

---

[6]The book recounts the story of Sadako Sasaki, a small girl at the time of the bombing who in 1955 succumbed to leukemia, at an age of 12 years.

[7]Considering that the 6th of August, as well as the subsequent days, had been hot and sunny, this episode of rain is rather peculiar. It is usually ascribed to the atmospheric disturbances caused by the nuclear detonation, but this explanation is of course incompatible with our thesis. Moreover, no such event is reported for Nagasaki.

According to accepted history, cloud seeding to produce rain was discovered by Langmuir and Schaefer very shortly after the war [291, p. 3 ff]. It is interesting to note that both investigators worked with the U.S. military during the war years. Furthermore, the groundwork for their discovery had been laid already before the war by Findeisen's seminal work [292]. We can speculate, but cannot prove, that the U.S. military was already in possession of the technology in 1945 and used it in the Hiroshima bombing. In this context, we may also note that, like other prominent scientists, Langmuir contributed a chapter to a nuclear scare propaganda booklet [293] discussed in Section 14.3.1.

13.2 The conventional attack and its concealment

13.2.1 Witness accounts of multiple detonations.
A nuclear bomb should produce only a single large explosion, whereas a conventional bombing will involve multiple smaller detonations. Before dissecting exactly how the conventional bombing was carried out, we note that reports of multiple detonations are not in short supply:[8]

Shigeru Tasaka, a schoolboy in third grade [14, p. 126]: *About noon, the people who had been out on labor service started coming back in twos and threes. ... Some of them thought the explosion was due to the arsenal blowing up, and in fact the thump of explosions could be heard. But others said that it must have been some new type of bomb.*

Yasuhiro Ishibashi, a schoolboy in fourth grade [14, p. 180]: *To the west, we would hear the sounds of explosions followed by flames rising high into the sky. I vacantly watched a big building burning, its iron framework collapsing in the heat.*

Ikuko Wakasa, a girl of 5 years at the time [14, p. 11]: *From the fields, I could see that not only the part of town where we lived but the whole city of Hiroshima was burning. There were clouds of black smoke and big explosions.*

Jesuit Father John Siemes [287]: *While we are attempting to put things in order, a storm comes up and it begins to rain. Over the city, clouds of smoke are rising and I hear a few slight explosions.*

Hisayo Yaguchi, a schoolgirl in fifth grade [14, p. 206]: *My big brother, the one who had been doing voluntary labor, said that an incendiary bomb had exploded right in front of him. His face was a burned mass. I looked at him once but I couldn't bear to look at him a second time.*

Wakaki describes an apparent napalm bomb [173, p. 87]: *It is reported that in a farm house near Koi an incendiary-like bomb dropped into a*

---

[8] In his book *The rising sun*, John Toland recounts the perceptions of Mrs. Yasuko Nukushina, a woman from Hiroshima [76, p. 783]: "People drifted by expressionless and silent like sleepwalkers in tattered, smoldering clothing. It was a parade of wraiths, an evocation of a Buddhist hell. She watched mesmerized until someone touched her. Grasping [her daughter] Ikuko's hand, she joined the procession. *In her confusion she had the illusion that vast numbers of planes were roaring over the city, dropping bomb after bomb without cessation.*"

While we may speculate that Ms. Nukushina's perception was interpreted as an illusion only by Toland but not by herself, this is now impossible to ascertain.

room through the roof and something adhesive, oily and combustible, derived from the bomb, adhered to pillers [sic] and began to burn.

We note, however, that only the last two of these witnesses state that the bomb in question actually hit the ground. This suggests that most bombs may have been detonated in the air. As pointed out before, the two key weapons used in the 'nuclear' bombings were napalm and mustard gas. We propose that both were delivered using M47 bomb casings which were fused for air burst. The M47 filled with napalm was one of the most commonly used incendiaries in Japan [13]. The same bomb casing was also available filled with mustard gas [188]; and according to Infield [105], it had been this very type of bomb that had been shipped to Bari in 1943. Air burst fuses for the M47 were available; thus, all the prerequisites for this scenario were met. We moreover propose that the attacks were carried out as follows:

1. Groves [40] states explicitly that the planes carrying the 'Pumpkins' were flying at high altitude and banked away immediately after releasing the bombs, without overflying the targets. Napalm and mustard bombs were likely delivered in the same manner.
2. The bombs were thrown into the cloud initially created by photoflash and smoke bombs.

We will now consider how this scenario fits the available evidence.

13.2.2 In-air detonation of napalm bombs. For the dispersal of napalm using M47 bombs, a special burster had been developed. It contained a TNT core to ensure a rapid burst of the bomb and the complete release of its cargo. The TNT was surrounded by white phosphorus to ignite the napalm, which was then dispersed in the form of large burning gobs. When such a bomb was detonated on the ground, the burning napalm was sprayed over a circular area about 50 yards in diameter [294, p. 35]. We submit that napalm bombs detonated in the air account for the following kinds of witness testimony:

1. Early on in the Nagasaki bombing, a Japanese lieutenant makes the following observations, as related by Weller et al. [166, p. 26]:

With the parachutes at perhaps a five thousand feet level there suddenly occurred below them, at about fifteen hundred feet, a burst of flame. Almost instantly the flame, yellow as gaslight, fell in a widening cone to earth, at the same time spreading wider in hoop skirt fashion.

This burst of flame is not, or not just, the photoflash bomb. Such a bomb would produce as its residue only a cloud of finely dispersed and already burned-up magnesium oxide; there would be nothing left to fall to the ground ablaze. Similarly, conventional explosives such as those contained in the Pumpkins would also burn up immediately. In contrast, burning napalm can account for the described falling flames.

2. A continued delivery of napalm bombs set to go off inside the cloud can account for the observed sustained red glow. Detonations of both napalm and mustard bombs can explain the secondary flashes within the cloud, as well as its continued growth. All of these features were noted by multiple witnesses—see the quote in Section 13.1.4, as well as interviews with allied POWs collected by Weller [166, p. 68 ff].

3. Raisuke Shirabe, a professor of surgery at Nagasaki University Hospital, recounts his perceptions at the beginning of the bombing [295]:

I could hear a dull drumming noise like the sound of heavy rain. It was probably caused by the falling of soil that had been sucked up into the sky by the explosion.

Shirabe's assumption that soil had been sent flying is not substantiated by any other testimony. We submit that the drumming noise he describes was instead caused by gobs of napalm raining down from the sky (likely accompanied by drops of mustard gas). The same effect can explain the otherwise puzzling statements by two of Keller's patients—namely, that at the time of the bombing they had heard a sound 'like rain' (see quote in Section 1.3).

4. Many witnesses describe buildings which were set afire early on in the attack, but which had neither collapsed themselves nor adjoined other buildings that had; see for example [167, 287]. Similarly, burned spots were noted in the woods near Hiroshima [32, 287]. In the absence of a 'nuclear' detonation, only some sort of incendiary can explain these fires; at the same time, the dearth of reports of explosions on or near the ground suggests that this incendiary was released in the air.

5. Takashi Nagai, a physician and writer from Nagasaki, includes this statement in his description of the bombing [296, p. 28]:

Fragments of incandescent metal rained down in balls of fire immediately setting everything alight.

Most likely, burning gobs of napalm had adhered to shards of bomb casings and heated them to a glow while falling down towards the ground.

6. John Toland [76, p. 803] recounts the story of Hajime Iwanaga, a boy from Nagasaki, who is struck by flying gobs of burning jelly in much the same way as acknowledged napalm victim Kim Phuc (see Section 9.4). Many other witnesses describe that they themselves or others were severely burned very shortly after the onset of the attack (see Section 9.3).

13.2.3 In-air detonation of mustard gas bombs. Sulfur mustard will not ignite readily or fall down in large, compact gobs; it is thus less conspicuous than napalm. Nevertheless, we can adduce some evidence to show that mustard gas was indeed released early on in the bombing:

1. Dr. Tsuzuki's statement that a 'white gas with stimulating odor' and causing 'suffocating pain' was perceived immediately after the onset of the bombing (see quote in Section 1.4.4);

2. Dr. Akizuki's encounter with patients displaying symptoms of mustard exposure only minutes after the bombing (see Section 10.1.1);

3. the actress Midori Naka, sometimes referred to as 'the first victim of radiation sickness', showed indeed clear and very early signs of mustard gas poisoning [297]:

She was trapped under the fallen building, but suffered neither burns nor serious injury. She managed to dig herself out and run to Kyobashigawa River to escape the fire ... by the time she arrived at the bank of Kyobashigawa River, she was feeling intense pain in her chest. She was vomiting violently, and there was blood in the vomit.[9]

---

[9] In his book *Children of the Ashes* [298], the writer Robert Jungk also describes Naka's travails. He purports to literally quote Naka herself in order to create an illusion of authenticity; however, he gravely distorts the story by omitting any mention of her immediate and severe symptoms, which don't fit the radiation sickness narrative. In his looseness with the facts, Jungk resembles Hersey [7], who was contradicted by two of the characters he featured in his famous work *Hiroshima* when these were interviewed a short while later by Clune [171].

13 How was it done?

It seems likely that the amount of explosive in these mustard bombs was carefully calibrated to achieve the best balance of effective dispersal of the fluid and rapid descent of the droplets to the ground. This would likely involve some degree of vaporization; vapors condensing again would form white 'contrails' on the way down. This effect could account for Ogura's observation that after a short while the white cloud column 'set down a foot' and reached all the way to the ground (see quote in Section 13.1.4). However, smoke from burning napalm would likely produce a similar impression.

13.2.4 Concealment of the napalm and mustard gas bombing. Bombs filled with mustard gas were apparently not used in any other attacks by the Americans, so that their use would not be readily suspected.[10] Napalm bombs, on the other hand, were exceedingly common; for example, the well-known raid on Tokyo used almost exclusively napalm bombs [13]. In these raids, however, the incendiaries had been detonated at or near the ground; detonating them several hundred meters above ground thus would have helped disguise their use. The fireworks—the photoflash bombs, followed by colored smoke bombs—hid both types of bombs behind a shroud of magic and mystery.

The smoke produced by all detonations, and also by the rapidly increasing fires on the ground, would also have concealed attacking airplanes from the people on the ground.[11] Thus, while early on in the attack it was necessary to use the minimum number of planes above the target, after a short while it should have become possible to employ a larger number of planes for delivering the amounts of napalm, mustard, and possibly other weapons which we may have failed to discern. Last, but not least, this would also include the planes needed to disperse the radioactive 'fallout', which were heard but not seen by the observers quoted above (see the first quote in Section 13.1.5).

13.2.5 Were thermate/magnesium bombs used as well? While napalm, filled into either the larger M47 bomb casing or the smaller M69

---

[10]If the use of mustard gas had been known, it is likely that a considerable number of victims contaminated with it could have been saved just by removing all contaminated clothes and a thorough washing of the skin. Exposure during rescue and recovery could have been mitigated by the use of proper gas masks.

[11]The US Strategic Bombing Survey [13], in describing large-scale attacks on Japanese cities, comments repeatedly on early fires on the ground hiding the targets from bombing squadrons arriving later on the scene. This would have worked both ways—attacking planes would likewise have been invisible to the people on the ground.

model, was the most widely used type of incendiary used in Japan, another major type was the M50 bomb. This bomb had a body of solid magnesium, with a cavity containing *thermate*, a powdered mixture of metallic aluminum, iron oxide, and some auxiliary additives, which accounted for one sixth of the bomb's overall weight [188]. Thermate burns easily and at very high temperature; it was ignited first and served to ignite the magnesium in turn. This bomb had been developed primarily for use against German cities, whose more heavily constructed buildings required incendiaries with greater penetration than the wooden buildings common in Japan.

Intriguingly, just four days before the Hiroshima bombing, a very large quantity—some 1,500 tons—of M50 bombs had been dropped on Hachioji, a small city near Tokyo. The U.S. Strategic Bombing Survey points out that "industrially, economically, militarily, and commercially the city was unimportant" [13, p. 192]. If there was no compelling military reason to destroy this city, could it be that this attack was merely a practice run for Hiroshima, and therefore that the bombs used here also played a major role in the 'nuclear' bombings?

While we have no hard evidence to reject this possibility, there is none to support it either. The magnesium bombs were designed to ignite only once they had smashed through the roofs and floors of houses on the ground; air burst fuses would seem to defeat the purpose and were apparently unavailable for this model. These bombs, small and numerous, would therefore have ignited on the ground. Moreover, in the Hachioji bombing, up to 20% of the magnesium bombs reportedly failed to ignite [13, p. 206]. Witness testimony from Hiroshima and Nagasaki mentions neither these duds nor magnesium bombs burning on the ground. In summary, therefore, it appears that this type of bomb was not used in the 'nuclear' bombings.

13.3 Japanese collusion

According to conventional historiography, the purpose of the 'nuclear' bombings was to shock the Japanese into surrender by demonstrating to them the United States' possession of a revolutionary weapon with apocalyptic power, against which any further resistance was futile. Of course, this could only have worked if the Japanese were really convinced that the bombings had indeed been nuclear. Conversely, the Japanese government would have had every reason to carefully examine the evidence before accepting the far-reaching implications of America's claim and conceding defeat.

As a matter of record, the Japanese government accepted the atomic tale very shortly after the Hiroshima bombing and did not reverse itself until the surrender. There seem to be three conceivable reasons for this:

1. the Japanese failed to notice the signs that the atomic bombs had been faked and were taken in;
2. while surprised by the fake nuclear bombings, the Japanese were not deceived by them, but they went along with the story nevertheless because they recognized it as a 'face-saving' way out of the war;
3. the Japanese were in on the stitch-up from the beginning and colluded with the Americans in staging the atomic bombings.

Scandalous though it may seem, we will here argue that only the third alternative can be reconciled with the facts.

13.3.1 The Japanese were not taken in. Immediately after the Hiroshima bombing, Truman addressed the world on the radio, claiming that 'the bomb' had had an explosive power equal to 20 kt of TNT [289, p. 241]. The Japanese would certainly have been able to estimate the extent of destruction that should result from such a powerful blast (see also Section 13.6.1 below). General Shunroku Hata, a high-ranking officer in the Japanese army and former minister of war who was stationed near Hiroshima, reported to the Emperor that "in his view the atomic bomb was not that powerful a weapon" [299]. This assessment echoes that of de Seversky, the engineer (see Section 1.1), who summed up his impressions as follows:

> *How strange, I thought, that in their concentration on the spectacle of damage observers should have overlooked the telltale evidence of structural survival!*

Had acceptance of the atomic tale not been a foregone conclusion, Hata's observation should have triggered a thorough investigation.

A second line of evidence on the ground that should have been pursued was that of poisonous gas. As early as August 7th, Hiroshima physician Hachiya notes in his diary [62]:

> *Did the new weapon I had heard about throw off a poison gas or perhaps some deadly germ?*

And on August 13th—still two days before Emperor Hirohito announces the surrender—he states:

The most popular explanation was still that some poison gas had been liberated and was still rising from the ruins.

Similar early reactions can be found in other testimony. In this context, we must also consider that the Japanese army was thoroughly familiar with chemical warfare. Japan had used poison gas against Chinese troops, including on occasion mustard [300]. Fear of overwhelming retaliation in kind would account for the avoidance of such tactics against the U.S. However, according to Grunden [301],

the training of Japanese soldiers in defense against gas warfare was well organized and well executed, and all Japanese troops and a large number of reservists received CW [chemical warfare] training.

Several thousand soldiers had been in Hiroshima when the city was bombed. While very many were killed, some survived. The survivors would surely have recognized the signs of poison gas use, and they may well have started the widespread 'rumor' that poison gas in fact *had* been used.

Nor would expertise on mustard gas have been hard to come by. As noted in Section 12.2.5, the Okunoshima factory, which manufactured large amounts of sulfur mustard and of several other poisons, was located only 50 km from Hiroshima; this means that specialists with intimate knowledge would have been close to hand. Under these circumstances, it is wholly incredible that the Japanese authorities were unable to ascertain the presence of poison gas, and more specifically of mustard, and to institute appropriate mitigating measures in a timely manner. Their failure to warn survivors and helpers of the danger is one of the most telling and damning indications of their collusion in the hoax.

13.3.2 The Japanese were not surprised but colluded from the outset.

A key consideration for deciding between Japanese acquiescence after the fact vs. collusion from the start is the American perspective. Without any prior mutual understanding, the Americans could not expect that the Japanese would go along. The Japanese government could have obtained proof of the poison gas attack and accused the U.S. of it before the world. Without prior assurance that this would not happen, why would the Americans have chanced it? As Alperovitz [68] and other historians have amply demonstrated, the American leadership clearly understood that Japan was defeated, and also that the Japanese government had long been trying to make peace on terms similar to those which were in the end implemented after the war.

Another important indication of the Japanese authorities' collusion is their failure to trigger an air alarm before the bombings, both at Hiroshima and at Nagasaki. The conventional explanation is that the small number of attacking planes—atomic bomb legend never tires of the *Enola Gay*, *Bock's Car*, the *Great Artiste*, and the exploits of their plucky crewmen—persuaded the Japanese that these were only flying reconnaissance missions. However, from the foregoing, it is clear that the number of planes in the sky must have been substantially larger.

The U.S. Strategic Bombing Survey of 1946 estimated that replicating the damage which had occurred in Hiroshima and Nagasaki would have required the use of 220 and 125 B-29 bombers, respectively, carrying incendiaries and explosives [302, p. 102]; similar numbers had previously been suggested by expert witness de Seversky [5]. Even assuming that the attack proceeded in stages, we had seen that multiple kinds of ordnance—the Pumpkins or equivalent high explosives, the napalm, and the mustard gas—were already deployed at the beginning of the attack. Thus, even the first stage must have involved a number of planes more than large enough to trigger an air alarm.

As is well known, however, in Hiroshima the alarm that had been in place earlier in the morning was *lifted* very shortly before the beginning of the attack. This measure caused many inhabitants to leave the air raid shelters and to take to the streets, which must have greatly increased the number of victims.[12] As noted above, this effect was compounded by the failure to issue appropriate warnings to survivors or protective equipment to early entrants, which caused avoidable casualties in the aftermath.

---

[12]Wakaki, the weapons engineer, estimates that lifting the air alarm caused a tenfold increase of the death toll [173, p. 103]. This may be a reasonable estimate if one considers the effects of explosives and incendiaries only. However, the mustard gas would likely have reached and killed many people inside the shelters also; cf. for example the number of victims among those who had been inside concrete buildings (Section 8.6).

13.3.3 Yoshio Nishina's mission to Hiroshima.

The leading Japanese nuclear physicist Yoshio Nishina, who during the war had himself been tasked with developing a nuclear bomb for the Japanese military, flew to Hiroshima two days after the bombing in order to 'investigate', accompanied by the head of military intelligence, General Arisue. According to Frank [303, p. 270], Nishina reached his verdict instantly:

As their plane circled the city, the vista of destruction told Nishina "at a glance that nothing but an atomic bomb could have inflicted such damages ... "

Toland [76, p. 794] relates that Arisue, too, was overwhelmed:

The general had seen many cities laid waste by fire bombings—usually there was smoldering debris, smoke from emergency kitchens and some signs of human activity—but below him stretched a lifeless desert. No smoke, no fires, nothing. There wasn't a street in sight.

Of course, these impressions contrast sharply with de Seversky's description of the scene. Which side is right? Fortunately, we don't have to guess, since de Seversky supports his case with photographs of his own; one of these, which shows a group of structurally intact concrete buildings very near the bomb's purported aiming point, is shown in Figure 13.1. The missing emergency kitchens or other 'signs of life' noted by Arisue would of course be accounted for by the contamination of the city center with mustard gas, which would have dissuaded people from spending more time in this area than necessary.

We had seen in Section 3.2 that Nishina's mission also involved the collection of soil samples. Even though these samples contained no detectable enriched uranium and only minuscule amounts of fission products, Nishina presented them as proof of a nuclear detonation. That the alternate interpretation of a 'dirty bomb' had immediately occurred to the Japanese physicists is evident from the report by Sakae Shimizu, whose group of Kyoto physicists conferred with Nishina upon their own arrival in Hiroshima on August 10th [37]. As demonstrated in Chapter 3, this interpretation would have fit the findings from Nishina's samples much better.[13]

---

[13] Nishina or his helpers may also have planted the radioactive pieces of evidence which were subsequently recovered and analyzed by Shimizu (see Section 4.2).

Figure 13.1: Photograph of downtown Hiroshima, taken by Alexander P. de Seversky during his visit in early September 1945. The original figure caption [5] reads as follows: "A cluster of concrete office buildings, standing erect and structurally intact amidst the ashes of the surrounding wooden houses, near 'ground zero' (B)."

Another example of how the atomic bomb story was implanted early on is found in the previously cited report by Wakaki. On August 8th, he and other officers are summoned to a conference at Kure, ostensibly to investigate the causes and mechanisms of Hiroshima's destruction. However, from Wakaki's account, it appears that nothing occurred at this conference but the exchange of speculations; no collection of further evidence is contemplated or resolved upon. In the end, one Captain Mitsui announces the verdict [173, p. 88 f]:

> *Judging from the conclusions reached in this debate, this explosion was most unusually powerful and cannot be taken to be an ordinary explosive. Most probably, this was an atomic bomb. In fact, although I did not tell you earlier, an enemy broadcast from the Marianas reported that a uranium bomb had been dropped on Hiroshima.*

Overall, it is apparent that the Japanese scientists and the military did not seriously investigate the Hiroshima bombing, but instead swiftly endorsed the tale of the atomic bomb. In its formal protest to the United States, communicated via the Swiss embassy on August 12th, the Japanese government reinforced the narrative [289, p. 244 f]:

On August 6, 1945, American airplanes released on the residential district of the town of Hiroshima bombs of a new type, killing and injuring in one second a large number of civilians and destroying a great part of the town. ... They now use this new bomb, having an uncontrollable and cruel effect much greater than any other arms or projectiles ever used to date. This constitutes a new crime against humanity and civilization.

We note in passing that this missive implies the use of multiple bombs at Hiroshima; this deviation from the imposed story also occurs in the first radio broadcast from Tokyo to announce the bombing (see quote in Section 13.1.3). Soon afterwards, however, the plural form was drowned out, never to resurface, by the incessant, breathless propaganda of 'The Bomb'.

13.3.4 How were the Japanese induced to collude? On this point, we can offer no more than conjecture. As will be discussed in Section 14.1, Japan had signaled its readiness to surrender several months before the bombings, demanding only that its monarchy and statehood be preserved. These signals had been sent through several different channels, including Japanese representatives in Switzerland and Sweden. However, these efforts did not come to fruition; the war dragged on, and the United States went through with the bombings. Alperovitz [68, p. 551] quotes Richard Hewlett, who interviewed Truman in 1959 concerning this decision:

I ... asked him ... whether there had been any consideration of putting a specific warning of the weapon in the Potsdam Declaration. His reply was immediate and positive. He said that certainly the Potsdam Declaration did not contain such a warning but that the Japanese had been warned through secret diplomatic channels by way of both Switzerland and Sweden. He said that this warning told the Japanese that they would be attacked by a new and terrible weapon unless they would surrender.

Hewlett professes surprise at this statement—which indeed could hardly have been entirely truthful. Firstly, the 'new and terrible weapon' did not exist, and would not come into existence soon enough. Secondly, by stating their warning publicly instead of through secret channels only, the U.S. could have avoided the opprobrium of having attacked without any warning at all.

According to Butow [304, p. 110], Allen Dulles, who oversaw the secret negotiations in Switzerland, let the Japanese side know that

> the United States could not make any firm commitments. All it could do was state its understanding that the imperial institution would be maintained if Japan surrendered.

The Japanese government would certainly have been vexed by such evasive language; nevertheless, in conjunction with the big stick of the new weapon, Dulles' statement should still have been enough of a carrot to evoke some speedy and substantial reaction. However, ostensibly, nothing came of it. In his book *Japan's Decision to Surrender* [304], Robert Butow gives a detailed account of the consultations between the Japanese decision makers, but he mentions neither Truman's alleged warning nor Dulles' averred 'understanding' as subjects of any internal Japanese discussions.

The lack of a Japanese reaction to the alleged American gambit strongly suggests that the offer of keeping the emperor and avoiding the 'terrible weapon' in return for surrendering speedily was never on the table. We speculate, but cannot prove, that instead of being 'warned' about the bombings through these secret channels, the Japanese were given demands and instructions for colluding in them. This unheard-of, abhorrent request then induced Japan to hold out for some more months, during which the country lay prostrate, exposed helplessly to the intensifying American bombing campaign.

It also appears that the Japanese government was not satisfied to have received, through these secret channels, an authoritative, binding statement by the highest levels of the U.S. government. This can be surmised from its subsequent diplomatic overture to Moscow—Stalin or Molotov would certainly have had Truman's ear and thus been able to present the Japanese government's proposals to him directly. The Soviet Union's refusal to mediate, and its increasingly obvious preparations for joining the war itself, likely compelled Tokyo to accept the American demand.[14]

---

[14] Alperovitz [68, p. 99] writes that the Americans reversed themselves three times with respect to the Russian entry into the war on Japan. Roosevelt had wanted them in; Truman initially wanted them out, then in again, and finally out. The first reversal

Could Japan have avoided the 'atomic' bombings by forthwith declaring unconditional surrender unilaterally? American self-interest would have urged that the institution of the emperor be preserved, since he was uniquely placed to secure the cooperation of his loyal subjects with the occupying troops; American leaders could be expected, or at least hoped, to act accordingly even without having given explicit guarantees. What reasons might have dissuaded Tokyo from following this path? The vengeful and unlawful treatment meted out by the Americans after the war to disarmed soldiers and civilians in Germany, which country *had* surrendered unconditionally, could certainly have been a powerful deterrent to the Japanese.[15]

In his biography of Hirohito, Toshiaki Kawahara quotes from a statement by the emperor, made before a Japanese press conference in 1975 [306, p. 201]:

I feel that it was truly regrettable that the atomic bomb was dropped. But it was in the midst of a war, and however tragic it may have been for the citizens of Hiroshima, I believe it was unavoidable.

According to Kawahara, Hirohito's use of the word "unavoidable"

drew sharp reaction from victims of the bombing and the citizens of Hiroshima, and strong protests from the Communist party.

The outrage would seem understandable on the premise that Hirohito had deemed unavoidable the choice made by *American* officials. However, considering what we can learn from credible sources [304, 306, 307] about his general good sense, grace, and sincerity, a thoughtless and callous statement of this kind would seem entirely out of character for the emperor.

---

may have been triggered by Japanese attempts to negotiate—peace seemed near, and keeping the Russians out would have denied them any claim to the spoils. The second reversal may have occurred when Japan initially refused to collude in the bombings, and the third one when Japan finally caved.

[15] See in particular James Bacque's book *Other losses: the shocking truth behind the mass deaths of disarmed German soldiers and civilians under General Eisenhower's command* [305], which thoroughly documents the deliberate starving to death of approximately one million German prisoners of war, as well as a number of civilians, in American and also in French prison camps. This starvation campaign was in full swing during the months preceding the 'atomic' bombings in Japan.

We posit that the subtext of Hirohito's statement is quite different. Caught off guard by a journalist's unexpected question about the Hiroshima bombing, he thought back to the time preceding it, and to the decision which *he* had then been forced to take. His unrehearsed reply meant that the bombing had been unavoidable to *him*—having exhausted all diplomatic channels, unable to protect the country from the relentless bombings and the impending Russian attack,[16] or even from starvation, Hirohito and his government had reached the end of the road and saw no other option than giving in to the Americans and playing their wretched, mortifying part in the staged atrocity.

13.4 Censorship and propaganda

In Section 1.4.4, we encountered the Australian journalist Wilfred Burchett, who had reported from Hiroshima four weeks after the bombing. Looking back on this episode in 1983, Burchett vividly describes the cunning and subterfuge he had had to use in order to reach the city, and then to relay his report to the editorial office of his newspaper; the American military was trying hard to thwart him at every step [165]. As noted earlier, his observations in the city clearly suggested the continued presence of mustard gas.

Burchett's news report in the *Daily Express* remained a rare exception in this period, however. When the Japanese news agency Domei released a worldwide broadcast in mid-September on the conditions then prevailing in Hiroshima and Nagasaki, it was promptly sanctioned with a one-day suspension. Shortly afterwards, Domei was permanently barred from broadcasting outside Japan altogether. In her book on American postwar censorship in Japan, Monica Braw relates how Domei's president and several other Japanese media executives were summoned at MacArthur's behest and given a dressing-down [308, p. 39]:

> *At a meeting called the next day, Japanese press people were told that the Supreme Commander was not satisfied with the manner in which they had carried out the [censorship] directive. "Freedom of the press is very dear to the Supreme Commander, and it is*

---

[16]While Japan's formal capitulation occurred after the Russians had entered the war, the real capitulation would have come before this event, namely, when Japan agreed to collude.

one of the freedoms for which the Allies have fought," the Civil Censorship officer told them.

Braw states one goal of American censorship as follows [308, p. 145]:

to draw a ring around Japan through which no unauthorized information slipped, either to or from Japan. Seen from this angle, Japan was a territory separated both from most of the world, including to a large extent the allies of the United States.

She also maintains that suppression of information on the effects of the atomic bombings was a key concern that drove such drastic measures, and she supports her case with rich detail on the bans imposed against specific books and news media. Particularly rigorous was the censorship of medical research on atomic bomb victims (see also Section 11.1).

13.4.1 The use of censorship to impose two different stories on two separate audiences. Concerning the reason for censoring all things 'atomic', Braw posits [308, p. 133]:

Above all there was concern about the reputation of the United States. An often-stated reason for suppression was that the material gave the impression that the United States was inhumane or barbaric in using the atomic bomb.

This does, however, not tell the entire story. If indeed the purpose had been to hide the horrors of the bombings from the world at large, Hersey's book *Hiroshima* [7] would not have been published as early as 1946, nor reprinted as often and generally promoted the way it was. Another early work of nuclear fear propaganda was the book *One World Or None: A Report to the Public on the Full Meaning of the Atomic Bomb* [293], which includes a fictional tale describing a nuclear attack on New York City by the physicist Morrison (see Section 13.5.2).

While both of the above works refrained from explicitly criticizing the United States for their use of the atomic bomb, independent minds in America were of course capable of making their own moral judgment. Alperovitz cites these trenchant words by Father James M. Gillis, editor of *Catholic World* [68, p. 438]:

I would call it a crime were it not that the word "crime" implies sin and sin requires consciousness of guilt ... the action taken by the

United States Government was in defiance of every sentiment and every conviction upon which our civilization is based.

When the chorus of critical voices grew louder, former Secretary of War Henry Stimson lent his name to a propaganda effort to shut them up [68].[17]

We can therefore conclude that censorship was not intended to protect the sensibilities of the American people or the reputation of their government.[18] It was not the American people's feelings in the matter that were to be suppressed, but their understanding of the facts. Information such as Burchett's, if independently confirmed and properly analyzed, would have undermined the official narrative. Instead, as illustrated by the incredulity and the brouhaha surrounding de Seversky's published first-hand observations (see Section 1.1), the American people were fed cartoonish and exaggerated misrepresentations of 'The Bomb's' effects.

While in America and generally overseas the presence of poison gas in the 'atom-bombed' cities could be hushed up, the same was apparently deemed unfeasible in those cities themselves. Most likely because very many survivors and rescue workers had experienced the effects for themselves, the authorities chose to 'explain' rather than deny the presence of poison gas. The story that seems to have been told in Japan can only be gleaned in outline from fragmentary information.

13.4.2 The 'atom-bomb gas'. In Section 1.4.4, we introduced several witnesses whose testimony we interpreted as evidence of poison gas use. Each of them draws a connection between the poison gas perceived and the atomic bomb or its radiation. Here are the pertinent excerpts again:

Dr. Masao Tsuzuki: *a part of it [the gas] might have originated from electrolytes generated by application of radioactivity to air ... At present we have no clue whether it [the bomb] was devised on purpose so as to radiate something like poisonous gas.*

---

[17]The result, published in 1947 in Harper's magazine (and reprinted in [289, p. 91]), went a long way to implant the still-popular myth that the atomic bomb accelerated the end of the war and thereby saved numerous American lives. Alperovitz's book [68] clearly refutes this myth (see Section 14.1).

[18]With respect to censorship inside Japan, of course, the stated motive of suppressing perceptions of the U.S. as barbaric seems a lot more convincing.

Wilfred Burchett: They believe it [the smell] is given off by the poisonous gas still issuing from the earth soaked with radioactivity released by the split uranium atom.

Hisato Itoh: ... we had breathed the gases when the atom bomb fell.

This list of examples can be extended from Arata Osada's collection of schoolchildren's testimony [14]:

Tokiko Wada: But Grandpa had breathed poisonous gas when the atom bomb fell and he got sick and went to the hospital. He died one night a little later and we had a funeral for him.

Satomi Kanekuni: On August 6 when the bomb fell, Father and Mother were living in Yanagi-machi. They were trapped by the house when it fell down and inhaled poisonous gas.

Junya Kojima: When I was five years old, there was the atom bomb explosion. My father was at his office then. I guess he breathed in poison gas ... he soon died.

Yohko Kuwabara: Just then, I was blinded for a moment by piercing flash of bright light, and the air filled with yellow smoke like poison gas.

Yoshiaki Wada: My mother ... breathed the poison gas from the atom bomb. That's why she was so bad.

In his foreword to the English edition of Osada's book, the translator Yoichi Fukushima comments on statements such as those quoted above [14, p. ix]:

Readers may often note in the children's accounts references to 'poison' being inhaled, and this is because in 1951 that was about the general level of comprehension regarding the effects of radiation.

It may be fair to assume that school children's understanding of the matter was indeed limited. Even here, however, the matter-of-fact style in which each of them draws a straight line from the atomic bomb to the poisonous gas is rather striking, and it does suggest that the children are in fact just repeating something they have been told.

Be that as it may, however—lack of education certainly cannot be blamed for Dr. Tsuzuki's valiant yet unfruitful effort to wring poison gas from radiation. Nor can it explain the following scientific misadventure [155, p. 464]:

> *Tsuzuki (1951) divided atom-bomb injuries into burns, traumas, and radiation injuries. Kajitano and Hatano (1953)... proposed a fourth type in addition: atom-bomb gas injuries, which they attributed to the effect of residual radioactivity.*

In this last example, two medical scholars blatantly conflate poison gas and residual radioactivity. They very likely would not have committed such a blunder without any outside encouragement.

Collectively, these examples strongly suggest that in the postwar period a narrative was forced upon the Japanese public, including the scientific community, in which bomb radiation or residual radioactivity had somehow given rise to poisonous gas—the 'atom-bomb gas'. While we do not know the full details of this tale, we can safely assume that it could not have survived worldwide exposure and scrutiny.

Thus, overall, we propose that censorship served to separate the people inside Japan from those outside, so that each audience could then be plied with its own made-to-measure propaganda. The people outside Japan received a yarn of instant wholesale annihilation and of an imminent worldwide nuclear war; this, apparently, in order to stampede them into submitting to an all-new and benevolent world government, which alone could save mankind from self-destruction (see Section 14.3). The Japanese, who had been near the events, were fed the 'atom-bomb gas' tale in order to hide from them the true meaning of what they had witnessed, so as to protect and consolidate the horror story of 'The Bomb'.

13.5 Special effects

Atomic mythology regales us with a number of remarkable phenomena, such as the shadows of people preserved on walls or pavements, which seem to prove the unique, awesome power of the nuclear bombs dropped on Hiroshima and Nagasaki. We may wonder whether these effects are physically plausible; some such aspects are discussed below (Section 13.6). However, more relevant in the current context is the question when and why they were created.

13.5.1 The timing. Alexander P. de Seversky, who examined Hiroshima for two days in early September, found no "traces of unusual phenomena" (see quote in Section 1.1). Another visitor to Hiroshima who arrived around the same time was Marcel Junod, a physician and official of the International Committee of the Red Cross. Junod's report [153], like de Seversky's, mentions no unusual signs.

In contrast, Averill Liebow, who arrived in mid-October as a member of the Joint Commission, describes in his diary a multitude of shadows and other special effects; he also includes a number of photographs [77]. Liebow makes a point of showing them to all of his visitors:

October 31: took Colonel Oughterson and Nagasaki guests on what we have now laid out as the "grand tour." This includes all of the fascinating evidences of blast and heat damage in the shrine area at the Chugoku Army headquarters, the "Korean Building" with the shadowing on the concrete there, and the remarkable view of the Commercial Museum[19] and the area of the hypocenter. All were fascinated by the outlines of men and vehicles on the Bantai Bridge.

When Liebow showed around another visitor (General Morgan) one month later, the shadows were already rapidly fading:

To our disappointment the shadows on the bridge were now only faintly visible, but they impressed the general.

Taken together, these reports of course suggest that the shadows were created sometime between de Seversky's visit and Liebow's arrival, and that they were meant for short-term effect but not to be preserved for posterity.[20]

13.5.2 The motivation. Also traveling in Junod's airplane was Philip Morrison, a physicist involved with the Manhattan Project. Junod relates [153, p. 291]:

In our plane the physicist Morrison was nervously going from one window to the other studying the scientific message the grim picture held for him. He compared photos he had with him with what he could see out of the windows, made hasty notes and sketched

---

[19]The remnants of this building have been preserved and are now known as the 'Atomic Dome'.

[20]The Bantai Bridge (named "Yorozuyo Bridge" on current maps) is located no more than 1 km from the hypocenter; it seems unlikely that it would not have been pointed out to de Seversky on his quest for unusual phenomena.

13 How was it done?

out a general plan. His nervousness and agitation contrasted with the rather shocked silence of General Newman.

Morrison must have seen what de Seversky saw—namely, the "telltale evidence of structural survival;" and, once on the ground, the absence of "unusual phenomena."[21] His apparent agitation may have been due to this realization; and it might well have been he to first propose that this appearance of ordinary, conventional destruction be spruced up with the various special effects in question. Whether or not the idea was indeed his, however—the obvious purpose was to fake the evidence of the nuclear bomb's specific and unique effects, so as to deceive the visitors who would shortly arrive in the city in numbers. Among these, the military men who were acquainted with, and inured to, the sights of cities destroyed by conventional bombing must have caused particular anxiety among the nuclear fakers. Treating each of them to Liebow's "grand tour" of special effects may have been more than mere courtesy.

13.6 Additional evidence against the nuclear detonation

The various observations presented earlier in this chapter provide some more evidence to show that no nuclear detonations took place. These aspects have been collected here so as to not disrupt the flow of this chapter's main argument.

13.6.1 The extent of destruction near to or far from the hypocenter.
As noted in Section 1.1, Alexander P. de Seversky had noted that flagpoles and "other fragile objects" had somehow withstood the "alleged super-hurricane thousand-mile-an-hour wind." This would indeed seem impossible—but should we expect a blast wave of such force?

Glasstone [90, p. 135] gives specific figures for a 'nominal bomb', that is, one with a yield of 20 kt and thus only slightly stronger than the supposed Hiroshima bomb. Near the hypocenter, the wind speed is indeed almost as high as stated by de Seversky—1280 km/h, or 800 mph,

---

[21] The second quote in Section 1.1 shows that mainstream atomic bomb propagandists were rather annoyed when de Seversky came forward with his findings, and they trained their guns on him. Morrison took this one step further in his contribution to the 'One World or None' propaganda pamphlet [293]. His fictional description of an atomic attack on New York City invites de Seversky for a cameo appearance: "A well-known aeronautical engineer who had managed to remain uninjured by the flash burn or the blast ... died in twelve days, while working on a report for the Air Forces on the extent of the damage to steel structures."

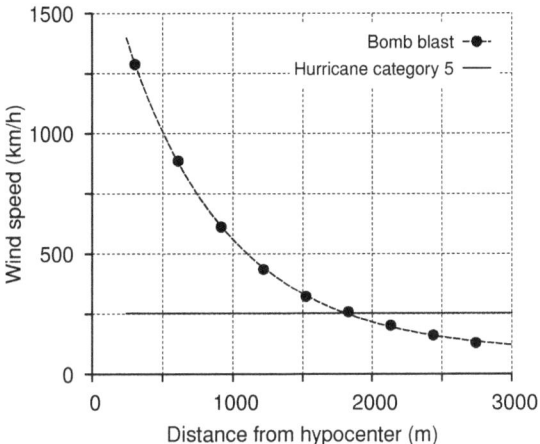

Figure 13.2: Wind speed of the pressure wave of a 'nominal' atomic bomb. Data points from Table 5.45 in [90]. Wind speed of a category 5 hurricane shown for comparison.

which is five times greater than a category 5 hurricane. Twice the speed of such a hurricane is exceeded beyond 1 km from the hypocenter; it is out of the question for wooden flagpoles etc., exposed on the roofs of tall buildings, to survive a blast of such strength. The wind speed does, however, drop rapidly with distance; the reference gives eight miles—the equivalent of 13 km, that is, the distance to Wakaki's residence—as the 'limit of light damage'. Thus, both the preservation of 'fragile objects' and Wakaki's experience of having been thrown to the ground by the blast are incompatible with the story of the nuclear blast.[22] Moreover, as noted earlier, the extent of destruction at the Jesuit convent (situated at 4 km from the hypocenter) was similar to that at Wakaki's residence; this, too, is incompatible with prediction.

13.6.2 The altitude of the epicenter. It is said that the epicenter of the Hiroshima bomb was determined by triangulation from shadows created by the flash. According to Liebow [77], one of the reference points on the ground was in fact the Bantai Bridge, which he places at "approximately 1,000 m from the hypocenter." On a high-resolution map appended to the official report of the Joint Commission [309], the

---

[22]When inspecting the damage in his neighborhood, Wakaki wonders [173, p. 60]: "why did the blast come from a direction at right angles to the flash?"

Figure 13.3: Shadows on the Bantai bridge: observation vs. prediction. Left: shadows of the railing on the pavement (photograph from Liebow [77]). Right: ray-tracing of expected shadows based on the official location of the epicenter. See text for details.

distance is 920 meters. The still-current DS02 report puts the altitude of the epicenter at 600 m.

Figure 13.3 shows a photograph of the shadows cast by the railing of the Bantai bridge on its pavement. The height of the individual pillars is approximately equal to the length of their shadows. For comparison, the figure also shows the expected length of the shadows in a simulated scene.[23] Here, the shadows appear longer by half than the height of the pillars—as of course they should, given that the ground distance of the epicenter is approximately 1.5 times greater than its altitude. Thus, the observed length of the shadows does not match the location of the epicenter allegedly inferred from them—the epicenter would have had to be at a steeper angle above the bridge in order to produce shadows such as these.

While the shadows suggest that the epicenter should have been higher than the 600 m claimed, another observation indicates that it should have been lower. Wakaki, who witnessed the flash from his home at Hatsukaichi, reports [173, p. 58]:

> *Then I gazed out at the Chugoku Mountains. At that moment I saw a flash-like lightning but brighter, far larger and much more*

---

[23] Scene generated with POV-ray. Ground distance between light source and scene: 920 m; altitude of light source: 600 m. The light source consisted of 100 'bulbs' arranged in a square with an edge length of 135 m, which approximates the cross-sectional area of a spherical fireball with diameter of 150 m; the latter number is based on Hubbell et al. [85].

Figure 13.4: Purported effects of the Hiroshima bomb on tombstones in the city. A: three tombstones said to have been bleached by the flash (cf. light shade on upper surface and on hollow square around base) and subsequently rotated around a vertical axis by the blast [86]. Stones in the background were apparently not rotated. B: light areas (chipped) and dark areas (unchipped) on a tombstone in Hiroshima [77]. Both locations are near the hypocenter.

blinding—just below the highest mountain and directly opposite our windows.

Hatsukaichi is 13 km to the southwest of the hypocenter, on the coast and thus near sea level. The mountain that should loom the highest above the hypocenter is at approximately $2/3$ of that distance to the northeast of it and rises to 682 m. Thus, the detonation would have occurred at an altitude of at most $3/5 \times 682$ m, that is, about 410 m— only $2/3$ of the officially claimed altitude.[24] Of note, this estimate is rather insensitive with respect to the location of the hypocenter—while shifting the hypocenter closer to the Bantai Bridge could remove the discrepancy concerning the shadows on the pavement, its effect on the detonation height inferred from Wakaki's observation would be negligible.

13.6.3 The improbable and ephemeral shadows. Nakatani [1] rightly ridicules dark, sooty shadows cast by humans and inanimate objects

---

[24] For discerning readers: taking into account the curvature of the Earth lowers this value by another 10 m.

on otherwise unblemished wooden walls or doors.[25] Another widely celebrated special effect is the flaking or chipping of polished granite surfaces by the bomb flash. The dividing lines of chipped and unchipped areas of such stone surfaces were also used in the attempts to locate the epicenter [85, 310].

Somewhat improbably, however, most of these outlines are said to have been weathered away a mere 20 years later [85]. Assuming that nobody disturbed the graveyard peace by night to polish up the chipped and flaked surface areas, this would mean that the unblemished parts had undergone weather-induced chipping to abolish the contrast. Considering the generally very high durability of polished granite, this seems quite unlikely.

13.6.4 The "Trinity" test detonation. In Section 13.1.4, we quoted Thomas Farrell on the "Trinity" test explosion at Alamogordo in New Mexico, whose flash he described as more blinding than the one at Hiroshima. Glasstone [90] shows a photograph which allegedly captured the "ball of fire" in progress, as it hugs the ground (see Figure 13.5A). However, the strange, splotchy object in the picture does not appear luminous at all; instead, it seems to be passively illuminated by a light source located off-image to the top left.

Glasstone also relates that the detonation occurred at the low altitude of 100 feet above ground, and that this caused the ground to become highly radioactive. He asserts that the radiation dose *measured* at the hypocenter, one hour after the detonation, was as high as 8,000 roentgens per hour. This is approximately equal to 80 Gy per hour; thus, any technicians without very heavy protection would have received deadly doses of radiation within mere minutes. Moreover, exact measurements of such enormous radiation intensities would certainly have required special-purpose instruments. On such equipment, Glasstone's otherwise highly technical book gives no technical explanation at all.[26]

---

[25] It is often intimated that the people whose outlines are preserved in such shadows were instantly 'atomized' or 'vaporized'. However, even the official estimates of the fictitious nuclear detonations do not provide enough energy for such a feat; the heat of the flash available directly at the hypocenter (cf. Figure 9.1A) would only have sufficed to inflict deep burns on a man but not to 'vaporize' him.

[26] Cf. also the related episode in Franklin Stahl's foreword to this book.

Figure 13.5: The "Trinity" bomb test. A: Alleged photograph of the ball of fire of the alleged nuclear detonation at Alamogordo, New Mexico, on July 16th, 1945. Taken from [90]. B: Oppenheimer and Groves standing near the remains of the tower on which the explosive device was allegedly mounted. From the Library of Congress catalogue. C: Detail from B, enlarged.

Had the ball of fire indeed enveloped the ground beneath the detonation, as the stated low altitude and the phony photograph suggest, then the temperature on the ground should have been high enough not merely to melt iron but even to evaporate it. This, however, did not happen, as is evident from the picture of Oppenheimer and Groves inspecting the wreckage of the tower on which the nuclear test device had allegedly been mounted (Figure 13.5B, C). The rods of construction steel are bent, but otherwise intact—even the regularly spaced circumferential ridges on their surfaces are still there. Thus, they evidently were not exposed to extreme heat.

The "Trinity" bomb test is discussed in more detail, and with rather dry humor, by Nakatani [1]. He relates that a conventional test detonation using 100 tons of trinitrotoluene (TNT) was carried out near the same test site shortly before the "atomic" one, and he suggests that more TNT was detonated in the "Trinity" test itself. While this may be so,[27] Farrell's description of the detonation as very bright and colorful suggests additional devices were deployed as well, as discussed above in Section 13.1.4. The event thus appears to have been a dress rehearsal for the fireworks used at Hiroshima.

---

[27]The word "trinitrotoluene," rather than any faith or interest in Christianity, may have been Oppenheimer's inspiration for naming the event "Trinity." Oppenheimer came from a Jewish family, but he seems to have been preoccupied with oriental religious ideas. After witnessing the test, he reportedly quoted Hindu scripture with "Now I am become Death, the destroyer of worlds."

14 Why was it done?

> The war might have ended weeks earlier, he [MacArthur] said, if the United States had agreed, as it later did anyway, to the retention of the institution of the emperor.
>
> Norman Cousins [311, p. 71]

Several hypothetical motives for staging the 'atomic' bombings are considered. The most widely espoused motive—namely, shocking Japan into surrender—is rejected for the following reasons:

1. Japan was not surprised but colluded in the bombings, and
2. Japan had long been ready to surrender on terms similar to those implemented after the war.

The alternate explanation that the bombings were staged in order to intimidate Stalin is dismissed, not only because Stalin was not intimidated, but also because such a plan could not even have been expected to work.

We propose that the 'atomic' bombings were acts of state terror, directed at the international general public: general fear of impending nuclear war should induce the people to voluntarily surrender their national sovereignty and submit to a world government. The motives behind this plan and the reasons for its failure are examined.

Having surveyed the available evidence, we assert that the 'nuclear' bombings were faked, in a manner that at this point does not need to be repeated. The one remaining question then of course is: Why?

14.1 The object was not to obtain Japan's surrender

Conventional historiography maintains that the atomic bombings were carried out for shock effect—Japan, which was refusing to give up, was in this way to be shocked into surrender, so that America would be spared the need to invade the Japanese home islands and the attendant losses. We reject this motive for two reasons:

1. It is incompatible with the thesis of this book. As was argued in Section 13.3, the Japanese actively colluded in staging the bombings and in managing their aftermath, and they can therefore not have been surprised by them.
2. Japan had been looking for ways out of the war since 1944 at the latest. As of early 1945, America's leadership was thoroughly informed of this, and indeed many persons of high rank, such as the Joint Chiefs of Staff and former president Herbert Hoover, implored Truman to realize the opportunity and conclude peace without delay.

The second reason does not depend on the fraudulent nature of the bombings, and accordingly it has been argued by several mainstream historians. The most thorough treatment has been given by Alperovitz [68]; his book, being more recent than most similar works, also benefits from access to a greater number of declassified documents. We will here only quote a few illustrative excerpts, mostly from Alperovitz' book; readers who remain unconvinced by these are encouraged to peruse his very comprehensive treatise for themselves.

14.1.1 The Japanese were ready for peace negotiations. Throughout most of the Pacific War, American intelligence was able to decode internal Japanese communications; the crucial role of this ability in America's resounding naval victory at Midway is well known. One report on the contents of such decoded cables, which was prepared in the War Department on August 11th 1944, contains the following statements [68, p. 23]:

> *Foreign Minister Shigemitsu has instructed Ambassador Sato [in Moscow] to find out whether Russia is willing to assist in bringing about a negotiated peace. Shigemitsu's instructions, although cautiously worded, clearly imply that he has in mind a move by Russia to initiate peace discussions between Japan and the Anglo-Americans. ... It seems hardly likely that he would have taken such a step without having consulted at least some of the more important members of the new Japanese Cabinet. This is the first time that the Japanese have been willing to suggest to Russia directly that they are ready for peace.*

Shigemitsu's message to the ambassador, which is appended to the report, is quoted as follows:

In the Pacific, the American offensive is becoming violent. The enemy has already broken into our territorial waters and by means of absolute superiority on the sea and in the air is steadily drawing nearer to our homeland itself with the intention of severing our sea communications and destroying our shore installations. This situation will become increasingly serious as Germany's military strength diminishes.

This quote implies that Shigemitsu has been given a realistic assessment of Japan's strategic situation by the country's military leadership. The latter is often alleged to have concealed the true state of affairs from the civilian government, and to have obstructed any and all peace efforts. We will not examine the extent of such obstruction in detail, but simply note that it had apparently ceased as of April 1945. A planning document prepared at this time in the Imperial General Headquarters contains the following statement [68, p. 116]:

The Greater East Asiatic War has now reached such critical point [that] it was [sic] definitely beyond the power of military strategy alone to save the situation.

Japanese peace initiatives continued. On January 30th 1945, the OSS informed the State Department of talks between the Japanese government and the Vatican, with a view to having the Pope act as an intermediary between the warring parties. Further 'peace feelers' were extended through Japan's diplomatic missions in Sweden, Switzerland, and also the Soviet Union. In March 1945, a new government was formed in Tokyo, which was led by Admiral Kantaro Suzuki. American naval intelligence officer Captain Ellis Zacharias [312] had predicted exactly this move even in 1944 and interpreted it as a sign that Japan was willing to give up.

14.1.2 Herbert Hoover's failed effort to facilitate peace negotiations.

Historian Jacques Launay [313] asserts that Admiral Suzuki was a personal friend of former U.S. president Herbert Hoover, and that upon the formation of Suzuki's government Hoover promptly approached Roosevelt and later Truman to facilitate negotiations; receiving, however, no useful reply from either. The memo which he presented in May 1945 to Truman makes the following arguments to suggest that negotiations with the Japanese appeared promising at this time and should be tried [68, p. 43]:

(a) *The appointment of Suzuki, a one-time anti-militarist elder statesman, as Prime Minister;*

(b) *The desire of the Japanese to preserve the Mikado [Emperor] who is the spiritual head of the nation;*

(c) *The sense they showed after the Russo-Japanese war [of 1905] of making peace before Russia organized her full might;*

(d) *The fear of complete destruction which by now they must know is their fate.*

Also illuminating in this context is a conversation between Hoover and General Douglas MacArthur of early May 1946. Alperovitz quotes from Hoover's diary [68, p. 350 f]:

I told MacArthur of my memorandum of mid-May 1945 to Truman, that peace could be had with Japan by which our major objectives would be accomplished. MacArthur said that was correct and that we would have avoided all of the losses, the Atomic bomb, and the entry of Russia into Manchuria.

14.1.3 American, not Japanese intransigence led to the 'atomic' bombings. Truman inherited the formula of 'unconditional surrender' from Roosevelt, who had initially pronounced it in 1943 at Casablanca. His proclamation was received with widespread consternation; many saw that this inflexible posture could not but prolong the war, leaving the Axis powers no choice but fight on to utter exhaustion. It is noteworthy that many of America's military leaders, and in particular the Joint Chiefs of Staff, tried to persuade Truman to drop this demand vis-a-vis Japan. The Joint Chiefs thought of Emperor Hirohito as an asset, considering him uniquely able to ensure the peaceful acquiescence of his loyal subjects in and after the surrender. Accordingly, retaining Hirohito was not only in Japan's but also in America's best interest; and extending the appropriate guarantees might bring the war to a speedy end. When Truman did not heed them, the Joint Chiefs approached their British counterparts to please ask Churchill if he would plead their case with Truman. Churchill obliged, but to no avail [68, p. 246 f].

Truman throughout held firm in demanding unconditional surrender right up to and including the Potsdam ultimatum, which was issued less than two weeks before the Hiroshima bombing (and one day after the bombing itself was purportedly ordered by him). The Joint Chief's pragmatic strategy of using rather than ousting Hirohito did of course prevail in the event, after Japan's ostensibly unconditional surrender.

This brief sketch may suffice to show that not Japan but the U.S. dragged out the war for as long as it lasted. Nobody has summed this up more succinctly than 'straight shooter' Harry Truman himself [68, p. 537]:

It was because of the unconditional surrender policy against Japan that Hiroshima and Nagasaki were wiped out.

14.1.4 The atomic bombings were not staged to let Japan 'save face'. The evidence of early and continued Japanese readiness for negotiations also disposes of another explanatory myth—namely, that the atomic bombings were necessary to give the Japanese a way to 'save face' in surrender; the idea being that, while surrendering to the enemy was inherently shameful, there would be no disgrace in submitting to the 'force of ten thousand suns'.

This explanation pictures the Japanese as uniquely, irrationally obsessed with honor—nay, not with honor, but only with its false *appearance*; for what could have been more dishonorable for valorous Japanese men than to sacrifice their women and children, in a cynical and macabre stage play, only to obscure their own responsibility for the defeat?

Not a few high-ranking Japanese soldiers, among them minister of war General Anami, committed ritual suicide after the surrender as a personal penance for their failure to protect the country. Whatever we may think of these men's role in history, their ability to tell true honor from false cannot be in doubt.

14.2 The purpose of the fake bombings was not to intimidate Stalin

Another school of thought starts from the premise that American leaders were aware of Japan's readiness to surrender on terms that also suited them, and it therefore looks for another motive for the atomic bombings. These historians, among them Alperovitz, posit that the true purpose was to subdue Stalin, whose tightening grip on Eastern Europe and ambitions in East Asia were troubling the Americans and the British.

14.2.1 American and British failure at Potsdam.

Adduced in support are several statements by Truman and by his war secretary Stimson, both of whom reacted with elation to Groves' report on the great success of the first 'nuclear' detonation at Alamogordo. On hearing the news while attending the Potsdam conference [68, p. 252],

> *Stimson ... was momentarily so moved by the initial indications of its power that he advised Truman the weapon might enable the United States to force the Soviet Union to abandon or radically alter its entire system of government.*

Stimson's diary records Churchill's impressions of how the Alamogordo report affected Harry Truman's posture in the negotiations [68, p. 260]:

> *"Now I know what happened to Truman yesterday. I couldn't understand it. When he got to the meeting after having read this report he was a changed man. He told the Russians just where they got on and off and generally bossed the whole meeting." Churchill said he now understood how this pepping up had taken place and that he felt the same way. His own attitude confirmed this admission.*

After one of the sessions at Potsdam, Truman walked up to Stalin to tell him about the new weapon, but in a deliberately casual manner. Stalin apparently betrayed no particular impression or emotion; Churchill, who was looking on, remained in doubt as to whether Stalin had even understood Truman's meaning. In any event, Stalin was certainly not at all intimidated by the revelation. Charles de Gaulle, who did not participate in the conference, commented as follows on its outcome [314, p. 230 f]:

> *Once the communiqué published by the conference appeared, we learned that it had concluded in a kind of uproar. Despite the wealth of conciliation lavished by Mr. Truman, despite Mr. Churchill's vehement protest, Generalissimo Stalin had agreed to no compromises of any kind ... the totalitarian character of the Warsaw government was in no way diminished ... In regard to Asia, Stalin ... managed to obtain for Russia the Kurile Archipelago and half of Sakhalin ... [dominance over North] Korea ... Outer Mongolia ... the Generalissimo promised not to intervene in China's internal affairs, but he was nonetheless to furnish the support and*

arms to Mao Tse-tung's Communists which were soon to permit them to seize the country.

Truman may have expected that the results of the Potsdam conference could swiftly be overturned on the strength of the 'atomic' bombs' use in 'combat'. On the day of Nagasaki's destruction [68, p. 266],

President Truman declared of Romania, Bulgaria, and Hungary that 'These nations are not to be spheres of influence of any one power.'

On its face, such a calculation on Truman's part would support Alperovitz' case that he ordered the bombings of Hiroshima and Nagasaki in order to put Stalin in his place and wring from him the concessions which he had withheld at Potsdam. The problem is, of course, that the gambit did not work—the Soviets gave up neither the three countries named by Truman nor any other of their postwar acquisitions. In short, Stalin called Truman's bluff and got away with it. What are we to make of these puzzling proceedings?

14.2.2 Who was being fooled? If we assume that the bombings which were to take place shortly after Potsdam would be faked, then we must wonder how much each of the negotiating parties knew about this at the time. Concerning Truman and his associates, there seem to be two possibilities:

1. Truman, Stimson, and Churchill knew that the bombings would be a bluff, but they feigned their way through the negotiations in order to keep Stalin in the dark and thereby extract the desired concessions from him.
2. They were honestly deceived, at least for the time being—rather than playacting, they were themselves being played by those who had organized the fraud.[1]

The palpable change in attitude displayed by Truman on receiving word of the Alamogordo test, and particularly also Churchill's reaction, appear to favor the second alternative—grotesque as it may seem that the 'leaders of the free world' would be made fools of in such

---

[1]In this context, we may recall the Interim Committee protocol that was discussed in Section 3.7.1, and which claimed that uranium bombs were "in production" as of May 1945. Stimson had been present at this meeting—it may well have been for his "benefit" that this wild claim had been made.

an egregious manner. It is noteworthy that Truman during this time was strongly influenced by his Secretary of State James F. Byrnes. When dismissing Byrnes in 1947, Truman accused him of 'duplicity' at Potsdam and of presuming to run the presidency over his head [68, p. 240]. According to Alperovitz, it was Byrnes who prevailed upon Truman to reject any and all proposals put to him by his subordinates for coming to terms with the Japanese before the 'nuclear' bombings. If indeed Byrnes represented a party that wished to stage the bombings for its own ends, but needed the president to take responsibility for it, then persuading Truman of their value as instruments of domination over the Soviets would have been a very clever ruse.

How much did Stalin know? It is of course extremely unlikely that he was deceived by the hoax for any length of time. If there is any truth at all to the lurid tales of atomic espionage—most of which, however, were cut from whole cloth, according to a contemporaneous book [315]—Stalin would have known the true state of nuclear weapons development as of 1945. Even if this source of information had failed him, the up to 400 officials in the Soviet embassy at Tokyo shortly after the war [308, p. 50] would most likely have soon found out what really had occurred in the two stricken cities.

That Stalin saw through the scam while at Potsdam or soon after explains the failure of the stratagem which, according to Alperovitz, had motivated the bombings. This outcome was of course inevitable; the perpetrators of the scam cannot seriously have expected anything else, nor could they have hoped to keep the truth for long from any other government which had a well-functioning secret service at its disposal.

14.3 The faked nuclear bombings as terror acts

We are thus left with the conclusion that the bombings were faked to stun and horrify a party without the means to see through the deception—a party with no secret service to provide it with reliable information and to protect it from being misled by the gruesome stage play. Since this rules out major state actors, the only plausible alternative is that the fraud was aimed at humanity at large—the bombings should be understood as two particularly vile and violent acts of state terrorism, disguised as 'military combat'.

14.3.1 What was the motive behind the terror attacks? Readers prepared to seriously consider the main thesis of this book are likely to have seen through the true nature, actors, and purpose of the terror attacks on September 11th, 2001. Those who have not can find out more from David Ray Griffin's excellent book *9/11 Ten Years Later: When State Crimes Against Democracy Succeed* [316]. However, they might for the moment accept the verdict of former Italian head of state Francesco Cossiga, who declared in 2007 with respect to a certain video that had surfaced in Italy [317]:[2]

> *The non-authenticity of the video is evidenced by the fact that Osama Bin Laden in it 'confesses' that Al-Qaeda was the author of the September 11 attack on the two towers in New York, while all democratic circles in America and Europe ... know that the disastrous attack was planned and carried out by the American CIA and Mossad with the help of the Zionist world to accuse the Arab countries and to induce the Western powers to intervene both in Iraq and Afghanistan.*

Having concluded that Hiroshima and Nagasaki were terror acts in the same vein as '9/11', we must look for the motive behind them. An important clue comes from the nuclear fear propaganda that sprang up soon afterwards. The people of the world, deeply traumatized by the war which had just ended, were told that even worse was soon to come—unless, that is, they accepted without delay the only possible solution: submission to a brand-new, benevolent, and unified world government that would henceforth guarantee eternal peace. This idea is captured in the title of the propaganda booklet *One World Or None: A Report to the Public on the Full Meaning of the Atomic Bomb* [293], a collection of essays advancing the scheme by leading scientists, several of whom took part in the 'Manhattan Project' and must be suspected of being in on the 'nuclear' scam. The following quote by one of them, Leo Szilard, captures the tenor of the book:

> *The issue that we have to face is not whether we can create a world government before this century is over. That appears to be very likely. The issue that we have to face is whether we can have such a world government without going through a third world war.*

---

[2]Text translated from the Italian original using the DeepL machine translation tool, with minor manual adjustments.

> *What matters is to create at once conditions in which the ultimate establishment of a world government will appear as inevitable to most men as war appears inevitable at present to many.*

You may have heard that it was Szilard, together with Eugene Wigner and Edward Teller, who had penned the famous 'Einstein' letter which was used to persuade Roosevelt of the atomic bomb's necessity. Thus, we see him involved first with the inauguration of the 'Manhattan Project' and now also with the political hay-making after its fraudulent 'triumph'. Nor was the world government agenda merely the obsession of a small circle of atomic scientists spooked by the awesome power of their own creations. It translated into specific policy proposals and diplomatic initiatives; for a while, it topped the agenda of the newly founded United Nations.

14.3.2 "World government is aim of imperialists." If world government was promoted by influential circles, why did the campaign fail in the event? As one might surmise, foiling the plan fell to the Soviets. Their dim view of the idea is spelled out in a 1947 article by Sergei Vavilov and three other prominent Russian scientists [318], presented as an 'open letter to Dr. Einstein', then a prominent and active promoter of world government. In a part of this letter, under the subheading "World government is aim of imperialists," they argue:

> *First of all the ideas of "world government" and "super state" are not at all a product of the "atom age." ... It is enough to recall they have already been promoted at the origin of the League of Nations.*
>
> *Furthermore in the present historic epoch such ideas were never progressive. They reflected the fact that capitalist monopolies which are dominant in the principal industrial countries ... need world markets, world sources of raw materials and regions for investment capital.[3] Domination of monopolies in political life and in the state machine of great powers permits use of this machine for their struggle for spheres of influence and for economic and political enslavement of foreign countries ...*
>
> *[T]he ideologists of imperialism are trying to discredit the very idea of national sovereignty. In doing so they often advance*

---
[3] The intended meaning may be 'capital investment.'

pompous plans of "world state" which would allegedly do away with imperialism, wars, enmity between nations, would secure realization of all human laws, etc. ...

This is the road to unlimited expansion of American imperialism and this is the way to disarm ideologically peoples who are defending their independence.

In short, world government, while palmed off by its promoters as mankind's only hope of survival in the 'atomic age', is depicted by these scientists as a new, worldwide colonial empire in disguise, dominated no longer by the British, who had effectively—and, it would seem, conveniently—lost their empire as a consequence of the war, but by American and international capital.

As the 'atomic' bombings had been fraudulent, so were the breathless portents of doom by Szilard, Einstein, and other boosters of world government. In contrast, while the four Soviet scientists quoted above can be assumed to have cleared their statements with the politburo, we have no reason to doubt their sincerity, nor does their argument give us cause to question their good sense.

14.4 Two competing views on modern history

The view of Western politics taken by the four Soviet scientists—namely, that the political life and 'the state machines' of 'great powers' have been subverted by monopolies—contrasts starkly with that of mainstream Western historiography. The latter, as a rule, admits as actors only national governments and their leaders, who pursue the best interests of their nations and their own ambitions, in varying proportion. Except in the politics of admitted 'banana republics', the role of financial and industrial interests and monopolies is rarely acknowledged or even mentioned. Which view is right? If capitalist interests do not figure in the history books, should we follow suit and dismiss them?

Let us examine the staged 'atomic' bombings, and their wider context, through the lens of national self-interest—in particular, American and British self-interest, since these two powers were ostensibly among the war's victors and thus should have seen to it that their national interests were realized.

14.4.1 The war, the faked 'atomic' bombings, and the American and British national interest. The observation is not novel that all Great

Britain got in return for its insistence on triggering a world war over the German-Polish conflict was to be deprived of its colonial empire, and also a demotion from a great power to a middling one. It is noteworthy that the loss of the empire was due to extortion on the part of Britain's American 'ally'.

While it can be argued that America emerged from the war with much enhanced stature and power, entering the war was certainly not willed by the American people; Roosevelt himself won reelection in 1940 by promising "again and again" that he would not send America's young men into the war. As to the 'nuclear' bombings and the national interest, we can defer to General MacArthur: concluding peace months earlier would have been possible and "avoided all of the losses, the Atomic bomb, and the entry of Russia into Manchuria."

Aside from aiding Soviet expansion and increasing the body count of American soldiers, the 'atomic' bombings affected the American psyche in a manner not to be taken lightly. If Japan got to play the victim, America had to portray the ignoble perpetrator. To assuage its guilty conscience, the convenient myth was invented that the bombs had shortened the war and saved many lives, which was of course the exact opposite of the truth.

Other than these feelings of guilt and the lies needed to numb them, the American people's only reward for their prolonged sacrifice was that, instead of being left alone to enjoy the peace when finally it came, they were transported instantly from the past war's sorrows to fear and dread of even more terrible bloodshed about to begin.

We could go on—the nuclear scare whipped up after the fake atomic bombs birthed the Cold War, with its vast expenditures on the 'military-industrial complex'; this treasure could have been spent in other ways, to greater benefit for civilian society.

14.4.2 Beyond the horizon. However, it should be sufficiently clear that any attempt to fit the story of the 'atomic' bombings into a framework of sound national self-interest is doomed to fail. Just as there is no nation state that can plausibly be named as the real target of the atomic hoax, so it is with the real perpetrator: the ostensible culprit, America, had no motive. If we insist, like many historians do, on granting agency in matters of peace and war only to national governments which pursue the national interest, we will not make sense of these events.

This brings us back to the point of view presented by Vavilov and his colleagues. Most history books never mention their postulated "domination of monopolies in political life and in the state machine." Is it possible nevertheless to find connections between such capitalist interests, the 'atomic' bombs, and the world government scheme?

The 'Einstein' letter was conveyed and pitched to Roosevelt by Alexander Sachs, a very wealthy Wall Street banker. Another financial tycoon, Bernard Baruch, was close to James F. Byrnes, who steered Truman through the rising tide of peace proposals to a successful conclusion of the atomic hoax; apparently going so far as keeping him deceived about the hoax as such—a rather brazen case of presidential puppetry.

Whether Baruch was indeed the gray eminence whose cover gave Byrnes such disproportionate influence over his peers and over Truman himself we do not know; there are, however, indications of Baruch's considerable sway in government affairs. As an example, consider the following quote from the diary of James Forrestal [319, p. 347]:

Had lunch with B. M. Baruch. ... He took the line of advising me not to be active in this particular matter and that I was already identified, to a degree that was not in my own interests, with opposition to the United Nations policy on Palestine.

The conversation took place on February 3rd, 1948. Baruch had at this time already resigned from his post at the U.N. (see below) and had no official role in government. And yet, he is seen here warning a government minister off the premises like a schoolboy. Forrestal took the hint.

Baruch had himself served as a presidential advisor to Roosevelt on economic measures to support the war effort. After the war, Truman appointed him as the U.S. representative in the newly created United Nations Atomic Energy Commission. On presenting to the United Nations the 'Baruch Plan' for an international ban on nuclear weapons, he outed himself as a lover of peace and enthusiast of world government:

We are here to make a choice between the quick and the dead. That is our business. Behind the black portent of the new atomic age lies a hope which, seized upon with faith, can work our salvation.

If we fail, then we have damned every man to be the slave of fear. Let us not deceive ourselves; we must elect world peace or world destruction.

Connections such as these are merely suggestive, not definitive. A fuller inquiry is needed into the men behind the Hiroshima and Nagasaki poison gas-cum-napalm terror attacks, and into how these men and these attacks fit into the wider context of the war. However, the task transcends the horizon of this author and this book—it must be left for other researchers to pursue.

Afterword

> All truth passes through three stages.
> First, it is ridiculed.
> Second, it is violently opposed.
> Third, it is accepted as being self-evident.
>
> Arthur Schopenhauer

This inquiry was a labor of love—exacting, but also rewarding. Some questions could be answered simply by taking the eyewitnesses at their word, rather than distorting their meaning to fit the dishonest 'atomic' narrative. Other insights occurred only after months of mulling over seemingly intractable enigmas. The hypothesis that took shape with time could ever better fit new evidence that it encountered; while some aspects of it may yet have to change, it has stabilized enough to face the test of public scrutiny. It is of course unlikely that fair, dispassionate scrutiny will be the predominant attitude of critics; I will be content with moving the needle to Schopenhauer's second stage—from ridicule to violent opposition.

Aside from the scientific understanding, I also gained a deep admiration for the survivors of Hiroshima and Nagasaki—moved by stories such as this one about two teenage boys: having set out in search of their relatives on the day of the Hiroshima bombing, they happened upon a shelter full of badly wounded people. Not finding their relatives among them, they nevertheless stayed on for an entire day to care for those sick and give them water. We learn of other adolescent boys and girls who, having lost both parents in the bombings, worked themselves to exhaustion in order to provide for their younger siblings, permitting them to go to school by abandoning their own. We read how Drs. Akizuki and Nagai, themselves affected by 'radiation' sickness, toiled unremittingly to relieve the suffering of others, regardless of the

Afterword

meager means at their disposal. We see the kindness of Dr. Hachiya and of the people near and dear to him:

> *I had been strongly attached to the patient they were cremating tonight. ... This woman had been loved and respected by her neighbors, and to the soldiers in the Second Corps she was the* baba-san *[grandmother] of Hiroshima. Her meagre pension as well as her savings had been spent to help one soldier or another. Her round, shapeless figure had cast a friendly shadow in the neighborhood and on the wards of our hospital. Many were the times when she and another* baba-san *had brought cheer to the sick and lonely. ...*
>
> *Shortly before she died I recalled stopping at her pallet to comfort her. She could not see me because her eyelids were swollen shut, but she recognized my voice.*
>
> *"Baba-san", I said, "your friends are around you. Hiroshima has been a good place to live in because you have been here to think of others before yourself. Death is approaching, but like an old soldier you can die with dignity in the knowledge that your wounds were received in line of duty."*

While this book focused on only those parts of the reports by Hachiya and by others which are germane to its scientific case, the works of these men are worth reading in full for being inspired by their genuine humanity. They personify these words by Mahatma Gandhi:

> *In the midst of death life persists,*
> *in the midst of untruth truth persists,*
> *in the midst of darkness light persists.*

References

[1] A. Nakatani: *Death Object: Exploding the Nuclear Weapons Hoax.* CreateSpace, 2017. URL: https://www.amazon.com/dp/B071NGKY17/.

[2] J. Bernstein: *Hitler's uranium club: the secret recordings at Farm Hall.* American Institute of Physics, 1996. URL: http://www.worldcat.org/oclc/932453089.

[3] M. Camac: *Morton Camac: Recollections of my participation in the Manhattan Project.* 1944. URL: https://tinyurl.com/atomic-heritage-camac.

[4] C. Hansen et al.: *The Swords of Armageddon.* Chukelea Publications, 2007. URL: http://www.worldcat.org/oclc/231585284.

[5] A. de Seversky: *Air Power: Key to Survival.* Simon and Schuster, 1950. URL: http://www.worldcat.org/oclc/925991274.

[6] K. Shizuma et al.: Isotope ratios of $^{235}U/^{238}U$ and $^{137}Cs/^{235}U$ in black rain streaks on plaster wall caused by fallout of the Hiroshima atomic bomb. *1204* 102 (2012), 154-60. PMID: 22217588.

[7] J. Hersey: *Hiroshima.* Vintage Books, 1989. URL: https://archive.org/details/hiroshima00hers_0.

[8] E. Ishikawa et al.: *Hiroshima and Nagasaki: the physical, medical, and social effects of the atomic bombings.* Harper Colophon Books, 1981. URL: http://www.worldcat.org/oclc/7278091.

[9] Z. R. Mathews and A. Koyfman: Blast Injuries. *J. Emerg. Med.* 49 (2015), 573-87. PMID: 26072319.

[10] P. D. Keller: A clinical syndrome following exposure to atomic bomb explosions. *J Am Med Assoc* 131 (1946), 504-6. PMID: 20983706.

[11] W. J. Broad: *The Hiroshima Mushroom Cloud That Wasn't.* 2016. URL: https://www.nytimes.com/2016/05/24/science/hiroshima-atomic-bomb-mushroom-cloud.html.

[12] T. Ogura: *Letters from the end of the world.* Kodansha International, 1997. URL: http://www.worldcat.org/oclc/760568964.

[13] Anonymous: *Effects of incendiary bomb attacks on Japan: a report on eight cities.* United States Strategic Bombing Survey, 1947. URL: http://www.worldcat.org/oclc/11827269.

[14] A. Osada, ed.: *Children of Hiroshima*. Publishing Committee for "Children of Hiroshima", 1980. URL: http://www.worldcat.org/oclc/8095388.

[15] S. Nishimura: Censorship of the atomic bomb casualty reports in occupied Japan. A complete ban vs temporary delay. *JAMA* 274 (1995), 520-2. PMID: 7629965.

[16] W. G. Burchett: The atomic plague. In: *Rebel journalism: the writings of Wilfred Burchett*. Ed. by G. Burchett and N. L. Shimmin. 2007, 2-5. URL: http://www.worldcat.org/oclc/172979873.

[17] J. C. Dacre and M. Goldman: Toxicology and pharmacology of the chemical warfare agent sulfur mustard. *Pharmacol. Rev.* 48 (1996), 289-326. PMID: 8804107.

[18] P. Dustin: Some new aspects of mitotic poisoning. *1264* 159 (1947), 794-7. PMID: 20248882.

[19] K. Kehe et al.: Acute effects of sulfur mustard injury—Munich experiences. *Toxicology* 263 (2009), 3-8. PMID: 19482056.

[20] P. Robinson and M. Leitenberg: *The problem of chemical and biological warfare: a study of the historical, technical, military, legal and political aspects of CBW, and possible disarmament measures*. Almquist & Wiksell, 1971. URL: http://www.worldcat.org/oclc/863435349.

[21] C. M. Pechura and D. P. Rall: *Veterans at Risk: The Health Effects of Mustard Gas and Lewisite*. Ed. by C. M. Pechura and D. P. Rall. National Academies Press, 1993. URL: https://www.nap.edu/download/2058.

[22] S. F. Alexander: Medical report on the Bari Harbor mustard casualties. *Mil. Surg.* 101 (1947), 1-17. PMID: 20248701.

[23] G. Southern: *Poisonous Inferno: World War II Tragedy at Bari Harbour*. Airlife, 2002. URL: http://www.worldcat.org/oclc/50272689.

[24] J. Hirsch: An anniversary for cancer chemotherapy. *397* 296 (2006), 1518-20. PMID: 17003400.

[25] J. F. Brodie: Radiation Secrecy and Censorship after Hiroshima and Nagasaki. *J. Soc. Hist.* 48 (2015), 842-864. DOI: 10.1093/jsh/shu150.

[26] W. Bloom: *Histopathology of iradiation from external and internal sources*. Ed. by W. Bloom. McGraw-Hill, 1948. URL: http://www.worldcat.org/oclc/251020532.

[27] F. Flury and H. Wieland: Über Kampfgasvergiftungen. VII. Die pharmakologische Wirkung des Dichloräthylsulfids. *1572* 13 (1921), 367-483. DOI: 10.1007/BF02998613.

[28] O. Heitzmann: Über Kampfgasvergiftungen. VIII. Die pathologisch-anatomischen Veränderungen nach Vergiftung mit Dichloräthylsulfid unter

Berücksichtigung der Tierversuche. *Z. Ges. Exp. Med.* 13 (1921), 484-522. DOI: 10.1007/BF02998614.

[29] S. Okajima et al.: Radiation doses from residual radioactivity. In: *US-Japan Joint Reassessment of Atomic Bomb Radiation Dosimetry in Hiroshima and Nagasaki: Final Report.* Ed. by W. Roesch. Vol. 1. Radiation Effects Research Foundation, 1987, 205-226. URL: https://www.rerf.or.jp/library/scidata/scids/ds86/images/v1/data/Chapter6/Chapter6.pdf.

[30] H. M. Cullings et al.: Dose estimation for atomic bomb survivor studies: its evolution and present status. *154* 166 (2006), 219-54. PMID: 16808610.

[31] M. Macià i Garau et al.: Radiobiology of the acute radiation syndrome. *Rep. Pract. Oncol. Radiother.* 16 (2011), 123-30. PMID: 24376969.

[32] F. W. Bilfinger: ICRC report on the effects of the atomic bomb at Hiroshima. *1553* 97 (2015), 859-882. DOI: 10.1017/s1816383116000114.

[33] A. W. Oughterson et al.: *Statistical Analysis of the Medical Effects of the Atomic Bombs: From the Report of the Joint Commission for the Investigatin of the Effects of the Atomic Bomb in Japan.* Technical Information Service, United States Atomic Energy Commission [prepared by the] Army Institute of Pathology, Office of the Air Surgeon, 1955. URL: https://www.osti.gov/biblio/4381263.

[34] S. Sutou: Rediscovery of an old article reporting that the area around the epicenter in Hiroshima was heavily contaminated with residual radiation, indicating that exposure doses of A-bomb survivors were largely underestimated. *1293* 58 (2017), 745-754. PMID: 29088449.

[35] K. Lohs: *Synthetische Gifte.* Militärverlag der Dt. Demokrat. Republik, 1958. URL: http://www.worldcat.org/oclc/1087882163.

[36] J. A. Auxier: *Ichiban: Radiation Dosimetry For The Survivors Of The Bombings Of Hiroshima And Nagasaki.* Energy Research and Development Administration, 1977. URL: http://www.worldcat.org/oclc/2694933.

[37] S. Shimizu: Historical sketch of the scientific field survey in Hiroshima several days after the atomic bombing. *Bull. Inst. Chem. Res. Kyoto Univ.* 60 (1982), 39-54. URL: http://hdl.handle.net/2433/76996.

[38] Anonymous: Cyclotron smashing: American soldiers demolish and sink precious Jap scientific equipment. *Life* 19 (1945), 26-27.

[39] Y. Nishina: A Japanese Scientist Describes the Destruction of his Cyclotrons. *1558* 3 (1947), 145-167. DOI: 10.1080/00963402.1947.11455874.

[40] L. R. Groves: *Now it can be told.* Harper & Row, 1962. URL: http://www.worldcat.org/oclc/654693371.

[41] M. Lindee: *Suffering Made Real: American Science and the Survivors at Hiroshima.* University of Chicago Press, 1994. URL: http://www.worldcat.org/oclc/537274978.

[42] A. A. Liebow et al.: Pathology of atomic bomb casualties. *661* 25 (1949), 853-1027. PMID: 18147964.

[43] J. Kopecky: *NGATLAS: Atlas of Neutron Capture Cross Sections.* 2001. URL: https://www-nds.iaea.org/ngatlas2/.

[44] Anonymous: *Cumulative fission yields.* 2006. URL: https://www-nds.iaea.org/sgnucdat/c3.htm.

[45] I. A. Likhtarev et al.: Thyroid cancer in the Ukraine. *1264* 375 (1995), 365. PMID: 7760928.

[46] Anonymous: *Atom (Wikipedia).* 2023. URL: https://en.wikipedia.org/wiki/Atom.

[47] M. Aitken: Thermoluminescence dating: Past progress and future trends. *Nuclear Tracks and Radiation Measurements (1982)* 10 (1985), 3-6. DOI: 10.1016/0735-245x(85)90003-1.

[48] M. S. Sasaki et al.: Experimental derivation of relative biological effectiveness of A-bomb neutrons in Hiroshima and Nagasaki and implications for risk assessment. *154* 170 (2008), 101-17. PMID: 18582156.

[49] E. J. Hall: Neutrons and carcinogenesis: a cautionary tale. *Bull. Cancer Radiother.* 83 Suppl (1996), 43s-6s. PMID: 8949750.

[50] A. Valota et al.: Modelling study on the protective role of OH radical scavengers and DNA higher-order structures in induction of single- and double-strand break by gamma-radiation. *Int. J. Radiat. Biol.* 79 (2003), 643-53. PMID: 14555347.

[51] H. Takata et al.: Chromatin compaction protects genomic DNA from radiation damage. *PLoS One* 8 (2013), e75622. PMID: 24130727.

[52] P. J. McHugh et al.: Repair of intermediate structures produced at DNA interstrand cross-links in *Saccharomyces cerevisiae. Mol. Cell. Biol.* 20 (2000), 3425-33. PMID: 10779332.

[53] R. G. Arneson: *Notes of the Interim Committee meeting, Thursday, 31 May 1945.* 1945. URL: https://archive.org/details/interim-committee-may31-1945.

[54] M. W. Carter: Off-site health and safety for nuclear weapons tests. In: *Health Physics: a Backward Glance.* Pergamon Press, 1980, 197-215. URL: http://www.worldcat.org/oclc/916232555.

[55] T. Matsunami and T. Mamuro: Uranium in Fallout Particles. *1264* 218 (1968), 555-556. DOI: 10.1038/218555a0.

[56] A. Sakaguchi et al.: Feasibility of using ^{236}U to reconstruct close-in fallout deposition from the Hiroshima atomic bomb. *Sci. Total Environ.* 408 (2010), 5392-8. PMID: 20797770.

[57] J. Takada et al.: Uranium isotopes in Hiroshima "black rain" soil. *1293* 24 (1983), 229-36. PMID: 6663539.

[58] A. Kudo et al.: Global transport rates of ^{137}Cs and $^{239+240}$Pu originating from the Nagasaki A-bomb in 1945 as determined from analysis of Canadian Arctic ice cores. *615* 40 (1998), 289-298. DOI: https://doi.org/10.1016/S0265-931X(97)00023-4.

[59] K. Shizuma et al.: Fallout in the hypocenter area of the Hiroshima atomic bomb. *1204* 57 (1989), 1013-6. PMID: 2584016.

[60] K. Shizuma et al.: ^{137}Cs concentration in soil samples from an early survey of Hiroshima atomic bomb and cumulative dose estimation from the fallout. *1204* 71 (1996), 340-6. PMID: 8698576.

[61] Y. Fujikawa et al.: Uranium and Plutonium Isotope Ratio Measurement as a Tool for Environmental Monitoring - Experiences in Osaka, Gifu and Hiroshima, Japan. *Journal of Nuclear Science and Technology* 39 (2002), 564-567. DOI: 10.1080/00223131.2002.10875531.

[62] M. Hachiya: *Hiroshima Diary: The Journal of a Japanese Physician, August 6-September 30, 1945*. University of North Carolina Press, 1955. URL: http://www.worldcat.org/oclc/471035728.

[63] M. Yamamoto et al.: Estimation of close-in fallout ^{137}Cs deposition level due to the Hiroshima atomic bomb from soil samples under houses built 1-4 years after the explosion. In: *Revisit the Hiroshima A-bomb with a database (Vol. 2)*. Vol. 2. 2013. URL: http://www.hisof.jp/03database/0222.pdf.

[64] A. Sakaguchi et al.: Preliminary results on ^{137}Cs in soil core samples collected from the under-floors of houses built 1-4 years after the Hiroshima atomic bomb. In: *Revisit the Hiroshima A-bomb with a database*. Vol. 1. 2011, 93-96. URL: http://www.hisof.jp/03database/0203.pdf.

[65] Y. Saito-Kokubu et al.: Depositional records of plutonium and ^{137}Cs released from Nagasaki atomic bomb in sediment of Nishiyama reservoir at Nagasaki. *J. Environ. Radioact.* 99 (2008), 211-7. PMID: 18171596.

[66] G. Trenear-Harvey: *Historical Dictionary of Atomic Espionage*. Scarecrow Press, 2011. URL: http://www.worldcat.org/oclc/695857029.

[67] M. Steenbeck: *Impulse und Wirkungen: Schritte auf meinem Lebensweg.* Verlag der Nation, 1977. URL: http://www.worldcat.org/oclc/804214668.

[68] G. Alperovitz: *The decision to use the atomic bomb.* Alfred A. Knopf, 1995.

[69] R. R. Wilson: On the Time Required for the Fission Process. *Phys. Rev.* 72 (1947), 98-100. DOI: 10.1103/physrev.72.98.

[70] R. R. Wilson: *On the Time Required for the Fission Process (draft).* 1946. URL: https://archive.org/details/wilson-1946-fission-time.

[71] D. L. Collins: Pictures from the past: Journeys into health physics in the Manhattan District and other diverse places. In: *Health Physics: a Backward Glance.* Ed. by R. Kathren and P. Ziemer. Pergamon Press, 1980, 37-71. URL: http://www.worldcat.org/oclc/916232555.

[72] O. Glasser: The Evolution of Dosimeters in Roentgen Ray Therapy. *Radiology* 37 (1941), 221-227. DOI: 10.1148/37.2.221.

[73] R. R. Wilson: Nuclear radiation at Hiroshima and Nagasaki. *Radiat. Res.* 4 (1956), 349-59. PMID: 13323257.

[74] M. Nakaidzumi: *The radioactivity of the atomic bomb from the medical point of view.* 1949. URL: https://www.osti.gov/biblio/4437504.

[75] T. Imanaka: Radiation survey activities in the early stages after the atomic bombing in Hiroshima. In: *Revisit the Hiroshima A-bomb with a database.* 2011, 69-81. URL: http://www.hisof.jp/03database/0201.pdf.

[76] J. Toland: *The rising sun.* Random House, 1970. URL: http://www.worldcat.org/oclc/1003083787.

[77] A. A. Liebow: *Encounter with disaster: a medical diary of Hiroshima, 1945.* Norton, 1985. URL: http://www.worldcat.org/oclc/12216042.

[78] K. Takeshita: Dose estimation from residual and fallout radioactivity. 1. Areal surveys. *J. Radiat. Res.* 16 Suppl (1975), 24-31. PMID: 1195199.

[79] *Final report of the findings of the Manhattan District atomic bomb investigating groups at Hiroshima and Nagasaki.* 1946. URL: https://www.genken.nagasaki-u.ac.jp/abcenter/manhattan/index_e.html.

[80] T. Higashimura et al.: Dosimetry of Atomic Bomb Radiation in Hiroshima by Thermoluminescence of Roof Tiles. *478* 139 (1963), 1284-5. PMID: 17757060.

[81] T. Hashizume et al.: Estimation of the air dose from the atomic bombs in Hiroshima and Nagasaki. *1204* 13 (1967), 149-61. PMID: 6029426.

[82] N. Kawano et al.: Mapping the fire field near the hypocenter of the Hiroshima A-bomb. In: *Revisit the Hiroshima A-bomb with a database*. Hiroshima City, 2011, 15-24. URL: http://www.hisof.jp/03database/0102.pdf.

[83] Y. Ichikawa et al.: Thermoluminescence dosimetry of gamma rays from atomic bombs in Hiroshima and Nagasaki. *1204* 12 (1966), 395-405. PMID: 5916800.

[84] S. D. Egbert and G. D. Kerr: Gamma-ray thermoluminescence measurements: a record of fallout deposition in Hiroshima? *476* 51 (2012), 113-31. PMID: 22421931.

[85] H. H. J. Hubbell et al.: *The epicenters of the atomic bombs*. Atomic Bomb Casualty Commission, 1969. URL: https://www.rerf.or.jp/library/scidata/tr_all/TR1969-03.pdf.

[86] T. Iwakura: *Hiroshima-Nagasaki: a pictorial record of the atomic destruction*. Hiroshima-Nagasaki Publishing Committee, 1978. URL: http://www.worldcat.org/oclc/6809565.

[87] W. E. Loewe and E. Mendelsohn: Neutron and Gamma-Ray Doses at Hiroshima and Nagasaki. *Nuclear Science and Engineering* 81 (1982), 325-350. DOI: 10.13182/nse82-a20278.

[88] R. W. Young and G. D. Kerr: *Reassessment of the atomic bomb radiation dosimetry for Hiroshima and Nagasaki: dosimetry system 2002*. 2002. URL: https://www.rerf.or.jp/library/scidata/scids/ds02/.

[89] V. Bond and J. Thiessen: *Reevaluations of dosimetric factors: Hiroshima and Nagasaki*. 1982. URL: http://www.worldcat.org/oclc/4434641227.

[90] S. Glasstone: *The Effects of Atomic Weapons*. Ed. by s. Glasstone. U.S. Government Printing Office, 1950. URL: http://www.worldcat.org/oclc/758274594.

[91] J. A. Auxier: Physical dose estimates for A-bomb survivors. Studies at Oak Ridge, U.S.A. *1293* 16 Suppl (1975), 1-11. PMID: 1195192.

[92] W. E. Loewe and E. Mendelsohn: Revised dose estimates at Hiroshima and Nagasaki. *1204* 41 (1981), 663-6. PMID: 7309523.

[93] W. C. Roesch, ed.: *US-Japan joint reassessment of atomic bomb radiation dosimetry in Hiroshima and Nagasaki: final report*. Radiation Effects Research Foundation, 1987. URL: https://www.rerf.or.jp/library/scidata/scids/ds86/ds86aa.html.

[94] T. Nakanishi et al.: ^{152}Eu in samples exposed to the nuclear explosions at Hiroshima and Nagasaki. *1264* 302 (1983), 132-134. URL: https://www.nature.com/articles/302132a0.

[95] T. Nakanishi et al.: Residual neutron-induced radionuclides in samples exposed to the nuclear explosion over Hiroshima: comparison of the measured values with calculated values. *1293* 32 Suppl (1991), 69–82. PMID: 1762133.

[96] K. Shizuma et al.: Residual ^{152}Eu and ^{60}Co activities induced by neutrons from the Hiroshima atomic bomb. *1204* 65 (1993), 272–82. PMID: 8244696.

[97] W. Rühm et al.: The neutron spectrum of the Hiroshima A-bomb and the Dosimetry System 1986. *Nucl. Instrum. Methods Phys. Res. B* 52 (1990), 557–562. DOI: 10.1016/0168-583x(90)90476-b.

[98] T. Straume et al.: Neutron discrepancies in the DS86 Hiroshima dosimetry system. *Health Phys.* 63 (1992), 421–6. PMID: 1526783.

[99] V. A. Voitovich: Adhesives and sealants based on sulfur. *Polymer Science. Series D* 3 (2010), 133–136. DOI: 10.1134/s1995421210020127.

[100] F. Yamasaki and A. Sugimoto: Radioactive ^{32}P produced in sulfur in Hiroshima. In: *Atomic Bomb Casualty Reports.* Science Council of Japan, 1953, 19–20.

[101] M. Hoshi et al.: A crack model of the Hiroshima atomic bomb: explanation of the contradiction of "Dosimetry system 1986". *1293* 40 Suppl (1999), 145–54. PMID: 10805003.

[102] M. Hoshi et al.: Intercomparison study on (152)Eu gamma ray and (36)Cl AMS measurements for development of the new Hiroshima-Nagasaki Atomic Bomb Dosimetry System 2002 (DS02). *476* 47 (2008), 313–22. PMID: 18389270.

[103] F. Yamasaki et al.: Radioactive ^{32}P found in human bones in Hiroshima. In: *Atomic Bomb Casualty Reports.* Science Council of Japan, 1953, 16–18.

[104] G. J. Fitzgerald: Chemical warfare and medical response during World War I. *Am. J. Public Health* 98 (2008), 611–25. PMID: 18356568.

[105] G. Infield: *Disaster at Bari.* Hale, 1971. URL: http://www.worldcat.org/oclc/18723781.

[106] E. Kilic et al.: Acute intensive care unit management of mustard gas victims: the Turkish experience. *Cutan. Ocul. Toxicol.* 37 (2018), 332–337. PMID: 29648477.

[107] C. B. Maynard: Bari revisited. MA thesis. 2003. URL: http://oasis.lib.tamuk.edu/search/?searchtype=o&searcharg=52636566.

[108] N. B. Munro et al.: The sources, fate, and toxicity of chemical warfare agent degradation products. *Environ. Health Perspect.* 107 (1999), 933–74. PMID: 10585900.

[109] A. S. Warthin and C. V. Weller: *The medical aspects of mustard gas poisoning.* Mosby, 1919. URL: http://www.worldcat.org/oclc/756441378.

[110] K. H. Lohs: *Delayed toxic effects of chemical warfare agents.* Almqvist and Wiksell, 1975.

[111] M. Goldman and J. C. Dacre: Lewisite: its chemistry, toxicology, and biological effects. *Rev. Environ. Contam. Toxicol.* 110 (1989), 75-115. PMID: 2692088.

[112] J. H. Folley et al.: Incidence of leukemia in survivors of the atomic bomb in Hiroshima and Nagasaki, Japan. *1004* 13 (1952), 311-21. PMID: 12985588.

[113] M. Ichimaru and T. Ishimaru: Review of thirty years study of Hiroshima and Nagasaki atomic bomb survivors. II. Biological effects. D. Leukemia and related disorders. *1293* 16 Suppl (1975), 89-96. PMID: 1104825.

[114] J. D. Laskin et al.: Oxidants and antioxidants in sulfur mustard-induced injury. *1128* 1203 (2010), 92-100. PMID: 20716289.

[115] R. F. Brown and P. Rice: Histopathological changes in Yucatan minipig skin following challenge with sulphur mustard. A sequential study of the first 24 hours following challenge. *Int. J. Exp. Pathol.* 78 (1997), 9-20. PMID: 9166101.

[116] R. P. Chilcott et al.: Human skin absorption of Bis-2-(chloroethyl)sulphide (sulphur mustard) in vitro. *J. Appl. Toxicol.* 20 (2000), 349-55. PMID: 11139165.

[117] G. Drasch et al.: Concentrations of mustard gas [bis(2-chloroethyl)sulfide] in the tissues of a victim of a vesicant exposure. *206* 32 (1987), 1788-93. PMID: 3430139.

[118] J. C. Boursnell et al.: Studies on mustard gas ($\beta\beta'$-dichlorodiethyl sulphide) and some related compounds: 5. The fate of injected mustard gas (containing radioactive sulphur) in the animal body. *Biochem. J.* 40 (1946), 756-64. PMID: 16748083.

[119] A. Maisonneuve et al.: Distribution of [^{14}C]sulfur mustard in rats after intravenous exposure. *Toxicol. Appl. Pharmacol.* 125 (1994), 281-7. PMID: 8171436.

[120] M. Batal et al.: DNA damage in internal organs after cutaneous exposure to sulphur mustard. *41* 278 (2014), 39-44. PMID: 24732442.

[121] L. Yue et al.: Distribution of DNA adducts and corresponding tissue damage of Sprague-Dawley rats with percutaneous exposure to sulfur mustard. *Chem. Res. Toxicol.* 28 (2015), 532-40. PMID: 25650027.

References

[122] E. B. Krumbhaar and H. D. Krumbhaar: The Blood and Bone Marrow in Yellow Cross Gas (Mustard Gas) Poisoning: Changes produced in the Bone Marrow of Fatal Cases. *J. Med. Res.* 40 (1919), 497-508.3. PMID: 19972497.

[123] M. Qi et al.: Simultaneous determination of sulfur mustard and related oxidation products by isotope-dilution LC-MS/MS method coupled with a chemical conversion. *J. Chromatogr. B Analyt. Technol. Biomed. Life Sci.* 1028 (2016), 42-50. PMID: 27322628.

[124] K. L. Dearfield et al.: Genotoxicity in mouse lymphoma cells of chemicals capable of Michael addition. *Mutagenesis* 6 (1991), 519-25. PMID: 1800900.

[125] D. R. Doerge et al.: Peroxidase-catalyzed S-oxygenation: mechanism of oxygen transfer for lactoperoxidase. *Biochemistry* 30 (1991), 8960-4. PMID: 1892813.

[126] R. Zojaji et al.: Delayed head and neck complications of sulphur mustard poisoning in Iranian veterans. *J. Laryngol. Otol.* 123 (2009), 1150-4. PMID: 19573255.

[127] L. N. Parker et al.: Thyroid carcinoma after exposure to atomic radiation. A continuing survey of a fixed population, Hiroshima and Nagasaki, 1958-1971. *1378* 80 (1974), 600-4. PMID: 4823811.

[128] W. E. Chiesman: Lesions due to Vesicants: Diagnosis and Treatment. *Br. Med. J.* 2 (1944), 109-12. PMID: 20785549.

[129] V. Vojvodić et al.: The protective effect of different drugs in rats poisoned by sulfur and nitrogen mustards. *Fundam. Appl. Toxicol.* 5 (1985), S160-8. PMID: 4092884.

[130] S. A. Grando: Mucocutaneous cholinergic system is targeted in mustard-induced vesication. *Life Sci.* 72 (2003), 2135-44. PMID: 12628470.

[131] A. Guffroy et al.: Systemic capillary leak syndrome and autoimmune diseases: A case series. *Semin. Arthritis Rheum.* 46 (2017), 509-512. PMID: 27637319.

[132] E. Siddall et al.: Capillary leak syndrome: etiologies, pathophysiology, and management. *Kidney Int.* 92 (2017), 37-46. PMID: 28318633.

[133] C. S. McElroy et al.: From the Cover: Catalytic Antioxidant Rescue of Inhaled Sulfur Mustard Toxicity. *1300* 154 (2016), 341-353. PMID: 27605419.

[134] W. Eisenmenger et al.: Clinical and morphological findings on mustard gas [bis(2-chloroethyl)sulfide] poisoning. *J. Forensic Sci.* 36 (1991), 1688-98. PMID: 1770337.

[135] M. D. McGraw et al.: Editor's Highlight: Pulmonary Vascular Thrombosis in Rats Exposed to Inhaled Sulfur Mustard. *Toxicol. Sci.* 159 (2017), 461-469. PMID: 28962529.

[136] B. Anderson and B. Anderson: Necrotizing uveitis incident to perfusion of intractraial malignancies with nitrogen mustard or related compounds. *Trans. Am. Ophthalmol. Soc.* 58 (1960), 95-104. PMID: 13683174.

[137] J. W. Conklin et al.: Comparative late somatic effects of some radiomimetic agents and x-rays. *154* 19 (1963), 156-68. PMID: 14022585.

[138] J. W. Conklin et al.: Further Observations On Late Somatic Effects Of Radiomimetic Chemicals And X-Rays In Mice. *Cancer Res.* 25 (1965), 20-8. PMID: 14254989.

[139] H. L. Gilchrist: *The residual effects of warfare gases.* 1933. URL: http://www.worldcat.org/oclc/785726.

[140] B. D. Pullinger: Some characters of coagulation necrosis due to mustard gas. *J. Pathol. Bacteriol.* 59 (1947), 255-9. PMID: 20266367.

[141] R. Björnerstedt et al.: *Napalm and other incendiary weapons and all aspects of their possible use: report of the Secretary-General.* United Nations, 1973. URL: http://www.worldcat.org/oclc/813339.

[142] L. N. Plaksin: [Keloid cicatrix after napalm burn]. *Stomatologiia Mosk* 46 (1967), 65-9. PMID: 5229472.

[143] V. A. Dolinin: [Clinical picture, organization and volume of medical aid in napalm lesions]. *1642* (1975), 33-7. PMID: 1216699.

[144] V. V. Mikhailov and V. E. Rosanov: [Pathogenetic mechanism of shock in napalm burns]. *Voen. Med. Zh.* (1985), 70-73.

[145] W. F. Pepper: The Children of Vietnam. *Ramparts* January (1967), 45-68. URL: https://www.ratical.org/CoV.

[146] A. Oughterson and S. Warren: *Medical effects of the atomic bomb in Japan.* McGraw-Hill, 1956. URL: http://www.worldcat.org/oclc/1914714.

[147] H. Kawamura et al.: Strontium-90 activity in bones exposed to the A-bomb in Hiroshima and exhumed on Ninoshima Island. *1293* 28 (1987), 109-116. PMID: 3598931.

[148] A. L. Carsten: Acute lethality—the hemopoietic syndrome in different species. In: ed. by J. J. Broerse and T. J. MacVittie. Martinus Nijhoff Publishers, 1984, 59-86.

[149] A. Barabanova et al.: *Diagnosis and treatment of radiation injuries.* International Atomic Energy Agency, 1998. URL: https://www-pub.iaea.org/MTCD/publications/PDF/P040_scr.pdf.

[150] E. Hall and A. Giaccia: *Radiobiology for the Radiologist.* Wolters Kluwer Health, 2019. URL: http://www.worldcat.org/oclc/1097855587.

[151] E. T. Arakawa: Radiation dosimetry in Hiroshima and Nagasaki atomic-bomb survivors. *840* 263 (1960), 488-93. PMID: 13794009.

[152] R. H. Ritchie and G. S. Hurst: Penetration of weapons radiation: aplication to the Hiroshima-Nagasaki studies. *1204* 1 (1959), 390-404. PMID: 13653555.

[153] M. Junod: *Warrior Without Weapons.* Macmillan, 1951. URL: http://www.worldcat.org/oclc/630905850.

[154] E. Barnouw: *Hiroshima-Nagasaki 1945.* 1969. URL: https://archive.org/details/hiroshimanagasakiaugust1945.

[155] S. Watanabe: Cancer and leukemia developing among atomic bomb survivors. In: *Handbuch der allgemeinen Pathology [Handbook of general pathology].* Ed. by E. Grundmann. Vol. 5 (Part 6). Springer, 1974, 461-577.

[156] G. Sekimori and G. Marshall: *Hibakusha.* Kosei Publishing Company, 1988. URL: http://www.worldcat.org/oclc/803547218.

[157] E. Yılmaz et al.: Gamma ray and neutron shielding properties of some concrete materials. *Ann. Nucl. Energy* 38 (2011), 2204-2212. DOI: 10.1016/j.anucene.2011.06.011.

[158] H. Yamada and T. D. Jones: *An Examination of A-Bomb Survivors Exposed to Fallout Rain and a Comparison to a Similar Control Population.* 1972. URL: https://www.osti.gov/biblio/4573543.

[159] S. Sawada: Cover-up of the effects of internal exposure by residual radiation from the atomic bombing of Hiroshima and Nagasaki. *Medicine, Conflict and Survival* 23 (2007), 58-74. DOI: 10.1080/13623690601084617.

[160] A. V. Peterson et al.: Investigation of circular asymmetry in cancer mortality of Hiroshima and Nagasaki A-bomb survivors. *154* 93 (1983), 184-99. PMID: 6823505.

[161] T. Tonda et al.: Investigation on circular asymmetry of geographical distribution in cancer mortality of Hiroshima atomic bomb survivors based on risk maps: analysis of spatial survival data. *Radiat. Environ. Biophys.* 51 (2012), 133-41. PMID: 22302183.

[162] M. Aoyama and Y. Oochi, eds.: *Revisit The Hiroshima A-bomb with a Database: Latest Scientific View on Local Fallout and Black Rain.* Hiroshima City, 2011. URL: http://www.hisof.jp/.

[163] E. S. Gilbert and J. L. Ohara: *Analysis of atomic bomb radiation dose estimation at RERF using data on acute radiation symptoms.* Radiation

Effects Research Foundation, 1983. URL: https://www.rerf.or.jp/library/scidata/tr_all/TR1983-09.pdf.

[164] T. M. Fliedner et al.: Pathophysiological principles underlying the blood cell concentration responses used to assess the severity of effect after accidental whole-body radiation exposure: an essential basis for an evidence-based clinical triage. *Exp. Hematol.* 35 (2007), 8-16. PMID: 17379081.

[165] W. G. Burchett: *Shadows of Hiroshima*. Verso, 1983. URL: http://www.worldcat.org/oclc/643923016.

[166] G. Weller et al.: *First Into Nagasaki: The Censored Eyewitness Dispatches on Post-atomic Japan and Its Prisoners of War*. Three Rivers Press, 2007. URL: http://www.worldcat.org/oclc/1030769123.

[167] T. Akizuki: *Nagasaki 1945: the first full-length eyewitness account of the atomic bomb attack on Nagasaki*. Quartet Books, 1982. URL: http://www.worldcat.org/oclc/8110733.

[168] Anonymous: *LSS Report 11 Mortality and Acute Effects Data Set*. 1995. URL: https://www.rerf.or.jp/en/library/data-en/lss11ma-en/.

[169] M. A. Block and M. Tsuzuki: Observations of burn scars sustained by atomic bomb survivors; a preliminary study. *Am. J. Surg.* 75 (1948), 417-34. PMID: 18908948.

[170] H. A. Dudley et al.: Civilian battle casualties in South Vietnam. *Br. J. Surg.* 55 (1968), 332-40. PMID: 4869678.

[171] F. Clune: *Ashes of Hiroshima: a post-war trip to Japan and China*. Angus and Robertson, 1952. URL: http://www.worldcat.org/oclc/34980133.

[172] J. Poolos: *The atomic bombings of Hiroshima and Nagasaki*. Chelsea House, 2008. URL: http://www.worldcat.org/oclc/183261128.

[173] H. Takayama: *Hiroshima in memoriam and today: Hiroshima as a testimony of peace for mankind-with the cooperation of Hiroshima citizens*. Society for the Publication of "Hiroshima in memoriam and today", 1973.

[174] T. Harada: Nuclear flash burns: A review and consideration. *Burns Open* 2 (2018), 1-7. DOI: 10.1016/j.burnso.2017.10.002.

[175] International Committee of the Red Cross: After the atomic bomb: *Hibakusha* tell their stories. *International Review of the Red Cross* 97 (2015), 507-525. DOI: 10.1017/s1816383116000242.

[176] J. W. Brooks et al.: A comparison of local and systemic effects following contact and flash burns. *Ann. Surg.* 144 (1956), 768-77. PMID: 13373261.

[177] E. I. Evans et al.: Flash burn studies on human volunteers. *Surgery* 37 (1955), 280-97. PMID: 13226167.

[178] G. Mixter: *Studies on flash burns: further report on the protective qualities of fabrics, as expressed by a protective index.* 1954. URL: https://www.osti.gov/servlets/purl/4387593.

[179] R. Shirabe: *A Physicians Diary of the Atomic Bombing and Its Aftermath.* Atomic Bomb Casualty Commission, 2002. URL: https://books.google.com/books?id=AWIXhCYSDEQC.

[180] Anonymous: *The day Man lost.* Kodansha International, 1972. URL: http://www.worldcat.org/oclc/838227278.

[181] N. K. Tahirkheli and P. R. Greipp: Treatment of the systemic capillary leak syndrome with terbutaline and theophylline. A case series. *Ann. Intern. Med.* 130 (1999), 905-9. PMID: 10375339.

[182] H. L. Fred and F. W. Chandler: Traumatic asphyxia. *Am. J. Med.* 29 (1960), 508-17. PMID: 13701562.

[183] P. Prodhan et al.: Orbital compartment syndrome mimicking cerebral herniation in a 12-yr-old boy with severe traumatic asphyxia. *Pediatr. Crit. Care Med.* 4 (2003), 367-9. PMID: 12831422.

[184] J. Dwek: Ecchymotic mask. *J. Int. Coll. Surg.* 9 (1946), 257-64. PMID: 20986861.

[185] B. A. Zikria et al.: Smoke and carbon monoxide poisoning in fire victims. *J. Trauma* 12 (1972), 641-5. PMID: 5055192.

[186] L. Freitag et al.: The role of bronchoscopy in pulmonary complications due to mustard gas inhalation. *Chest* 100 (1991), 1436-41. PMID: 1935306.

[187] P. Enkhbaatar et al.: Pathophysiology, research challenges, and clinical management of smoke inhalation injury. *74* 388 (2016), 1437-1446. PMID: 27707500.

[188] Anonymous: *U.S. Explosive Ordnance.* Vol. 2. U.S. Navy Bureau of Ordnance, 1947. URL: https://archive.org/details/OP1664USExplosiveOrdnanceVolume2/.

[189] J. Carter and K. Torgerson: *Group 3 SWMUs Site Reconnaissance Trip Report, Deseret Chemical Depot, Tooele, Utah.* 1998. URL: https://archive.org/details/carter-1998.

[190] K. Yamamoto et al.: An acute fatal occupational cadmium poisoning by inhalation. *Z. Rechtsmed.* 91 (1983), 139-43. PMID: 6666383.

[191] D. H. Yates and K. P. Goldman: Acute cadmium poisoning in a foreman plater welder. *Br. J. Ind. Med.* 47 (1990), 429-31. PMID: 2378822.

[192] L. L. Brunton et al.: *Goodman and Gilman's The pharmacological basis of therapeutics*. McGraw Hill, 2005.

[193] J. J. Flick: Ocular lesions following the atomic bombing of Hiroshima and Nagasaki. *1519* 31 (1948), 137-54. PMID: 18905669.

[194] H. W. Rose et al.: Human chorioretinal burns from atomic fireballs. *AMA Arch. Ophthalmol.* 55 (1956), 205-10. PMID: 13282545.

[195] V. A. Byrnes et al.: Chorioretinal burns produced by atomic flash. *1539* 53 (1955), 351-64. PMID: 14349443.

[196] J. J. Vos: A theory of retinal burns. *Bull. Math. Biol.* 24 (1962), 115-128. PMID: 13926801.

[197] A. Oyama and T. Sasaki: A case of corneal burns by the atomic bomb. *Ganka rinsho iho* 40 (1946), 177-178.

[198] T. F. Schlaegel: Ocular histopathology of some Nagasaki atomic-bomb casualties. *Am. J. Ophthalmol.* 30 (1947), 127-35. PMID: 20284412.

[199] H. C. Wilder: Pathology of the eye in atomic bomb casualties. *Am. J. Pathol.* 23 (1947), 890. PMID: 20344734.

[200] M. Rimbaş and M. R. Voiosu: Significant Delay Posed by the Ileocecal Valve in Videocapsule Endoscopy Small Bowel Transit Time. 40 (2017), 287-290. PMID: 26458267.

[201] J. V. Neel: *Unprecedented challenge faced in early years*. 1988. URL: https://www.rerf.or.jp/en/about/history_e/psnacount_e/neel-en/.

[202] F. W. Putnam: Symposium Paper: The Atomic Bomb Casualty Commission in retrospect. *569* 95 (1998), 5426-5431. DOI: 10.1073/pnas.95.10.5426.

[203] F. M. Snell et al.: Hematologic studies in Hiroshima and a control city 2 years after the atomic bombing. *AMA Arch. Intern. Med.* 84 (1949), 569-604. PMID: 18141734.

[204] W. J. Schull: The somatic effects of exposure to atomic radiation: the Japanese experience, 1947-1997. *Proc. Natl. Acad. Sci. U. S. A.* 95 (1998), 5437-41. PMID: 9576900.

[205] T. Francis et al.: *Report of ad hoc committee for appraisal of ABCC program*. Atomic Bomb Casualty Commission, 1955. URL: https://www.rerf.or.jp/library/scidata/tr_all/TR1959-33.pdf.

[206] J. V. Neel et al.: The effect of exposure to the atomic bombs on pregnancy termination in Hiroshima and Nagasaki: preliminary report. *Science* 118 (1953), 537-41. PMID: 13113170.

[207] S. Jablon et al.: *RBE of neutrons in atomic bomb survivors Hiroshima—Nagasaki*. Atomic Bomb Casualty Commission, 1970. URL: https://www.rerf.or.jp/library/scidata/tr_all/TR1970-12.pdf.

[208] S. Jablon: *Atomic bomb radiation estimation at ABCC*. Atomic Bomb Casualty Commission, 1971. URL: https://www.rerf.or.jp/library/scidata/tr_all/TR1971-23.pdf.

[209] R. C. Milton and T. Shohoji: *Tentative 1965 radiation dose estimation for atomic bomb survivors*. Atomic Bomb Casualty Commission, 1968. URL: https://www.rerf.or.jp/library/scidata/tr_all/TR1968-01.pdf.

[210] *The Effects on populations of exposure to low levels of ionizing radiation*. National Academy of Sciences, 1980. DOI: 10.17226/21287.

[211] *Health effects of exposure to low levels of radiation*. National Academies Press, 1990. DOI: 10.17226/1224.

[212] T. J. MacVittie et al.: The Hematopoietic Syndrome of the Acute Radiation Syndrome in Rhesus Macaques: A Systematic Review of the Lethal Dose Response Relationship. *1204* 109 (2015), 342–66. PMID: 26425897.

[213] J. J. Broerse and J. Zoetelief: The Occurrence of Radiation Syndromes in Rodents and Monkeys in Dependence on Dose Rate and Radiation Quality. In: *Response of Different Species to Total Body Irradiation*. Ed. by J. J. Broerse and T. J. MacVittie. Martinus Nijhoff Publishers, 1984, 175–187.

[214] M. Bauchinger et al.: *Cytogenetic analysis for radiation dose assessment*. International Atomic Energy Agency, 2001. URL: https://www-pub.iaea.org/MTCD/publications/PDF/TRS405_scr.pdf.

[215] A. Léonard et al.: Usefulness and limits of biological dosimetry based on cytogenetic methods. *1064* 115 (2005), 448–54. PMID: 16381765.

[216] A. Léonard et al.: Persistence of chromosome aberrations in an accidentally irradiated subject. *1064* 22 (1988), 55–57. DOI: 10.1093/oxfordjournals.rpd.a080089.

[217] A. D. Bloom et al.: Cytogenetic investigation of survivors of the atomic bombings of Hiroshima and Nagasaki. *74* 2 (1966), 672–4. PMID: 4162352.

[218] A. D. Bloom et al.: Cytogenetics of the in-utero exposed of Hiroshima and Nagasaki. *74* 2 (1968), 10–2. PMID: 4172681.

[219] M. S. Sasaki and H. Miyata: Biological dosimetry in atomic bomb survivors. *Nature* 220 (1968), 1189–93. PMID: 5725977.

[220] M. Otake: Dose-response relationship of neutron and gamma rays to chromosomally aberrant cells among atomic bomb survivors in Hiroshima and Nagasaki. *1293* 20 (1979), 307–21. PMID: 536952.

[221] A. A. Awa: Review of thirty years study of Hiroshima and Nagasaki atomic bomb survivors. II. Biological effects. G. Chromosome aberrations in somatic cells. *1293* 16 Suppl (1975), 122-31. PMID: 1195195.

[222] A. A. Awa et al.: Relationship between the radiation dose and chromosome aberrations in atomic bomb survivors of Hiroshima and Nagasaki. *1293* 19 (1978), 126-40. PMID: 712662.

[223] C. Lindholm et al.: Persistence of translocations after accidental exposure to ionizing radiation. *413* 74 (1998), 565-71. PMID: 9848275.

[224] L. F. Povirk and D. E. Shuker: DNA damage and mutagenesis induced by nitrogen mustards. *Mutat. Res.* 318 (1994), 205-26. PMID: 7527485.

[225] F. A. Shakil et al.: Cytogenetic abnormalities of hematopoietic tissue in retired workers of the Ohkunojima poison gas factory. *Hiroshima J. Med. Sci.* 42 (1993), 159-65. PMID: 8014068.

[226] D. L. Preston et al.: *Comparison of the dose-response relationships for chromosome aberration frequencies between the T65D and DS86 dosimetries.* Radiation Effects Research Foundation, 1988. URL: https://www.rerf.or.jp/library/scidata/tr_all/TR1988-07.pdf.

[227] D. Huff: *How to lie with statistics.* Norton, 1993. URL: http://www.worldcat.org/oclc/492609885.

[228] A. A. Awa and T. Teramoto: *Minutes of the second ABCC/RERF history forum.* 2013. URL: https://www.rerf.or.jp/uploads/2017/09/historyforum03e.pdf.

[229] H. H. Rossi and C. W. Mays: Leukemia risk from neutrons. *1204* 34 (1978), 353-60. PMID: 669955.

[230] E. J. Grant et al.: Radiation unlikely to be responsible for high cancer rates among distal Hiroshima A-bomb survivors. *32* 14 (2009), 247-9. PMID: 19568834.

[231] L. B. Russell and W. L. Russell: An analysis of the changing radiation response of the developing mouse embryo. *1674* 43 (1954), 103-49. PMID: 13174630.

[232] E. M. Otis and R. Brent: Equivalent ages in mouse and human embryos. *Anat. Rec.* 120 (1954), 33-63. PMID: 13207763.

[233] S. P. Hicks: The effects of ionizing radiation, certain hormones, and radiomimetic drugs on the developing nervous system. *1674* 43 (1954), 151-78. PMID: 13174631.

[234] A. S. Dekaban: Abnormalities in children exposed to x-radiation during various stages of gestation: tentative timetable of radiation injury to the human fetus. I. *J. Nucl. Med.* 9 (1968), 471-7. PMID: 5747864.

[235] N. Sanjarmoosavi et al.: Teratogenic effects of sulfur mustard on mice fetuses. *Iran. J. Basic Med. Sci.* 15 (2012), 853-9. PMID: 23493485.

[236] M. L. Murphy et al.: The comparative effects of five polyfunctional alkylating agents on the rat fetus, with additional notes on the chick embryo. *Ann. N. Y. Acad. Sci.* 68 (1958), 762-81; discussion 781-2. PMID: 13627731.

[237] J. W. Wood et al.: In utero exposure to the Hiroshima atomic bomb. An evaluation of head size and mental retardation: twenty years later. *Pediatrics* 39 (1967), 385-92. PMID: 6066886.

[238] M. Otake and W. J. Schull: In utero exposure to A-bomb radiation and mental retardation; a reassessment. *Br. J. Radiol.* 57 (1984), 409-14. PMID: 6539140.

[239] R. W. Miller: Delayed effects occurring within the first decade after exposure of young individuals to the Hiroshima atomic bomb. *510* 18 (1956), 1-18. PMID: 13335315.

[240] J. N. Yamazaki et al.: A study of the outcome of pregnancy in women exposed to the atomic bomb blast in Nagasaki. *J. Cell. Physiol. Suppl.* 43 (1954), 319-28. PMID: 13174637.

[241] G. Plummer: Anomalies occurring in children exposed in utero to the atomic bomb in Hiroshima. *510* 10 (1952), 687-93. PMID: 13003418.

[242] J. W. Wood et al.: Mental retardation in children exposed in utero to the atomic bombs in Hiroshima and Nagasaki. *Am. J. Public Health Nations Health* 57 (1967), 1381-1389. DOI: 10.2105/ajph.57.8.1381.

[243] W. J. Blot: Growth and development following prenatal and childhood exposure to atomic radiation. *1293* 16 Suppl (1975), 82-8. PMID: 1195206.

[244] R. W. Miller and J. J. Mulvihill: Small head size after atomic irradiation. *Teratology* 14 (1976), 355-7. PMID: 996782.

[245] R. Rugh: Low levels of x-irradiation and the early mammalian embryo. *Am. J. Roentgenol. Radium Ther. Nucl. Med.* 87 (1962), 559-66. PMID: 14495197.

[246] A. Stewart et al.: Malignant disease in childhood and diagnostic irradiation in utero. *74* 271 (1956), 447. PMID: 13358242.

[247] A. Stewart and G. W. Kneale: Radiation dose effects in relation to obstetric x-rays and childhood cancers. *74* 1 (1970), 1185-8. PMID: 4192374.

[248] E. B. Harvey et al.: Prenatal x-ray exposure and childhood cancer in twins. *N. Engl. J. Med.* 312 (1985), 541-5. PMID: 3969117.

[249] R. Wakeford: Childhood leukaemia following medical diagnostic exposure to ionizing radiation in utero or after birth. *Radiat. Prot. Dosimetry* 132 (2008), 166-74. PMID: 18922822.

[250] S. Jablon and H. Kato: Childhood cancer in relation to prenatal exposure to atomic-bomb radiation. *74* 2 (1970), 1000–3. PMID: 4098041.

[251] H. Kato: Mortality in children exposed to the A-bombs while in utero, 1945-1969. *1480* 93 (1971), 435–42. PMID: 5562716.

[252] K. van Calsteren et al.: Substantial variation in transplacental transfer of chemotherapeutic agents in a mouse model. *Reprod. Sci.* 18 (2011), 57–63. PMID: 20826505.

[253] H. Kato et al.: Risk of cancer among children exposed to atomic bomb radiation in utero: a review. *IARC Sci. Publ.* (1989), 365–74. PMID: 2680953.

[254] L. M. Anderson et al.: Critical windows of exposure for children's health: cancer in human epidemiological studies and neoplasms in experimental animal models. *714* 108 Suppl 3 (2000), 573–94. PMID: 10852857.

[255] S. Sasaki: Influence of the age of mice at exposure to radiation on life-shortening and carcinogenesis. *1293* 32 Suppl 2 (1991), 73–85. PMID: 1823369.

[256] J. Meyne and M. S. Legator: Clastogenic effects of transplacental exposure of mouse embryos to nitrogen mustard or cyclophosphamide. *Teratog. Carcinog. Mutagen.* 3 (1983), 281–7. PMID: 6137084.

[257] M. Nakano et al.: Chromosome aberrations do not persist in the lymphocytes or bone marrow cells of mice irradiated in utero or soon after birth. *154* 167 (2007), 693–702. PMID: 17523844.

[258] M. Nakano et al.: Fetal irradiation of rats induces persistent translocations in mammary epithelial cells similar to the level after adult irradiation, but not in hematolymphoid cells. *154* 181 (2014), 172–6. PMID: 24512615.

[259] K. Ohtaki et al.: Human Fetuses do not Register Chromosome Damage Inflicted by Radiation Exposure in Lymphoid Precursor Cells except for a Small but Significant Effect at Low Doses. *154* 161 (2004), 373–379. DOI: 10.1667/3147.

[260] I. Schmitz-Feuerhake: Dose revision for A-bomb survivors and the question of fallout contribution. *1204* 44 (1983), 693–5. PMID: 6853199.

[261] I. Schmitz-Feuerhake and P. Carbonell: Evaluation of low-level effects in the Japanese A-bomb survivors after current dose revisions and estimation of fallout contribution. In: *Biological effects of low-level radiation*. International Atomic Energy Agency, 1983, 45–53.

[262] T. Watanabe et al.: Hiroshima survivors exposed to very low doses of A-bomb primary radiation showed a high risk for cancers. *Environ. Health Prev. Med.* 13 (2008), 264–70. PMID: 19568913.

[263] M. Matsuura et al.: Survival analyses of atomic bomb survivors in Hiroshima Prefecture, Japan, 1968-1982—cancer mortality risk among early entrants. *1511* 44 (1995), 29-38. PMID: 7591838.

[264] J. D. Rizzo et al.: Solid cancers after allogeneic hematopoietic cell transplantation. *Blood* 113 (2009), 1175-83. PMID: 18971419.

[265] Anonymous: *Genetic and somatic effects of ionizing radiation: United Nations Scientific Committee on the Effects of Atomic Radiation: 1986 report to the General Assembly, with annexes.* United Nations, 1986.

[266] S. Wada et al.: Mustard gas as a cause of respiratory neoplasia in man. *Lancet* 1 (1968), 1161-3. PMID: 4172287.

[267] J. E. Norman: Lung cancer mortality in World War I veterans with mustard-gas injury: 1919-1965. *496* 54 (1975), 311-7. PMID: 1113317.

[268] M. Ghanei and A. A. Harandi: Lung carcinogenicity of sulfur mustard. *Clin. Lung Cancer* 11 (2010), 13-7. PMID: 20085862.

[269] V. K. Ivanov et al.: Radiation-epidemiological studies of thyroid cancer incidence among children and adolescents in the Bryansk oblast of Russia after the Chernobyl accident (1991-2001 follow-up period). *476* 45 (2006), 9-16. PMID: 16544150.

[270] M. D. Tronko et al.: A cohort study of thyroid cancer and other thyroid diseases after the Chornobyl accident: thyroid cancer in Ukraine detected during first screening. *J. Natl. Cancer Inst.* 98 (2006), 897-903. PMID: 16818853.

[271] Y. Shimizu et al.: Studies of the mortality of atomic bomb survivors. Report 12, part II. Noncancer mortality: 1950-1990. *154* 152 (1999), 374-89. PMID: 10477914.

[272] M. P. Little: Cancer and non-cancer effects in Japanese atomic bomb survivors. *J. Radiol. Prot.* 29 (2009), A43-59. PMID: 19454804.

[273] S. C. Darby et al.: Radiation-related heart disease: current knowledge and future prospects. *Int. J. Radiat. Oncol. Biol. Phys.* 76 (2010), 656-65. PMID: 20159360.

[274] T.-M. Pham et al.: Radiation exposure and the risk of mortality from noncancer respiratory diseases in the life span study, 1950-2005. *154* 180 (2013), 539-45. PMID: 24148011.

[275] R. Seltser and P. E. Sartwell: The Influence Of Occupational Exposure To Radiation On The Mortality Of American Radiologists And Other Medical Specialists. *Am. J. Epidemiol.* 81 (1965), 2-22. PMID: 14246078.

[276] B. Darvishi et al.: Investigating Prevalence and Pattern of Long-term Cardiovascular Disorders in Sulphur Mustard-exposed Victims and

Determining Proper Biomarkers for Early Defining, Monitoring and Analysis of Patients' Feedback on Therapy. *Basic Clin. Pharmacol. Toxicol.* 120 (2017), 120–130. PMID: 27607565.

[277] N. J. Kleiman: Radiation cataract. *Ann. ICRP* 41 (2012), 80–97. PMID: 23089007.

[278] P. J. Gehring: The cataractogenic activity of chemical agents. *Crit. Rev. Toxicol.* 1 (1971), 93–118. PMID: 4266286.

[279] G. R. Merriam and E. F. Focht: A clinical study of radiation cataracts and the relationship to dose. *1664* 77 (1957), 759–85. PMID: 13411351.

[280] G. Wilde and J. Sjöstrand: A clinical study of radiation cataract formation in adult life following gamma irradiation of the lens in early childhood. *Br. J. Ophthalmol.* 81 (1997), 261–6. PMID: 9215051.

[281] D. G. Cogan et al.: Atom bomb cataracts. *478* 110 (1949), 654. PMID: 15396017.

[282] F. Kandori and Y. Masuda: Statistical observations of atom-bomb cataracts. *1519* 42 (1956), 212–4. PMID: 13354691.

[283] R. E. Shore et al.: Epidemiological studies of cataract risk at low to moderate radiation doses: (not) seeing is believing. *154* 174 (2010), 889–94. PMID: 21128813.

[284] A. Minamoto et al.: Cataract in atomic bomb survivors. *413* 80 (2004), 339–45. PMID: 15223766.

[285] Anonymous: *Bomb, photoflash, AN-M46.* 0. URL: http://65.175.100.54/uxofiles/mulvaney/techdatasheets/Bomb,AN-M46,Photoflash,100lbs.pdf.

[286] L. De Jong: *Het Koninkrijk der Nederlanden in de Tweede Wereldoorlog/Deel 11B, Nederlands-Indië II: tweede helft.* Staatsuitgeverij, 1985. URL: http://www.worldcat.org/oclc/769195196.

[287] J. A. Siemes: *Eyewitness account of Hiroshima.* 1945. URL: http://www.atomicarchive.com/Docs/Hiroshima/Hiroshima_Siemes.shtml.

[288] R. S. Norris: *Racing for the bom: General Leslie R. Groves, the Manhattan Project's indispensable man.* Steerforth Press, 2002.

[289] T. L. Roleff: *The atom bomb.* Greenhaven Press, 2000. URL: http://www.worldcat.org/oclc/41628179.

[290] M. Nasu: *Children of the Paper Crane.* M. E. Sharpe, 1991. URL: http://www.worldcat.org/oclc/1015606007.

[291] W. R. Cotton and R. A. Pielke: *Human impacts on weather and climate.* Cambridge University Press, 1995.

References

[292] T. Storelvmo and I. Tan: The Wegener-Bergeron-Findeisen process - Its discovery and vital importance for weather and climate. *Meteorologische Zeitschrift* 24 (2015), 455–461. DOI: 10.1127/metz/2015/0626.

[293] D. Masters and K. Way: *One World Or None: A Report to the Public on the Full Meaning of the Atomic Bomb.* New Press, 1946. URL: https://archive.org/details/oneworldornonere00mast.

[294] R. M. Neer: *Napalm: an American biography.* Belknap Press of Harvard University Press, 2013. URL: http://www.worldcat.org/oclc/965388191.

[295] R. Shirabe: *My Experience and Damages.* 1986. URL: https://www-sdc.med.nagasaki-u.ac.jp/abcenter/shirabe/index_e.html.

[296] T. Nagai: *The bells of Nagasaki.* Kodansha International, 1994. URL: http://www.worldcat.org/oclc/31221284.

[297] Anonymous: *The first special exhibition of FY 2003: Damage surveys in post-war turmoil.* 2003. URL: http://www.pcf.city.hiroshima.jp/virtual/VirtualMuseum_e/exhibit_e/exh0307_e/exh03075_e.html.

[298] R. Jungk: *Children of the Ashes.* Pelican Books, 1963. URL: http://www.worldcat.org/oclc/20711493.

[299] L. Rees: *Horror in the East.* Ebury Press, 2011. URL: http://www.worldcat.org/oclc/1023316760.

[300] B. T. Wakabayashi: Documents on Japanese poison gas warfare in China. *Sino-Jpn. Stud.* 7 (1994), 3–33. URL: http://www.chinajapan.org/articles/07.1/07.1wakabayashi3-33.pdf.

[301] W. E. Grunden: No retaliation in kind: Japanese chemical warfare policy in World War II. In: *One Hundred Years of Chemical Warfare: Research, Deployment, Consequences.* Ed. by B. Friedrich et al. Springer International Publishing, 2017. DOI: 10.1007/978-3-319-51664-6.

[302] F. D'Olier et al.: *United States Strategic Bombing Survey: Pacific War.* U.S. Government, 1946. URL: https://archive.org/details/unitedstatesstra00cent/.

[303] R. B. Frank: *Downfall: the end of the Japanese empire.* Penguin, 2001.

[304] R. J. C. Butow: *Japan's Decision to Surrender.* Stanford University Press, 1954.

[305] J. Bacque: *Other losses: the shocking truth behind the mass deaths of disarmed German soldiers and civilians under General Eisenhower's command.* Prima Publishing, 1992. URL: http://www.worldcat.org/oclc/45377004.

[306] T. Kawahara: *Hirohito and his times: a Japanese perspective*. Kodansha International, 1990.

[307] M. Shigemitsu: *Japan and her destiny: my struggle for peace*. E. P. Dutton, 1958.

[308] M. Braw: *The atomic bomb suppressed: American censorship in Japan 1945-1949*. Sharpe, 1991.

[309] A. W. Oughterson et al.: *Medical Effects Of Atomic Bombs The Report Of The Joint Commission For The Investigation Of The Effects Of The Atomic Bomb In Japan Volume 1*. 1951. DOI: 10.2172/4421057.

[310] E. Arakawa et al.: *Determination of the burst point and hypocenter of the atomic bomb in Hiroshima*. Atomic Bomb Casualty Commission, 1959. URL: https://www.rerf.or.jp/library/scidata/tr_all/TR1959-12-B.pdf.

[311] N. Cousins: *The pathology of power*. Norton & Company, 1987.

[312] E. M. Zacharias: *Secret missions: the story of an intelligence officer*. G. P. Putnam's Sons, 1946.

[313] J. de Launay: *Secret diplomacy of World War II*. Simmons-Boardman, 1963.

[314] C. de Gaulle: *The war memoirs of Charles de Gaulle: Salvation (1944-1946)*. Simon and Schuster, 1946. URL: https://archive.org/details/salvation19441940000unse/.

[315] W. A. Reuben: *The atom spy hoax*. Action Books, 1954. URL: http://www.worldcat.org/oclc/869495241.

[316] D. R. Griffin: *9/11 Ten Years Later: When State Crimes Against Democracy Succeed*. Olive Branch Press, 2011. URL: http://www.unz.com/book/david_ray_griffin__911-ten-years-later/.

[317] F. Cossiga: *Osama-Berlusconi? "Trappola giornalistica"*. 2007. URL: https://preview.tinyurl.com/cossiga911.

[318] S. Vavilov et al.: Open Letter to Dr. Einstein—From Four Soviet Scientists. *Bull. At. Sci.* 4 (1948), 34-37. DOI: 10.1080/00963402.1948.11460160.

[319] W. Millis: *The Forrestal Diaries*. Cassell & Company, 1952. URL: https://archive.org/details/theforrestaldiarieswaltermillised/.

www.ingramcontent.com/pod-product-compliance
Lightning Source LLC
Chambersburg PA
CBHW060028180426
43195CB00051B/2224